THE ACCESSION OF THE EUROPEAN UNION TO THE EUROPEAN CONVENTION ON HUMAN RIGHTS

After more than 30 years of discussion, negotiations between the Council of Europe and the European Union on the EU's accession to the European Convention on Human Rights have resulted in a Draft Accession Agreement. This will allow the EU to accede to the Convention within the next couple of years. As a consequence, the Union will become subject to the external judicial supervision of an international treaty regime. Individuals will also be entitled to submit applications against the Union, alleging that their fundamental rights have been violated by legal acts rooted in EU law, directly to the Strasbourg Court.

As the first comprehensive monograph on this topic, this book examines the concerns for the EU's legal system in relation to accession and the question of whether and how accession and the system of human rights protection under the Convention can be effectively reconciled with the autonomy of EU law. It also takes into account how this objective can be attained without jeopardising the current system of individual human rights protection under the Convention. The main chapters deal with the legal status and rank of the Convention and the Accession Agreement within Union law after accession; the external review of EU law by Strasbourg and the potential subordination of the Luxembourg Court; the future of individual applications and the so-called co-respondent mechanism; the legal arrangement of inter-party cases after accession and the presumable clash of jurisdictions between Strasbourg and Luxembourg; and the interplay between the Convention's subsidiarity principle (the exhaustion of local remedies) and the prior involvement of the Luxembourg Court in EU-related cases.

The analysis presented in this book comes at a crucial point in the history of European human rights law, offering a holistic and detailed enquiry into the EU's accession to the ECHR and how this move can be reconciled with the autonomy of EU law.

Volume 39 in the series Modern Studies in European Law

Modern Studies in European Law
Recent titles in this series:

**For the complete list of titles in this series, see
'Modern Studies in European Law' link at
www.hartpub.co.uk/books/series.asp**

The Accession of the European Union to the European Convention on Human Rights

Paul Gragl

·HART·
PUBLISHING

OXFORD AND PORTLAND, OREGON
2013

Published in the United Kingdom by Hart Publishing Ltd
16C Worcester Place, Oxford, OX1 2JW
Telephone: +44 (0)1865 517530
Fax: +44 (0)1865 510710
E-mail: mail@hartpub.co.uk
Website: http://www.hartpub.co.uk

Published in North America (US and Canada) by
Hart Publishing
c/o International Specialized Book Services
920 NE 58th Avenue, Suite 300
Portland, OR 97213-3786
USA
Tel: +1 503 287 3093 or toll-free: (1) 800 944 6190
Fax: +1 503 280 8832
E-mail: orders@isbs.com
Website: http://www.isbs.com

British Library Cataloguing in Publication Data
Data Available

ISBN: 978-1-84946-460-4

Typeset by Hope Services, Abingdon
Printed and bound in Great Britain by
TJ International Ltd

For Jennifer and My Parents

Acknowledgements

It is not an easy thing to say thank you. In order to express my gratitude for the support in a work like this book, I would like to say a sincere and thousandfold 'thank you' to all the people who directly and indirectly supported and helped me finish my work. I will try hard to reciprocate not only with words, but with my own support for these people in the future. But beyond that, it is difficult not to forget any colleagues or friends (sometimes those two categories overlap of course) who accompanied me along the way.

The first thank you goes to *Renate Kicker*. Without her, my doctoral thesis and thus the book at hand would most probably have been of a completely different nature. On my second day at the Institute of International Law of the University of Graz, she approached me and suggested the very topic of my thesis, the European Union's accession to the European Convention on Human Rights. She therefore gave my work the initial spark for future development. Any comments or complaints as to why I did not choose another topic must consequently be addressed to her, not me. Seriously, all joking aside, thank you again for such a wonderful and intriguing topic which accompanied me for two years and eventually became an important part of my life.

I also owe my gratitude to *Wolfgang Benedek* and *Kirsten Schmalenbach*, my doctoral thesis supervisors. They both are, in a manner of speaking, my international law 'mentors' and their influence made me what I am today, a sincere and diligent international law devotee. During my graduate studies, my interest in international law was mainly deepened by *Kirsten Schmalenbach's* classes on various topics in the field of International Law, European Union law and the intricate interplay of those two legal systems. Moreover, she supervised my diploma thesis on the US Alien Tort Claims Act and thus helped me finish my legal studies with excellent grades not only on my diploma thesis, but also on several classes in the final and specialised phase of my studies. Thank you very much for your inspiring help. I guess I would not be what I am today without your help. Beyond that, I have had the opportunity to work as a research and teaching assistant at the Institute of International Law and International Relations with the nicest and most reputable superior I have ever worked with, *Wolfgang Benedek*. By employing me, he gave me the opportunity to continue and improve my legal knowledge on a daily basis, mostly by doing research (both thesis-related and non-thesis-related) and by working with students, which was an entirely new experience for me. He always gave me sufficient space and time for the work on my thesis and, at the same time, effectively integrated me into the Institute and its team, for which I am sincerely grateful. Furthermore, I would like to express my gratitude and appreciation for his help and constant support in all matters, again for both thesis-related and non-thesis-related aspects.

Another big thank you goes to *Tobias Lock* whom I became acquainted with through his academic articles on the very topic of this book. A personal meeting with him at the IHR Conference at the University College London in May 2011 gave me a major breakthrough in my work and effectively helped me finish the substantial parts of my thesis and this book throughout the following summer. Therefore, I would like to say thank you for showing me the argumentative Ariadne's thread through the multi-dimensional maze of European human rights protection. A big part of this book's structure is owed to *Tobias Lock's* help and support.

Besides the purely academic help, I would also like to thank my dear colleagues *Julia Cortolezis, Elisabeth Hoffberger, Heike Montag, Matthias C Kettemann* and *Reinmar Nindler* for sharing hundreds of coffees while talking shop. With them, I enjoyed the dearly needed coffee, tea and lunch breaks which helped me reorganise my overloaded brain before resuming my work.

A huge amount of thanks is owed to my lovely and enchanting girlfriend *Jennifer Kaier* who endured my stress and (I guess, in her view extremely boring) explications about this book. Not only did she patiently survive this time, she also provided me with constant moral support and helped me with the linguistic subtleties and delicacies of the English language by proofreading my thesis and this book (please note that she does not study law and that her enthusiasm for reading more than 270 pages of legal stuff was inversely proportional to this fact). Thank you so much my dear Jenny for all your help.

I also owe a lot of gratitude to the people of Hart Publishing, Oxford, especially to *Rachel Turner* for her prompt and professional help in our frequent email correspondence, and to *Richard Hart* for our personal meeting in August 2012. This also includes the anonymous reviewer of this book who helped me during the final round of drafting.

My sincerest apologies go to my friends *Stefan Kreiner and Herwig Brunnegger*, with whom I could not spend as much time as I wanted to while I was writing this book.

Last, but of course not least, thank you to *my parents* who have always supported me, both financially and morally, during my studies (which took me, altogether, more than 10 years to finish). Thank you for believing in me this whole time.

Paul Gragl, November 2012

Contents

Table of Figures

List of Abbreviations

ACP	African, Caribbean and Pacific States
BVerfG	Bundesverfassungsgericht
CFI	Court of First Instance
CFSP	Common Foreign and Security Policy
ChFR	Charter of Fundamental Rights of the European Union
CJEU	Court of Justice of the European Union
CoE	Council of Europe
CSDP	Common Security and Defence Policy
EC	European Community/Communities
ECHR	European Convention for the Protection of Human Rights and Fundamental Freedoms
ECommHR	European Commission of Human Rights
ECSC	European Coal and Steel Community
ECtHR	European Court of Human Rights
EEA	European Economic Area
EEC	European Economic Community
EFTA	European Free Trade Association
EU	European Union
EUSA	European Union Studies Association
GATT	General Agreement on Tariffs and Trade
GC	General Court
ICCPR	International Covenant on Civil and Political Rights
ICJ	International Court of Justice
ITLOS	International Tribunal for the Law of the Sea
OJ	Official Journal of the European Union
OSPAR	Convention for the Protection of the Marine Environment of the North-East Atlantic
PCA	Permanent Court of Arbitration
PCIJ	Permanent Court of International Justice
TEC	Treaty establishing the European Community
TEU	Treaty on European Union (consolidated version after the Treaty of Lisbon [2010] OJ C 83/13)
TFEU	Treaty on the Functioning of the European Union (consolidated version after the Treaty of Lisbon [2010] OJ C 83/47)
TRNC	Turkish Republic of Northern Cyprus
UN	United Nations
UNCLOS	United Nations Convention on the Law of the Sea

UNSC	United Nations Security Council
VCLT	Vienna Convention on the Law of Treaties
VCLTIO	Vienna Convention on the Law of Treaties between States and International Organisations or between International Organisations
VfGH	Verfassungsgerichtshof
WTO	World Trade Organisation

Table of Cases

Court of First Instance/General Court

Opinions of the Court of Justice

European Commission of Human Rights

European Court of Human Rights

Permanent Court of International Justice

International Court of Justice

Arbitral Tribunals

Permanent Court of Arbitration

International Tribunal for the Law of the Sea

Miscellaneous Courts and Tribunals

NATIONAL COURTS

Austria

Czech Republic

France

Germany

Italy

Poland

Spain

United States of America

Table of Legislation

EUROPEAN UNION

UNITED NATIONS

Part I

Introduction—A Tale of Two Courts

1

Setting the Scene for Accession

I. THE EU AND THE EUROPEAN CONVENTION ON HUMAN RIGHTS

'The European courts were never supposed to meet.'[1]

GIVEN THE SUBSTANTIAL legal issues the European Union's accession to the European Convention on Human Rights (ECHR) brings about for the European system of human rights protection, the introductory quotation seems to give a succinct and condensed account of the legal questions the book at hand tries to analyse and solve. Literally speaking, this book will tell the tale of two courts[2] whose legal regimes are intricately intertwined with each other. The issues examined hereinafter are principally rooted in the fact that European integration rests on two different legal orders.[3] Firstly, it is based on the protection of human rights enshrined in the Convention which was drafted by the Council of Europe and which is interpreted and applied by the European Court of Human Rights (ECtHR) in Strasbourg. It is the sole duty of this international court, by virtue of Article 1 ECHR, to observe whether the high contracting parties to the Convention are actually securing to everyone within their jurisdiction the rights and freedoms defined in the Convention. If a high contracting party fails to comply with this requirement, the Court may declare a certain legal act or measure to be in violation of the Convention and that the respondent state is required under its international obligations to redress this human rights violation.

Secondly, the system of European integration rests on the European Union (EU) and its historical predecessors which, in the beginning, merely focused on the economic integration and welfare of the Member States. In contrast to the ECtHR, the Court of Justice of the European Union (CJEU) in Luxembourg 'shall ensure that in the interpretation and application of the Treaties the law is observed' (Art 19 (1) TEU)). The broad jurisdiction of the CJEU, which goes far beyond the protection

---

[1] See Laurent Scheeck, 'The Relationship between the European Courts and Integration through Human Rights' (2005) 65 *Zeitschrift für ausländisches öffentliches Recht und Völkerrecht* 837, 843.

[2] The inspiration for the title of Part I, 'A Tale of Two Courts', is indebted to Charles Dickens, *A Tale of Two Cities* (first published 1859; London, Penguin 2012) and Sionaidh Douglas-Scott, 'A Tale of Two Courts: Luxembourg, Strasbourg and the Growing European Human Rights *Acquis*' (2006) 43 *Common Market Law Review* 629, 629ff.

[3] See Carl Lebeck, 'The European Court of Human Rights on the Relation between ECHR and EC-Law: The Limits of Constitutionalisation of Public International Law' (2007) 62 *Zeitschrift für Öffentliches Recht* 195, 196.

of fundamental rights and encompasses almost the entirety of the Union's policies and legal fields, significantly shaped the Union's legal system. In this context, the Council of Europe and the EU have sometimes been metaphorically referred to as 'twins separated at birth'[4] since both of them were created as international organisations at approximately the same time, especially for the purpose of reinforcing transnational and intergovernmental cooperation in Europe, but with entirely different objectives. Therefore, one might say that in the past, the landscape of European human rights protection seemed simple and easily comprehensible. The European continent was home to two distinct 'European' organisations and two distinct courts—on the one hand, the ECtHR in Strasbourg to watch over alleged human rights violations by the contracting states, and on the other hand, the CJEU in Luxembourg which had other matters to deal with.[5]

However, even though these two legal regimes are distinct and independent, they do not operate in complete isolation from each other.[6] Despite their different origins and destinations, these two European 'siblings' have virtually been compelled to grow closer together during the last few decades.[7] The main reason for this inter-organisational consolidation was the fact that the European Union's precursor organisations started out as purely economic entities. Thence, the Treaties of Paris and Rome established an organisation completely devoid of its own 'Bill of Rights' or any other catalogue of fundamental rights. Any account of the European Union's commitment to human rights thus begins with the absence of any reference to such rights in the Union's founding treaties.[8] Yet, although the Member States had no difficulty in accepting the supremacy of EU law developed by Luxembourg's case law in its renowned judgment *Costa v ENEL*,[9] the discussion on the issue of fundamental rights protection within the Union's legal system and the eventual accession to the Convention was mainly triggered by the German Constitutional Court and its *Solange I* decision.[10] This decision did not necessarily imply that the Community had to accede to the Convention,[11] but rather it pointed out that the Member States would not allow for Union law to take precedence over national fundamental rights.

Since the European Union became more powerful in terms of political output,[12] the CJEU took recourse to the Convention and developed its own

---

[4] See Gerard Quinn, 'The European Union and the Council of Europe on the Issue of Human Rights: Twins Separated at Birth' (2001) 46 *McGill Law Journal* 849, 849.

[5] See Douglas-Scott (n 2) 629.

[6] See Guy Harpaz, 'The European Court of Justice and its Relations with the European Court of Human Rights: The Quest for Enhanced Reliance, Coherence and Legitimacy' (2009) 46 *Common Market Law Review* 105, 106.

[7] A more detailed account of the intricate interplay between Strasbourg and Luxembourg will be given in ch 5.

[8] See Gráinne De Búrca, 'The Road Not Taken: The European Union as a Global Human Rights Actor' (2011) 105 *American Journal of International Law* 649, 649ff.

[9] See Case 6/64 *Costa v ENEL* [1964] ECR 585.

[10] See BvL 52/71 *Solange I* BVerfGE 37, 271.

[11] See Jean-Paul Jacqué, 'The Accession of the European Union to the European Convention on Human Rights and Fundamental Freedoms' (2011) 48 *Common Market Law Review* 995, 998.

[12] See Scheeck (n 1) 837.

system of fundamental rights protection, based on its case law in which the Court repeatedly referred to the rights and freedoms enshrined in the Convention.[13] Thereby, the legal interface between the two courts and between the legal regimes of the Convention and the European Union were established. However, the CJEU's increasing use of the Convention to deduce its own fundamental rights protection turned out to be problematic. In fact, it has led to a situation where the two courts interpret the same text in different contexts and in different ways, without possessing any formal instruments for mutual coordination. A divergence in the courts' human rights jurisprudence seemed inevitable.

Moreover, after the EU continued to acquire competences in fields which had previously been the *domaine réservé* of the Member States but without acceding to the Convention, it became apparent that individuals seeking a judgment from Strasbourg were deprived of this right once these powers had been transferred into Union law. More precisely, in cases where an EU Member State was obliged to implement Union law in violation of the Convention, the legal status quo would not lead to a conviction of the actual 'perpetrator', namely the Union, but of the Member State implementing Union law. Thus, given the ECtHR's lack of jurisdiction *ratione personae* over the Union and the enduring desire for its own fundamental rights catalogue for the European Union, accession seemed a viable option to close the lacunae within the European system of human rights protection. Most importantly, by acceding to the Convention, the European Union and its institutions would become subject to the same system of external judicial review which all EU Member States are already subject to. Yet, first and foremost, it is contradictory that the Union, without itself being a contracting party to the Convention, urges candidate countries aspiring to EU membership to ratify the Convention and to protect human rights in accordance with it.

Accession would accordingly remove the increasing contradiction between the human rights commitments requested from future EU Member States and the Union's lack of accountability vis-à-vis the ECtHR.[14] Otherwise, it remains highly hypocritical to make ratification of the Convention a condition for EU membership, when the Union itself is entirely exempt from Strasbourg's judicial review.[15] As a result, in 1979 the European Commission issued a Memorandum on the then-Community's possible accession to the Convention. Since all the EU Member States were already contracting parties to the Convention, the Commission argued in this document that the EU itself should also accede to the Convention in order to restore the legal position in which the citizens of Member States found

---

[13] See especially Case 29/69 *Stauder v City of Ulm* [1969] ECR 419; Case 11/70 *Internationale Handelsgesellschaft mbH v Einfuhr- und Vorratsstelle für Getreide und Futtermittel* [1970] ECR 1125; and Case 4/73 *Nold v Ruhrkohle Aktiengesellschaft* [1977] ECR 1.

[14] See Hans Christian Krüger, 'Reflections Concerning Accession of the European Communities to the European Convention on Human Rights' (2002) 21 *Penn State International Law Review* 89, 94.

[15] See Philip Alston and JHH Weiler, 'The European Union and Human Rights: Final Project Report on an Agenda for the Year 2000' in Antonio Cassese (ed), *Leading by Example: A Human Rights Agenda for the European Union for the Year 2000* (Florence, European University Institute, 1998) 55.

themselves before the transfer of certain powers to the European Union.[16] This proposal was unheeded and hence lay dormant until 1993 when an ad hoc working group was formed under the Belgian Presidency to examine the following three key issues of accession: The competence to accede, the preservation of the autonomy of European Union law, and the exclusive jurisdiction of the CJEU.[17] However, the Luxembourg Court's seminal *Opinion 2/94* dealt a detrimental blow to these efforts. In this opinion, the Court simply held that, as the law stood back then, the Union had no competence to accede to the Convention,[18] and disregarded the other aforementioned issues such as its own exclusive jurisdiction and the autonomy of European Union law.

But now, after several decades of discussions and setbacks, accession is finally legally possible. With the entry into force of the Treaty of Lisbon on the part of the European Union and Protocol No 14 to the Convention on the part of the Council of Europe, both the EU Treaties and the Convention have been amended to the effect that the EU is now in the legal position to accede to the Convention. Article 6 (2) TEU sets out the obligation that the European Union shall accede to the ECHR, while Article 59 (2) ECHR[19] now reads that the European Union may accede to the Convention. Eventually, after it was agreed that 'the rapid accession of the Union to the European Convention for the Protection of Human Rights and Fundamental Freedoms is of key importance',[20] the European Union and the Council of Europe began negotiations on accession in summer 2010.[21] At the time of writing, these negotiations have principally been concluded and resulted in a Draft Agreement on Accession[22] which will be thoroughly and critically explored in Part III of this book.

---

[16] See Commission of the European Communities, 'Memorandum on the Accession of the European Communities to the Convention for the Protection of Human Rights and Fundamental Freedoms' Bulletin Supplement 2/79, COM (79) 210 final, para 15.

[17] See Commission of the European Communities, 'Memorandum from the Commission to the Working Group' SEC (93) 1678. See also Jacqué, 'Accession' (n 11) 1001f.

[18] See Opinion 2/94 *Accession by the Community to the European Convention for the Protection of Human Rights and Fundamental Freedoms* [1996] ECR I-1759, para 36.

[19] See also art 17 of Protocol No 14 to the Convention.

[20] See European Council, 'The Stockholm Programme—An Open and Secure Europe Serving and Protecting Citizens' [2010] OJ C115/1, 8.

[21] See, inter alia, Council of Europe, 'Press Release 545 (2010)'; Council of the European Union, 'Draft Council Decision Authorising the Commission to negotiate the Accession Agreement of the European Union to the European Convention for the Protection of Human Rights and Fundamental Freedoms (ECHR)' Doc 9689/10 (partly classified); Council of Europe, '1st Meeting of the CDDH Informal Working Group on the Accession of the European Union to the European Convention on Human Rights (CDDH-UE) with the European Commission' CDDH-UE(2010)01.

[22] See Council of Europe, '8th Meeting of the CDDH Informal Working Group on the Accession of the European Union to the European Convention on Human Rights (CDDH-UE) with the European Commission' CDDH-UE(2011)16. For the official report of this agreement, see Council of Europe, 'Steering Committee for Human Rights—Report to the Committee of Ministers on the Elaboration of Legal Instruments for the Accession of the European Union to the European Convention on Human Rights' CDDH-UE(2011)009.

By mid-2012, the Council of Europe's Committee of Ministers is still awaiting the conclusion of the internal discussions between the EU and its Member States on the Draft Accession Agreement,[23] which have been described as 'very intense'.[24] For instance, the United Kingdom and France proposed several substantial amendments and modifications to the Agreement, which, however, have been dismissed by the other Member States.[25] Therefore, it seems unlikely that these proposals will be integrated into the final Accession Agreement and thence they will not be taken into consideration in the legal analysis of this book.

In a nutshell, there are many reasons why the European Union's accession to the ECHR would enhance the protection of human rights in Europe. Firstly, by rendering the Convention legally binding for the Union, potential divergences in human rights standards between the Convention and European Union and between the case law of the Luxembourg and Strasbourg courts can be prevented.[26] Secondly, the Union and its institutions will become subject to external judicial supervision where the respect for and the protection of human rights is concerned. This also means that even though fundamental rights are now well protected by means of the EU's own Charter of Fundamental Rights, accession is still necessary. In fact, accession will guarantee that alleged human rights violations will be reviewed externally, whereas the Charter will internally ensure that the EU and its court, the CJEU, may prevent such violations in the first place, according to the Convention's principle of subsidiarity.[27] Lastly, and most importantly for the effective judicial protection of individuals, EU citizens will have direct access to the ECtHR and may bring complaints against European Union institutions before the Strasbourg Court directly.[28]

II. ACCESSION AND AUTONOMY: THE RESEARCH QUESTION OF THIS BOOK

At this point, critical readers might ask why an entire book on this very matter is necessary when accession just seems to be a walk in the park for European human rights law. Yet, this book does not primarily deal with the benefits and

---

[23] See Stian Øby Johansen, 'The EU's Accession to the ECHR: Negotiations to resume after 7 Month Hiatus', available at<http://blogg.uio.no/jus/smr/multirights/content/the-eus-accession-to-the-echr-negotiations-to-resume-after-7-month-hiatus#sdfootnote10sym> accessed 1 November 2012.

[24] Council of the European Union, 'Accession of the European Union to the European Convention for the Protection of Human Rights and Fundamental Freedoms—State of Play' 18117/11, FREMP 112, para 9.

[25] See Council of the European Union, 'Accession of the EU to the ECHR—Working Document from the Presidency' DS 1675/11, paras 8, 10, 11, 14 and 17.

[26] See Siegbert Alber/Ulrich Widmaier, 'Die EU-Charta der Grundrechte und ihre Auswirkungen auf die Rechtsprechung' (2000) 27 *Europäische Grundrechte-Zeitschrift* 497, 503f.

[27] See Hans Christian Krüger/Jörg Polakiewicz, 'Vorschläge für ein kohärentes System des Menschenrechtsschutzes in Europa' (2001) 28 *Europäische Grundrechte-Zeitschrift*, 100f.

[28] See Krüger, 'Reflections' (n 14) 94.

advantages of accession, but rather with the objections which have been raised against accession and its legal consequences. Sceptics have primarily argued that accession would bring about considerable risks for the autonomy of the European Union's specific legal order, including the possible incompatibility of a CJEU subordinated to the ECtHR, the external judicial control of the Union,[29] loss of jurisdiction and competences, and possible Treaty amendments by means of the final Accession Agreement, which would bypass the Union's internal revision procedure under Article 48 TEU.

In this context, it is trite to say that questions of jurisdiction and competence are questions of authority and power.[30] Certainly, the European Union and its Court of Justice in Luxembourg are anxious about the ramifications of the impending accession on their competences and jurisdiction vis-à-vis the Strasbourg Court. It would be naïve to expect these institutions to willingly forfeit their comprehensive competences which they have acquired from sovereign nation states over the last 50 years. As a result, certain provisions have been inserted into European Union law by means of the Treaty of Lisbon[31] which demand that the Union's competences are not affected by the accession and that the specific characteristics of European Union law are preserved. Nevertheless, despite these legal safeguards which have been put in place to prevent any loss of competence or jurisdiction on the part of the Union, sceptics still fear that Strasbourg may detrimentally encroach upon the EU's legal order after accession, for example by reviewing Union law allegedly in violation of the Convention. If this assumption was indeed true, the Union's legal autonomy, vigilantly guarded by the Luxembourg Court, would be in serious danger and accession could not be achieved in a smooth, rapid and uncomplicated manner.

It is therefore evident that accession in general and the Accession Agreement in particular have to be compatible with the EU Treaties and must not obstruct the autonomy of Union law—requirements which several past draft agreements have failed to satisfy.[32] The book at hand thus examines whether the European Union's accession to the ECHR is in fact compatible with the specific characteristics of the Union's autonomous legal order. Accordingly, it is the objective of this book to answer the central research question with regard to accession, namely *whether and how accession and the system of human rights protection under the Convention can be effectively reconciled with the autonomy of European Union law.* It must be

---

[29] See eg, Court of Justice of the European Union, 'Discussion Document of the Court of Justice of the European Union on certain aspects of the accession of the European Union to the European Convention for the Protection of Human Rights and Fundamental Freedoms', 5 May 2010, paras 4f.

[30] See eg, Ingolf Pernice, 'Kompetenzabgrenzung im Europäischen Verfassungsverbund' (2000) 55 *JZ* 866, 866, and Christian Starck, 'Der Vertrag über eine Verfassung für Europa' in Reinhard Hendler/Martin Ibler/José Martínez Soria (eds), *Für Sicherheit, für Europa. Festschrift für Volkmar Götz* (Göttingen, Vandenhoeck & Ruprecht, 2005) 79.

[31] In particular art 6 (2) TEU and Protocol No 8 to the Treaties.

[32] See Tobias Lock, 'Walking on a Tightrope: The Draft Accession Agreement and the Autonomy of the EU Legal Order' (2011) 48 *Common Market Law Review* 1025, 1028.

understood at this point that the accession of one international organisation (the European Union) to another international treaty regime (the Convention) and its judicial enforcement machinery (the Strasbourg Court) represents an unprecedented step in the history of international law. Under these special circumstances, several legal problems and challenges are expected to arise, especially in the light of the EU's prominent legal autonomy. This book aims to explore the question of how accession and autonomy can effectively be reconciled with one another, which is crucial to the future multi-level architecture of European human rights protection. The reader will therefore come across this leading question in every single chapter and, of course, the respective answers to it as well, with particular regard to individual legal issues in the context of the EU's accession to the Convention.

As the European Union's legal autonomy is upheld and preserved by the CJEU, the essence of this book's research question can be reduced to a potential jurisdictional conflict between Strasbourg and Luxembourg over which court has the last say in human rights cases involving European Union law. In other words, it is a tale of two courts struggling for the upper hand in interpreting and applying human rights law and particularly Luxembourg's efforts in shielding European Union law from any external interference. Hence, the legal analysis in this book is not principally concerned with the *vertical* jurisdictional relationship between the domestic courts of the Member States and the European courts, but with the *horizontal* jurisdictional competition[33] between the CJEU and other international courts and tribunals in general (especially Part II) and between the CJEU and the ECtHR in particular, both before (Part II) and after accession (Part III). Thereby, the two protagonists in this tale of two courts are the CJEU in Luxembourg as the observant guardian of the Union's legal autonomy, and the ECtHR in Strasbourg which is entrusted with the judicial protection of human rights by virtue of the Convention.

The importance of the European Union's legal autonomy, as developed by Luxembourg's case law, is a given and self-evident fact. This principle thus represents the crucial premise this book builds upon. This also means that the EU's autonomy principle is not called into question, since a critical review of this concept would firstly go beyond the scope of the analysis at hand and secondly deserve its own scientific and analytical examination. With respect to the autonomy of European Union law, the CJEU has emphasised in its respective decisions and opinions that the EU's legal order is a self-referential system which means that the interpretation and application of its legal rules exclusively depend on the system of which these rules constitute an indispensable part.[34] However, the reader's attention must be drawn to an important *caveat* at the beginning: This

---

[33] See also Nikolaos Lavranos, *Jurisdictional Competition. Selected Cases in International and European Law* (Groningen, Europa Law Publishing, 2009) 4.

[34] See René Barents, *The Autonomy of Community Law* (The Hague, Kluwer Law, 2004) 171.

very autonomy is, of course, of utmost importance for the future development of the European Union's legal system and thus the further economic, legal and political integration of the EU's Member States. However, when bearing in mind that the Union's legal autonomy is merely a means of achieving this noble end, it becomes clear that—in the reverse words of *Immanuel Kant*[35]—autonomy itself does not hold any intrinsic value. Autonomy itself is merely the vehicle by which to attain the objective of legal and political integration. The aforementioned research question must hence be broadened and extended to the effect that it must also encompass the addendum whether and how accession and the system of human rights protection under the Convention can be effectively reconciled with the autonomy of European Union law *without jeopardising the current system of individual human rights protection under the Convention*. One must not forget that accession is not an end in itself. The objective and purpose of accession is rather to enhance the legal protection of human rights in Europe, and not to adjust the Convention system to the legal order of the European Union. In the end, it is the EU acceding to the Convention and not vice versa. But on the other hand, the specific characteristics of European Union law must be taken into account as accurately as possible, in order to allow for a smooth, rapid and effective integration of the Union into the Convention system.

In other words, this book investigates how both the EU's legal autonomy and the effective protection of individuals can be upheld after accession at the same time. If, at the end of the day, accession preserved the autonomy of Union law, but lowered the standards of human rights protection guaranteed by the Convention system, the entire procedure of integrating the European Union into an external judicial monitoring system would be to no avail and run afoul of the original purpose of accession—closing gaps in the European system of human rights protection and subjecting the Union to the control of a specialised international court. This book hence aims at presenting viable solutions in order to reconcile the EU's legal autonomy and the effective protection of human rights under Strasbourg's judicial protection machinery in order to make this accession as viable and efficient as possible.

Therewith, this introduction has come full circle, back to the introductory statement that the two European courts were never supposed to meet. Prima facie, the Union's accession to the ECHR is a welcome and worthwhile step in the right direction, but the legal issues involved cannot be easily dismissed. They deserve a thorough, detailed and systematic analysis in order to reconcile two unruly principles and to bring about a new and improved landscape of human rights protection in Europe. This book will take up this task.

---

[35] See Immanuel Kant, *Grundlegung zur Metaphysik der Sitten* (first published 1785; Berlin, Walter de Gruyter Akademie-Ausgabe, 1900) 429.

III. A CAVEAT ON LEGAL DEFINITIONS

An extensive study such as this comprises a plethora of legal terms and thus a comprehensive and characteristic terminology. At the outset, this short subchapter thence advises the reader on the book's specific terminology in order to avoid confusion or uncertainty, as legal precision and clarity are of utmost importance for a thorough understanding of the issues presented here.

It is a well-known fact that the legal construction of the European Union's predecessor organisations was, even for legal professionals, intricate and difficult to grasp. After the entry into force of the Treaty of Maastricht in 1993, the EU's three pillar structure was introduced which led to the distinction between the European Union itself (virtually as an 'umbrella organisation') and its three constituent pillars, among them the European Communities and the European Community (EC) itself. In fact, it was the Community which enjoyed legal personality and which was the main protagonist of European integration and legal communitarisation. However, the deconstruction of the Union's pillar structure via the Treaty of Lisbon and the EU's newly won international legal personality by virtue of Article 47 TEU left the European Union as a single international organisation,[36] without the further need for temples, roofs, pillars or any other architectural metaphors. Today, the European Union is not merely the successor of the European Community, but rather it has absorbed both the Community and the former 'umbrella' or 'temple' construction of the EU.[37] Therefore, and for the sake of clarity and legibility, only the European Union (and its abbreviated form EU) are referred to in this book, even if the terms 'European Economic Community' (EEC) or 'European Community' (EC) were legally and historically correct in lieu thereof. The only exceptions to this rule are explicit references, for instance in judgments. Otherwise, the historical terms are encompassed by the term EU.

Furthermore, it must be clarified beforehand that this tale of two courts actually tells the tale of even more courts or quasi-judicial organs. When there is reference to the Court of Justice of the European Union (CJEU) or to its toponymic designation 'Luxembourg' or 'the Luxembourg Court', this term, in general, not only includes the Court of Justice itself, but also the General Court (GC; the successor of the Court of First Instance (CFI))[38] and specialised courts within the meaning of Article 19 (1) TEU. Only in cases where the GC or the former CFI have adjudicated on a case, explicit reference to those courts will be

---

[36] See Matthias Ruffert, 'Art 47 EUV' in Christian Calliess and Matthias Ruffert (eds), *EUV/AEUV. Kommentar*, 4th edn (Munich, Beck, 2011) para 1, and Rudolf Geiger, 'Art 1 EUV' in Rudolf Geiger, Daniel-Erasmus Kahn and Markus Kotzur (eds), *EUV/AEUV. Kommentar*, 5th edn (Munich, Beck, 2010) paras 6f.

[37] See Bruno De Witte, 'European Union Law: How Autonomous is its Legal Order?' (2010) 65 *Zeitschrift für Öffentliches Recht* 141, 143.

[38] See European Convention, 'Final Report of the Discussion Circle on the Court of Justice' CONV 636/03, 25 March 2003, para 14.

made. If not, the reader must be aware that CJEU or 'Luxembourg' stands for the Union's entire judicial system, not for one single court. The wording 'Court of Justice of the European Union' might not be a favourable choice for a regime of various courts,[39] but it nonetheless describes the Union's judicial system which comprises the Court of Justice, the General Court and specialised courts.

The same is true for the European Court of Human Rights (ECtHR) and its toponyms 'Strasbourg' or 'Strasbourg Court'. Regarding past cases, this term covers the now defunct two-tiered system of the Court itself and the former European Commission of Human Rights which was abolished in 1998 by Protocol No 11 to the Convention.[40] For more current cases and of course all cases after 1998, the terms ECtHR and 'Strasbourg' only denote the Court itself. The use of these toponymic or sometimes personalising notions—'Luxembourg' and 'Strasbourg'—is not a mere didactic device. In fact, these designations might help people to understand that these courts are composed of real human beings, ie judges, who (although they are prohibited from deciding on cases *contra legem*) are still more or less free to further develop the respective legal order they are working in by means of judicial activism. As a result, the personifications used in this book should exemplify that courts occasionally act like one single personal entity (when disregarding dissenting opinions) which aim at strengthening and consolidating the legal system which created them in the first place.

The last aspect to be clarified at this point pertains to the terms 'human rights' and 'fundamental rights'. Usually, the term 'human rights' is used within the context of international law and thus refers to the external dimension of this notion. The term 'fundamental rights', conversely, is generally used within the legal framework of national or domestic legal orders and thence denotes the internal dimension of this term. In this book, these terms will be used in this traditional manner, except for ambiguous situations in which it is indeterminate what term would be the correct one. In these cases, these two terms will be used interchangeably and without the established dichotomy of distinguishing between rights under international or national law.

---

[39] See Bernhard W Wegener, 'Art. 19 EUV' in Christian Calliess and Matthias Ruffert (eds), *EUV/ AEUV. Kommentar*, 4th edn (Munich, Beck, 2011) para 5.

[40] See generally on this topic David Harris, Michael O'Boyle, Ed Bates and Carla Buckley (eds), *Law of the European Convention on Human Rights*, 2nd edn (Oxford, Oxford University Press, 2009) 4, and Christoph Grabenwarter, *Europäische Menschenrechtskonvention*, 4th edn (Munich, Beck, 2009) § 6, para 2.

2

Scope of this Book

I. A SURVEY OF THE STATUS QUO

A PROJECTION OF the new legal order to come is, without doubt, not easy to imagine. For that reason, it is essential to examine the past and current relationship between the two European courts in order to extrapolate the future impact of accession. By analysing past events, the current and future development of European human rights law will become clearer and easier to understand.

Part II of this book thence examines the legal status quo, ie the situation before accession and the relationship between the autonomy of European Union law, international law and international courts in general in order to identify Luxembourg's attitude vis-à-vis external influences and courts. The notion 'legal autonomy' is defined in chapter three in order to understand what the term means and how it is devised and used in the CJEU's case-law. After that, chapter four provides an insight into the complicated and almost opposing relationship between the Luxembourg Court and other international courts and tribunals which may or may not give a foretaste of the relationship between the CJEU and the European Court of Human Rights (ECtHR) after accession. Beyond that, this chapter illustrates Luxembourg's seminal case law which is also of utmost significance for the accession procedure and which is constantly referred to in the later parts of this book. The most prominent decisions which accompany the reader throughout this entire legal analysis are, inter alia, *Opinion 1/91*,[1] the *Commission v Ireland (MOX Plant)* case[2] and the famous *Kadi and Al Barakaat v Council and Commission* judgment.[3] These decisions and opinions represent the theoretical backbone of the European Union's legal autonomy and must be taken into consideration for the successful preservation of the EU's autonomy principle.

---

[1] See Opinion 1/91 *EEA I (Draft agreement between the Community, on the one hand, and the countries of the European Free Trade Association, on the other, relating to the creation of the European Economic Area)* [1991] ECR I-6079.

[2] See Case C-459/03 *Commission v Ireland (MOX Plant)* [2006] I-4635.

[3] See Joined Cases C-402/05 P and C-415/05 P *Kadi and Al Barakaat v Council and Commission* [2008] ECR I- 6351.

A major portion of Part II, however, is dedicated to the current relationship between Luxembourg and Strasbourg and their 'cross-fertilising'[4] judicial interplay. Accordingly, chapter five illustrates how the CJEU took recourse to the Convention in order to establish the Union's case law-based fundamental rights catalogue; what role the European Union's Charter of Fundamental Rights plays in light of accession; how the ECtHR reacted to alleged human rights violations by EU institutions, especially in its decisions in *Matthews v United Kingdom*[5] and *Bosphorus v Ireland*;[6] and how Luxembourg's *Opinion 2/94*[7] might still be relevant for accession and the legal issues involved. As aforementioned, this profound analysis of past and current cases illustrates the ambiguous relationship between Strasbourg and Luxembourg. Beyond that, chapter six raises questions regarding the EU's accession to the Convention which Part III eventually examines in detail.

II. THE SHAPE OF THINGS TO COME

Part III, the centrepiece of this book, follows the road from Luxembourg to Strasbourg and goes into more detail regarding the abovementioned research question, namely how accession and autonomy can effectively be reconciled. Over the course of five chapters, this research question is broken down into more specific questions which are then answered within the respective line of reasoning and with due reference to the theoretical findings of Part II.

Chapter seven ('The Accession Agreement and the Status of the Convention after Accession') analyses what rank the Convention and the Accession Agreement—as international treaties—will have within the European Union's legal order after accession. Clarifying the Convention's future status within EU law is crucial in terms of its possible legal consequences, which are dependent on the Convention's rank, be it primary law, secondary law, something in between or none of the above. The general research question is therefore adapted to the issue of whether the Convention's legal rank after accession may jeopardise the autonomy of Union law or may even help overcome some legal problems of the past, for example alleged human rights violations by EU law itself.

Chapter eight ('External Review by Strasbourg: A Subordination of the Luxembourg Court?') examines the question of whether the European Union's subjection under Strasbourg's external review may violate the Union's autonomy principle. To this end, the general research question is split up into two parts; the

---

[4] See Francis G Jacobs, 'Judicial Dialogue and the Cross-Fertilization of Legal Systems: The European Court of Justice' (2003) 38 *Texas International Law Journal* 547, 548f, and Laurent Scheeck, 'The Relationship between the European Courts and Integration through Human Rights' (2005) 65 *Zeitschrift für ausländisches öffentliches Recht und Völkerrecht* 837, 868f.

[5] See *Matthews v United Kingdom* App no 24833/94 (ECtHR, 18 February 1999).

[6] See *Bosphorus v Ireland* App no 45036/98 (ECtHR, 30 June 2005).

[7] See Opinion 2/94 *Accession by the Community to the European Convention for the Protection of Human Rights and Fundamental Freedoms* [1996] ECR I-1759.

first debates whether the ECtHR would have to interpret Union law in a binding manner (which would in fact interfere with the EU's legal autonomy), and the second dealing with the issue of whether a judgment by Strasbourg, ruling that EU legislation infringed the rights enshrined in the Convention, would be compatible with the autonomy of EU law. Moreover, this chapter scrutinises to what extent EU primary law and secondary law are subject to Strasbourg's judicial review.

Chapter nine ('Individual Applications after Accession: Introducing the Co-Respondent Mechanism') explores how the system of individual applications under Article 34 ECHR) will be arranged and organised after accession. To be exact, this chapter takes a closer look at the issue of individuals wishing to challenge a legal act allegedly in violation of human rights who may not know against which entity (Member State and/or the European Union) their applications must be directed. Therefore, it presents and critically analyses the solution found in the Draft Accession Agreement, namely the so-called 'co-respondent mechanism' which allows the Union and the Member States to join proceedings as equal respondent parties. Nevertheless, this chapter also asks what dangers this new mechanism may trigger for the EU's legal autonomy and through which legal safeguards these risks can be reduced or even entirely eliminated.

Chapter 10 ('Inter-Party Cases after Accession') deals with disputes between the high contracting parties under Article 33 ECHR (the so-called inter-state cases) in a twofold manner: Firstly, the book investigates the internal dimension of Article 33 ECHR after accession and the problem of inter-state cases (or *inter-party* cases as they should appropriately be called after the EU's accession to the Convention) potentially causing a major jurisdictional conflict between Luxembourg and Strasbourg. Since both courts claim exclusive jurisdiction for disputes between their Member States or contracting parties, respectively, a clash between them seems unavoidable. In its reformulated version, the general research question thus asks whether the provisions of the Draft Accession Agreement are capable of solving this conflict and whether the internal Union mechanisms for dispute settlement may hold the key to this solution. Secondly, chapter 10 examines the external scope of Article 33 ECHR and asks whether the European Union has the competence to emerge as a prominent human rights litigator after accession, in order to remind candidate countries of their obligations under the so-called *Copenhagen Criteria*, for example, and thus to put them on the right track towards EU accession.

The last chapter of Part III, chapter 11 ('The Exhaustion of Domestic Remedies and the Prior Involvement of the Luxembourg Court'), looks into the intricate interplay between the 'exhaustion of local remedies rule' under Article 35 ECHR and those situations in which Strasbourg may end up adjudicating on alleged human rights violations by European Union law, but where the CJEU had no prior opportunity to pronounce itself on the said violations. In the past, it has been argued that such a situation would gravely endanger the EU's legal autonomy, since an external court would decide on Union law without the involvement of the Luxembourg Court, which would, in turn, violate the CJEU's exclusive jurisdiction. This book therefore suggests various solutions to this problem by taking into account both the autonomy principle and the effective protection of individuals. Furthermore, this chapter also analyses whether individuals, claiming a human rights violation by Union law, are obliged under Article 35 ECHR to first exhaust all internal Union remedies, ie the action for annulment or a reference for a preliminary ruling, before calling upon the Strasbourg Court.

III. CONCLUSIONS AND OUTLOOK

The last part, Part IV, summarises and assesses the findings of the previous parts. Most importantly, it will answer the research question of this book and conclude that the EU's legal autonomy is in fact reconcilable with the European Union's accession to the ECHR and its subjection to Strasbourg's external review. Beyond that, it shows what impact the accession will have on the European Union's legal order; on the relationship between the Luxembourg and Strasbourg Courts; on the role of the domestic courts; and, above all, on the existing and complicated multi-level framework of human rights protection in Europe. It also depicts potential weaknesses identified within this book, for example the effective yet complicated mechanisms introduced by the Accession Agreement, and calls upon the European Union and its Member States to adopt internal rules particularly designed to address and solve these issues in order to make the EU's accession to the Convention as effective as possible for the protection of human rights in Europe.

Part II

The Autonomy of European Union Law versus International Law and Courts

3

The Notion of Legal Autonomy

I. THE LEGAL FRAMEWORK: THE CJEU'S EXCLUSIVE JURISDICTION

IN ORDER TO understand the concerns about upholding the autonomy of the Union's legal order and the subsequent difficulties arising from the European Union's accession to the Convention, it is primarily crucial to define the term 'legal autonomy', namely from the Court of Justice of the European Union's (CJEU) point of view, and its implications for EU law, especially relating to international law in general, international treaties and international courts and tribunals.

Principally, the word αὐτό-νομος (*autónomos*) means self-legislation or the legal authority to govern domestic affairs without external interference,[1] which, in the case of the Union, leads to the notion of an entirely independent, quasi-state like legal order. Since its renowned judgment in *Costa v ENEL*,[2] it is a well-established fact that Luxembourg regards the Union's supranational legal order to be autonomous, in order to ensure first and foremost the *effet utile*[3] of the Treaties and thus the supremacy of EU law over the domestic legal orders of the Member States. The CJEU's teleological interpretation[4] of the Treaties is consequently considered the first step in establishing a functioning constitutional order of its own that is autonomous from the national legal systems of the Union's Member States.[5] In every case in which the CJEU resorted to this formula, the invocation of the autonomy of the Union's legal order was related to the affirmation of the abovementioned supremacy of European Union law over conflicting rules of

---

[1] See Anne Peters, *Elemente einer Theorie der Verfassung Europas* (Berlin, Duncker & Humblot, 2001) 243.

[2] See Case 6/64 *Costa v ENEL* [1964] ECR 585 where the CJEU ruled that the Treaties have created 'their own legal system'.

[3] See Case 41/74 *Van Duyn v Home Office* [1974] ECR 1337, para 2.

[4] See Art 31 (1) of the Vienna Convention on the Law of Treaties; see also Mark E Villiger, *Commentary on the 1969 Vienna Convention on the Law of Treaties* (Leiden, Brill Academic Publishers, 2009) 427ff, and Pieter Jan Kuijper, 'The European Courts and the Law of Treaties: The Continuing Story' in Enzo Cannizzaro (ed), *The Law of Treaties Beyond the Vienna Convention* (Oxford, Oxford University Press, 2011) 256ff.

[5] For questions related to the degree of the EU's legal autonomy from the legal systems of its Member States, see generally René Barents, *The Autonomy of Community Law* (The Hague, Kluwer Law, 2004).

domestic law.[6] For instance, in *Internationale Handelsgesellschaft*, the Luxembourg Court declared that

> the validity of an EC measure or its effect within a Member State cannot be affected by allegations that it runs counter to either fundamental rights as formulated by the constitution of that State or the principles of a national constitutional structure.[7]

Prima facie, the Member States had no difficulty in accepting the supremacy of EU law. However, the issue that caused some problems was the question raised by the German Constitutional Court, over whether EU law could take priority over the inalienable fundamental rights contained in the German Basic Law.[8] In the subsequent years, the CJEU attempted to clarify its position and to give assurances to the Member States. In the subsequent cases, Luxembourg explained that basic human rights form part of Union law.[9] These basic rights are not only general principles of European Union law, but are also inspired by the constitutional traditions of the Member States, the European Convention on Human Rights and Strasbourg's case law as well. On the grounds of this constitutional nature, all EU legislation can be traced back to a sole norm as the definitive source of validity, ie the Treaties.[10] Therefore, it is obvious that EU law must necessarily be tantamount to a legal order entirely autonomous from the law of its Member States. Most importantly, due to pragmatic reasons, the uniformity and efficacy of Union law would be jeopardised if domestic courts used their respective constitutions to bridle the enforcement of EU law within the Member States.[11] The Treaties are autonomous in the sense that they are not determined by the legal orders from which they are derived. In other words, once they have been concluded, they take on a life of their own.[12]

Although the drafters of the Treaties did not include an explicit autonomy or supremacy clause,[13] there are two provisions relating to the CJEU's exclusive jurisdiction and thence the Union's legal autonomy. After the entry into force of the Treaty of Lisbon, one implicit reference to the Union's legal autonomy can be found in Article 19 (1) TEU), which entrusts the CJEU with the observance of the law in the interpretation and application of the Treaties, thereby making it the

---

[6] See Bruno De Witte, 'European Union Law: How Autonomous is its Legal Order?' (2010) 65 *Zeitschrift für Öffentliches Recht* 141, 142.

[7] Case 11/70 *Internationale Handelsgesellschaft mbH v Einfuhr- und Vorratsstelle für Getreide und Futtermittel* [1970] ECR 1125, para 3.

[8] See BvL 52/71 *Solange I* BVerfGE 37, 271, and 2 BvR 197/83 *Solange II* BVerfGE 73, 339.

[9] See especially Case 29/69 *Stauder v City of Ulm* [1969] ECR 419; Case 11/70 *Internationale Handelsgesellschaft* (n 7); and Case 4/73 *Nold v Ruhrkohle Aktiengesellschaft* [1977] ECR 1.

[10] See Aida Torres Pérez, *Conflicts of Rights in the European Union: A Theory of Supranational Adjudication* (Oxford, Oxford University Press, 2009) 52.

[11] See Jan Wouters, 'National Constitutions and the European Union' (2000) 27 *Legal Issues of Economic Integration* 25, 64f.

[12] See Theodor Schilling, 'The Autonomy of the Community Legal Order: An Analysis of Possible Foundations' (1996) 37 *Harvard International Law Journal* 389, 404.

[13] Such a clause was included, for example, in art VI, cl 2 of the Constitution of the United States of America.

sole and ultimate authority[14] on the interpretation and the uniform application for all EU law.[15] Article 19 (1) TEU is thus sometimes regarded as the archetypal inflexible exclusive jurisdiction clause.[16] So far, the Luxembourg Court's concern about the uniform application of Union law has dominated most of its case law.[17] Article 19 (1) subsequently guarantees Luxembourg's exclusive jurisdiction to rule on EU law, as it must have the last say over national courts in order to ensure legal uniformity within the Union.

Another reference to the European Union's legal autonomy and hence the CJEU's exclusive jurisdiction is set forth in Article 344 of the Treaty on the Functioning of the European Union (TFEU). According to this provision, the Luxembourg Court is the sole authority to settle disputes between Member States or a Member State and the Union's institutions concerning the interpretation or application of the Treaties, thus barring Member States from submitting a dispute relating to EU law to any form of settlement other than those provided for therein. In other words, once a dispute arises relating to the 'interpretation or application' of the Treaties, the Member States have no other way than to bring the case before the CJEU[18] which will ensure the uniform interpretation and application of Union law. This merely leaves the Member States with an action for failure to fulfil obligations under Article 259 TFEU in order to bring alleged infringements of Union law by other Member States before the Court.

Thus, the main objective of Article 344 TFEU is to exclude other international courts or tribunals from adjudicating on cases involving the Union's Member States and, most significantly, Union law. The inclusion of this provision was particularly intended to exclude the jurisdiction of the International Court of Justice in disputes between Member States that have accepted its jurisdiction either on the basis of a special ad hoc agreement under Article 36 (1) of the Statute of the International Court of Justice ('ICJ Statute') or by the use of an Optional Clause Declaration, according to Article 36 (2) of the ICJ Statute.[19] Otherwise, Member States could bring actions involving the interpretation and application of EU law before the ICJ which would subsequently foster the fragmentation of the Union's

---

[14] See Hans Christian Krüger, 'Reflections Concerning Accession of the European Communities to the European Convention on Human Rights' (2002) 21 *Penn State International Law Review* 89, 95.

[15] See, eg Franz C Mayer, 'Art 19 EUV' in Eberhard Grabitz, Meinhard Hilf and Martin Nettesheim (eds), *Das Recht der Europäischen Union. Band I* (Munich, Beck, 2010) para 33.

[16] See Yuval Shany, *The Competing Jurisdictions of International Courts and Tribunals* (Oxford, Oxford University Press, 2003) 180.

[17] See especially Case 106/77 *Simmenthal II* [1978] ECR 629, para 14; Case 44/79 *Hauer v Land Rheinland-Pfalz* [1979] ECR 3727, para 14; Joined Cases C-6/90 and C-9/90 *Francovich v Italian Republic* [1991] ECR I-5357, paras 38ff; Opinion 1/91 *EEA I (Draft agreement between the Community, on the one hand, and the countries of the European Free Trade Association, on the other, relating to the creation of the European Economic Area)* [1991] ECR I-6079, para 35; Case C-228/92 *Roquette Frères SA v Hauptzollamt Geldern (Roquette Frères I)* [1994] ECR I-1445, para 27.

[18] See Koen Lenaerts, Dirk Arts, Ignace Maselis and Robert Bray, *Procedural Law of the European Union*, 2nd edn (London, Sweet & Maxwell, 2006) 492.

[19] See Tobias Lock, *Das Verhältnis zwischen dem EuGH und internationalen Gerichten* (Tübingen, Mohr Siebeck, 2010) 156.

legal order and thus obstruct its uniformity. Article 344 TFEU is accordingly considered a *lex specialis* provision to the principle of loyal cooperation enshrined in Article 4 (3) TEU, thence excluding both national and international courts from interpreting Union law.[20]

Still, the only example to date where Article 344 TFEU was explicitly invoked by the Luxembourg Court is the illustrious *Commission v Ireland (MOX Plant)*[21] case which will be examined in detail later on.[22] Moreover, as the scope of Article 19 (1) TEU and Article 344 TFEU forms the essence of the CJEU's 'interpretative autonomy',[23] these two provisions will consequently play a very important role in relation to international law and thus the accession to the Convention.

II. ACCESSION AND AUTONOMY: JUSTIFIED CONCERNS
OR MUCH ADO ABOUT NOTHING?

Given the aforementioned significance of Luxembourg's exclusive jurisdiction and the legal autonomy for the European Union's legal order, it is of utmost importance to examine whether the European Union's future accession to the Convention, a treaty-based system of human rights protection with a judicial body to assess potential human rights violations, will detrimentally affect the EU's legal autonomy or not. Over the past decades, a sceptical view towards foreign influences on EU law has raised many objections against the accession, most notably concerning the risks involved for the autonomy of the EU's specific legal system and the incompatibility of a CJEU subordinated to the Strasbourg Court and its external judicial control.[24] To prevent any interference with the Union's legal autonomy in the first place, a couple of legal safeguards were put in place. One of them is Article 6 (2) TEU, which succinctly states that '[t]he Union shall accede to the European Convention for the Protection of Human Rights and Fundamental Freedoms. *Such accession shall not affect the Union's competences as defined in the Treaties*.'[25]

But beyond this short and concise wording, this provision does not describe the exact modalities of the accession or the future relationship between Luxembourg and Strasbourg, nor does it mention the EU's specific features; its legal autonomy first and foremost, or how this characteristic legal trait can be upheld after accession.[26] However, Article 6 (2) TEU must be read in conjunction with Protocol No 8

---

[20] See ibid 157.
[21] Case C-459/03 *Commission v Ireland (MOX Plant)* [2006] ECR I-4635.
[22] See ch 4. See also ch 10 for an analysis of art 344 TFEU after accession.
[23] See Schilling, 'Autonomy' (n 12) 398f.
[24] See, eg Court of Justice of the European Union, 'Discussion Document of the Court of Justice of the European Union on certain aspects of the accession of the European Union to the European Convention for the Protection of Human Rights and Fundamental Freedoms', 5 May 2010, paras 4ff.
[25] Emphasis added.
[26] See Paul Gragl, 'Accession Revisited: Will Fundamental Rights Protection Trump the European Union's Legal Autonomy' in Wolfgang Benedek, Florence Benoît-Rohmer, Wolfram Karl and Manfred Nowak (eds), *European Yearbook on Human Rights 2011* (Vienna, NWV, 2011) 160.

which readdresses the autonomy issue and states that an accession agreement 'shall make provision for preserving the specific characteristics of the Union and Union law, [...]',[27] especially with regard to the Union's participation in the Convention control bodies (lit a) and to the creation of mechanisms which are necessary to ensure that inter-party complaints by non-Member States and individual applications are correctly addressed to Member States and/or the Union as appropriate (lit b).

Moreover, according to Article 2 of Protocol No 8, the agreement on accession 'shall ensure that accession of the Union shall not affect the competences of the Union or the powers of its institutions'. This also includes the obligation of the Member States under Article 344 TFEU not to submit a dispute concerning the interpretation or application of the Treaties to any other court or tribunal than the Luxembourg Court. Consequently, Article 3 of Protocol No 8 sets forth that nothing in the accession agreement shall affect Article 344 TFEU. Besides, Declaration No 2 on Article 6 (2) TEU also calls for the accession agreement to be arranged in 'such a way as to preserve the specific features of Union law'.[28] Yet, whereas the Treaties aim to enshrine the Union's legal autonomy as much as possible, the receiving end, namely the Convention, merely states that the Union 'may accede' to the Convention (Art 59 (2) of the European Convention on Human Rights (ECHR)).[29] No reference to preserving the autonomy of European Union law can be found in the Convention.

In a nutshell, these provisions represent a short but concise list of elements which are indispensable in regards to the Union's legal system. However, it is still doubtful whether the drafters' intention to preserve the European Union's legal autonomy, particularly by constantly reiterating that the EU's powers and competences shall not be affected by the accession, will eventually be complied with in the legal reality of international courts and divided competences between the Union and its Member States.[30] When dealing with this particular topic, certain scholars and experts continuously argue that accession will not, in any way, call into question the autonomy of Union law,[31] since the CJEU will remain the sole

---

[27] See Art 1 of Protocol No 8 relating to Art 6, para 2 of the TEU on the accession of the European Union to the European Convention on the Protection of Human Rights and Fundamental Freedoms.

[28] See Declarations Concerning Provisions of the Treaties, 2. Declaration on Article 6 (2) of the Treaty on European Union [2010] OJ C83/335, 3.

[29] See Jonas Christoffersen, *Institutional Aspects of the EU's Accession to the ECHR*. European Parliament, Committee on Constitutional Affairs, Hearing on the Institutional Aspects of the European Union's Accession to the European Convention on Human Rights, 18 March 2010, 2.

[30] See Gragl, 'Accession Revisited' (n 26) 160f.

[31] See, eg Olivier De Schutter, *L'adhésion de l'Union européenne à la Convention européenne des droits de l'homme: feuille de route de la négociation.* European Parliament, Committee on Constitutional Affairs, Hearing on the Institutional Aspects of the European Union's Accession to the European Convention on Human Rights, 10 April 2010, 10; Krüger, 'Reflections' (n 14) 95f.; Hans Christian Krüger and Jörg Polakiewicz, 'Vorschläge für ein kohärentes System des Menschenrechtsschutzes in Europa' (2001) 28 *Europäische Grundrechte-Zeitschrift* 92, 100f; Siegbert Alber and Ulrich Widmaier, 'Die EU-Charta der Grundrechte und ihre Auswirkungen auf die Rechtsprechung' (2000) 27 *Europäische Grundrechte-Zeitschrift* 497, 506f.

Supreme Court adjudicating on all cases related to European Union law and the validity of the Union's legal acts.[32] Furthermore, the Strasbourg Court

> could not be regarded as a superior Court but rather as a specialised Court exercising external control over the international law obligations of the Union resulting from the accession to the Convention. The position of the Court of Justice would be analogous to that of national Constitutional or Supreme Courts in relation to the Strasbourg Court at present.[33]

In addition, these scholars opine that under no circumstances would the European Court of Human Rights (ECtHR) review all the judgments arriving from Luxembourg, just those cases raising issues involving the protection of human rights under the Convention. These cases would thus merely represent a small percentage of those brought before the Strasbourg Court.[34] Luxembourg would not be subordinated to Strasbourg for another simple reason: When drawing parallels with national Supreme Courts, one can see that Strasbourg does not have the power to annul their judgments, but only to give declaratory rulings on the conformity of these judgments with the Convention.[35] Lastly, the ECtHR would be obliged to apply the principle of subsidiarity[36] in every case, which defines the Court's relationship vis-à-vis the authorities of the contracting parties to the Convention. It is thence a logical consequence that the CJEU would principally be responsible for guaranteeing an effective protection of fundamental rights within the EU, according not only to the Charter of Fundamental Rights of the European Union (ChFR), which is virtually the Union's internal 'Bill of Rights',[37] but under the Convention as well.

Given the similarities between the European Union and the other contracting parties to the Convention, this point of view is very plausible. Moreover, prima facie, these arguments seem remarkably convincing. The Luxembourg Court can certainly be regarded as a quasi-domestic court, analogous to a Supreme Court of any other Convention party. This position was also reconfirmed at the first meeting of the 'Informal Working Group on the Accession' between the EU and the

---

[32] See European Parliament, 'Resolution on the Institutional Aspects of Accession by the European Union to the European Convention for the Protection of Human Rights and Fundamental Freedoms' P7_TA-PROV(2010)0184, para 1.

[33] See European Convention, 'Final Report of Working Group II' CONV 354/02, WG II 16, 12. For a similar approach, see also European Parliament, 'Resolution on the Institutional Aspects of Accession' (n 32) para 1; and Krüger, 'Reflections' (n 14) 97.

[34] See Alber and Widmaier (n 31) 506.

[35] See René Van der Linden, *Accession of the EC/EU to the European Convention on Human Rights*. European Parliament, Committee on Constitutional Affairs, Hearing on the Institutional Aspects of the European Union's Accession to the European Convention on Human Rights, 18 March 2010, 5.

[36] See art 35 ECHR and the 'exhaustion of local remedies rule' which represents a basic principle of international law; see eg Jens Meyer-Ladewig, *Europäische Menschenrechtskonvention. Handkommentar*, 3rd edn (Baden-Baden, Nomos, 2011) art 35, para 7.

[37] See Serhiy Holovaty, *Institutional Aspects of the EU's Accession to the ECHR*. European Parliament, Committee on Constitutional Affairs, Hearing on the Institutional Aspects of the European Union's Accession to the European Convention on Human Rights, 18 March 2010, 3.

Council of Europe.[38] The Luxembourg Court, like any other national Supreme or Constitutional Court, observes the proper interpretation and application of the law within its jurisdiction. After the entry into force of the Treaty of Lisbon, this law also encompasses the European Union's principal fundamental rights document, the Charter of Fundamental Rights, which is, by virtue of Article 6 (1) TEU, part of the Union's primary law.[39] And, of course, after the successful accession to the Convention, the Convention will form an integrative part of the EU as well. This means that the CJEU will apply the Convention in fundamental rights cases and take into account the case law of the Strasbourg Court.[40] By properly protecting the rights set forth in the Charter and the Convention, the CJEU is— analogously speaking—no more or less powerful than any other domestic court of the Convention's contracting parties, overseeing the accurate application of a legal provision in accordance with 'constitutionally' assured fundamental rights.[41] Lastly, when regarding the importance and the original purpose of the future accession, it is highly doubtful whether absolute legal autonomy in respect of the protection of human rights under an international legal system such as the Convention is desirable at all.[42]

However, this point of view conveniently ignores the fact that the European Union is neither a purely international organisation (or at least that, at some point in history, it ceased to exist as such and became a supranational organisation), nor a federation or federal republic. The European Union is, indisputably, a special creation *sui generis* whose integration into another system of international law, namely into Strasbourg's judicial protection system, deserves special consideration. Even though these problems have largely been dismissed out of hand, both in the Treaties themselves[43] and in academic contributions,[44] the EU's unique features, most notably the specific division of competences between the Union and its Member States and the role of the CJEU as the exclusive and ultimate arbiter of Union law,[45] will certainly cause some serious problems regarding the EU's legal autonomy.

[38] See Council of Europe, '1st Meeting of the CDDH Informal Working Group on the Accession of the European Union to the European Convention on Human Rights (CDDH-UE) with the European Commission. Summary of Discussions of the Informal Meeting of Member States' Representatives in the CDDH' CDDH-UE (2010)01, para 18.

[39] See for more details, eg Frank Schorkopf, 'Art 6 EUV' in Eberhard Grabitz, Meinhard Hilf and Martin Nettesheim (eds), *Das Recht der Europäischen Union. Band I* (Munich, Beck, 2010) paras 28ff.

[40] See Olivier De Schutter in Council of Europe—Parliamentary Assembly, *The Accession of the European Union/European Community to the European Convention on Human Rights*, Doc 11533 (Committee on Legal Affairs and Human Rights) 18 March 2008, 30.

[41] See Gragl, 'Accession Revisited' (n 26) 164.

[42] See, eg Lock, *Verhältnis* (n 19) 291.

[43] See, as aforementioned, art 6 (2) TEU, and Protocol No 8 to the Treaties.

[44] See, eg Krüger, 'Reflections' (n 14) 96, and Council of Europe—Parliamentary Assembly, *Accession of the European Union* (n 40) 10f, 28f, and 35f.

[45] See Jean-Paul Jacqué, *L'adhésion à la Convention européenne des droits de l'homme*. Note à l'attention de la Commission institutionnelle en vue de l'audition du 18 mars 2010. European Parliament, Committee on Constitutional Affairs, Hearing on the Institutional Aspects of the European Union's Accession to the European Convention on Human Rights, 18 March 2010, 2.

III. THE UNION'S LEGAL AUTONOMY AND INTERNATIONAL LAW

For the purpose of this book, it is crucial to take a closer look at the relationship between the Union's legal autonomy and international law in general, especially when examining the European Union's accession to the Convention, an international human rights treaty. In order to understand and solve the jurisdictional issues the accession will entail for the Union's concept of legal autonomy, the EU's past and present relationship with international law must first be thoroughly scrutinised. This section therefore emphasises the meaning of the autonomy of EU law in its *external* aspect, ie the international legal system in general. Moreover, the expansion of the Union's competences, encompassing ever more policy areas and thereby the expansion of the CJEU's jurisdiction, might lead to jurisdictional conflicts with other international courts or quasi-judicial bodies in the future. In particular, due to the renowned *AETR*-formula[46] pronounced by the Luxembourg Court, the Union automatically acquires exclusive external competence in a policy field in which it has already promulgated legislation. This development has resulted in an enormous expansion of the European Union's activities on the international level, predominantly through the ratification of several international agreements and memberships in international organisations.[47]

Despite the CJEU's ruling in *Van Gend en Loos v Netherlands Inland Revenue Administration*, stating that the 'Community constitutes a new legal order of international law',[48] the European Economic Community was undoubtedly, at least at its inception, a creature of international law,[49] arguably an international organisation,[50] which, allegedly from the 1960s onwards, was transformed into a constitutional legal order *sui generis*.[51] The CJEU's main intention of delineating Union law from international law, however, was again to uphold the supremacy of EU law over the domestic application of international law. As a result, Member

---

[46] See Case 22/70 *Commission v Council (AETR)* [1971] ECR 263, para 19.

[47] See Nikolaos Lavranos, 'Concurrence of Jurisdiction between the CJEU and other International Courts and Tribunals, EUSA Ninth Biennial International Conference', March 31–April 2, 2005, Austin, Texas, Conference Paper 1, 12; see also, more extensively on this topic, Piet Eeckhout, *EU External Relations Law* (Oxford, Oxford University Press, 2011).

[48] Case 26/62 *Van Gend en Loos v Netherlands Inland Revenue Administration* [1963] ECR 1, para 25.

[49] See JHH Weiler, 'The Transformation of Europe' (1991) 100 *Yale Law Journal* 2403, 2413ff; see also Schilling, 'Autonomy' (n 12) 403.

[50] But see JHH Weiler and Ulrich R Haltern, 'Constitutional or International? The Foundations of the Community Legal Order and the Question of Judicial Kompetenz-Kompetenz' in Anne-Marie Slaughter, Alec Stone Sweet and JHH Weiler (eds), *The European Courts and National Courts: Doctrine and Jurisprudence* (Oxford, Hart Publishing, 1998) 342, who argue that continuing to refer to the EU as an international organisation is 'to try to push the toothpaste back in the tube'.

[51] See JHH Weiler and Ulrich R Haltern, 'The Autonomy of the Community Legal Order—Through the Looking Glass' (1996) 37 *Harvard International Law Journal* 411, 420. Arguing against this opinion, see Axel Marschik, *Subsysteme im Völkerrecht. Ist die Europäische Union ein 'Self-Contained Regime'?* (Berlin, Duncker & Humblot, 1997) 220ff.

States with dualistic constitutions, relying on the concept of transformation to implement non-municipal law into their own legal order, could not extenuate or even nullify the efficacy of Union law by passing a derogating *lex posterior*.[52] But even as an autonomous legal system, European Union law has not ceased to be part of international law. The Union courts perceive the EU to be bound by international law, especially by treaties to which the EU itself is a party,[53] but also to other treaties,[54] and customary international law.[55] Moreover, the Luxembourg Court held that it will interpret secondary legislation[56] in accordance with international law.[57]

In this context, the United Nations and its Charter, sometimes regarded as a constitution for the world community,[58] take on a special position. But the European Union is not a member of the United Nations and it cannot become a member since the United Nations is, according to Article 4 of its Charter, only open to nation-states. This means that, from a formal point of view, the EU is not obliged to implement Security Council Resolutions. On several occasions, however, these resolutions have also called upon international organisations to abide by them.[59] For instance, in its *Kadi and Al Barakaat v Council and Commission* judgment,[60] which is accurately acclaimed as a strong corroboration of the autonomy of EU law in relation to international law, the Luxembourg Court examined the effects of such a Security Council Resolution and discussed what is called 'the relationship between the international legal order under the United Nations and the Community legal order'.[61]

---

[52] See Peters (n 1) 244.

[53] See art 218 TFEU and Case 104/81 *Kupferberg & Cie KG (Kupferberg I)* [1982] ECR 3641, para 11.

[54] For example, according to art 78 (1) TFEU, the common policy on asylum, subsidiary protection and temporary protection must comply with the principle of *non-refoulement* and the Geneva Convention of 28 July 1951 and the Protocol of 31 January 1967 relating to the status of refugees.

[55] See art 3 (5) TEU, and art 21 (1) and (2) TEU, implicitly referring to customary international law. See also Case C-162/96 *Racke GmbH v Hauptzollamt Mainz* [1998] ECR I-3655, paras 25ff; and Case T-115/94 *Opel Austria GmbH v Council* [1998] ECR II-2739, para 77.

[56] See eg, Case C-286/90 *Poulsen* [1992] ECR I-6019, para 9; see also Case C-377/98 *Netherlands v European Parliament and Council* [2001] ECR I-7079, para 55.

[57] See Marco Bronckers, 'The Relationship of the EC Courts with other International Tribunals: Non-Committal, Respectful or Submissive?' (2007) 44 *Common Market Law Review* 601, 602; see also Lavranos, 'Concurrence' (n 47) 12.

[58] See Bardo Fassbender, 'The United Nations Charter as Constitution of the International Community' (1998) 36 *Columbia Journal of Transnational Law* 531, 542.

[59] See Lavranos, 'Concurrence' (n 47) 20.

[60] For an extensive account of the case's background, see, eg Albert Posch, 'The *Kadi* Case: Rethinking the Relationship between EU Law and International Law?' (2009) 15 *The Columbia Journal of European Law Online* 1, 1ff.

[61] Joined Cases C-402/05 P and C-415/05 P *Kadi and Al Barakaat v Council and Commission* [2008] ECR I- 6351, para 290.

In *Kadi*, the CJEU recalled the abiding and inextricable divide between the Union's 'domestic' legal order and international law.[62] By following the Opinion of Advocate General Maduro,[63] the Luxembourg Court ruled that

> the review by the Court of the validity of any Community measure in the light of fundamental rights must be considered to be the expression, in a community based on the rule of law, of a constitutional guarantee stemming from the EC Treaty as an *autonomous legal system* which is not to be prejudiced by an international agreement.[64]

The nucleus of this judgment is that an international agreement cannot affect the allocation or division of powers fixed by the Treaties which, in fact, represent the European Union's constitutional basis. The autonomy of the EU's legal system, especially vis-à-vis international law, is consequently observed and thus ensured by the Luxembourg Court by virtue of the exclusive jurisdiction conferred on it by Article 19 (1) TEU—a jurisdiction that the CJEU has already held to form part of the very foundations of the Union.[65] Thence, Luxembourg made it clear that an international agreement—in the *Kadi* case the UN Charter—cannot have the effect of prejudicing the constitutional principles of the European Union.[66] This assertion accordingly links the EU's legal autonomy to its hierarchy of norms, with primary law taking priority over Union agreements and secondary law.[67]

The *Kadi* judgment of the CJEU is arguably the most important decision to date on the subject of the relationship between the European Union's legal order and international law in general. Luxembourg's judgment in *Kadi* conceptually marks a leap in the constitutionalism of the European Union's legal order.[68] In addition, another piece of evidence for this constitutional approach can be found in the Court's confirmation of the *Kadi* ruling in the more recent *Hassan v Council and Commission and Chafiq Ayadi v Council* case, where a contested EU regulation was annulled by, again, referring to the EU's autonomous legal order.[69]

---

[62] See Jean D'Aspremont and Frédéric Dopagne, '*Kadi*: The CJEU's Reminder of the Elementary Divide between Legal Orders' (2008) 5 *International Organisations Law Review* 317, 371.

[63] See Joined Cases C-402/05 P and C-415/05 P, *Kadi and Al Barakaat v Council and Commission* [2008] ECR I-6351, Opinion of AG Maduro, para 24, stating that the 'relationship between international law and the Community legal order is governed by the Community legal order itself, and international law can permeate that legal order only under the conditions set by the constitutional principles of the Community'.

[64] Joined Cases C-402/05 P and C-415/05 P *Kadi and Al Barakaat v Council and Commission* (n 61) para 316 (emphasis added).

[65] See ibid para 282. See also Opinion 1/91 *EEA I* (n 17) paras 35 and 71; and Case C-459/03 *Commission v Ireland (MOX Plant)* (n 21) para 123.

[66] Joined Cases C-402/05 P and C-415/05 P *Kadi and Al Barakaat v Council and Commission* (n 61) paras 333–34.

[67] See Case C-122/95 *Germany v Council (Framework Agreement on Bananas)* [1998] ECR I-973, paras 53ff; see also De Witte (n 6) 153.

[68] See Katja S Ziegler, 'Strengthening the Rule of Law, but Fragmenting International Law: The *Kadi* Decision from the Perspective of Human Rights' (2009) 9 *Human Rights Law Review* 288, 288.

[69] See Joined Cases C-399/06 P and C-403/06 P *Hassan v Council and Commission and Chafiq Ayadi v Council* [2009] ECR I-11393, paras 34 and 80ff.

By validating its view on European constitutionalism, Luxembourg effectively 'killed two birds with one stone': Not only did it corroborate the Union's concept of legal autonomy from the UN system and international law, it also prevented a resurgence of the *Solange*-doctrine from the German Constitutional Court or any other domestic Supreme Court[70] and thus shielded the autonomy of EU law both *externally* and *internally*.

Moreover, by adopting a sharply dualist tone in its approach to international law, the CJEU identified itself with the interpretation and approach of the US Supreme Court in various cases, such as *Medellin v Texas*,[71] which examined the gap between the domestic constitutional order and the absence of any national judicial role in shaping the relationship between the two different legal orders.[72] In brief, primary Union law still remains the 'supreme law of the land' for the European Union and its Member States, whereas obligations under international law continue to be subordinated to primary EU law.[73] This may possibly result in conflicting obligations resulting from European Union law and the UN Charter, especially in light of Article 103 of the UN Charter,[74] and in the further fragmentation of international law. Of course, the main purpose of the CJEU's judgment was not to undermine the UN system, but to protect the applicants' fundamental rights. In fact, the Court imposed a higher fundamental rights standard concerning the measures implementing UN law as would have otherwise been the case.[75] But at the same time, the Luxembourg Court delineated the internal legal order of the Union from international law by again coining it 'an autonomous legal system', mostly to the end of maintaining its supremacy over its Member States and their international obligations.

Luxembourg's objective to protect its exclusive jurisdiction is apparently a means of preserving the autonomy of the Union's legal order.[76] However, in reality, it seems to be the other way round: The concept of the Union's legal autonomy is brought forward as a rhetorical shield to help protect the CJEU's own exclusive

---

[70] See Giacomo Di Federico, 'Fundamental Rights in the EU: Legal Pluralism and Multi-Level Protection after the Lisbon Treaty' in Giacomo Di Federico (ed), *The EU Charter of Fundamental Rights. From Declaration to Binding Document* (Dordrecht, Springer Netherlands, 2011) 37.

[71] See 552 US 491 (2008) *Medellin v Texas*. In fact, this case did not deal with a Security Council Resolution, but with a judgment of the ICJ. The US Supreme Court ruled that '[w]hile a treaty may constitute an international commitment, it is not binding domestic law unless Congress has enacted statutes implementing it or the treaty itself conveys an intention that it be "self-executing" and is ratified on that basis'. (Syllabus, para 1(a)).

[72] See Gráinne De Búrca, 'The European Court of Justice and the International Legal Order after *Kadi*' Jean Monnet Working Paper No.1/09, 2009, 2ff <http://centers.law.nyu.edu/jeanmonnet/papers/09/090101.html> accessed 1 November 2012.

[73] See Nikolaos Lavranos, 'Judicial Review of UN Sanctions by the European Court of Justice' (2009) 78 *Nordic Journal of International Law* 343, 358.

[74] Art 103 of the UN Charter reads: 'In the event of a conflict between the obligations of the Members of the United Nations under the present Charter and their obligations under any other international agreement, their obligations under the present Charter shall prevail.'

[75] See Lavranos, 'Judicial Review' (n 73) 358.

[76] See Case C-459/03 *Commission v Ireland (MOX Plant)* [2006] ECR I-4635, Opinion of AG Maduro, para 10.

jurisdiction in EU law matters.[77] One might argue that the Luxembourg Court's overprotective attitude in its claims for absolute legal autonomy is rather dualistic and unfriendly towards international law, although the European Union is, according to the Court's own case law, generally bound by it.[78] However, Luxembourg's attitude is worrisome if it does indeed aspire to create a barrier around EU law, therewith running the risk of positioning the Union outside international law.[79]

The pivotal questions in this context are, firstly, what this 'isolationist' approach means for the European Union's accession to the Convention; secondly, whether the *Kadi* case will serve as an example of the CJEU's behaviour towards international law and the ECtHR in the future; and lastly, whether Luxembourg will and can thereby uphold this strict delineation of European Union law and international law after the accession to the Convention, particularly towards the legal protection regime created by the Convention. The next two chapters will therefore further analyse the legal status quo by examining the CJEU's relationship with other international courts and tribunals and, of course, above all, with the ECtHR whose role will be of utmost importance after accession.

[77] See De Witte, 'European Union Law' (n 6) 150.
[78] See eg, Joined Cases 21/72–24/72, *International Fruit Company and Others v Produktschap voor Groenten en Fruit* [1972] ECR 1219, para 7; see also Joined Cases 3/76, 4/76 and 6/76 *Kramer and Others (Biological Resources of the Sea)* [1976] ECR 1279, para 30.
[79] See Jan Klabbers, *Treaty Conflict and the European Union* (Cambridge, Cambridge University Press, 2009) 148.

4

The EU and International Courts and Tribunals

A
S MENTIONED IN chapter three, the European Union's legal autonomy and the exclusive jurisdiction of the Luxembourg Court are confronted with conflicting, sometimes even irreconcilable rules of international law. The Court of Justice of the European Union (CJEU) will therefore, according to Article 19 (1) of the Treaty on European Union (TEU) and Article 344 of the Treaty on the Functioning of the European Union (TFEU), vigilantly observe the uniform interpretation and application of Union law, in order to avoid interferences from any other regime, international court or tribunal, especially—in regards to the aim of this book—the European Court of Human Rights. The CJEU's well-known reputation for this approach stems from several judgments and opinions in the past which pursue one major end, namely upholding and safeguarding Luxembourg's exceptional position within the Union's legal order. This section therefore gives an account of different cases[1] in the past that bear some similarities with the jurisdictional issues brought about by accession. Moreover, it shows that the arguments the CJEU found in these cases, while defending its judicial monopoly and the Union's legal autonomy, are equally applicable to the impending consequences of the accession and the jurisdictional and procedural problems involved.

Due to the proliferation of international judicial bodies within the last decades[2] and in order to understand the overall picture of an increasingly judicial international system, the general relationship between the Union courts and other international courts is illustrated in this chapter. The proliferation of international courts is closely connected to the increased use of international agreements and the creation of numerous international organisations. To monitor

---

[1] See, for a more detailed analysis on the topic of jurisdictional conflicts in international law, Nikolaos Lavranos, *Jurisdictional Competition. Selected Cases in International and European Law* (Groningen, Europa Law Publishing, 2009).

[2] See Yuval Shany, *The Competing Jurisdictions of International Courts and Tribunals* (Oxford, Oxford University Press, 2003) 1ff; see Tobias Lock, *Das Verhältnis zwischen dem EuGH und internationalen Gerichten* (Tübingen, Mohr Siebeck, 2010) 14ff, see also Chester Brown, 'The Proliferation of International Courts and Tribunals: Finding Your Way through the Maze' (2002) 3 *Melbourne Journal of International Law* 453, 453ff.

the compliance with these new rules of international law and the subsequent enforcement of them, international treaties usually envisage the establishment of a dispute settlement mechanism or an international court or tribunal.[3]

A detailed scrutiny of the pertinent CJEU jurisprudence and the subsequent analysis of the legal effects of decisions issued by other international courts or tribunals help to shed light on the question of whether the CJEU's view is entitled to a more cooperative acclaim in the future.[4] Because of the special situation regarding the Luxembourg and Strasbourg Courts, primarily in view of accession, an exhaustive description of this unique judicial relationship is deliberately omitted in this chapter and will be given in the subsequent chapter five.

I. EUROPEAN UNION LAW AT RISK: THE CJEU AND THE EEA COURT

A. CJEU Opinion 1/91

Since 1960, the European Free Trade Association (EFTA) has worked as an economic community besides the European Union, primarily for those European countries that were either unable or unwilling to join the then European Economic Community (EEC). However, it has always been in the interest of both organisations that the legal system of the EFTA should be in line with EU law. The ultimate goal was to completely integrate all EFTA Member States into the Union's internal market with liberal trade and competition laws,[5] but without granting them full membership.[6] To this end, an agreement on the European Economic Area (EEA) between the Union and the EFTA Member States was drafted in 1990 which, in its initial version, envisaged the creation of an EEA Court. The EEA Court was, inter alia, intended to have the competence to settle disputes between the EEA 'Contracting Parties'. Moreover, the EEA Court and the CJEU were instructed to pay due regard to each other's rulings when interpreting provisions from the EEA Agreement, the Union Treaties or secondary legislation that were substantially identical. The EEA Agreement was to be concluded by the Union as a 'mixed agreement', which meant that both the Union and the Member States still

---

[3] See Nikolaos Lavranos, 'Das Rechtsprechungsmonopol des EuGH im Lichte der Proliferation internationaler Gerichte' (2007) 42 *Europarecht* 440, 442.

[4] See Kirsten Schmalenbach, 'Struggle for Exclusiveness: The CJEU and Competing International Tribunals' in Isabelle Buffard, James Crawford, Alain Pellet and Stephan Wittich (eds), *International Law between Universalism and Fragmentation. Festschrift in Honour of Gerhard Hafner* (Leiden, Brill, 2008) 1045.

[5] See Marco Bronckers, 'The Relationship of the EC Courts with other International Tribunals: Non-Committal, Respectful or Submissive?' (2007) 44 *Common Market Law Review* 601, 606.

[6] See generally on this topic Trevor C Hartley, 'The European Court and the EEA' (1992) 41 *International and Comparative Law Quarterly* 841, 841ff.

shared a decision-making competence.[7] On the Union's side, both the Union and its individual Member States would therefore sign the EEA Agreement.[8]

The European Commission however, was aware of the fact that the Luxembourg Court was extremely critical of the EEA, especially of the planned EEA Court,[9] and requested, prior to the ratification, an opinion on the agreement, pursuant to Article 218 (11) TFEU. At large, the CJEU confirmed that the establishment of an adjudicating system in an agreement, according to which another court would settle disputes between the contracting parties, is basically compatible with the EU Treaties. The decisions of the EEA Court would be binding on the CJEU, inter alia, 'where the Court of Justice is called upon to rule on the interpretation of the international agreement'.[10] Due to this provision, Luxembourg had the opportunity to apply Article 19 (1) TEU[11] and argued, however, that the establishment of such a dispute settlement institution was incompatible with the Treaties. The principles stipulated in this opinion go far beyond the scope of the agreement actually in question.[12] The Court rather took the opportunity to define the notion of autonomy with regard to the correlation between EU law and international law and held that

> [t]o confer [the jurisdiction to rule on the respective competences of the Community and the Member States as regards the matters governed by the provisions of the agreement creating the EEA to the EEA Court], is incompatible with Community Law since it is likely adversely to affect the allocation of responsibilities defined in the Treaties and the autonomy of the Community legal order, respect for which must be assured exclusively by the Court of Justice pursuant to Article [19 (1) TEU]. This exclusive jurisdiction of the Court of Justice is confirmed by Article [344 TFEU], under which Member States undertake not to submit a dispute concerning the interpretation or application of that Treaty to any method of settlement other than those provided for in the Treaty.[13]

Consequently, it did not bother Luxembourg that such a dispute settlement mechanism had the competence to interpret an agreement that, as an integral part of Union law,[14] would be subject to judicial interpretation by the CJEU. But nonetheless, if such an agreement contained provisions that altogether were duplications of primary and secondary EU law, the CJEU could not accept the creation of such a dispute settlement body. The insertion of parts of Union law into the EEA, linked with the agreement's purpose of uniform application,

---

[7] See generally on the topic of 'mixed agreements', Piet Eeckhout, *EU External Relations Law* (Oxford, Oxford University Press, 2011) 212ff.

[8] See Bronckers (n 5) 606.

[9] See Barbara Brandtner, 'The 'Drama' of the EEA. Comments on Opinions 1/91 and 1/92' (1992) 3 *European Journal of International Law* 300, 304, fn 19.

[10] See Opinion 1/91 *EEA I (Draft agreement between the Community, on the one hand, and the countries of the European Free Trade Association, on the other, relating to the creation of the European Economic Area)* [1991] ECR I-6079, para 39.

[11] Then art 219 TEC.

[12] See Brandtner (n 9) 300.

[13] Opinion 1/91 *EEA I* (n 10) para 35.

[14] See Case 181/73 *Haegeman v Belgian State* [1974] ECR 449, para 5.

must necessarily and automatically lead to the future interpretation of Union law being conditioned upon the EEA Court's interpretation.[15] To guarantee the CJEU's exclusive jurisdiction in applying and interpreting Union law and thus the EU's legal autonomy, it is intolerable for the CJEU that two entirely different courts have jurisdiction to interpret and apply literally identical, yet essentially different laws.[16] By settling disputes between the 'Contracting Parties' to the EEA Agreement, the EEA Court could end up ruling on the division of competences between the Union and its Member States. Such a course of action, however, would be contrary to the Treaties which assigned the allocation of such internal competences exclusively to the Luxembourg Court.[17] Thus, this draft agreement shook the very foundations of the Union and clashed with the Treaties that entrusted the interpretation of EU law to the Union courts.[18] This approach by the CJEU is often regarded as the creation of high-ranking core principles whose derogation is outside the legal limits of the Union's Member States.[19] Thence, according to Luxembourg, the autonomy of the EU's legal order, as well as the CJEU's exclusive jurisdiction, are part of these 'eternal' core principles[20] and entirely autonomous from international law.[21]

B. Aftermath: A Question of Legal Hierarchy

After *Opinion 1/91* brought about these devastating conclusions for the EEA, the agreement was amended to comply with these aforementioned principles of European Union law. This new, amended version was then resubmitted to the CJEU and finally found the Court's approval,[22] especially concerning the revocation of the EEA Court. However, as regards alternative dispute settlement mechanisms with the legal authority to bind the Union, the CJEU declared that when confronted with partially identical provisions in an international agreement and the Treaties, it must be ensured that the newly created joint committee, established to settle disputes concerning the agreement's interpretation or application, strictly adheres to the CJEU's rulings.[23] If they are not adhered to, the powers of the international dispute settlement body must be limited *ratione*

---

[15] See Brandtner (n 9) 310.

[16] See Schmalenbach, 'Struggle for Exclusiveness' (n 4) 1046.

[17] See Opinion 1/91 *EEA I* (n 10) paras 33–36.

[18] See ibid para 46.

[19] See José Luis Da Cruz Vilaça and Nuno Piçarra, 'Y a-t-il des limites matérielles à la révision des Traités instituant les Communautés européennes?' (1993) 29 *Cahiers de Droit Européen* 3, 3.

[20] See Schmalenbach, 'Struggle for Exclusiveness' (n 4) 1047.

[21] For a sceptical view of the CJEU's approach, see Trevor C Hartley, 'International law and the Law of the European Union—A Reassessment' (2001) 72 *British Year Book of International Law* 1, 1ff.

[22] See Opinion 1/92 *EEA II (Draft agreement between the Community, on the one hand, and the countries of the European Free Trade Association, on the other, relating to the creation of the European Economic Area)* [1992] ECR I-2821.

[23] See ibid para 25.

materiae to those treaty provisions which are not substantially identical to Union law.[24]

Subsequently, the EEA Court was replaced by the EFTA Court,[25] competent only for dispute settlements between EFTA Member States, but not for disputes to which the Union would be a party.[26] This means that EU law is applied and interpreted only by the CJEU, whereas the interpretation of identical EEA law is left to the EFTA Court.[27] Furthermore, according to Article 3 (2) of the ESA/Court Agreement,[28] the EFTA Court has to

> pay due account to the principles laid down by the relevant rulings by the Court of Justice of the European Communities given after the date of signature of the EEA Agreement and which concern the interpretation of that Agreement or of such rules of the Treaty establishing the European Economic Community and the Treaty establishing the European Coal and Steel Community in so far as they are identical in substance to the provisions of the EEA Agreement [...].

Notwithstanding the institutional detachment of the two courts, no conflicting case law has resulted so far.[29] The reasons for the successful cooperation between Luxembourg and the EFTA Court go far beyond the similarities and parallels of their respective competences, the pertinent statutory provisions or the geographic proximity of their seat in Luxembourg, which helped develop an intricate system of cooperation. The prevention of conflicting case law primarily stems from a very high level of mutual understanding between the two courts which not only led to homogeneity and coherence in their case law, but also to the further development of their jurisprudence.[30]

At the end of the day, it is indisputable that the CJEU was primarily concerned about the legal certainty within the Union's legal order. The EU's basically monistic approach in conjunction with the hierarchical position of international treaty law, forming an integral part of the Union's legal order[31] and ranking between primary and secondary EU law,[32] would have granted the EEA Court some critical influence on the functioning of Union law, as this integrative approach implies pivotal consequences for the CJEU's jurisdiction. If the planned

---

[24] See ibid para 36. See also Schmalenbach, 'Struggle for Exclusiveness' (n 4) 1047.

[25] See art 108 (2) of the EEA Agreement. See also, generally on the EEA's judicial system, Leif Sevón, 'The EEA Judicial System and the Supreme Courts of the EFTA States' (1992) 3 *European Journal of International Law* 329, 329ff.

[26] See Opinion 1/92 *EEA II* (n 22) para 19.

[27] See Vassilios Skouris, 'The ECJ and the EFTA Court under the EEA Agreement: A Paradigm for International Cooperation between Judicial Institutions' in Carl Baudenbacher, Per Tresselt and Thorgeir Örlygsson (eds), *The EFTA Court. Ten Years On* (Oxford, Hart Publishing, 2005) 123.

[28] Agreement between the EFTA States on the Establishment of a Surveillance Authority and a Court of Justice.

[29] See Schmalenbach, 'Struggle for Exclusiveness' (n 4) 1048.

[30] See Skouris (n 27) 129.

[31] See Case 181/73 *Haegeman* (n 14) para 5.

[32] See Case C-61/94 *Commission v Germany (International Dairy Arrangement)* [1996] ECR I-3989, para 52.

EEA Court had interpreted EEA rules as substantially identical to primary EU law, the Luxembourg Court's interpretation of the parallel primary EU law would have proven superior, because of the higher position of this law within the Union's legal order. Yet if, on the other hand, the EEA Court had interpreted EEA law as substantially identical to secondary EU law, EEA law, as an integral part of the Union's legal order, would have prevailed over the CJEU's interpretation of the parallel secondary EU law, simply due to the latter's lower rank. More precisely, the authoritative and, most notably, exclusive interpretation of secondary Union law by the CJEU was at risk of being undermined by substantially identical EEA law.[33]

In a nutshell, this depiction of a very specific jurisdictional conflict shows that an agreement between the Union and another international organisation must not affect the EU's division of competences or allocation of powers in a twofold manner. First, it is impermissible to interfere with the *internal* division of competences between the Union and its Member States;[34] and second, and more importantly in the context of this book, it is considered unacceptable that an international court, such as the planned EEA Court, should be enabled to encroach upon Luxembourg's innermost right to observe the law within the proper interpretation and application of the Treaties, and thus to affect the *external* allocation of powers by transferring them to another international organisation. According to the notion of the Union's legal autonomy, the CJEU must remain competent for the interpretation of international agreements in their entirety, but this fact does not completely exclude jurisdiction by international tribunals. As long as the interpretation of the Union's innermost legal core—namely, primary and secondary Union law and international dispositions identical to its substance—remains the Court's prerogative, the CJEU is willing to allow the establishment of other dispute settlement bodies by international agreements.[35]

II. COMPETING JURISDICTIONS: THE *MOX PLANT* CASE

The previous chapter demonstrated in detail how the CJEU guards its exclusive jurisdiction over Union law, which has been substantially reduplicated in an international agreement, from the interpretation of another international court or tribunal. This subchapter, in contrast, will present a very specific case in order to illustrate the legal issues associated with the case of competing jurisdiction between the Luxembourg Court and another international court. More specifically, the consequences of the CJEU's expanding jurisdiction in regards to other international courts or tribunals will be discussed on the basis of the *Commission v Ireland (MOX Plant)* case. In this case, a lack of coordination between the various

---

[33] See Schmalenbach, 'Struggle for Exclusiveness' (n 4) 1048f.
[34] As set forth in arts 4 and 5 TEU and arts 2 to 4 TFEU.
[35] See Brandtner (n 9) 328.

international judicial bodies led to legal complications further aggravated by the involvement of the CJEU.[36] This means, *in concreto*, that a disagreement involving legal issues relating to both international law and European Union law can be brought before both the CJEU and an international court or tribunal. Classified in a systematic context, such a circumstance leads to the concurrence of jurisdiction between a court of universal jurisdiction *ratione personae* and general or specialised competence *ratione materiae* and a regional court with specialised competence *ratione materiae*.[37] In the framework of the analysis pursued in this book, this case will present the background to the subsequent line of reasoning as to why or why not Luxembourg, after the accession, might exclude Strasbourg from disputes between EU Member States that involve the Convention, in order to uphold its exclusive jurisdiction and the Union's legal autonomy.[38]

The *MOX Plant* case concerned a dispute pertaining to international law and European Union law and was first brought before international arbitral tribunals, but not the CJEU, although, in this case, the parties to the dispute were EU Member States. This fact raises the crucial question—which court or tribunal should be the appropriate arbiter to rule on the disputes, the Luxembourg Court or the international arbitral tribunal?[39] The answer can be found in Article 344 TFEU which provides that all disputes between European Union Member States involving Union law must be brought exclusively before the CJEU. This provision and the corresponding CJEU case law are sufficient *caveats* for EU Member States to keep their hands off arbitral tribunals and other international courts in the future.[40]

A. Factual Background and Procedures

As the factual and procedural details of this renowned case have already been exhaustively described in the works of other scholars,[41] this section will be confined to a brief summary of the facts which are relevant in the context of this book. In the *MOX Plant* dispute Ireland filed a complaint against the United Kingdom relating to the radioactive waste efflux of the MOX plant in Sellafield,

---

[36] Case C-459/03 *Commission v Ireland (MOX Plant)* [2006] ECR I-4635. See Nikolaos Lavranos, 'The *MOX Plant* and *IJzeren Rijn* Disputes: Which Court Is the Supreme Arbiter?' (2006) 19 *Leiden Journal of International Law* 223, 223.

[37] See Shany, *Competing Jurisdictions* (n 2) 44.

[38] For an analysis of this specific issue see ch 10.

[39] See Lavranos, '*MOX Plant* and *IJzeren Rijn*' (n 36) 224.

[40] See Schmalenbach, 'Struggle for Exclusiveness' (n 4) 1049.

[41] See, eg M Bruce Volbeda, 'The MOX Plant Case: The Question of "Supplemental Jurisdiction" for International Environmental Claims Under UNCLOS' (2006) 42 *Texas International Law Journal* 211, 211; Yuval Shany, 'The First *MOX Plant* Award: The Need to Harmonise Competing Environmental Regimes and Dispute Settlement Procedures' (2004) 17 *Leiden Journal of International Law* 815, 815; Robin Churchill and Joanne Scott, 'The *MOX Plant* Litigation: The First Half-Life' (2004) 53 *International and Comparative Law Quarterly* 643, 643.

England, and argued that certain provisions of the United Nations Convention on the Law of the Sea (UNCLOS) allow Convention tribunals to enforce not only UNCLOS directives, but 'other rules of international law not incompatible with this Convention'[42] as well. Consequently, the dispute involved two different facets. Firstly, Ireland alleged that the released radioactive pollution of the MOX Plant contaminated the waters of the Irish Sea and thus violated the environmental standards of the UNCLOS. Secondly, Ireland believed that the United Kingdom had additionally infringed its right to information regarding the MOX Plant by relying on provisions enshrined in the Convention for the Protection of the Marine Environment of the North-East Atlantic (OSPAR Convention).[43] After lengthy diplomatic negotiations had failed, Ireland and the United Kingdom agreed to establish two arbitral tribunals, one to rule on the alleged infringement under the UNCLOS provisions and one to decide on the violation of the OSPAR rules.[44] Moreover, Ireland requested that the International Tribunal for the Law of the Sea (ITLOS) issue provisional measures, pursuant to Article 290 (5) UNCLOS.[45]

The ITLOS ruled that it had prima facie jurisdiction over this case, as the dispute settlement procedure under the UNCLOS only deals with the application and interpretation of that Convention.[46] Similarly, the OSPAR Arbitral Tribunal confirmed its jurisdiction, but dismissed the case on its merits.[47] The United Kingdom, however, argued that the CJEU may have exclusive jurisdiction under Article 344 TFEU, since various aspects of EU law were also possibly involved,[48] which could limit the jurisdiction of the tribunal. Due to the presumable violation of the said provision, the European Commission had already initiated an infringement procedure against Ireland. The Arbitral Tribunal subsequently suspended its proceedings to allow for the resolution of potentially conflicting international obligations and dispute settlement procedures under the Union's legal order[49] and to explain the issues relating to possible CJEU jurisdiction.

---

[42] *MOX Plant Case (Ireland v United Kingdom)* PCA, Written Pleadings, Memorial of Ireland, Part 2, 26 July 2002, 113.

[43] Art 9 (2) of the OSPAR Convention requires the contracting parties to make all information available 'on the state of the maritime area, on activities or measures adversely affecting or likely to affect it'.

[44] See Lavranos, 'MOX Plant and IJzeren Rijn' (n 36) 225.

[45] See *MOX Plant Case (Ireland v United Kingdom)*, Provisional Measures, Request for Provisional Measures and Statement of Case of Ireland of 9 November 2001, ITLOS Reports 2001.

[46] See *MOX Plant Case (Ireland v United Kingdom)*, Provisional Measures, Order of 3 December 2001, ITLOS Reports 2001, 95, paras 48–53.

[47] See *MOX Plant Case (Ireland v United Kingdom)* PCA, Dispute Concerning Access to Information under Article 9 of the OSPAR Convention, Final Award of 2 July 2003, paras 106f.

[48] See *MOX Plant Case (Ireland v United Kingdom)* PCA, Written Pleadings, Counter-Memorial of the United Kingdom, 9 January 2003, 100ff.

[49] See *MOX Plant Case (Ireland v United Kingdom)* PCA, Procedural Order No 3, 24 June 2003, paras 29–31. For a broader approach, see Natalie Klein, *Dispute Settlement in the UN Convention on the Law of the Sea* (Cambridge, Cambridge University Press, 2005) 44ff.

B. The UNCLOS Arbitral Decision

A special feature of the UNCLOS, which is sometimes considered an inherent problem leading to concurring jurisdictions,[50] is that Articles 282 and 287 UNCLOS provide a list of various fora[51] which can be selected by the contracting parties for dispute settlement. In fact, the UNCLOS explicitly accepts the jurisdiction of regional courts, such as the CJEU.[52] However, in any case, the Arbitral Tribunal's decision to discontinue the proceedings was not entirely based on the UNCLOS provisions, as the Tribunal overtly accounted for the 'internal operation of a separate legal order',[53] ie European Union law. In this context, the Arbitral Tribunal's decision can be considered a demonstration of judicial comity rather than a legal obligation or necessity.[54] Even though the Tribunal first confirmed that it had prima facie jurisdiction,[55] it then considered it necessary to verify whether it had definite jurisdiction or whether, according to the United Kingdom's objection, the CJEU had exclusive jurisdiction in this case, since EU environmental legislation was involved. Eventually, the Tribunal decided to suspend its proceedings and requested the parties to expedite the resolution within the legal framework of the Union and thus to find out whether the CJEU had exclusive jurisdiction.[56]

This exceptional move of the Tribunal is most noteworthy, particularly due to the following two reasons. Firstly, it did not address the legal requirements of Article 282 UNCLOS which is, in fact, as a residual jurisdiction clause,[57] the basis of the jurisdictional conflict, principally from the viewpoint of the UNCLOS.[58] Secondly, the Tribunal therefore left it to Luxembourg to decide whether the Union's infringement proceedings under Article 258 TFEU (which is undoubtedly a regional dispute settlement mechanism, according to Article 282 UNCLOS), would take precedence in this case. Since this overly restrictive reading of Article 282 UNCLOS renders the text of this provision basically meaningless,[59]

---

[50] See Nikolaos Lavranos, 'Concurrence of Jurisdiction between the CJEU and other International Courts and Tribunals, EUSA Ninth Biennial International Conference', 31 March—2 April 2005, Austin, Texas, Conference Paper 1, 42.

[51] Namely, dispute settlement mechanisms established by a general, regional or bilateral agreement (art 282) or the ITLOS, the ICJ, arbitral tribunals and 'special' arbitration (art 287).

[52] See Lavranos, '*MOX Plant* and *IJzeren Rijn*' (n 36) 225.

[53] *MOX Plant Case (Ireland v United Kingdom)* (n 49) para 24.

[54] See Schmalenbach, 'Struggle for Exclusiveness' (n 4) 1050.

[55] See *MOX Plant Case (Ireland v United Kingdom)* (n 49) para 14.

[56] See ibid para 26 and Tribunal's Order, No 6, 20.

[57] See Shany, *Competing Jurisdictions* (n 2) 238.

[58] See Klein, *Dispute Settlement* (n 49) 46f.

[59] See Shany, *Competing Jurisdictions* (n 2) 238. But see against, *MOX Plant Case (Ireland v United Kingdom)*, Provisional Measures, Separate Opinion of Judge Wolfrum, ITLOS Reports 2001, stating that 'the interpretation of article 282 of the Convention outlined here does not render this provision devoid of substance. The possibility exists that States Parties agree on a system for the settlement of disputes under the Convention different from that envisaged in Part XV, section 2, of the Convention.'

this form of jurisdictional renouncement seems to be relatively unusual for an international judicial court that should be, first and foremost, competent in interpreting its own legal basis for its jurisdiction. Because of the special nature of the Union's legal order, the problem persists in that the Luxembourg Court cannot be easily integrated into the dispute settlement system of Article 282.[60] Yet, as the CJEU is the Court of an autonomous legal order of 'trans-national dimension, [...] beholden to, but distinct from the existing legal order of public international law',[61] it is pre-eminently designed to interpret and apply Union law. The Union's judicial system is not designed to interpret or apply the UNCLOS in *inter-se* disputes of states, which are, at the same time, EU Member States, where no legal issue related to Union law is called into question and where the UNCLOS therefore is the sole legal basis.[62]

However, the UNCLOS was concluded as a so-called mixed agreement[63] and thus concerns the competences of the Union and the Member States as well. Upon conclusion, such an international agreement becomes a self-executing part of the Union's legal order by virtue of Article 216 TFEU.[64] Thus, it could also be argued that infringement proceedings according to Article 259 TFEU are a suitable instrument in settling disputes between Member States about the interpretation and application of mixed agreements. The Arbitral Tribunal's decision to suspend the proceedings can be seen as a pragmatic way of avoiding any dealings with the intricate entanglement of UNCLOS provisions and EU law, mainly due to the concurrent partaking of the Union and its Member States in the UNCLOS.[65] This argument is also in line with the United Kingdom's point of view that there was a restriction on jurisdiction by virtue of Article 282 UNCLOS for disputes between EU Member States in cases where the dispute affects a subject matter over which competence has already been transferred to the Union. If practically all the claims of Ireland were to fall within the competence of the European Union to such extent that provisions of international agreements impose obligations or bestow rights on the Union, then the CJEU would have exclusive jurisdiction to interpret these provisions. In the *MOX Plant* case, this meant that Luxembourg was

---

[60]   See Schmalenbach, 'Struggle for Exclusiveness' (n 4) 1050.

[61]   Case C-459/03 *Commission v Ireland (MOX Plant)* [2006] ECR I-4635, Opinion of AG Maduro, para 21.

[62]   See Volker Röben, 'The Order of the UNCLOS Annex VII Arbitral Tribunal to Suspend Proceedings in the Case of the MOX Plant at Sellafield: How Much Jurisdictional Subsidiarity?' (2004) 73 *Nordic Journal of International Law* 223, 242.

[63]   Council Decision of 23 March 1998 concerning the conclusion by the European Community of the United Nations Convention of 10 December 1982 on the Law of the Sea and the Agreement of 28 July 1994 relating to the Implementation of Part XI thereof (98/392/EC) [1998] OJ L179/1.

[64]   See Case 104/81 *Kupferberg & Cie KG (Kupferberg I)* [1982] ECR 3641, especially paras 11–14.

[65]   See *MOX Plant Case (Ireland v United Kingdom)* PCA, Procedural Order No 3, 24 June 2003, para 26, stating that 'whatever the Parties may agree in these proceedings as to the scope and effects of European Community law applicable in the present dispute, the question is ultimately not for them to decide but is rather to be decided within the institutions of the European Communities, and particularly by the European Court of Justice'.

competent to apply and interpret the relevant UNCLOS provisions, as UNCLOS had become part of EU law and was hence justiciable before the CJEU.[66]

Certainly, the UNCLOS Arbitral Tribunal did not foresee this situation. In its position as an international tribunal, it was neither able nor permitted to discern and to rule on the division of competences between the Union and its Member States. If the Arbitral Tribunal had decided on the jurisdictional objections of the United Kingdom, the Tribunal would have been required to assess, inter alia, whether the Union or its Member States had competence in relation to some or even all of the matters raised by the UNCLOS provisions invoked in this specific dispute.[67] A first guideline for third UNCLOS parties to detect the correct addressee of their claims and thus the right respondent is the declaration on the division of competences within the scope of UNCLOS between the Union and the Member States.[68] As regards maritime pollution, the declaration provides that

> with regard to the provisions on maritime transport, safety of shipping and the prevention of marine pollution [...] the Community has exclusive competence only to the extent that such provisions of the Convention or legal instruments adopted in implementation thereof affect common rules established by the Community. When Community rules exist but are not affected, in particular in cases of Community provisions establishing only minimum standards, the Member States have competence, without prejudice to the competence of the Community to act in this field. Otherwise competence rests with the Member States.[69]

In conclusion, however, this declaration is of little avail in practice. Firstly, disputing EU Member States cannot invoke this declaration to contest possible extensions of exclusive Union competences,[70] especially due to Luxembourg's *AETR* case law.[71] Secondly, and most importantly, the clauses of this declaration are ambiguous and vague.[72] Thus, a ruling of the CJEU on the extent of the exclusive external competences of the Union was an indispensable prerequisite to clarify *ex ante* whether this concrete dispute pertained to the exclusive jurisdiction of the CJEU,[73] mainly because of the absence of any mechanism in the international legal system to resolve situations of overlapping jurisdictions. Falling back on the

---

[66] See Klein, *Dispute Settlement* (n 49) 49.

[67] See *MOX Plant Case (Ireland v United Kingdom)* PCA, Statement by the President, 13 June 2003, para 9. See also generally Klein, *Dispute Settlement* (n 49) 50.

[68] Declaration Concerning the Competence of the European Community with regard to Matters Governed by the United Nations Convention on the Law of the Sea of 10 December 1982 and the Agreement of 28 July 1994 relating to the Implementation of Part XI of the Convention [1998] OJ L179/129.

[69] See ibid para 2 ('Matters for which the Community shares competence with its Member States').

[70] See Schmalenbach, 'Struggle for Exclusiveness' (n 4) 1052.

[71] See Case 22/70 *Commission v Council (AETR)* [1971] ECR 263, para 19.

[72] See Martin Björklund, 'Responsibility in the EC for Mixed Agreements—Should Non-Member Parties Care?' (2001) 70 *Nordic Journal of International Law* 373, 378.

[73] See Schmalenbach, 'Struggle for Exclusiveness' (n 4) 1052.

principles of subsidiarity[74] or comity, respectively, was therefore the most realistic instrument for reconciling potential conflict between judicial proceedings.[75]

C. The Judgment of the Court of Justice of the European Union

As aforementioned, the European Commission initiated infringement proceedings against Ireland before it could abide by the UNCLOS Arbitral Tribunal's request to expedite the resolution of this issue within the legal framework of the Union and to clarify whether the CJEU had exclusive jurisdiction in this case. The Commission argued that Ireland had instituted the proceedings against the United Kingdom without taking due account of the fact that the European Union is a party to the UNCLOS as well. Most notably, the Commission alleged that by submitting the dispute to an international tribunal outside the Union's legal order, Ireland had violated the exclusive jurisdiction of the CJEU, as set forth in Article 344 TFEU. Additionally, Ireland had also failed to comply with its duty of cooperation under Article 4 (3) TEU, which means that it first had to inform or consult with the competent Union institutions.[76]

At large, the Luxembourg Court followed the Commission's legal opinion and decided that Ireland's reference to a judicial dispute settlement mechanism outside of the Union's legal order was tantamount to an infringement of Article 344 TFEU, since 'this dispute is clearly covered by one of the methods of dispute settlement established by the [...] Treaty within the terms of Article [344 TFEU], namely the procedure set out in Article [259 TFEU].'[77] Thereby the Court confirmed that infringement proceedings under Articles 258 and 259 TFEU represented a departure from the classic dispute settlement mechanisms of public international law.[78] The CJEU also declared that the UNCLOS was concluded by the Union and all the Member States on the basis of shared competence.[79] As a result, mixed agreements have the same status in the Union's legal order as pure EU agreements, since these are provisions coming from within the scope of Union competence,[80] and thus, these agreements form an integral part of Union law.[81] The Luxembourg Court accordingly concluded that the subject matter covered by the UNCLOS provisions, relied on by Ireland before the Arbitral Tribunal, are largely regulated by Union measures, several of which are expressively mentioned

---

[74] See Röben (n 62) 243.

[75] See Klein, *Dispute Settlement* (n 49) 51.

[76] See Case C-459/03 *Commission v Ireland (MOX Plant)* [2006] I-4635, paras 55 and 59.

[77] ibid, para 128.

[78] See Case 39/72 *Commission v Italian Republic (Slaughtering Premiums)* [1973] ECR 101, paras 11 and 24. See also Anthony Arnull, *The European Union and its Court of Justice*, 2nd edn (New York, McGraw-Hill Books, 2006) 44.

[79] See Case C-459/03 *Commission v Ireland (MOX Plant)* (n 76) para 83.

[80] See ibid para 84. See also Case C-13/00 *Commission v Ireland (Berne Convention)* [2002] ECR I-2943, para 14.

[81] See Case C-459/03 *Commission v Ireland (MOX Plant)* (n 76) para 69.

in the abovementioned Declaration[82] on the Division of Competences concerning UNCLOS.[83] After affirming that Ireland's claim against the United Kingdom was based on UNCLOS rules within the scope of the Union's external competences, the CJEU held that the dispute in this case was in fact a dispute pertaining to the interpretation or application of the Treaties, and most importantly, within the terms of Article 344 TFEU.[84]

Luxembourg also ruled that all disputes relating to provisions of international agreements, even those entirely concluded on a competence shared between the Union and the Member States, necessitate the CJEU's exclusive jurisdiction to decide the disputes on their merits.[85] By referring to its approach in *Opinion 1/91* on the EEA Agreement, the Court asserted that

> [t]he Court has already pointed out that an international agreement cannot affect the allocation of responsibilities defined in the Treaties and, consequently, the autonomy of the Community legal system, compliance with which the Court ensures under Article [19 (1) TEU]. That exclusive jurisdiction of the Court is confirmed by Article [344 TFEU], by which Member States undertake not to submit a dispute concerning the interpretation or application of the EC Treaty to any method of settlement other than those provided for therein [...].[86]

The Luxembourg Court additionally pointed out that such a flagrant breach of Article 344 TFEU involves an evident risk of adversely affecting the jurisdictional order laid down in the Treaties and, consequently, the autonomy of the Union's legal system.[87] Furthermore, the Court was not content with reaffirming its exclusive jurisdiction, but also highlighted two other important aspects in this case. Firstly, it is exclusively the competence of the Luxembourg Court, should the need arise, to identify the elements of the dispute which relate to provisions of the international agreement in question and which fall outside its jurisdiction, thus allowing these provisions to be interpreted and applied by other international courts.[88] As a consequence, if EU Member States ponder whether a dispute involves Union law, they are de facto obliged to obtain an answer from the CJEU before submitting the case to any other international court or tribunal.[89]

Secondly, the Court conceived Article 344 TFEU as a specific expression of the Member States' general duty of loyalty resulting from Article 4 (3) TEU.[90] According to this view, the obligation of close cooperation within the framework of a mixed agreement entails a duty to inform and consult with the competent

---

[82] See n 68.

[83] See Case C-459/03 *Commission v Ireland (MOX Plant)* (n 76) para 110.

[84] See ibid para 127.

[85] See Schmalenbach, 'Struggle for Exclusiveness' (n 4) 1053.

[86] See Case C-459/03 *Commission v Ireland (MOX Plant)* (n 76) para 123.

[87] See ibid para 154.

[88] See ibid para 135.

[89] See Nikolaos Lavranos, 'The Scope of Exclusive Jurisdiction of the Court of Justice' (2007) 32 *European Law Review* 83, 89.

[90] See Case C-459/03 *Commission v Ireland (MOX Plant)* (n 76) para 169.

Union institutions prior to instituting dispute settlement proceedings before any other international court or tribunal.[91] Hereby it can be guaranteed that the European Commission and the CJEU are informed in due time of proceedings which may possibly clash with Article 344 TFEU.[92]

By and large, the CJEU's approach amounts to a strong reassertion and a maximal expansion of its jurisdiction, especially regarding mixed agreements. Furthermore, the Court restrains the right of Member States to use other dispute settlement mechanisms of their choice. It thereby pre-empts the exercise of the jurisdiction of other international courts and tribunals in all cases that possibly involve Union law.[93]

III. LEGAL ANALYSIS

A. Elements of the European Union's Legal Autonomy

The most noteworthy facet of *Opinion 1/91*, the *MOX Plant* and *Kadi and Al Barakaat v Council and Commission*[94] judgments, particularly in the context of the European Union's accession to the European Convention on Human Rights, is the extensively defined scope of Luxembourg's exclusive jurisdiction. This extensive interpretation is mainly based on the following four primary elements of the European Union's legal autonomy:

(1) An international court or tribunal must not be given the power to rule on the internal division of competences between the EU and the Member States.
(2) The decisions of an international court or tribunal must not internally bind the CJEU and the other Union institutions.
(3) An international agreement must not alter the functional nature of the EU institutions.
(4) An international agreement must not contain hidden amendments to the Union Treaties.

If one or more of these principles is breached, the European Union's legal autonomy is inevitably violated.

As a result, Luxembourg has to follow an active approach to maintain these imperatives and thereby the autonomy of EU law. To put this approach into practice, the CJEU aims at (a) protecting both the autonomy of the Union's legal order and the CJEU's own exclusive jurisdiction; (b) limiting the choice and

---

[91] See ibid para 179.
[92] See Lavranos, 'Rechtsprechungsmonopol des EuGH' (n 3) 450.
[93] See Lavranos, 'Scope of Exclusive Jurisdiction' (n 89) 84f.
[94] Joined Cases C-402/05 P and C-415/05 P *Kadi and Al Barakaat v Council and Commission* [2008] ECR I-6351.

utilisation of other international courts and tribunals by the EU Member States; and (c) constraining the jurisdiction of other international courts and tribunals.[95] As the supreme adjudicator of EU law under Article 19 (1) TEU, Luxembourg is reasonably concerned with the uniform application and interpretation of the Union's legal order. However, some critics have questioned the CJEU's *modus operandi* in this case, mainly in relation to the issue of whether the extensive understanding of its exclusive jurisdiction is proportionate[96] or whether the CJEU has simply expanded Article 344 TFEU for its own sake,[97] ie thereby confirming the *effet utile* principle.

B. Protecting Legal Autonomy and Exclusive Jurisdiction

Through the extensive interpretation of its jurisdiction in *Opinion 1/91* and in the *MOX Plant* case, the Luxembourg Court left no room for doubt about its exclusive competence in interpreting and applying European Union law. Moreover, it is absolutely unacceptable that another domestic or international court may encroach upon the CJEU's jurisdictional 'monopoly' enshrined in Article 19 (1) TEU and Article 344 TFEU. In addition, the CJEU thereby protects both its exclusive jurisdiction and the autonomy of EU law—two virtually axiomatic principles that are closely intertwined.[98]

With *Opinion 1/91* and the *MOX Plant* judgment, the CJEU has applied and confirmed the concept of the Union's legal autonomy most explicitly towards international law. Therefore, international law in general, not only in international agreements, but also in the form of jurisdiction and adjudication of international courts or tribunals, cannot in any way interfere with the autonomy of the EU's legal system. If the Member States wish to modify that legal autonomy, they have to amend or revise the existing Treaties. More specifically, the concept of the Union's legal autonomy must be considered to be immune from intrusions caused by the external relational activities of the EU and its Member States.[99] Only Luxembourg is entrusted to observe the aspired consistency and uniformity of EU law in all Member States under the provisions of the Treaties. As the Court ruled in its seminal judgment in *Foto-Frost v Hauptzollamt Lübeck-Ost*, the main purpose of the powers, given to it by the Treaties, is to ensure that Union law is uniformly applied.[100] The jurisdiction of the CJEU consequently encompasses

---

[95] See Lavranos, 'Rechtsprechungsmonopol des EuGH' (n 3) 458f.

[96] See Lavranos, 'Scope of Exclusive Jurisdiction' (n 89) 89.

[97] See Schmalenbach, 'Struggle for Exclusiveness' (n 4) 1053.

[98] See Bruno De Witte, 'European Union Law: How Autonomous is its Legal Order?' (2010) 65 *Zeitschrift für Öffentliches Recht* 141, 150.

[99] See Lavranos, 'Scope of Exclusive Jurisdiction' (n 89) 90.

[100] See Case 314/85 *Foto-Frost v Hauptzollamt Lübeck-Ost* [1987] ECR 4199, para 15.

all Union law[101] and thus also 'unionised' international law.[102] Considering these arguments, the requirement of exclusive and final jurisdiction of the CJEU as set forth in Article 19 (1) TEU and Article 344 TFEU is an evident and necessary provision for ensuring the supremacy, unity and consistency of European Union law. If Member States settled their disputes involving Union law before an international court or tribunal of their choice, the chances of fragmenting EU law would be exceedingly high.[103]

The *MOX Plant* judgment was therefore a true landmark decision. It fell 'squarely on the oldest and most conservative trajectory of European thinking about the role of international law and its relations with national law'.[104] The most innovative aspect of this judgment is the fact that Member States, questioning Luxembourg's jurisdiction in a concrete case, must refrain from submitting the dispute to an international court or arbitral tribunal before consulting with the CJEU.[105] One possible consequence might be that this course of action will leave a lacuna in the system of judicial protection. For example, if a dispute involving both Union law and international law could only be submitted to the CJEU, but the CJEU were reluctant to interpret or apply international law, the result would be a considerable and undesirable gap in the protection of human rights.[106] Nevertheless, according to its unvarying and consistent case law, the Luxembourg Court will remain the sole arbiter competent to answer jurisdictional questions in all cases involving EU law.

C. Limiting the Choice and Utilisation of International Courts

The abovementioned rationale also leads to a serious restriction for the EU Member States in settling disputes with each other. Their competence to use other dispute settlement mechanisms established by international agreements which they have ratified is significantly limited by the expanding exclusive jurisdiction of the CJEU.[107] The Luxembourg Court expands its exclusive jurisdiction under Article 19 (1) TEU and Article 344 TFEU due to the complex internal distribution of external competences in the Union, or, in other words, the competence to enter into international agreements with third parties and international organisations.

---

[101] But see the last sentence of art 24 (1) of the TEU, which exempts most of the Union's common foreign and security policy from the jurisdiction of the Court.

[102] See eg Case 181/73 *Haegeman* (n 14) para 5; Case C-280/93 *Germany v Council (Bananas— Common Organisation of the Markets)* [1994] ECR I-4973, para 144; Case C-149/96 *Portugal v Council (Market Access in Textile Products)* [1999] ECR I-8395, para 47ff.

[103] See Lavranos, '*MOX Plant and IJzeren Rijn*' (n 36) 234.

[104] Martti Koskenniemi, 'International Law: Constitutionalism, Managerialism and the Ethos of Legal Education' (2007) 1 *European Journal of Legal Studies* 1, 1.

[105] See Joni Heliskoski, *Mixed Agreements as a Technique for Organising the International Relations of the European Community and its Member States* (The Hague, Kluwer Law, 2001) 61ff.

[106] See Jan Klabbers, *Treaty Conflict and the European Union* (Cambridge, Cambridge University Press, 2009) 148.

[107] See Lavranos, 'Scope of Exclusive Jurisdiction' (n 89) 91.

This situation entails complex legal issues, since the *inter se* relationships between European Union Member States are twofold. Of course, the Member States interact as sovereign actors on the international level, with reciprocal rights and duties under international law. But as EU members, they also have reciprocal rights and duties under Union law.[108] If Union Member States submit a case which involves provisions of a mixed agreement falling within the European Union's exclusive competence to an international court, the claim is, from the perspective of an international court or tribunal, inadmissible, as the states would have no standing under the international agreement in question.[109] From the perspective of Luxembourg, a dispute between EU Member States can only affect their reciprocal rights and duties according to Article 216 (2) TFEU, stating that agreements concluded by the European Union are not only binding upon its institutions, but also on the Member States.[110] In other words, the CJEU's claim for exclusive jurisdiction reduces the *inter se* relationship between EU Member States to one legal regime, namely that of the European Union.[111]

One may ask whether the CJEU is even authorised to encroach upon the Member States' sovereignty to such an extent or whether such an approach constitutes an ultra vires action.[112] The legal issue in this case is the duplication of the international reciprocal duties and rights of the EU Member States in the European legal order, since the Union is—due to its concerted action with its Member States in the field of parallel competences—legally bound to the same set of international rules.[113] In the *MOX Plant* case, the CJEU only took into consideration the question of whether an agreement comes within the Union's competence, and not whether this competence is of an exclusive or shared nature.[114] The Union's secondary legislation in the field of a shared competence (in this case, the protection of the maritime environment[115]) does not per se pre-empt the Member States to solve a dispute by means of an international court or tribunal. If their actions, however, would affect the operation of EU legislation, then the CJEU would enjoy exclusive jurisdiction by virtue of Article 344 TFEU.[116] In its *Opinion 2/00* on the *Cartagena Protocol*, Luxembourg upheld its findings of the *Commission v Council (AETR)* judgment[117] and concluded that the EU holds exclusive external competence when secondary legislation within the framework of the EU has already been adopted in the same field, since secondary law is liable to be affected if the Member States participate in executing the same external competence.[118]

---

[108] See Schmalenbach, 'Struggle for Exclusiveness' (n 4) 1054.
[109] See Röben (n 62) 239.
[110] See Lock, *Verhältnis* (n 2) 177.
[111] See Schmalenbach, 'Struggle for Exclusiveness' (n 4) 1054.
[112] See Lavranos, 'Rechtsprechungsmonopol des EuGH' (n 3) 460.
[113] See Schmalenbach, 'Struggle for Exclusiveness' (n 4) 1054.
[114] See Case C-459/03 *Commission v Ireland (MOX Plant)* (n 76) para 93.
[115] See art 191 (4) TFEU.
[116] See Röben (n 62) 238.
[117] See Case 22/70 *Commission v Council (AETR)* (n 71) para 22.
[118] See Opinion 2/00 *Cartagena Protocol* [2001] ECR I-9713, para 45.

However, the EU Member States were not entirely discouraged from using other international courts or arbitral tribunals after the *MOX Plant* judgment. In the *IJzeren Rijn* case, the Netherlands and Belgium both argued that their dispute only involved international law. Yet, at the same time, they also requested that the Arbitral Tribunal take into account their obligations under Article 344 TFEU.[119] Another example is a more recent dispute submitted to the International Court of Justice (ICJ), instigated by Germany against Italy for failing to respect its jurisdictional immunity as a sovereign state. In its application, Germany asserted that, although the present case involves two EU Member States, the CJEU has no jurisdiction to entertain it, since the dispute is not governed by any of the jurisdictional clauses in the Treaties. Moreover, 'outside of that specific framework' the Member States 'continue to live with one another under the regime of general international law'.[120] Obviously, the ICJ did not engage in this matter, as the final judgement does not contain any references to the CJEU or its potential jurisdiction in this case.[121] These two examples plainly illustrate that the Member States disapprove of judicial limitations of their sovereign rights and that they are therefore prone to circumvent the exclusive jurisdiction of the CJEU by submitting cases to other courts and tribunals.[122] In the *IJzeren Rijn* case, it was particularly easy for the Member States to sideline the CJEU's exclusive jurisdiction, as they consulted with the Commission on their dispute beforehand.[123] No infringement procedures under Article 258 TFEU have so far been initiated in such a situation, thereby barring the Luxembourg Court from executing and protecting its exclusive jurisdiction.[124]

D. Constraining the Jurisdiction of International Courts and Tribunals

At this point, it is apparent that the actual or potential jurisdiction of other international courts or tribunals can be limited or will (presumably) be completely excluded when the CJEU is involved in the same dispute that might touch upon Union law. Such a situation, in which multiple fora can be seized by the parties to the same international dispute, may give rise to some important issues.[125] International courts and tribunals are advised to suspend the proceedings in the same dispute in order to avoid jurisdictional competition with the CJEU. Moreover, they should request that the Member States ascertain whether or not Luxembourg has jurisdiction

[119] See *Iron Rhine Arbitration (Belgium v Netherlands)* PCA, Arbitration Agreement, 22 July 2003, para 3.

[120] *Jurisdictional Immunities of the State (Germany v Italy)* (Application by Germany of 23 December 2008) 2.

[121] See *Jurisdictional Immunities of the State (Germany v Italy; Greece Intervening)* ICJ Rep [2012] 1.

[122] See Lavranos, 'Scope of Exclusive Jurisdiction' (n 89) 91.

[123] See *Iron Rhine Arbitration (Belgium v Netherlands)* PCA, Memorial by the Kingdom of Belgium of 1 October 2003, paras 39ff.

[124] See Lavranos, 'Scope of Exclusive Jurisdiction' (n 89) 91.

[125] See generally Shany, *Competing Jurisdictions* (n 2) 77.

in a concrete case.[126] As a consequence, international courts and tribunals are bereft of any competence to decide a case *in fine* without prior reassurance that the CJEU does not have jurisdiction, particularly because of the supremacy and binding effect of Union law, which includes CJEU judgments as well.[127] According to the principle of the supremacy of Union law,[128] a judgment by Luxembourg would therefore supplant the ruling of any international court or tribunal, rendering their judgments superfluous. This approach will consequently hinder the Member States from bringing cases before international judicial bodies and thus obligate them in taking up a subordinate role in the European legal order.[129] The question remains whether other international courts would easily and willingly accept such a limitation of their jurisdiction by the CJEU. More importantly, this jurisdictional limitation of other international courts will eventually weaken the dispute settlement mechanisms set forth in the international treaties which established these courts, whose task is to interpret and apply these international treaties.[130]

The CJEU's approach vis-à-vis other international judicial bodies may represent a real risk of incoherence arising from jurisdictional overlaps and competition. Nevertheless, informed and mutually respectful decision-making by international courts may help mitigate this risk.[131] Of course, the more international law provides for explicit and unambiguous rules on jurisdictional conflicts (for instance, in the form of principles such as *forum non conveniens*, *lis alibi pendens*, *electa una via* etc),[132] the fewer preventive mechanisms are necessary to preclude Member States from using alternative dispute settlement bodies. In this regard, the CJEU is perhaps best advised to show more trust in the capability of other international courts to apply their rules accurately[133] and thus more comity towards their jurisdiction. An excellent example in the context of this book is set by utilising the '*Solange*' model of the German Constitutional Court[134] by the ECtHR with regard to the CJEU in its *Bosphorus v Ireland* judgment,[135] which will be discussed in detail in the following chapter of this book.

---

[126] See Lavranos, 'Scope of Exclusive Jurisdiction' (n 89) 92.

[127] See Lavranos, 'Concurrence' (n 50) 46.

[128] See, for instance, the most recent cases confirming the principle of supremacy: Case C-409/06 *Winner Wetten GmbH v Bürgermeisterin der Stadt Bergheim* [2010] ECR I-8015; Case C-2/08 *Amministrazione dell'Economia e delle Finanze v Fallimento Olimpiclub* [2009] ECR I-7501; Case C-314/08 *Filipiak v Dyrektor Izby Skarbowej w Poznaniu* [2009] ECR I-11049.

[129] See Franz C Mayer, 'Verfassungsgerichtsbarkeit' in Armin von Bogdandy and Jürgen Bast (eds), *Europäisches Verfassungsrecht. Theoretische und dogmatische Grundzüge* (Berlin Heidelberg, Springer, 2009) 588.

[130] See Lavranos, 'Scope of Exclusive Jurisdiction' (n 89) 92.

[131] See Philippa Webb, 'Scenarios of Jurisdictional Overlap among International Courts' (2006) 19 *Revue québecoise de Droit International* 277, 285.

[132] See generally on these principles of international law, Shany, *Competing Jurisdictions* (n 2) 135ff and 212ff; see also International Law Association, 'Third Interim Report: Declining and Referring Jurisdiction in International Litigation' (London Conference, 2000).

[133] See Schmalenbach, 'Struggle for Exclusiveness' (n 4) 1056.

[134] See 2 BvR 197/83 *Solange II* BVerfGE 73, 339.

[135] See *Bosphorus v Ireland* App no 45036/98 (ECtHR, 30 June 2005) para 155.

5

A Special Case: The Court of Justice of the European Union and the European Court of Human Rights

THE PRECEDING EXTENSIVE analysis illustrates the Court of Justice of the European Union's (CJEU) sceptical approach vis-à-vis international courts and tribunals and its ambitious undertakings to protect its exclusive jurisdiction over European Union law. The present chapter, however, will substantiate these findings and focus on a judicial relationship which is of utmost importance to this book. The current situation, namely the status quo of the relationship between the European Court of Justice and the European Court of Human Rights (ECtHR) is, in a manner of speaking, the linchpin for the further line of reasoning in Part III of this book. This exceptional judicial interface mainly results from the fact that both courts have comparable jurisdiction *ratione personae,* despite their differing human rights protection mechanisms.[1] By presenting this relationship, this enquiry serves as a starting point for the subsequent analysis of the different legal problems arising from the EU's accession to the Convention. Firstly, this chapter will look at how the case law of the two courts is intertwined at present; secondly, how these two courts are therefore dealing with jurisdictional conflicts or even rivalry[2] resulting from the 'multi-layered labyrinth'[3] of human rights protection in Europe; and lastly, of course, how the European Union's lack of jurisdiction *ratione personae* before the ECtHR affects the mutual judicial dialogue between Luxembourg and Strasbourg. Even before the European Union has actually acceded to the Convention, this exceptional judicial relationship deserves thoughtful consideration. Certainly, the two regimes are distinct and mostly independent from each other (as regards, for instance, their legal bases), but still they

---

[1] See Yuval Shany, *The Competing Jurisdictions of International Courts and Tribunals* (Oxford, Oxford University Press, 2003) 68.

[2] See Kirsten Schmalenbach, 'Struggle for Exclusiveness: The CJEU and Competing International Tribunals' in Isabelle Buffard, James Crawford, Alain Pellet and Stephan Wittich (eds), *International Law between Universalism and Fragmentation. Festschrift in Honour of Gerhard Hafner* (Leiden, Brill, 2008) 1063.

[3] See Andreas Haratsch, 'Die *Solange*-Rechtsprechung des Europäischen Gerichtshofs für Menschenrechte. Das Kooperationsverhältnis zwischen EGMR und EuGH' (2006) 66 *Zeitschrift für ausländisches öffentliches Recht und Völkerrecht* 927, 927 and 946.

do not operate in complete isolation from each other. Rather, they developed both a formal and informal relationship[4] and thereby became part of a larger European 'community of law', leading to a complex system of legal actors interacting with one another on the grounds of both self-interest and shared values.[5]

However, a *caveat* in the beginning might lead the way. The history of the complex relationship between the European Union and the Convention and of the Luxembourg and Strasbourg Courts in particular has already been comprehensively scrutinised in a plethora of academic articles and books.[6] Therefore, another lengthy and extensive examination of this topic *ab ovo* is omitted at this point, since this would go beyond the scope of the discussion presented in this book. The following sections merely give a fragmentary synopsis of the substantial interaction between the two courts in order to comprehend the legal implications of accession.

I. THE CONVENTION AND THE EU: A VIEW FROM LUXEMBOURG

A. **Luxembourg's Case Law: Recourse to the Convention**

Today, according to Article 6 (1) of the Treaty on European Union (TEU), fundamental rights within the EU are primarily protected by the provisions set forth in the Charter of Fundamental Rights of the European Union.[7] Yet it was not until the entry into force of the Lisbon Treaty that the Charter became legally binding. The EU's precursor organisations, the European Coal and Steel Community (ECSC) and the European Economic Community (EEC) were created as economic organisations first and foremost, and thus their founding treaties did not provide for the protection of fundamental rights.[8]

In the following decades, the CJEU was not reluctant to develop a system of fundamental rights protection based on case law. The main objective[9] of this

---

[4] See Guy Harpaz, 'The European Court of Justice and its Relations with the European Court of Human Rights: The Quest for Enhanced Reliance, Coherence and Legitimacy' (2009) 46 *Common Market Law Review* 105, 106.

[5] See Laurence Helfer and Anne-Marie Slaughter, 'Toward a Theory of Effective Supranational Adjudication' (1997) 107 *Yale Law Journal* 273, 276.

[6] See, eg Jan Hendrik Wiethoff, *Das konzeptuelle Verhältnis von EuGH und EGMR* (Baden-Baden, Nomos, 2008); Paul Craig and Gráinne De Búrca, *EU Law. Text, Cases and Materials*, 5th edn (Oxford, Oxford University Press, 2011) 399–407; Tobias Lock, *Das Verhältnis zwischen dem EuGH und internationalen Gerichten* (Tübingen, Mohr Siebeck, 2010) 243–307; Walter Frenz, *Handbuch Europarecht. Band 4: Europäische Grundrechte* (Berlin Heidelberg, Springer, 2009) paras 32–119.

[7] The intriguing, yet complex relationship between the Convention and the Charter will be examined in more detail later on in ch 5.

[8] See JHH Weiler, 'Eurocracy and Distrust: Some Questions Concerning the Role of the European Court of Justice in the Protection of Fundamental Human Rights within the Legal Order of the European Communities' (1986) 61 *Washington Law Review* 1103, 1110, for an extensive analysis of the historical reasons why no codified 'Bill of Rights' was included in the EEC Treaty.

[9] See Jason Coppel and Aidan O'Neill, 'The European Court of Justice: Taking Rights Seriously?' (1992) 29 *Common Market Law Review* 669, 669ff, for a comprehensive presentation of the CJEU's motives to embrace human rights law.

step was to respond to the pressure from domestic Constitutional Courts which criticised the then deficient system of human rights protection,[10] particularly by questioning the unconditioned application of the supremacy principle by invoking fundamental rights as the ultimate limit to that principle (the so-called counter-limits doctrine).[11] Certainly, it would have been easier for the Union to claim allegiance to the Convention in the first place, but this option was flawed with two major problems. Firstly, at that time, some of the EU's Member States had not ratified the Convention or had not recognised the individual right of petition under the Convention, or even both. Under these special circumstances, it would have been difficult to accept the Convention as an anterior treaty protected by the provisions of Article 351 of the Treaty on the Functioning of the European Union (TFEU)[12] and, where appropriate, to allow it to be invoked by individuals under European Union law where no such invocation would be permissible under the Convention itself. Secondly, and considerably more significant in the context of this book, Article 19 (1) TEU appoints the CJEU as the vigilant guardian for interpreting and applying Union law. By substantially accepting the authority of the Convention and the case law of the ECtHR, however, without putting certain legal safeguards in place to prevent external interference, the EU would have run the risk of subjecting itself to another legal order.[13]

Consequently, neither court had the legal competence to protect human rights at EU level. This is exactly where Europe's human rights conundrum was located. As the Union had become more powerful in terms of political output and administrative competence, it had also obtained the power to violate human rights.[14] In the following years, the CJEU had to resort to other sources of law[15] and adopted the formula that fundamental human rights are enshrined in the general principles of Union law and therewith protected by the Luxembourg Court.[16] To further protect fundamental rights, the CJEU drew inspiration from both 'constitutional traditions common to the member states'[17] and 'international treaties

---

[10] See BvL 52/71 *Solange I* BVerfGE 37, 271; see also Corte Costituzionale 183/73 *Frontini*, 27 December 1973.

[11] See Giacomo Di Federico, 'Fundamental Rights in the EU: Legal Pluralism and Multi-Level Protection after the Lisbon Treaty' in Giacomo Di Federico (ed), *The EU Charter of Fundamental Rights. From Declaration to Binding Document* (Dordrecht, Springer Netherlands, 2011) 19.

[12] See Pietro Manzini, 'The Priority of Pre-Existing Treaties of EC Member States within the Framework of International Law' (2001) 12 *European Journal of International Law* 781, 782, defining this provision as one of two subordination clauses codified in art 30 (4) of the Vienna Convention on the Law of Treaties.

[13] See Jan Klabbers, *Treaty Conflict and the European Union* (Cambridge, Cambridge University Press, 2009) 163f.

[14] See Laurent Scheeck, 'The Relationship between the European Courts and Integration through Human Rights' (2005) 65 *Zeitschrift für ausländisches öffentliches Recht und Völkerrecht* 837, 837.

[15] See, for a general and concise overview, Andreas Haratsch, 'Der kooperative Grundrechtsschutz in der Europäischen Union' in Andreas Haratsch and Peter Schiffauer (eds), *Grundrechtsschutz in der Europäischen Union* (Berlin, BWV, 2007) 10f.

[16] See Case 29/69 *Stauder v City of Ulm* [1969] ECR 419, para 7.

[17] See Case 11/70 *Internationale Handelsgesellschaft mbH v Einfuhr- und Vorratsstelle für Getreide und Futtermittel* [1970] ECR 1125, para 4.

for the protection of human rights on which the member states have collaborated or of which they are signatories, [...] including the [Convention]'[18] and the International Covenant on Civil and Political Rights.[19] Later, Luxembourg referred to the Convention more explicitly[20] and emphasised its importance with regard to the ECtHR's interpretation of it.[21] The CJEU's case law was then adopted as Article F (2) of the TEU in primary law via the Treaty of Maastricht. Today, reference to the Convention can be found in Article 6 (3) TEU, which reads:

> Fundamental rights, as guaranteed by the European Convention for the Protection of Human Rights and Fundamental Freedoms and as they result from the constitutional traditions common to the Member States, shall constitute general principles of the Union's law.

This means that even before the Union's accession to the European Convention of Human Rights (ECHR), the Convention itself, but only in the form of general principles of law, had already become a substantial and integral part of EU law. Thus the interface between the so-called Luxembourg and Strasbourg regimes was established, the former relying on and referring to the latter as a source of inspiration and guidance in human rights matters.[22]

B. General Principles Derived from the Convention as Part of EU Law

Despite the Convention's quasi-implementation in the form of general principles of law into the Union's legal order, the Convention is not a primary source of Union law, but merely a source of law-determining principles to fill lacunae within the case law-based system of fundamental rights protection. The CJEU has no jurisdiction to apply the Convention directly[23] and is accordingly not formally bound by it. This fact allows the CJEU to adapt and apply the Convention very flexibly[24] and to interpret it in an integrative way in order to bolster the *effet utile* principle.[25]

---

[18] Case 4/73 *Nold v Ruhrkohle Aktiengesellschaft* [1977] ECR 1, paras 12–13.

[19] See Case 374/87 *Orkem v Commission* [1989] ECR 3283, para 18.

[20] See Case 36/75 *Rutili v Ministre de l'Intérieur* [1975] ECR 1219, para 32.

[21] See Case C-540/03 *European Parliament v Council (Immigration Policy)* [2006] ECR I-5769, paras 46–55, 85, and 96–98.

[22] See Harpaz (n 4) 108.

[23] See Case T-347/94 *Mayr-Melnhof v Commission* [1998] ECR II-1751, paras 9 and 311; Case T-112/98 *Mannesmannröhren-Werke v Commission* [2001] ECR II-729, para 59; Case T-99/04 *AC-Treuhand AG v Commission* [2008] ECR II-1501, para 45.

[24] See Jürgen Kühling, 'Grundrechte' in Armin von Bogdandy and Jürgen Bast (eds), *Europäisches Verfassungsrecht. Theoretische und dogmatische Grundzüge* (Berlin Heidelberg, Springer, 2009) 663.

[25] See Eckart Klein, 'Das Verhältnis des Europäischen Gerichtshofs zum Europäischen Gerichtshof für Menschenrechte' in Detlef Merten and Jürgen Papier (eds), *Handbuch der Grundrechte in Deutschland und Europa. Band VI/1, Europäische Grundrechte I* (Heidelberg, CF Müller, 2010) 1276.

However, it is most notable that the CJEU judges are now less cautious than a couple of years ago in regularly referring to the case law of the ECtHR when a question concerning the interpretation of EU fundamental rights arises.[26] In such cases, Luxembourg recurrently uses the formula 'as interpreted by the European Court of Human Rights',[27] which led to the view that the Convention's status within the Union's legal order had evolved from 'gentle integration to absorption', or from a status of being 'borrowed towards appropriation'.[28] In fact, since the beginning of the judicial interface between Luxembourg and Strasbourg, the CJEU has frequently referred to both the Convention and Strasbourg's jurisprudence. The Luxembourg judges have not cited any other international court or tribunal with such regularity.[29] The CJEU has undoubtedly used the ECtHR's jurisprudence as an interpretive tool with respect to the lawfulness of acts and omissions of EU institutions and organs.[30]

Nevertheless, despite this deferential and virtually cooperative approach, the CJEU does not feel itself formally bound by the rulings of the ECtHR.[31] This course of action is legally consistent, since the general principles mentioned in Article 6 (3) TEU, derived by the CJEU from the Convention, can only bind the EU in their capacity as EU law, but not as provisions of international law. The former President of the Luxembourg Court, Rodríguez Iglesias, similarly asserted that the EU was never legally bound by the Convention. Rather, it has confined itself to emphasising the Convention's significance besides other international human rights treaties in ascertaining the general principles of law in the field of fundamental rights protection.[32] As a result, the EU and the CJEU will not be legally bound by the Convention and the ECtHR's rulings before the Union has formally acceded to the Convention. Consequently, according to Article 19 (1) TEU, the CJEU remains the ultimate arbiter of these provisions to the extent that they are already part of EU law.[33]

---

[26] See Scheeck (n 14) 857f.

[27] See eg, Case C-540/03 *European Parliament v Council* (n 21) para 85; Case C-105/03 *Criminal Proceedings against Maria Pupino* [2005] ECR I-5285, para 60; Case C-303/05 *Advocaten voor de Wereld* [2007] ECR I-3633, para 50, see generally Walter Berka, 'EU-Recht und EMRK' in Werner Schroeder (ed), *Europarecht als Mehrebenensystem* (Baden-Baden, Nomos, 2008) 114.

[28] See Denys Simon, 'Des influences réciproques entre CJCE et CEDH: "Je t'aime, moi non plus?"' (2001) 96 *Pouvoirs, Les cours européennes* 31, 37.

[29] See Sionaidh Douglas-Scott, 'A Tale of Two Courts: Luxembourg, Strasbourg and the Growing European Human Rights *Acquis*' (2006) 43 *Common Market Law Review* 629, 650. See also Case C-555/07 *Kücükdeveci* [2010] ECR I-365, paras 3–4.

[30] See Harpaz (n 4) 109.

[31] See Marco Bronckers, 'The Relationship of the EC Courts with other International Tribunals: Non-Committal, Respectful or Submissive?' (2007) 44 *Common Market Law Review* 601, 604.

[32] See Gil Carlos Rodríguez Iglesias, 'Zur Stellung der Europäischen Menschenrechtskonvention im europäischen Gemeinschaftsrecht' in Ulrich Beyerlin (ed), *Recht zwischen Umbruch und Bewahrung. Völkerrecht, Europarecht, Staatsrecht, Festschrift für Rudolf Bernhardt* (Berlin Heidelberg, Springer, 1995) 1274.

[33] See Klein, 'Verhältnis des EuGH zum EGMR' (n 25) 1278.

C. Consequences for the EU Member States

Since the Member States play an instrumental role in the application and implementation of European Union law,[34] the Luxembourg judges have ruled that the fundamental rights recognised by the CJEU in its case law are also binding on the Member States when they implement Union rules.[35] The same rights that the CJEU 'borrowed' from national and international legal systems have been applied or, more critically speaking, instrumentalised[36] vis-à-vis the Member States. Therewith, national fundamental rights law has been applied through European Union law and CJEU jurisprudence in a circular looping route or, metaphorically speaking, Escherian image,[37] demonstrating a system which might be described as a relationship of inversely commutative[38] or tangled hierarchies.[39] Still, this did not prevent Luxembourg from obligating Member States to give effect to the Convention, as interpreted by the CJEU, in all cases which fall within the ambit of Union law, therewith increasing its competences at the expense of those of the Member States.[40]

In concreto, the CJEU held that Member States are also bound by the Union's fundamental rights when derogating from EU law,[41] for example by breaching fundamental freedoms. Moreover, within the course of the *ERT* case, the CJEU modified its view to the effect that it had no power to examine the compatibility of national legislation with the Convention,[42] but also ruled that, in cases which fell within the scope of Union law, it would determine whether national rules were compatible with the fundamental rights that derive from the Convention. Luxembourg will thus require the Member States to comply with EU fundamental rights in all Union-related cases.[43] This decision is a very broad interpretation of the term 'scope of Union law', since this formula applies in all cases in which Member States limit fundamental freedoms on the grounds of public policy, public morality, public security and public health[44]— all domains which basically fall within the member states' competence.[45] By interpreting the Member States' limitation of fundamental freedoms in light

---

[34] See, eg Thomas von Danwitz, *Europäisches Verwaltungsrecht* (Berlin Heidelberg, Springer, 2008) 315ff.

[35] See Case 5/88 *Wachauf* [1989] ECR 2609, paras 18–19.

[36] See Scheeck (n 14) 853f.; see also Sebastian Winkler, *Der Beitritt der Europäischen Gemeinschaften zur Europäischen Menschenrechtskonvention* (Baden-Baden, Nomos, 2000) 26f.

[37] See Klabbers, *Treaty Conflict* (n 13) 173f.

[38] See Douglas-Scott (n 29) 634.

[39] See Mireille Delmas-Marty, *Towards a Truly Common Law. Europe as a Laboratory for Legal Pluralism* (Cambridge, Cambridge University Press. 2002) 65.

[40] See Coppel and O'Neill (n 9) 692.

[41] See Case 36/75 *Rutili* (n 20) para 27.

[42] See Joined Cases 60/84 and 61/84 *Cinéthèque SA* [1985] ECR 2605, para 26.

[43] See Case C-260/89 *ERT* [1991] ECR I-2925, para 42.

[44] See arts 36, 52 and 62 TFEU.

[45] See Di Federico (n 11) 29.

of the general principles of law and of fundamental rights in particular,[46] the CJEU used the Convention-derived fundamental rights to considerably extend the field of application of European Union law to other areas of national law.[47] Given the increasing EU legislation in the form of secondary Union law and the extensive interpretation of its jurisdiction,[48] Luxembourg might interfere with competences which are exclusively reserved to the Member States.[49]

Nonetheless, the CJEU continuously expanded its so-called *ERT* doctrine in a very problematic way.[50] In *Carpenter v Secretary of State*, the Court applied Article 8 ECHR, the right to respect for private and family life, to substantiate Mr Carpenter's fundamental freedom to provide services under Article 56 TFEU against the deportation of his wife, a third-country national, who also worked as his children's nanny which allowed Mr Carpenter to travel for business.[51] Similarly, in *Karner GmbH v Troostwijk GmbH*, the CJEU applied Article 10 ECHR, the right to freedom of expression, to corroborate the free movement of goods under Article 28 TFEU against a restriction on the advertising of goods from an insolvent company.[52] But even in situations where the Luxembourg Court decided not to expand its Convention-derived human rights jurisdiction, another interesting development occurred regarding the Member States and their fundamental rights obligations within the scope of Union law. In *Omega Spielhallen*,[53] the principle of human dignity took precedence over the freedom to provide services, and in *Schmidberger v Austria*,[54] the freedom of expression prevailed over the free movement of goods. Moreover, in these cases, the Luxembourg Court understood fundamental rights and fundamental freedoms to be on par with one another. This conceptualisation apparently solved the conflict between Union law and a different set of rules by transforming this conflict between the Treaties and the Convention to a conflict between rules of the same legal system.[55] It therefore seems that the CJEU did not act as the guardian of EU law; it rather acted as the guardian of the Convention,[56] thereby bestowing priority to fundamental rights over fundamental freedoms.[57]

---

[46] See Case C-62/90 *Commission v Germany (Medicinal Products)* [1992] ECR I-2575, para 23.

[47] See Douglas-Scott (n 29) 634.

[48] See Stefan Storr, 'Rechtsstaat und Grundrechte in Europa' in Österreichische Juristenkommission (ed), *Grundrechte im Europa der Zukunft* (Vienna, Linde, 2010) 35.

[49] See Peter Szczekalla, 'Grenzenlose Grundrechte' (2006) 25 *Neue Zeitschrift für Verwaltungsrecht* 1019, 1020.

[50] See Paul Gragl, 'Anwendungsbereich und Tragweite der Europäischen Grundrechte' (2011/2012) 22 *Juristische Ausbildung und Praxisvorbereitung* 47, 47ff.

[51] See Case C-60/00 *Carpenter v Secretary of State* [2002] ECR I-6279, paras 40–46.

[52] See Case C-71/02 *Karner GmbH v Troostwijk GmbH* [2004] ECR I-3025, paras 50–53.

[53] See Case C-36/02 *Omega Spielhallen* [2004] ECR I-9609.

[54] See Case C-112/00 *Schmidberger v Austria* [2003] ECR I-5659.

[55] See Klabbers, *Treaty Conflict* (n 13) 165.

[56] See Robert Uerpmann-Wittzack, 'Völkerrechtliche Verfassungselemente' in Armin von Bogdandy and Jürgen Bast (eds), *Europäisches Verfassungsrecht. Theoretische und dogmatische Grundzüge* (Berlin Heidelberg, Springer, 2009) 219ff.

[57] See Douglas-Scott (n 29) 635.

Of course, Luxembourg's ultimate objective of centralising the judicial control over fundamental rights law demonstrates its desire to ensure compliance with fundamental rights in all cases falling within the scope of EU law, virtually acting like a federal constitutional court. However, this daring *modus operandi* also placed a predominant responsibility on the CJEU, namely that of combining the national, supranational and international level of fundamental rights protection, whilst concurrently preserving the Union's legal autonomy.[58] This led to concomitant obligations on the part of the Member States to abide by both the Convention itself and fundamental EU rights derived from the Convention. Still, to make things more complicated, the standard protection instituted by the CJEU is not the minimum, as defined by the ECtHR. On the contrary, in some cases—for instance, if fundamental rights clash with free movement rights or the Union's fundamental freedoms in general[59]—fundamental Union rights claim to be both the floor and the ceiling which states are required to comply with under the principle of supremacy.[60] In other words, in such cases fundamental EU rights in the form of general principles, derived from the Convention, do not just set the bottom threshold of human rights protection, but, as an integral part of EU law, take precedence over domestic law at the same time.

This means that the CJEU construed the Union's legal bond to human rights as flowing from Union law itself rather than from an external obligation,[61] as the EU lacked the legal basis and therefore the competence to accede to the Convention at that time.[62] After accession, however, the potential conflicts between the European Union and domestic legal systems in the field of fundamental rights protection might not just disappear. According to the principle of subsidiarity, laid down in Article 35 ECHR[63] and Article 52 (6) of the Charter of Fundamental Rights (ChFR),[64] respectively, Member States may still guarantee a higher level of protection than the ECtHR and the CJEU. This is certainly permitted by the Convention system, but might collide with the EU's principle of supremacy, despite the aforementioned assurance in Article 52 (6) ChFR. By and large, the system of human rights protection in Europe is being largely 'disaggregated',[65] which means that the function of protecting human rights

---

[58] See Di Federico (n 11) 29.

[59] See eg, Case C-112/00 *Schmidberger v Austria* (n 54) or Case C-438/05 *Viking Line* [2007] ECR I-10779.

[60] See Aida Torres Pérez, *Conflicts of Rights in the European Union: A Theory of Supranational Adjudication* (Oxford, Oxford University Press, 2009) 36.

[61] See Klabbers, *Treaty Conflict* (n 13) 166.

[62] See Opinion 2/94 *Accession by the Community to the European Convention for the Protection of Human Rights and Fundamental Freedoms* [1996] ECR I-1759, para 36.

[63] See Wolfgang Peukert, 'Art 35' in Jochen Frowein and Wolfgang Peukert (eds), *EMRK-Kommentar* (Kehl am Rhein, NP Engel, 2009) para 1.

[64] See Explanations relating to the Charter of Fundamental Rights [2007] OJ C303/35.

[65] See Christian Walter, 'Constitutionalising (Inter)national Governance—Possibilities for and Limits to the Development of an International Constitutional Law' (2001) 44 *German Yearbook of International Law* 170, 196ff.

is currently allocated to various institutions from different and thus possibly overlapping and conflicting legal spheres.[66] Therefore, the question remains whether the CJEU will use the accession to the Convention to further expand its jurisdiction at the expense of the Member States.

D. The Charter of Fundamental Rights: Incorporation of the Convention

Another question, regarding the legal status of the Convention within European Union law before accession, arises with the ChFR's entry into force which refers to the Convention in several articles. In its present form, the Charter is a *desideratum* of several legal 'layers', ie international law, EU law and domestic constitutional law of the Member States. Articles 52 and 53 ChFR take this exceptional circumstance into account by referring to these different layers of law (Article 52) and by preventing legal conflicts between them (Article 53).[67] Consequently, this section examines the changes which are to be expected in respect to the Charter and the subsequent co-existence of two binding human rights documents which are deemed admissible under both the Convention and European Union law.[68] The complementary nature of these two documents can therefore be deduced from these abovementioned provisions, which are thoroughly discussed below.

i. Article 52 (3) of the Charter

The first provision to be examined is Article 52 (3) ChFR which governs the important relationship between the Charter and the Convention. According to this clause,[69] the meaning and scope of the rights enshrined in the Charter shall be the same as those laid down in the Convention, insofar as those rights correspond to the rights guaranteed in the Convention.[70] In a *Joint Communication from the Presidents of the CJEU and the ECtHR*, it was also emphasised that the 'greatest coherence' between the Convention and the Charter shall be ensured, especially insofar as the Charter contains corresponding rights. In addition, according to Article 52 (3) ChFR, the 'parallel interpretation' of the two documents could prove useful.[71] This means that the provisions of the Convention are virtually mirrored in the Charter, leading to the interesting fact that these two documents

---

[66] See Torres Pérez (n 60) 37.

[67] See Christoph Grabenwarter, 'Die Grundrechte im Verfassungsvertrag der Europäischen Union' in Stefan Hammer, Alexander Somek, Manfred Stelzer and Barbara Weichselbaum (eds), *Demokratie und sozialer Rechtsstaat in Europa, Festschrift für Theo Öhlinger* (Vienna, WUV, 2004) 476.

[68] See Di Federico (n 11) 41f.

[69] For the first reference by the Court to art 52 (3) ChFR after the Lisbon Treaty's entry into force, see Joined Cases C-92/09 and C-93/09 *Schecke und Eifert* [2010] ECR I-11063, para 51.

[70] A list of these corresponding rights can be found in the Explanations relating to the Charter (n 64).

[71] See Joint Communication from Presidents Costa and Skouris, 17 January 2011, 1.

must be read in conjunction with each other. So, for instance, if the right to private and family life is infringed, Article 7 ChFR must be read in the light of Article 8 ECHR,[72] and legislation must comply with the same standards enshrined in the Convention and those determined by the case law of both the CJEU and the ECtHR.[73] Hence, this provision aims to create consistency[74] and to harmonise the Union's system of fundamental rights protection with the Convention[75] by establishing the Convention as the minimum standard of human rights protection in the EU, however, without thereby adversely affecting the autonomy of Union law and the exclusive jurisdiction of the Luxembourg Court.[76] The preservation of the Union's legal autonomy is equally laid down in the second sentence of Article 52 (3) ChFR, stating that 'this provision shall not prevent Union law from providing a more extensive fundamental rights protection'.[77]

Given this special proviso, Article 52 (3) ChFR will not automatically preclude all conflicting decisions between Luxembourg and Strasbourg. Basically, Article 52 (3) ChFR can be regarded as a kind of 'dynamic norm of reference' to the ECtHR's jurisprudence. But this view also leads to the question of whether the CJEU, when referring to the Strasbourg Court, is also bound by the latter's case law. Some argue that the ECtHR's case law already binds the Luxembourg Court when the latter is interpreting the Convention rights which are incorporated in the Charter, even before the Union's accession to the Convention.[78] Since the CJEU is the main interpreter of the Charter, such a presumption would lead to the CJEU being bound by the case law of the ECtHR when interpreting the Charter, which is EU law. Concurrently, this would result in a legal hierarchy of the two courts with Strasbourg at the top of this European court system.[79] However, the wording of the Charter in Article 52 (7) ChFR, which merely contains the duty to duly regard the Strasbourg Court's case law, does not sustain a binding force of Strasbourg's case law on Luxembourg when interpreting the Charter.[80]

But still, the reference to the ECtHR's case law does not necessarily imply any risks to the Union's legal autonomy. Firstly, Luxembourg already tends to

---

[72] See Uerpmann-Wittzack (n 56) 224.

[73] See Explanations relating to the Charter (n 64) 33.

[74] On the topic of creating consistency, see generally Thomas von Danwitz, 'Art 52' in Peter J Tettinger and Klaus Stern (eds), *Kölner Gemeinschaftskommentar zur Europäischen Grundrechte-Charta* (Munich, Beck, 2006) paras 51ff.

[75] See Klein, 'Verhältnis des EuGH zum EGMR' (n 25) 1281.

[76] See Explanations relating to the Charter (n 64) 33.

[77] See Martin Borowsky, 'Art 52' in Jürgen Meyer (ed), *Charta der Grundrechte der Europäischen Union* (Baden-Baden, Nomos, 2010) para 30b.

[78] See ibid para 37. See also Koen Lenaerts and Eddy De Smijter, 'The Charter and the Role of the European Courts' (2001) 8 *Maastricht Journal of European and Comparative Law* 90, 99.

[79] See Tobias Lock, 'The ECJ and the ECtHR: The Future Relationship between the Two European Courts' (2009) 8 *Law and Practice of International Courts and Tribunals* 375, 383.

[80] See ibid 385.

accept Strasbourg's leading role in the field of human rights protection[81] and the Charter simply codifies this practice.[82] This also prevents the European Union from adopting measures affording less extensive protection.[83] Reciprocally, the ECtHR diligently considers the special features of both EU law in general and the Charter in particular, most likely by applying its 'margin of appreciation' principle, thus contributing to a veritably cooperative relationship between the two courts.[84] Secondly, this does not grant the Strasbourg Court any jurisdiction to interpret and apply the respective Charter provisions as a quasi-court of last resort. In fact, it will be the CJEU that decides on both the interpretation and scope of the fundamental rights enshrined in the Charter.[85] Particularly in respect of the European Union's legal autonomy, it must certainly be permissible for the Luxembourg Court to derogate from a specific interpretation by the ECtHR, provided the limitations of fundamental rights are in accordance with Article 52 (1) ChFR and therefore 'meet objectives of general interest recognised by the Union or the need to protect the rights and freedoms of others'.[86] Moreover, the CJEU is merely bound by the ECtHR's case law to the extent that it is not allowed to fall below the Strasbourg Court's guaranteed level of protection.[87]

In this context, it must remain the CJEU's prerogative to adjust and adapt these incorporated provisions of the Convention, especially in light of the Convention's subsidiary principle, laid down in Article 35 (1) ECHR. Luxembourg may, for example, prioritise one right over another by means of teleological interpretation (under the general rules of Article 31 (1) of the Vienna Convention of the Law of Treaties (VCLT) and therewith take into account the abovementioned special features of Union law. This typical *effet utile* approach may very well violate the Convention as interpreted by the Strasbourg Court, for instance in the field of antitrust law where the Commission's effective investigations may take precedence over the fundamental right of defence in an administrative procedure,[88] as the ECtHR would be given jurisdiction to review such cases after accession anyway. Such EU-related interpretations of potential fundamental rights limitations have already been envisaged in some working papers on the Union's future accession.[89]

---

[81] See eg, the following recent cases: Case C-279/09 *DEB v Germany* [2010] ECR I-13849, paras 37ff; Joined Cases C-92/09 and C-93/09 *Schecke und Eifert* (n 69) para 59; Case T-49/07 *Fahas v Council* [2010] ECR II-5555, para 72.

[82] See Olivier De Schutter, 'Art 52—Portée des droits garantis' in EU Network of Independent Experts on Fundamental Rights, *Commentary of the Charter of Fundamental Rights of the European Union* (2006) 401.

[83] See Case C-120/10 *European Air Transport SA v Collège d'Environnement de la Région Bruxelles-Capitale* [2011] ECR I-0000, Opinion of AG Villalón, para 79.

[84] See Borowsky, 'Art 52' (n 77) para 37.

[85] See von Danwitz, 'Art 52' (n 74) para 58.

[86] See Di Federico (n 11) 42.

[87] See von Danwitz, 'Art 52' (n 74) para 58.

[88] See Di Federico (n 11) 42 and n 149.

[89] See Commission of the European Communities, 'Memorandum on the Accession of the European Communities to the Convention for the Protection of Human Rights and Fundamental

ii. Article 53 of the Charter

Article 53 ChFR is the second provision which is of utmost importance in regards to the judicial interface between Luxembourg and Strasbourg. The interaction of the aforementioned different legal layers will, in the case of concurrence or conflict, be resolved in favour of the Convention.[90] This can be deduced from the wording of this article, stating that:

> [n]othing in this Charter shall be interpreted as restricting or adversely affecting human rights and fundamental freedoms as recognised, in their respective fields of application, by Union law and international law and by international agreements to which *the Union or all the Member States are party*, including the *European Convention for the Protection of Human Rights and Fundamental Freedoms*, and by the Member States' constitutions.[91]

The rights enshrined in the Convention and the respective case law of the Strasbourg Court therefore represent the minimum threshold of fundamental rights protection by which the Union is obliged to abide.[92] It is consequently argued that Article 53 ChFR might be seen as a conflict rule, according to which the legal order with the highest and most extensive fundamental rights protection should always prevail.[93]

Yet, unlike other international human rights treaties that are intended to complement the national systems of protection, the Charter is part of Union law which is construed as an autonomous legal order and which tends to suppress or even remove the legal disparities between the Member States by means of the supremacy principle.[94] Therefore, Article 53 ChFR is not an exception to the supremacy of Union law, since the scope of the Charter is only governed by Article 51 ChFR.[95] Furthermore, it does not imply any 're-nationalisation' of fundamental rights protection[96] or any review of primary or secondary EU law by the standards of national fundamental rights. In light of the Union's legal autonomy, the Charter neither invites the courts of the Member States to alleviate or soften

Freedoms' Bulletin Supplement 2/79, COM (79) 210 final, para 20; see also Steering Committee for Human Rights (CDDH), 'Study of Technical and Legal Issues of a Possible EC/EU Accession to the European Convention on Human Rights' DG-II(2002)006 of 28 June 2002, para 79.

[90] See Grabenwarter, 'Grundrechte im Verfassungsvertrag' (n 67) 476.

[91] Emphasis added.

[92] See Luzius Wildhaber, 'About the Co-Existence of Three Different Legal Systems and Three Jurisdictions' (2005) 60 *Zeitschrift für Öffentliches Recht* 313, 319.

[93] See eg, Koen Lenaerts and Eddy De Smijter, 'A "Bill of Rights" for the European Union' (2001) 38 *Common Market Law Review* 273, 287ff; Matthias Ruffert, 'Schlüsselfragen der Europäischen Verfassung der Zukunft: Grundrechte—Institutionen—Kompetenzen—Ratifizierung' (2004) 39 *Europarecht* 165, 174; for a critical approach, see R Alonso García, 'The General Provisions of the Charter of Fundamental Rights of the European Union' (2002) 8 *European Law Journal* 492, 513f.

[94] See García (n 93) 507f.

[95] See Martin Borowsky, 'Art 53' in Jürgen Meyer (ed), *Charta der Grundrechte der Europäischen Union* (Baden-Baden, Nomos, 2010) para 11.

[96] See Olivier De Schutter, 'Art 53—Niveau de protection' in EU Network of Independent Experts on Fundamental Rights, *Commentary of the Charter of Fundamental Rights of the European Union* (2006) 411.

the supremacy of EU law within its scope of application, nor to question the CJEU's exclusive jurisdiction.[97]

By and large, Article 53 ChFR thus gives an answer to the question of '*Quis judicabit?*' Even though it attempts to prevent any conflicts with the Convention and the Strasbourg Court, the Charter is ultimately interpreted and applied by the Luxembourg Court and, when implementing Union law, the courts of the Member States.[98] As the Union will not be legally bound by the Convention before accession, Luxembourg's jurisdictional autonomy will thereby remain entirely unaffected.[99]

iii. Legal Issues in Relation to the Accession and the Union's Legal Autonomy

In the context of the foregoing analysis, it is notable that even before the European Union's actual accession to the Convention, the Convention has such a preeminent significance within the Union's legal order. Article 6 TEU incorporates the Convention in a threefold manner. Firstly, in paragraph 1, by making it an integral part of the Charter and therewith part of EU law; secondly, in paragraph 2, by entitling and obliging the European Union to accede to it;[100] and thirdly, in paragraph 3, by referring to the provisions of the Convention as general principles of European Union law. The Union's subsequent obligation to adhere to the Convention, stemming from Article 6 TEU, is thence sometimes considered an '*in toto* incorporation'[101] or even a 'substantial accession' to the Convention,[102] but without subordinating the CJEU to the ECtHR. The Luxembourg Court is not bound by Strasbourg's case law when interpreting rights corresponding to those of the Convention.[103] Metaphorically speaking, one might even say that 'Ulysses may have tied himself to the mast, but this time he has made sure that the knots remain within his own reach.'[104]

However, this fact does not absolve the Union from *formally* acceding to the Convention. Even if the European Union implicitly abided by the Convention in any case before accession, individuals could not submit applications to Strasbourg in order to bring claims against the EU. An external judicial control by Strasbourg is therefore currently not possible. Additionally, divergences in judicial interpretation might still arise, particularly due to the existence of two differently

---

[97] See Borowsky, 'Art 53' (n 95) para 10.

[98] See art 51 ChFR and Preamble of the Charter, para 5.

[99] See Klein, 'Verhältnis des EuGH zum EGMR' (n 25) 1281f.

[100] See Uerpmann-Wittzack (n 56) 224.

[101] See Borowsky, 'Art 52' (n 77) paras 30 and 30a.

[102] See eg, Siegbert Alber and Ulrich Widmaier, 'Die EU-Charta der Grundrechte und ihre Auswirkungen auf die Rechtsprechung' (2000) 27 *Europäische Grundrechte-Zeitschrift* 497, 505.

[103] See Lock, 'Future Relationship' (n 79) 387.

[104] See Rick Lawson, 'Confusion and Conflict? Diverging Interpretations of the European Convention on Human Rights in Strasbourg and Luxembourg' in Rick Lawson and Matthijs De Bois (eds), *The Dynamics of the Protection of Human Rights in Europe: Essays in Honour of Henry G. Schermers, Vol 3* (Leiden, Martinus Nijhoff, 1994) 227.

worded documents on the same subject-matter and their interpretation by two different courts. Similarly, the provisions of Articles 52 (3) and 53 ChFR will not suffice in order to avoid the risk of contradictions, and especially not where the CJEU interprets the respective Convention provisions in a teleological manner, ie *in dubio pro integratione*, and where the application and interpretation of the Charter and the Convention by national courts is concerned.[105] Uniformity is therefore only ensured by the eventual accession of the EU to the Convention.[106]

The impact of the Charter should be examined against this interesting background. Article 19 (1) TEU sets out that the CJEU must guarantee compliance with the Treaties and therewith, via the provision of Article 6 (1) TEU, the Charter. The Luxembourg Court will therefore enjoy a more extensive competence in relation to acts purportedly in breach of fundamental rights. This pertains to Article 263 (4) TFEU especially, according to which individuals may institute proceedings 'against a regulatory act which is of direct concern to them and does not entail implementing measures'. Besides that, by following Article 67 TFEU and its own judgment in the *Kadi and Al Barakaat v Council and Commission* case, the CJEU will have to carefully balance economy-based fundamental freedoms and international security with effective fundamental rights protection.[107] It will be intriguing to observe whether the CJEU maintains this mostly Convention-based course of fundamental rights protection after accession. If it does, potential divergences in interpreting the Convention between Luxembourg and Strasbourg would presumably occur only on rare occasions.

Yet the Charter also impacts the national plane. The second sentence of Article 19 (1) TEU obliges the Member States to 'provide remedies sufficient to ensure effective legal protection in the fields covered by Union law'. Furthermore, according to Article 291 (1) TFEU, the Member States must also 'adopt all measures of national law necessary to implement legally binding Union acts'. These two provisions codify the consistent case law on the procedural autonomy of the Member States,[108] the right to an effective remedy and the right to a fair trial, stemming from the Articles 6 and 13 ECHR which are now laid down in Article 47 ChFR. They equally assign to the national legislators the primary responsibility of ensuring that the Charter is respected, but first and foremost they emphasise the principal role the domestic courts play in the multilevel European system of fundamental rights protection. The preliminary reference procedure under Article 267 TFEU consequently represents a crucial and indispensable tool in the prevention of fundamental rights violations in the Union's legal system.[109] Thus,

---

[105] See Steering Committee for Human Rights (CDDH), 'Study of Technical and Legal Issues' (n 89) para 80.

[106] See European Convention, 'Final Report of Working Group II' CONV 354/02, WG II 16, 12.

[107] Joined Cases C-402/05 P and C-415/05 P *Kadi and Al Barakaat v Council and Commission* [2008] ECR I- 6351; see Di Federico (n 11) 44.

[108] See Diana-Urania Galetta, *Procedural Autonomy of EU Member States: Paradise Lost?* (Berlin Heidelberg, Springer, 2010) 21.

[109] See Di Federico (n 11) 44f.

Article 6 (1) TEU has definitely put 'new flesh on the bones of the *Foto-Frost*[110] formula.'[111] But, at the same time, this raises new questions in relation to accession, in particularly how the CJEU's exclusive jurisdiction and the autonomy of EU law can be effectively maintained in fundamental rights cases related to Union law where a domestic court decides *not* to request a preliminary ruling from the Luxembourg Court and the claimant directly applies to the Strasbourg Court.[112] Such questions will be dealt with and answered later on in Part III of this book.

II. VIOLATIONS OF THE CONVENTION BY EU LAW: THE STRASBOURG PERSPECTIVE

A. Inescapable Obligations of the Member States

The fact that the Convention takes up a different legal status within the Member States' legal systems[113] and that these states are also Member States of other international or supranational organisations such as the European Union[114] does not release them from the obligation to uphold and protect the provisions enshrined in the Convention. However, the supremacy of EU law over conflicting and incompatible domestic legislation requires the Member States to fully comply with their obligations resulting from the Treaties, including the CJEU's case law. Additionally, it is also certain that, due to the lack of jurisdiction *ratione personae*, the ECtHR cannot review Union acts allegedly breaching the Convention until the Union has actually acceded to the Convention.[115] This lacuna within the protection system of the Convention raised the 'spectre' of the Luxembourg Court deciding cases which would subsequently obligate the Member States to enact legislation and implement measures in direct violation of the Convention.[116] So when Strasbourg eventually received applications alleging infringements of the Convention by the European Union it did not remain idle. Whilst the Convention was substantially implemented in the Union's legal order via both the CJEU's case law and primary law, Strasbourg was eventually compelled to take a stand vis-à-vis

---

[110] See Case 314/85 *Foto-Frost v Hauptzollamt Lübeck-Ost* [1987] ECR 4199.

[111] Di Federico (n 11) 45.

[112] For an analysis of this specific legal issue, see ch 11.

[113] See generally Dirk Ehlers, 'Allgemeine Lehren der EMRK' in Dirk Ehlers (ed), *Europäische Grundrechte und Grundfreiheiten* (Berlin, De Gruyter, 2009) 30ff; for an overview of the Convention's legal rank within the Member States with special regard to the accession, see Winkler (n 36) 119ff.

[114] See Kerstin Holzinger, *EMRK und internationale Organisationen* (Baden-Baden, Nomos, 2010) 71ff.

[115] See Di Federico (n 11) 25.

[116] See Joseph R Wetzel, 'Improving Fundamental Rights Protection in the European Union: Resolving the Conflict and Confusion between the Luxembourg and Strasbourg Courts' (2003) 71 *Fordham Law Review* 2823, 2824f.

the Union and focused its attention on European Union law, thereby permeating the legal system of the Union.[117]

i. No Jurisdiction ratione personae: *Inadmissibility of Applications against the EU*

From the outset,[118] Strasbourg was indeed very reluctant to mention anything related to EU law,[119] as illustrated by the decision in the *Confédération Française Démocratique du Travail (CFDT) v The European Communities* case. The application was concurrently directed against the then European Communities or, put another way, against all the Member States, both collectively and individually. The European Commission of Human Rights[120] held that, to the extent that the application was directed against the EU as such, the consideration of the applicant's complaint lay outside the Commission's jurisdiction *ratione personae*, since the Union never was (and still is not) a contracting party to the Convention.[121] Moreover, the Commission decided that the applicant had not defined the term 'the member states jointly' and considered that the application was instead directed against the Council of the EC. Nevertheless, this institution did not fall under the Commission's jurisdiction either.[122] The Commission also rejected the subsidiary application appertaining to the individual responsibility of the EU Member States, which were at the same time contracting parties to the Convention, as it could not answer the question whether the act carried out by an EU organ could also involve the responsibility of the then nine Member States.[123] This question was further complicated by the fact that France, at the time, had not yet recognised the right of individual petition under the Convention.[124] The Commission and the subsequently newly installed permanent Court continuously repeated this jurisprudence in several other cases[125] in relation to the Union.[126]

In a nutshell, the European Commission of Human Rights dispelled any doubts regarding the question as to whether the Strasbourg organs had jurisdiction

---

[117] See Scheeck (n 14) 857.

[118] For a general overview of the ECtHR's early case law on violations of the ECHR by EU law, see Patrick Schäfer, *Verletzungen der Europäischen Menschenrechtskonvention durch Europäisches Gemeinschaftsrecht und dessen Vollzug. Verantwortlichkeit und Haftung der Mitgliedstaaten* (Baden-Baden, Nomos, 2006) 65ff.

[119] See Klabbers, *Treaty Conflict* (n 13) 167.

[120] The European Commission of Human Rights was abolished and replaced with a new permanent Court of Human Rights by the 11th Protocol to the ECHR that entered into force on 1 November 1998.

[121] See *Confédération Française Démocratique du Travail (CFDT) v The European Communities, alternatively: Their Member States a) jointly and b) severally* App no 8030/77 (Commission Decision, 10 July 1978) para 3.

[122] See ibid para 4.

[123] See ibid para 5.

[124] See ibid para 6.

[125] See eg, *Dufay v The European Communities, alternatively: Their Member States a) jointly and b) severally* App no 13539/88 (Commission Decision, 19 January 1989); *Garzilli v Member States of the EU* App no 32384/96 (Commission Decision, 22 October 1998); *Société Guérin Automobiles v the 15 Member States of the EU* App no 51717/99 (ECtHR, 4 July 2000).

[126] See Scheeck (n 14) 858.

ratione personae over the European Union or its organs. As the Union is not a contracting party to the Convention, it does not have standing to be sued before the Commission or the Court. Still, this result consequently raised the question as to whether the Union's Member States are in some way responsible for the legal acts they implement in order to give effect to EU law.

ii. Applications against States for Giving Effect to Supranational Law

In the *M & Co v Federal Republic of Germany* case, the European Commission of Human Rights had to decide whether Germany would carry any responsibility for an act which was exclusively based on an EU regulation.[127] It held that a transfer of powers to a supranational organisation did not automatically absolve a state from its responsibilities under the Convention in relation to the exercise of the transferred powers. Nonetheless, the transfer of powers to an international organisation was not completely prohibited. Such a transfer was compatible with the Convention, provided that within that organisation, ie the European Union, fundamental rights would receive an 'equivalent protection'.[128] The Commission concluded that the legal system of the Union not only secured fundamental rights, but also provided for control of their observance, especially by referring to a Joint Declaration by the European Parliament, the Council and the Commission[129] in which they stressed that 'they attach prime importance to the protection of fundamental rights, as derived in particular from the Constitution of the Member States and the European Convention for the Protection of Human Rights and Fundamental Freedoms'.[130] Furthermore, it would also be contrary to the idea of transferring powers to an international organisation to hold the Member States responsible for checking whether the rights laid down in the Convention were duly respected. The application was thus incompatible with the provisions of the Convention *ratione materiae*.[131] By and large, the European Commission on Human Rights thereby introduced a new concept concerning the relationship between the two legal orders, namely the '*Solange*' principle[132] which states that a transfer of competences to another international or supranational organisation is not prohibited 'as long as' fundamental rights receive an equivalent protection within the legal order of this organisation.[133]

---

[127] *M & Co v Federal Republic of Germany* App no 13258/87 (Commission Decision, 9 February 1990). For a more detailed analysis of the factual background, see Carl Lebeck, 'The European Court of Human Rights on the Relation between ECHR and EC-Law: The Limits of Constitutionalisation of Public International Law' (2007) 62 *Zeitschrift für Öffentliches Recht* 195, 209ff.

[128] See *M & Co v Federal Republic of Germany* App no 13258/87 (n 127) 152ff.

[129] Joint Declaration by the European Parliament, the Council and the Commission Concerning the Protection of Fundamental Rights and the European Convention for the Protection of Human Rights and Fundamental Freedoms [1977] OJ C103/1.

[130] See *M & Co v Federal Republic of Germany* App no 13258/87 (n 127) 153.

[131] See ibid 153.

[132] See 2 BvR 197/83 *Solange II* BVerfGE 73, 339.

[133] See Scheeck (n 14) 858. See also Schäfer (n 118) 99ff.

Even though the *M & Co* judgment proved significant and seemingly acknowledged the Union's legal system as a separate and, most importantly, autonomous system of human rights protection, it did not obstruct the ECtHR from reviewing acts of Member States which in fact implemented EU law.[134] In the *Procola v Luxembourg* and *Cantoni v France* cases, the Strasbourg Court eventually reached a turning point in its relationship with the EU.[135] In *Procola*,[136] the ECtHR decided on the merits of a case involving European Union law and reviewed an act by Luxemburgish authorities that had incorporated two EU regulations regarding the fixation of milk quotas. Certainly, the Strasbourg Court ostensibly examined the domestic legal acts and found a violation of Article 6 ECHR, but implicitly, it also scrutinised the two almost identical EU regulations. Similarly, in *Cantoni*,[137] the ECtHR held that national laws, based almost verbatim on an EU directive,[138] were still within the ambit of the Convention and thus that of the Strasbourg Court.[139] This bold step is remarkable since the ECtHR indirectly controlled the conformity of an EU directive with the Convention. Moreover, the Strasbourg Court also showed a general tendency to monitor EU activities in an increasingly detailed manner before concluding that these Union-related applications were inadmissible *ratione personae*.[140] The ECtHR, however, maintained a stony silence concerning the question as to what extent the Member States' margin of discretion (under Article 288 (3) TFEU) must be taken into account when incorporating directives into domestic law. However, in contrast to *Cantoni*, Germany did not have such a margin of discretion in the *M & Co* case, since, according to Article 299 (2) TFEU, it simply enforced an act by the European Commission to impose a fine. As a result, it remained uncertain to which extent the ECtHR would review the Convention's conformity of *all* legal acts of the Member States which had originated in European Union law or merely of those in which the Member States enjoyed a broad margin of appreciation.[141]

iii. Responsibility of States for Concluding International Treaties

Cantoni has sometimes been considered to be Strasbourg's 'warning shot'[142] across the European Union's bow in order to restrain its gradually

---

[134] See Douglas-Scott (n 29) 637.

[135] See Nina Philippi, 'Divergenzen im Grundrechtsschutz zwischen EuGH und EGMR' (2000) 3 *Zeitschrift für Europarechtliche Studien* 97, 105.

[136] See *Procola v Luxembourg* App no 14570/89 (ECtHR, 28 September 1995).

[137] See *Cantoni v France* App no 17862/91 (ECtHR, 15 November 1996).

[138] Council Directive 65/65/EEC of 26 January 1965 on the approximation of provisions laid down by Law, Regulation or Administrative Action relating to proprietary medicinal products [1965] OJ L369/1.

[139] See *Cantoni v France* App no 17862/91 (n 137) para 30.

[140] See Scheeck (n 14) 859.

[141] See Lock, *Verhältnis* (n 6) 253.

[142] See Dean Spielmann, 'Human Rights Case Law in the Strasbourg and Luxembourg Courts: Conflicts, Inconsistencies, and Complementarities' in Philipp Alston, Mara Bustelo and James Heenan (eds), *The EU and Human Rights* (Oxford, Oxford University Press, 1999) 773.

increasing powers and thence to prevent human rights violations which the ECtHR could not review in the face of its lack of jurisdiction *ratione personae*. In its now renowned *Matthews v United Kingdom*[143] judgment, Strasbourg took a step further and implicitly asserted that it would not wait until the EU had formally acceded to the Convention.[144] In this case, Denise Matthews, a resident of Gibraltar, alleged a violation of Article 3 of Protocol No 1 to the Convention, the right to free elections. Within the context of the Treaty of Maastricht, the Member States of the European Union had concluded the Direct Elections Act as an international treaty[145] to govern the direct elections of representatives to the European Parliament. When Ms Matthews applied to be registered as a voter at the European elections, the authorities denied her application since Gibraltar was not part of the United Kingdom, but a dependent territory and, according to Annex II of the Act, the provisions of the Act would only be applied in respect of the United Kingdom.[146] Consequently, Matthews alleged a violation of her right to free elections and brought an action against the United Kingdom.

The ECtHR initially referred to Article 1 ECHR and held that Gibraltar was in fact within the jurisdiction of the United Kingdom.[147] But beyond that, it was still questionable whether the United Kingdom could be held responsible for the absence of elections to the European Parliament in Gibraltar, since the Parliament is an organ of the Union.[148] Strasbourg reiterated that the acts of the Union as such could not be challenged before the Court, as the EU was not a contracting party to the Convention and thereby lacked any standing. The ECtHR further held that the Convention did not exclude the transfer of competences to other organisations provided that the rights enshrined in the Convention rights were effectively secured. The responsibility of the Member States would therefore continue even after such a transfer.[149] Moreover, the Direct Elections Act and its Annexes were indeed an international treaty, freely entered into by the United Kingdom, and not an act within the Union's legal order. For that very reason, the Act could not be challenged before the CJEU and the United Kingdom was responsible *ratione materiae* under Article 1 ECHR and especially under Article 3 of Protocol No 1 to the Convention.[150]

There are two features of the *Matthews* judgment which are of utmost significance. Firstly, it shows that the ECtHR feels responsible for implicitly controlling legal acts in relation to European Union law, even though the Union is

---

[143] See *Matthews v United Kingdom* App no 24833/94 (ECtHR, 18 February 1999).
[144] See Scheeck (n 14) 859.
[145] Act concerning the Election of the Representatives of the Assembly by Direct Universal Suffrage [1976] OJ L278/5.
[146] See *Matthews v United Kingdom* App no 24833/94 (n 143) paras 7–8.
[147] See ibid paras 29–30.
[148] See ibid para 31.
[149] See ibid para 32.
[150] See ibid para 33.

not a contracting party to the Convention. But secondly, and more importantly, Strasbourg is also able to convict a Member State in this context, whereas in *Cantoni* it did not find a violation of the Convention.[151] The main difference between this case and previous ones is the fact that the Direct Elections Act was a matter of national regulation and not related to any decision of the EU itself. This consideration was explicitly stated in *Matthews*,[152] but not in any other case.[153] The Treaty of Maastricht and the Direct Elections Act were indeed concluded as part of primary Union law, but as international treaties and not as legal acts which were derived from Union law.[154] Accordingly, as the CJEU is not competent in invalidating primary law, it could neither review this case nor offer any remedy.[155] The very essence of *Matthews* is that in fields where the EU Member States retain a competence or some discretionary power in implementing European Union law, they will be held responsible for violations of the Convention, even if these violations are caused by some Union act.[156] However, the Strasbourg Court did not clarify how it will react in situations where the EU Member States have no competence or discretionary power left. It was not before the *Bosphorus*[157] judgment that any answers were given.

B. The *Bosphorus* Case: Strasbourg's Solange Approach

The impact the *Bosphorus* judgment had on the relationship between Strasbourg and Luxembourg is not to be underestimated, especially when considering the abundant literature analysing and examining the case.[158] Yet, this section will not unnecessarily dwell on the details of this judgment, but rather give a concise summary of the factual background to the proceedings. Furthermore, it will scrutinise the repercussions the judgment had on the judicial interface between the Union and the ECtHR, what privileged status was conceded to European Union law by

---

[151] See Scheeck (n 14) 859f.
[152] See *Matthews v United Kingdom* App no 24833/94 (n 143) para 33.
[153] See Lebeck (n 127) 210.
[154] See also Lock, *Verhältnis* (n 6) 255.
[155] See *Matthews v United Kingdom* App no 24833/94 (n 143) para 33.
[156] See Klabbers, *Treaty Conflict* (n 13) 170.
[157] *Bosphorus v Ireland* App no 45036/98 (ECtHR, 30 June 2005).
[158] See, for example, the following selection of articles dealing with the *Bosphorus* case: Cornelia Janik, 'Die EMRK und Internationale Organisationen. Ausdehung und Restriktion der *equivalent protection*-Formel in der neuen Rechtsprechung des EGMR' (2010) 70 *Zeitschrift für ausländisches öffentliches Recht und Völkerrecht* 127–79; Tobias Lock, 'Beyond Bosphorus: The European Court of Human Rights' Case Law on the Responsibility of Member States of International Organisations under the European Convention on Human Rights' (2010) 10 *Human Rights Law Reports* 529–45; Jürgen Bröhmer, 'Die Bosphorus-Entscheidung des Europäischen Gerichtshofs für Menschenrechte' (2006) 17 *Europäische Zeitschrift für Wirtschaftsrecht* 71–76; Haratsch, '*Solange*-Rechtsprechung' (n 3) 927–47; Frank Schorkopf, 'The European Court of Human Rights' Judgment in the Case of *Bosphorus Hava Yollari Turizm v. Ireland*' (2005) 6 *German Law Journal* 1255–64.

Strasbourg, and, most certainly, what *Bosphorus* implies for the European system of human rights protection after accession.

i. Factual Background and Procedures

Due to grave human rights violations during the war in Yugoslavia in the early 1990s, the United Nations Security Council adopted Resolution 820 (1993)[159] under Chapter VII of the United Nations Charter. This Resolution provided that states should impound, inter alia, all aircraft in their territories 'in which a majority or controlling interest is held by a person or undertaking in or operating from the Federal Republic of Yugoslavia'.[160] Within the EU, this Resolution was then implemented as Council Regulation 990/93.[161] On this legal basis, the Irish authorities impounded two passenger aircraft which *Bosphorus Airways*, a Turkish airline company, had leased from the Yugoslavian airline company *JAT*. The applicant company *Bosphorus* challenged this impoundment before the Irish courts and, eventually, the Irish Supreme Court requested a preliminary ruling from the CJEU. The Luxembourg Court, however, ruled that the infringement of the company's fundamental rights, particularly the right to peaceful enjoyment of property and the freedom to pursue a commercial activity, was appropriate and proportionate, as compared to the objective of putting an end to the state of war and the massive violations of human rights in Yugoslavia.[162] *Bosphorus Airways* subsequently filed an application against Ireland before the ECtHR, claiming that the impoundment of the two aircraft amounted to a violation of the right to property under Article 1 of Protocol No 1 to the Convention.[163]

ii. Strasbourg's Judgment: The 'Equivalent Protection'-Formula

The first question the ECtHR had to deal with concerned Ireland's responsibility for the alleged breach of the Convention. Strasbourg succinctly held that the impoundment of the two aircraft was implemented by the Irish authorities on Irish territory, therefore, according to Article 1 ECHR, the impugned act fell within the jurisdiction of Ireland.[164] But still, this brief and concise statement did not answer the predominant question as to where this infringement had originated from.[165] As aforementioned, the impoundment was based on an EU Regulation and thus

---

[159] UNSC Res 820 (17 April 1993) UN Doc S/RES/820.

[160] See ibid para 24. See also *Bosphorus v Ireland* App no 45036/98 (n 157) para 16.

[161] Council Regulation (EEC) No 990/93 of 26 April 1993 concerning trade between the European Economic Community and the Federal Republic of Yugoslavia (Serbia and Montenegro) [1993] OJ L102/14.

[162] See Case C-84/95 *Bosphorus v Minister for Transport, Energy and Communications* [1996] ECR I-3953, paras 19 and 26.

[163] See *Bosphorus v Ireland* App no 45036/98 (n 157).

[164] See *Bosphorus v Ireland* App no 45036/98 (n 157) paras 135ff.

[165] See Bröhmer (n 158) 72.

on a binding and directly applicable legal act that had left no discretion to the Irish authorities.[166] The Irish Government was hence stuck between a rock and a hard place or, in other words, it had to choose between violating its obligations flowing from the Convention or those flowing from European Union law.[167] In such a situation, the Member States are merely left with the ironic and paradoxical 'alternative'[168] to either breach Treaty A (the Convention) or Treaty B (European Union law). If Ireland had chosen not to impound the aircraft, it would have infringed its obligations as a Member State of the Union, which most likely would have led to infringement procedures under Article 258 TFEU.

The ECtHR was therefore faced with the question as to whether compliance with EU obligations could justify the impugned interference by the Irish authorities with the applicant company's property rights, as the Convention has to be interpreted in light of any relevant rules and principles of international law applicable in relations between the contracting parties,[169] including the principle of *pacta sunt servanda* under Article 26 of the Vienna Convention on the Law of Treaties (VCLT).[170] To solve this treaty conflict, Strasbourg reverted to principles it had already applied in previous cases—as in *Matthews*, the ECtHR emphasised that the Convention did not prohibit contracting parties from transferring powers or competences to international or supranational organisations. Moreover, according to its *CFDT* judgment, the said organisations could not be held responsible under the Convention as long as they were not contracting parties.[171] Yet, even though the ECtHR acknowledged the contracting states' obligations flowing from their membership in other organisations, it also stated that it could not completely absolve them from their Convention responsibilities following such a competence transfer, since such an exemption would be incompatible with the purpose of the Convention.[172]

To reconcile these two diametrically opposed principles—on the one hand, the states' sovereignty and autonomy to enter into international agreements, and on the other their obligations under the Convention to protect human rights—Strasbourg conceived a simple but innovative solution. It ruled that

> State action taken in compliance with such legal obligations is justified as long as the relevant organisation is considered to protect fundamental rights, as regards both the substantive guarantees offered and the mechanisms controlling their observance, in a manner which can be considered at least equivalent to that for which the Convention provides [...]. By 'equivalent' the Court means 'comparable'; any requirement that the organisation's protection be 'identical' could run counter to the interest of international

---

[166] See *Bosphorus v Ireland* App no 45036/98 (n 157) para 147ff.

[167] See ibid para 148.

[168] See Christian Busse, 'Die Geltung der EMRK für Rechtsakte der EU' (2000) 53 *Neue Juristische Wochenschrift* 1074, 1079.

[169] See art 31 (3) lit c VCLT.

[170] See *Bosphorus v Ireland* App no 45036/98 (n 157) paras 150–51.

[171] See ibid para 152.

[172] See ibid para 154.

cooperation pursued [...]. However, any such finding of equivalence could not be final and would be susceptible to review in the light of any relevant change in fundamental rights protection.[173]

Strasbourg added that this newly devised '*equivalent protection*' formula can always be rebutted if it is considered that the protection of Convention rights within the legal order of the international organisation in question is 'manifestly deficient'. But nevertheless, such equivalent protection would only be presumed in cases where the state has no discretion at all in implementing a legal act.[174] Vice versa, if a state were to exercise its discretionary power, it would remain fully responsible under the Convention for all acts falling outside its strict international legal obligations.[175] As a result, Strasbourg presumed *in concreto* that the European Union provided for an equivalent protection of fundamental rights, in particular as the Union's legal system envisaged a complementary role for national courts within its control mechanisms, to be exact in the form of the preliminary reference procedure under Article 267 TFEU.[176] Moreover, although it had not entered into force at that point in time, the ECtHR also referred to the Charter in general and Article 52 (3) ChFR in particular.[177] Since the protection of fundamental rights by Union law could be considered equivalent to that of the Convention system, Ireland had not infringed the Convention when it had implemented legal obligations flowing from its membership of the EU.[178] Therefore, the Court did not find a violation of Article 1 of Protocol No 1 to the Convention and dismissed the case.

iii. The Future of the Bosphorus Formula and Ramifications for Accession

In a nutshell, the preceding cases imply that the ECtHR will exercise its jurisdiction in the following three situations. Firstly, if primary EU law is challenged before the Strasbourg Court, the responsibility to guarantee the rights set forth in the Convention lies with the Member States, since primary law cannot be challenged before the CJEU. Moreover, primary law represents a special form of international treaty, freely entered into by the Member States. Secondly, in cases where Member States execute or implement Union law and enjoy some discretionary power in doing so, they are fully responsible for violations of the Convention as well. Thirdly, unless the Member States retain any discretionary power, they remain only partially responsible in accordance with the *Bosphorus* formula.[179]

---

[173] Ibid para 155.
[174] See ibid para 156.
[175] See ibid para 157.
[176] See ibid para 164.
[177] See ibid paras 80f.
[178] See ibid para 165.
[179] See Jessica Baumann, 'Auf dem Weg zu einem doppelten EMRK-Schutzstandard? Die Fortschreibung der Bosphorus-Rechtsprechung des EGMR im Fall Nederlandse Kokkelvisserij' (2011) 38 *Europäische Grundrechte-Zeitschrift* 1, 3.

However, even though the *Bosphorus* judgment put the relationship between the Convention and Union law on a firm footing, the ECtHR has wisely refused to be dragged into a power game with the CJEU.[180] By deciding not to review legal acts of the Member States which stem from obligations rooted in European Union law and which had left them no discretionary power at all, Strasbourg generally recognised the importance of international cooperation and particularly the sovereignty of the Convention contracting parties to freely enter into other international agreements, including their right to transfer powers to supranational organisations. This led to the notion that Strasbourg was especially open-minded and tolerant towards international law and Union law.[181] The ECtHR thereby respected the jurisdiction of the CJEU and took 'a leap of faith'[182] that Luxembourg would correctly interpret and apply both the Convention and the jurisprudence of the ECtHR. Strasbourg's '*Solange*' approach is thus simply an embodiment of the international legal principle of comity.[183] Hereby, the ECtHR was able to circumnavigate the delicate question of which court should be the supreme human rights court in Europe.[184] Strasbourg also acknowledged the crucial role of international cooperation in the context of international organisations in general and both the legitimacy and specificity of the European Union's integration project, including its implications for the protection of fundamental rights.[185]

However, Strasbourg's 'leap of faith' towards European Union law also gives rise to a major legal problem, namely the privileged status of both Union law itself and of legal acts of Member States within the field of Union law.[186] In the current situation, Strasbourg lacks jurisdiction *ratione personae* to review such Union-induced acts. This fact, of course, does not give the Member States *carte blanche* to haphazardly violate the Convention, but still, it bestows them with some form of privileged status, since other contracting parties to the Convention that are *not* at the same time Member States of the European Union do not enjoy this privilege. Nonetheless, to hold the EU Member States responsible for infringing the Convention, even in cases where they do not have any discretionary power at their disposal, would lead to an indirect or *de facto* accession to the Convention.[187]

---

[180] See Klabbers, *Treaty Conflict* (n 13) 170.

[181] See Haratsch, '*Solange*-Rechtsprechung' (n 3) 932f.

[182] See Peter Szczekalla, 'Vertrauensvorschuss aus Straßburg: Der Europäische Gerichtshof für Menschenrechte klärt sein Verhältnis zum Europäischen Gerichtshof—Anmerkungen zu EuGHMR (Große Kammer), Urteil vom 30. Juni 2005, 45036/98' (2005) 2 *Zeitschrift für Gemeinschaftsprivatrecht* 176, 178.

[183] See Nikolaos Lavranos, 'Das Rechtsprechungsmonopol des EuGH im Lichte der Proliferation internationaler Gerichte' (2007) 42 *Europarecht* 440, 467.

[184] See Iris Canor, '*Primus inter pares.* Who is the Ultimate Guardian of Fundamental Rights in Europe?' (2000) 25 *European Law Review* 1, 3f.

[185] See Luzius Wildhaber, 'The European Convention on Human Rights and International Law' (2007) 56 *International and Comparative Law Quarterly* 217, 230.

[186] See Geoff Sumner, 'We'll Sometimes Have Strasbourg: Privileged Status of Community Law Before the European Court of Human Rights' (2008) 16 *Irish Student Law Review* 127, 127ff.

[187] See Baumann (n 179) 4.

But without putting some procedural safeguards in place, this step would most certainly interfere with the Union's legal autonomy.

The question remains whether this virtually Kafkian situation[188] will be perpetuated in the future. Of course, after the Union's eventual accession to the Convention there will be no further need to apply the '*equivalent protection*' presumption on EU-related cases, as the risk of conflicting treaty obligations will be eliminated in the course of formal accession.[189] The Strasbourg Court would, most likely, promptly revise or entirely reverse the *Bosphorus* formula in its future jurisprudence.[190] If the ECtHR applied this presumption after accession, it would be difficult to justify this undue preference of the Union over the other contracting parties to the Convention.[191] Furthermore, the objective of accession is to subject the Union to Strasbourg's external control and to put the CJEU on par with the other domestic Supreme or Constitutional Courts. At present, Strasbourg does not apply the *Bosphorus* formula on any other national legal order, although the protection of fundamental rights is, in some cases, more effectively guaranteed on the national plane than on the Union level.[192]

In fact, expanding and applying the formula on national courts seems very appealing, especially in order to rid Strasbourg of its immense backlog of pending applications. But still, this move would cast doubt on the ECtHR's very existence, as it would negate its role in protecting human rights on the basis of case-by-case reviews.[193] In a recent judgment, the ECtHR resisted this 'temptation' and did not apply the '*equivalent protection*' presumption on a national legal act involving Union law. Moreover, Strasbourg proved to be very shrewd in holding a Member State responsible under the Convention without interfering with the Union's legal order. In the *MSS v Belgium and Greece* case,[194] the ECtHR had to decide whether Belgium had violated Article 3 ECHR by deporting an asylum seeker from Afghanistan to Greece where fair and effective asylum proceedings could not be guaranteed.[195] Belgium had invoked Article 3 (1) of the EU's Dublin

---

[188] See Torres Pérez (n 60) 34.

[189] See Christine Heer-Reißmann, *Die Letztentscheidungskompetenz des Europäischen Gerichtshofs für Menschenrechte in Europa* (Frankfurt am Main, Peter Lang, 2007) 289ff, arguing that the CJEU would be obliged to abide by the judgments of the ECtHR under art 46 ECHR.

[190] See Gregor Heißl, 'Happy End einer unendlichen Geschichte? Der Beitritt der EU zur EMRK und seine Auswirkungen auf Österreich' in Michael Holoubek, Andrea Martin and Stephan Schwarzer (eds), *Die Zukunft der Verfassung—Die Verfassung der Zukunft? Festschrift für Karl Korinek zum 70. Geburtstag* (Vienna New York, Springer, 2010) 137.

[191] See Baumann (n 179) 10.

[192] See Lock, *Verhältnis* (n 6) 301.

[193] See Luzius Wildhaber, 'Bemerkungen zum Vortrag von BVerfG-Präsident Prof. Dr. H.-J. Papier auf dem Europäischen Juristentag 2005 in Genf' (2005) 32 *Europäische Grundrechte-Zeitschrift* 743, 743.

[194] See *MSS v Belgium and Greece* App no 30696/09 (ECtHR, 21 January 2011).

[195] For more details on the background of the case and the case itself, see ch 8 and Ronald Frühwirth and Joachim Stern, 'Vorabentscheidungsverfahren und einstweiliger Rechtsschutz. Zur Pflicht, Abschiebungen nach Griechenland im Rahmen der Dublin II-VO auszusetzen' (2010) 22 *juridikum* 274, 274ff.

II-Regulation[196] which obliges Member States—in this case Greece—to examine the application of third-country nationals for asylum submitted at their borders or in their territory. In its judgment, Strasbourg referred to the *Bosphorus* case, but concluded that under Article 3 (2) of the Regulation, the so-called 'sovereignty clause', Belgium could have considered the fact that Greece was not fulfilling its obligations under the Convention. Consequently, Belgium itself could have examined the asylum application and thus refrained from transferring the applicant to Greece. The ECtHR accordingly held that the challenged measure taken by the Belgian authorities did not strictly fall within Belgium's international legal obligations, ie its obligations under the EU Treaties. Thence, the presumption of equivalent protection did not apply in this case,[197] since Article 3 (2) of the Regulation grants the Member States some discretionary power in examining asylum applications.

Yet, the *MSS* case is just one recent example. Currently, there is no telling how Strasbourg will decide until the Union accedes to the Convention. Certainly, at the end of the day, it would be consistent to completely repeal the presumption the ECtHR devised in the *Bosphorus* case after the Union's eventual accession to the Convention. This step would finally remedy the anomaly of the European Union being a legal order which is not subject to Strasbourg's external control and put it on par with the national systems of human rights protection.[198] Maybe, however, there is no further need to apply the *Bosphorus* formula before accession, as the Luxembourg Court might bring the Union into line with the Convention on its own accord. In its judgment on a most recent asylum case involving the applicant's transfer from the United Kingdom to Greece, the CJEU explicitly referred to the *MSS* case and argued that a Member State in which an asylum application has been lodged would be obliged to exercise its right to examine that asylum application itself under Article 3 (2) of the Regulation, if deportation to the Member State primarily responsible for the application were to expose the asylum seeker to a serious risk of violation of his or her fundamental rights.[199] It seems that the pressure of Strasbourg's judgments involving European Union law and the impending accession to the Convention can in fact help overcome gaps within the European Union's system of human rights protection and thus redress violations rooted in the intricate interplay of Member States and EU law, but without granting the Union undue privileges in the form of the *'equivalent protection'* presumption.

---

[196] Council Regulation (EC) No 343/2003 of 18 February 2003 Establishing the Criteria and Mechanisms for Determining the Member State Responsible for Examining an Asylum Application Lodged in one of the Member States by a Third-Country National [2003] OJ L50/1.

[197] See *MSS v Belgium and Greece* App no 30696/09 (n 194) para 340.

[198] See Baumann (n 179) 11.

[199] See Joined Cases C-411/10 and C-493/10 *NS v Secretary of State for the Home Department and ME and Others v Refugee Applications Commissioner* [2011] ECR I-0000, paras 90 and 107.

III. OPINION 2/94: OBSOLETE CONCERNS OR AUTONOMY AT RISK?

To conclude the illustration of the special interface between Strasbourg and Luxembourg, this section analyses *Opinion 2/94* which had been requested by the Council and then issued by the CJEU in 1996 to answer the question as to whether the Union could accede to the Convention. Of course, it is well known that the CJEU held that Article 253 of the EEC Treaty[200] did not provide a proper legal basis for accession to the Convention, since this would go beyond the scope of this provision.[201] As a result, as Union law back then stood, the Union had no competence to accede to the Convention,[202] since such accession required prior Treaty amendments first and foremost.[203] However, it is also a well-established fact that the Treaties have been amended by the entry into force of the Treaty of Lisbon and thus, a legal basis for accession was created in Article 6 (2) TEU which, according to its wording, also obligates the Union to accede to the Convention:

> The Union *shall* accede to the European Convention for the Protection of Human Rights and Fundamental Freedoms. Such accession shall not affect the Union's competences as defined in the Treaties. (emphasis added).[204]

Given this premise, one may ask why *Opinion 2/94* would be of any relevance today, more than 15 years after its publication and after the Lisbon Treaty entered into force, which clearly provides the Union with the necessary competence for accession. Yet, in relation to the Union's legal autonomy, the Opinion of the Luxembourg Court and particularly the submissions of the Member States' governments proved to be more dramatic than first thought. Some of these statements are still highly topical, especially in the context of this book, as the governments emphasised that accession to the Convention would endanger the autonomy of the Union's legal order and the CJEU's exclusive jurisdiction. This contentious issue is therefore scrutinised below.

A. The Statements of the Governments

i. Reference to Opinion 1/91: Legal Autonomy at Risk

In the proceedings, the governments of France, Portugal, Spain, Ireland and the United Kingdom argued that the Union's accession to the Convention was

---

[200] Now, in amended form, art 352 TFEU.
[201] See Opinion 2/94 *Accession to the ECHR* (n 62) para 35.
[202] See ibid para 36.
[203] See ibid para 34.
[204] See also Rudolf Geiger, 'Art 6 EUV' in Rudolf Geiger, Daniel-Erasmus Kahn and Markus Kotzur (eds), *EUV/AEUV. Kommentar*, 5th edn (Munich, Beck, 2010) para 21; Frank Schorkopf, 'Art 6 EUV' in Eberhard Grabitz, Meinhard Hilf and Martin Nettesheim (eds), *Das Recht der Europäischen Union. Band I* (Munich, Beck, 2010) paras 35ff; Hans D Jarass, *Charta der Grundrechte der Europäischen Union. Kommentar* (Munich, Beck, 2010) Einleitung, para 44.

incompatible with the Treaties, primarily with Article 19 TEU and Article 344 TFEU.[205] One of the principal arguments put forward against the accession was that *Opinion 1/91* would 'backfire'[206] on the Council, since 'the envisaged accession calls into question the autonomy of the Community legal order and the Court of Justice's monopoly of jurisdiction'.[207] Spain asserted that, contrary to the criteria defined by the CJEU in *Opinion 1/91* and *Opinion 2/91*, the ECtHR would not simply interpret EU law, but rather examine its legality in light of the Convention, which would most certainly have an impact on the case law of the Court of Justice.[208] The French Government added that the Union's legal order has an autonomous and specific judicial organisation at its disposal.[209] Ireland explicitly supported this view and stated that accession would call into question the exclusive jurisdiction of the Luxembourg Court under Articles 19 TEU and 344 TFEU, to settle any dispute relating to the application and interpretation of the Treaties.[210] Portugal stressed that Strasbourg was competent to apply and interpret provisions with a horizontal effect, which would inevitably lead to interference with the application and interpretation of Union law. But most importantly, by interpreting Union law, the ECtHR would be moved to decide on the competence of the Union. It would thus be difficult to devise practicable machinery enabling the Union and the Member States to resolve questions of competence.[211] Spain and the United Kingdom also emphasised the legal effects of decisions made by the Strasbourg Court, in particular its competence to grant just satisfaction to the injured party which may take the form of monetary compensation. Thus, if the European Union acceded to the Convention, the CJEU would surrender, within the scope of application of the Convention, its ultimate and exclusive authority to interpret Union law. The ECtHR would subsequently not limit itself to the interpretation and application of an international agreement, ie the Convention, but it would additionally be involved in the interpretation and application of EU law and would have to rule on the division of competences between the Union and its Member States.[212]

ii. *Exhaustion of Local Remedies and Individual Applications*

In this context, the French Government underscored problems regarding the prior exhaustion of local remedies under Article 35 (1) ECHR. Within the European Union's legal system, actions open to individuals are limited and only available under Articles 263 (4) and 265 (3) TFEU (action for annulment and action for failure to act). However, even these provisions are difficult to invoke,

---

[205] Back then arts 164 and 219 of the EEC Treaty.
[206] See Schmalenbach, 'Struggle for Exclusiveness' (n 2) 1065.
[207] Opinion 2/94 *Accession to the ECHR* (n 62) c VI.2., para 1.
[208] See ibid c VI.2., para 2.
[209] See ibid c VI.2., para 3.
[210] See ibid c VI.2., para 6.
[211] See ibid c VI.2., para 7.
[212] See ibid c VI.2., para 8.

since they require certain legal preconditions which are sometimes difficult to comply with.[213] As a result, the CJEU is, in the majority of cases, seized by way of reference for a preliminary ruling procedure according to Article 267 TFEU. Still, the question arose whether the Strasbourg Court would require the Union to widen access to the preliminary reference procedure for individuals and whether the ECtHR would consider this procedure when assessing the requirement that domestic remedies be exhausted. France also mentioned that it would be easier to amend Article 263 (4) TFEU in order to enable individuals to challenge Union acts affecting their fundamental rights.[214] This concern strikes as noble and very desirable in terms of effective fundamental rights protection. However, although a limited Treaty revision is imminent in order to establish the European Stability Mechanism by means of Article 136 (3) TFEU,[215] another (major) Treaty amendment is highly unlikely in the near future after the failure of the EU Constitutional Treaty and the long struggle to adopt the Treaty of Lisbon. Portugal supported this approach and added that, when determining whether domestic remedies had in fact been exhausted, the Strasbourg Court could even rule on the jurisdiction of the Luxembourg Court. Consequently, Strasbourg would have to decide whether an individual could have brought an action for annulment against a Union act which directly and individually concerned them.[216]

iii. Inter-State Cases

With regard to inter-state cases, the Spanish Government was obviously gifted with legal finesse or some sort of prophetic providence with respect to the future *Commission v Ireland (MOX Plant)* case. It argued that Article 55 ECHR, which obligates the contracting parties to submit all disputes between them concerning the interpretation or application of the Convention to a means of settlement laid down therein, was incompatible with Article 344 TFEU[217] which, using similar wording, prohibits EU Member States from submitting a dispute concerning the interpretation and application of the Union Treaties to any method of settlement other than those provided for therein, ie the CJEU. It would thus be necessary to provide for a reservation on the part of the Union or any other special agreement to exclude disputes between Member States *inter se* or with the Union.[218] In this context, the Portuguese Government stressed that the control bodies of the

---

[213] See eg, for art 263 (4) TFEU, Joined Cases 16/62 and 17/62 *Confédération Nationale des Producteurs de Fruits et Légumes v Council* [1962] ECR 471, 477; Case 25/62 *Plaumann v Commission* [1962] ECR 95, 106. For art 265 (3) TFEU, see eg, Case 6/70 *Borromeo v Commission* [1970] ECR 815, paras 4–7; Joined Cases 83/84 and 84/84 *NM v Commission and Council* [1984] ECR 3571, paras 9–12. See also ch 11 for more details.

[214] See Opinion 2/94 *Accession to the ECHR* (n 62) c VI.2., para 4.

[215] See European Council, 'Conclusions 16-17 December 2010' EUCO 30/1/10 REV 1.

[216] See Opinion 2/94 *Accession to the ECHR* (n 62) c VI.2., para 7.

[217] Case C-459/03 *Commission v Ireland (MOX Plant)* [2006] ECR I-4635; see Opinion 2/94 *Accession to the ECHR* (n 62) c VI.2., para 2.

[218] See Opinion 2/94 *Accession to the ECHR* (n 62).

Convention were competent to apply and interpret provisions with a horizontal effect, which would inevitably interfere with the interpretation and application of European Union law. Portugal admitted that Article 55 ECHR would enable inter-state action under Article 33 ECHR to be excluded in order to respect Article 344 TFEU. However, the *ratio legis* of this article could not be limited to proceedings between Member States. In fact it means that no method of judicial resolution of disputes other than that applied by the Luxembourg Court may interfere with the interpretation and application of the Treaties. In the case of accession, the Strasbourg Court would be moved to interpret Union law and take decisions on the division of competences between the Union and its Member States.[219]

B. Luxembourg's Opinion

i. *Union's Lack of Competence to Accede to the Convention*

When scrutinising the CJEU's Opinion,[220] the reader may get the impression that the judges might have heeded Lord Polonius' advice in Shakespeare's *Hamlet*, sug-gesting that 'brevity is the soul of wit'.[221] Whereas Luxembourg busied itself with the question as to whether the request for an opinion was admissible over the length of 22 paragraphs,[222] it dealt with the substantive issue of accession rather concisely. It deftly avoided any comment on the aforementioned concerns of the governments by stating that

> the Court has been given no detailed information as to the solutions that are envisaged to give effect in practice to such submission of the Community to the jurisdiction of an international court.

> It follows that the Court is not in a position to give its opinion on the compatibility of Community accession to the Convention with the rules of the Treaty.[223]

Moreover, the CJEU did not take up its concerns again with respect to the European Union's legal autonomy as in *Opinion 1/91*,[224] but simply indicated that the EU's accession to the Convention would lead to substantial changes in the Union's system for human rights protection insofar as that step would entail the entry of the Union into a different institutional system of international law, as

---

[219] See ibid c VI.2., para 7.

[220] For a lengthy and detailed discussion of the Opinion in all its aspects, see eg, Siofra O'Leary, 'Current Topic: Accession by the European Community to the European Convention on Human Rights—The Opinion of the CJEU' [1996] *European Human Rights Law Review* 362, 362ff.

[221] See William Shakespeare, *Hamlet* (Oxford, Oxford University Press, 2008) Act II, Scene II: 'Therefore, since brevity is the soul of wit, and tediousness the limbs and outward flourishes, I will be brief [...].'

[222] See Opinion 2/94 *Accession to the ECHR* (n 62) paras 1–22.

[223] See ibid paras 21 and 22.

[224] See also ch 4 of this book.

well as the integration of all the provisions of the Convention into the EU's legal order:[225]

> Such a modification of the system for the protection of human rights in the Community, with equally fundamental institutional implications for the Community and for the Member States, would be of constitutional significance and would therefore be such as to go beyond the scope of Article [352 TFEU]. It could be brought about only by way of Treaty amendment.[226]

However, as aforementioned, it was not until the Lisbon Treaty and the inclusion of Article 6 (2) TEU that this Treaty amendment became a legal reality. The Luxembourg Court therefore held that, as Union law stood back then, the Union had no competence to accede to the Convention.[227]

ii. Analysis

As the succinct wording suggests, the CJEU's reasoning in *Opinion 2/94* is not very straightforward. It only reveals one single and crucial argument against accession which implicitly draws on the concerns of the governments of the Member States. An external review by the Strasbourg Court of the Union institutions, including the Luxembourg Court itself, may interfere with the legal autonomy of the EU.[228] Given the fact that the deliberations of the CJEU judges remain unpublished and thus secret, there is no telling whether or not these judges who voted in favour of the known outcome consciously intended to protect the European Union's legal order from Strasbourg's external interference.[229]

One issue, however, became clear—the concerns which the various governments of the Member States expressed before the CJEU in 1994 are still remarkably relevant and problematic, even today, virtually on the eve of accession. The difficulties of an EU accession to the Convention are less about substantive fundamental rights protection than about organising and structuring the procedural framework between two different legal systems[230] without jeopardising the autonomy of the European Union's legal order. The ultimate authority in interpreting and applying the Convention lies with the ECtHR. This provision will presumably clash with Article 19 (1) TEU and Article 344 TFEU, and thus with Luxembourg's role as the final arbiter of Union law, since, after accession, the Convention becomes part of European Union law and will consequently be interpreted and applied by the Luxembourg Court as well. The accession agreement between the

---

[225] See Opinion 2/94 *Accession to the ECHR* (n 62) para 34.
[226] See ibid para 35.
[227] See ibid para 36.
[228] See Piet Eeckhout, *EU External Relations Law* (Oxford, Oxford University Press, 2011) 100.
[229] See Scheeck (n 14) 865.
[230] See Rudolf Bernhardt, 'Probleme eines Beitritts der Europäischen Gemeinschaft zur Europäischen Menschenrechts-Konvention' in Ole Due, Marcus Lutter and Jürgen Schwarze (eds), *Festschrift für Ulrich Everling. Band I* (Baden-Baden, Nomos, 1995) 110f.

EU and the Convention contracting parties must therefore include provisions to delineate the respective jurisdictions of the two courts[231] and to reconcile the procedures available under the Convention with the European Union's principle of legal autonomy and the CJEU's exclusive jurisdiction under Article 19 (1) TEU and Article 344 TFEU. It will basically be the procedural instruments of the Convention, namely inter-state cases, individual applications and the exhaustion of the local remedies rule, which are most apt to sideline the Luxembourg Court and to exclude it from any prior involvement in deciding on EU-related cases, thereby encroaching on its jealously and well-protected exclusive jurisdiction. But moreover, it is still to be seen how the CJEU will consider the European Union's position between the conflicting poles of an open-minded monism towards international law and the preservation of the EU Treaties and their legal specificities in the future and after accession.[232]

---

[231] See Matthias Ruffert, 'Anmerkung zu Gutachten 2/94' [1996] *Juristenzeitung* 624, 626.
[232] See Daniel Thym, 'Auswärtige Gewalt' in Armin von Bogdandy and Jürgen Bast (eds), *Europäisches Verfassungsrecht. Theoretische und dogmatische Grundzüge* (Berlin Heidelberg, Springer, 2009) 458.

6

The EU, International Law and International Courts: An Anticipating Assessment for Accession

I. LESSONS OF THE PAST

The principal and most dominant question of Part II was to define the term the Luxembourg Court itself had coined in numerous judgments and opinions, namely the significance and notion of the Union's legal autonomy. Furthermore, this part of the book examined how the Court viewed the principle of legal autonomy vis-à-vis international law and international courts in general and towards the European Court of Human Rights (ECtHR) in particular. This extensive analysis was thence necessary to identify the 'gateways' through which this specific concept may be infringed by the Union's future accession to the Convention.

As shown in the previous chapters, the concept of 'legal autonomy' is entirely the Court of Justice of the European Union's (CJEU) creation; it is nowhere to be explicitly found in the text of the founding Treaties,[1] but rather in Luxembourg's extensive case law. Starting with the twin judgments that ensured the future functioning of the Treaties,[2] *Van Gend en Loos v Netherlands Inland Revenue Administration* and *Costa v ENEL* (constituting the Union as a new legal order of international law[3] and an autonomous system with supremacy over the laws of the Member States[4]), the Luxembourg Court used Article 19 (1) of the Treaty on European Union (TEU) and Article 344 of the Treaty on the Functioning of the European Union (TFEU) to establish, extend and uphold its exclusive jurisdiction over Union law.

---

[1] See Bruno De Witte, 'European Union Law: How Autonomous is its Legal Order?' (2010) 65 *Zeitschrift für Öffentliches Recht* 141, 150.

[2] See Nial Fennelly, 'The European Court of Justice and the Doctrine of Supremacy: *Van Gend en Loos*; *Costa v ENEL*; *Simmenthal*' in Miguel Poiares Maduro and Loïc Azoulai (eds), *The Past and Future of EU Law. The Classics of EU Law Revisited on the 50th Anniversary of the Rome Treaty* (Oxford, Hart Publishing, 2010) 39.

[3] See Case 26/62 *Van Gend en Loos v Netherlands Inland Revenue Administration* [1963] ECR 1, para 25.

[4] See Case 6/64 *Costa v ENEL* [1964] ECR 585.

In its *Opinion 1/91* on the EEA Draft Agreement, the CJEU perpetuated the autonomy principle and held that conferring jurisdiction over the division of competences between the Union and its Member States to an external court was incompatible with Union law, since such a step is likely to adversely affect the allocation of responsibilities defined in the Treaties and the autonomy of the Union's legal order. The respect for this autonomy must be assured exclusively by the CJEU, in accordance with Article 19 (1) TEU. Moreover, under Article 344 TFEU, the Member States are obliged not to submit a dispute concerning the interpretation or application of the Treaties to any method of settlement other than those provided for therein.[5] In other words, it is the CJEU's exclusive power to interpret and apply Union law. The creation of and submission to mechanisms of dispute settlements between the parties in an external, international agreement may jeopardise the CJEU's own interpretation of EU law provisions and may thus constrain its judicial competences by rival interpretations of the same provisions by another court.[6]

In its *Commission v Ireland (MOX Plant)* judgment, the Luxembourg Court referred to *Opinion 1/91* and reiterated the importance of Article 19 (1) TEU and, in this special case, of Article 344 TFEU for the Court's exclusive jurisdiction and the autonomy of the Union's legal order.[7] Submitting a dispute relating to EU law to any court or quasi-judicial body other than the CJEU involves a manifest risk that the jurisdictional order enshrined in the Treaties and thus the Union's legal autonomy, may be adversely affected.[8] Therefore, such a course of action constitutes both a breach of Article 344 TFEU and of the Court's exclusive jurisdiction,[9] subjecting the Member State in question to infringement procedures under Articles 258 or 259 TFEU. In *Kadi and Al Barakaat v Council and Commission*, a most recent judgment on the delineation between European Union law and international law, the Luxembourg Court stated that constitutional guarantees stemming from the Treaties as an autonomous legal system could not be prejudiced by an international agreement.[10] Again, the CJEU stressed that an international agreement could not affect the allocation or division of powers as set forth in the Treaties. The Union's legal autonomy, particularly towards international law, is thus carefully observed and guaranteed by the CJEU on the basis of Article 19 (1) TEU.

---

[5] See Opinion 1/91 *EEA I (Draft agreement between the Community, on the one hand, and the countries of the European Free Trade Association, on the other, relating to the creation of the European Economic Area)* [1991] ECR I-6079, para 35.

[6] See De Witte (n 1) 150.

[7] See Case C-459/03 *Commission v Ireland (MOX Plant)* [2006] I-4635, para 123.

[8] See ibid, para 154.

[9] See ibid, para 153.

[10] See Joined Cases C-402/05 P and C-415/05 P *Kadi and Al Barakaat v Council and Commission* [2008] ECR I-6351, para 316.

In conclusion, the term 'autonomy of European Union law' comprises the following four subsequent imperatives, elaborated on by the Luxembourg Court in the course of its jurisprudence:

(1)   An international court or tribunal must not be given the power to rule on the internal division of competences between the EU and the Member States.

(2)   The decisions of an international court or tribunal must not internally bind the CJEU and the other Union institutions.

(3)   An international agreement must not alter the functional nature of the EU institutions.

(4)   An international agreement must not contain hidden amendments to the Union Treaties.

If one or more of these principles is violated, the European Union's legal autonomy is concurrently compromised.

Accordingly, there are three major ramifications for the relationship between international law and international courts on the one hand and the Union and its Court of Justice on the other hand:

(1)   By virtue of Article 19 (1) TEU, Article 344 TFEU and its respective case law, the CJEU will vigilantly protect both the legal autonomy of the Union and its own exclusive jurisdiction.

(2)   The Luxembourg Court thus limits the choice and utilisation of other international courts and tribunals by the EU Member States.

(3)   Lastly, the CJEU thereby attempts to constrain the jurisdiction of other international courts and tribunals.[11]

In a nutshell, this means that an agreement between the Union and another international organisation, such as the agreement on the EU's accession to the Convention, must not affect the Union's internal division of competences or allocation of powers in two ways. First, interference with the *internal* division of competences between the Union and its Member States is not permitted;[12] and second, and more importantly in the context of this book, it is unacceptable that an international court, such as the Strasbourg Court, should be able to encroach upon Luxembourg's innermost right to observe the law in the proper interpretation and application of the Treaties, and thus to affect the *external* allocation of powers by transferring them to another international organisation.[13]

---

[11] See Nikolaos Lavranos, 'Das Rechtsprechungsmonopol des EuGH im Lichte der Proliferation internationaler Gerichte' (2007) 42 *Europarecht* 440, 458f.

[12] As set forth in arts 4 and 5 TEU and arts 2 to 4 TFEU.

[13] See Paul Gragl, 'Accession Revisited: Will Fundamental Rights Protection Trump the European Union's Legal Autonomy' in Wolfgang Benedek, Florence Benoît-Rohmer, Wolfram Karl and Manfred Nowak (eds), *European Yearbook on Human Rights 2011* (Vienna, NWV, 2011) 162.

Yet, in comparison to other international courts and tribunals, the relationship between Luxembourg and Strasbourg has been significantly more cooperative. In its quest for its own codified catalogue of fundamental rights, the CJEU 'borrowed'[14] these rights from the Convention by reverting to its explicit provisions and Strasbourg's case law, thereby enshrining fundamental rights as general legal principles in primary law. Additionally, the Convention has now effectively been incorporated by the Lisbon Treaty on the basis of Article 6 (1) TEU and Article 52 (3) of the Charter of Fundamental Rights of the European Union (ChFR), respectively. This shows a tendency towards the appreciation of the Convention as a fully-fledged human rights instrument in contrast to the reluctance expressed towards other international agreements and courts.[15] Strasbourg, on the other hand, has exercised due care when dealing with human rights violations related to European Union law by, eventually, granting the Union enormous privileges in the form of the '*Bosphorus*'-formula of '*equivalent protection*'. This particular *modus operandi* is a perfect example of judicial deference and informal dialogue. The question remains, however, whether this 'institutional truce' between Luxembourg and Strasbourg will come to an end when the Union accedes to the Convention.[16]

II. QUESTIONS FOR THE FUTURE

The actual accession will, after all, drastically change the landscape of human rights protection in Europe. The conflict between legal autonomy and effective individual human rights protection essentially amounts to the question of who will be the ultimate guardian of human rights after accession or, put differently, whether the Luxembourg Court will be subordinated to the Strasbourg Court and whether it will thereby lose its exclusive jurisdiction when Strasbourg implicitly or even explicitly interprets and applies European Union law. This general question also relates to more detailed questions that are crucial with respect to the autonomy of the Union legal order and its concurrent integration into the protection system of the Convention. There are several situations and scenarios in which the Strasbourg Court might end up actually adjudicating on Union law—a position that is entirely unacceptable for the CJEU. The most pressing question therefore

---

[14] See Laurent Scheeck, 'The Relationship between the European Courts and Integration through Human Rights' (2005) 65 *Zeitschrift für ausländisches öffentliches Recht und Völkerrecht* 837, 849f.

[15] See Robert Uerpmann-Wittzack, 'Völkerrechtliche Verfassungselemente' in Armin von Bogdandy and Jürgen Bast (eds), *Europäisches Verfassungsrecht. Theoretische und dogmatische Grundzüge* (Berlin Heidelberg, Springer, 2009) 222.

[16] See Kirsten Schmalenbach, 'Struggle for Exclusiveness: The CJEU and Competing International Tribunals' in Isabelle Buffard, James Crawford, Alain Pellet and Stephan Wittich (eds), *International Law between Universalism and Fragmentation. Festschrift in Honour of Gerhard Hafner* (Leiden, Brill, 2008) 1064.

is how to avoid such scenarios and how to reconcile the CJEU's special position with the procedures available under the Convention.

This book therefore asks what legal status the Convention and the Accession Agreement will have within the EU's legal order; whether Strasbourg should exert some sort of external control over the Union and whether the CJEU, according to its own case law in *Opinion 1/91*, would be bound by the ECtHR's jurisprudence. This book also asks how the correct respondent in individual complaint procedures under Article 34 of the European Convention on Human Rights (ECHR) is found in EU-related cases and whom to hold responsible in cases where Member States implement EU law. Moreover, what mechanisms may be envisaged to identify the correct respondent and to avoid a scenario in which the ECtHR rules on the internal division of competences between the EU and its Member States; how Article 344 TFEU and Article 55 ECHR can be reconciled with one another and whether inter-party cases between the EU and its Member States and between Member States *inter se* should be excluded, especially in the light of EU-internal dispute settlement mechanisms such as the infringement procedures under Articles 258 and 259 TFEU. Lastly, this book asks how Strasbourg will interpret the local remedies rule within the EU's legal system and how a prior involvement of the CJEU can be guaranteed in EU-related human rights cases, in order to avoid a situation in which Strasbourg might rule on EU law before Luxembourg has the chance to do so. The final Accession Agreement must take into account all of these problems in order not to affect the essential powers of the Union institutions.

Part III

The Road from Luxembourg to Strasbourg: Reconciling Accession and Autonomy

7

The Status of the Accession Agreement and the Convention after Accession

I. THE LEGAL BASIS: ARTICLE 218 TFEU AND THE COURT OF JUSTICE

SINCE THE EXISTING provisions envisaging accession (Art 6 (2) TEU) and Art 59 (2) ECHR), respectively) are not sufficient in substance to allow for immediate accession, preceding negotiation procedures under the general rules of international law, most notably under those enshrined in the Vienna Convention on the Law of Treaties between States and International Organisations or between International Organisations (VCLTIO) were necessary.[1] These procedures eventually led to the drafting of an international treaty—the Draft Accession Agreement.[2] This Agreement represents the legal basis for accession and must subsequently be ratified by all parties in accordance with their respective domestic provisions for treaty ratification.[3] On the part of the EU, these internal decision-making procedures are set forth in Article 218 (1) of the Treaty on the Functioning of the European Union (TFEU), which states that 'agreements between the Union and [...] international organisations shall be negotiated and concluded in accordance with the following procedure.'[4]

By virtue of Article 218 (6) lit a (ii) TFEU, the Council shall, after obtaining the consent of the European Parliament, adopt a decision concluding the agreement

---

[1] Even though the VCLTIO is not in force, its provisions may be considered declaratory of customary international law; see eg, Michael Akehurst, 'Custom as a Source of International Law' (1974/1975) 47 *British Yearbook of International Law* 1, 12. See also Case C-327/91 *France v Commission* [1994] ECR I-3641, para 25.

[2] See for the finalised Draft Agreement on the Accession of the EU to the Convention and the Draft Explanatory Report, Council of Europe, '8th Meeting of the CDDH Informal Working Group on the Accession of the European Union to the European Convention on Human Rights (CDDH-UE) with the European Commission' CDDH-UE(2011)16, and Council of Europe, 'Steering Committee for Human Rights—Report to the Committee of Ministers on the Elaboration of Legal Instruments for the Accession of the European Union to the European Convention on Human Rights' CDDH(2011)009.

[3] See Frank Schorkopf, 'Art 6 EUV' in Eberhard Grabitz, Meinhard Hilf and Martin Nettesheim (eds), *Das Recht der Europäischen Union. Band I* (Munich, Beck, 2010) para 38.

[4] For more details, see eg, Piet Eeckhout, *EU External Relations Law* (Oxford, Oxford University Press, 2011) 193ff; see also Delano Verwey, *The European Community, the European Union and the International Law of Treaties* (The Hague, Asser Press, 2004) 87ff.

on Union accession to the Convention.[5] Furthermore, under Article 218 (8) TFEU, the Council must act unanimously for this agreement, and its decision concluding accession will enter into force after it has been approved by the EU's Member States in accordance with their respective constitutional requirements.

However, with particular regard to the Union's legal autonomy, it should also be noted that, according to Article 218 (11) TFEU, the CJEU may—and most probably will[6]—be asked by a Member State, the European Parliament, the Council or the Commission to issue an opinion as to whether the envisaged accession agreement is compatible with the Treaties. Previous statements by the Court of Justice of the European Union (CJEU), such as *Opinion 1/91*,[7] *Opinion 2/94*[8] and *Opinion 1/09*,[9] prove that the finalised Accession Agreement will not be waved through automatically.[10] In case Luxembourg's opinion is adverse, the agreement cannot enter into force unless it is amended or the Treaties are revised. Given the political reality and burdensome constitutional barriers for Treaty amendments in some Member States, the latter alternative is highly unlikely. In other words, if the CJEU detects any risk to the Union's legal autonomy in the provisions of the Accession Agreement, it will render a negative opinion and the agreement shall not enter into force until it is redrafted and thus made compatible with the EU Treaties. As Part II of this book has shown, most of the draft agreements of the past failed[11] to clear the difficult hurdle of legal autonomy.[12] The high demands for international agreements stipulated by the CJEU have most recently been emphasised in *Opinion 1/09*,[13] where the Luxembourg Court ruled that an agreement providing for the creation of a court responsible for the interpretation of its

---

[5] For more details, see eg, Daniel-Erasmus Khan, 'Art 218 AEUV' in Rudolf Geiger, Daniel-Erasmus Khan and Markus Kotzur (eds), *EUV/AEUV. Kommentar*, 5th edn (Munich, Beck, 2010) para 11.

[6] See Giacomo Di Federico, 'Fundamental Rights in the EU: Legal Pluralism and Multi-Level Protection After the Lisbon Treaty' in Giacomo Di Federico (ed), *The EU Charter of Fundamental Rights. From Declaration to Binding Document* (Dordrecht, Springer Netherlands, 2011) 45.

[7] Opinion 1/91 *EEA I (Draft agreement between the Community, on the one hand, and the countries of the European Free Trade Association, on the other, relating to the creation of the European Economic Area)* [1991] ECR I-6079.

[8] Opinion 2/94 *Accession by the Community to the European Convention for the Protection of Human Rights and Fundamental Freedoms* [1996] ECR I-1759.

[9] Opinion 1/09 *European and Community Patents Court* [2011] ECR I-1137.

[10] See Noreen O'Meara, '"A More Secure Europe of Rights?" The European Court of Human Rights, the Court of Justice of the European Union and EU Accession to the ECHR' (2011) 12 *German Law Journal* 1813, 1827.

[11] See, for the most prominent examples of failed draft agreements, Opinion 1/91 *EEA I (Draft agreement between the Community, on the one hand, and the countries of the European Free Trade Association, on the other, relating to the creation of the European Economic Area)* [1991] ECR I-6079; see also Opinion 2/94 *Accession by the Community to the European Convention for the Protection of Human Rights and Fundamental Freedoms* [1996] ECR I-1759, even though no actual accession agreement has been submitted for review by the CJEU in this case.

[12] See for one of the few positive examples, Opinion 1/00 *European Common Aviation Area* [2002] ECR I-3493.

[13] For a detailed analysis of *Opinion 1/09*, see Tobias Lock, 'Walking on a Tightrope: The Draft Accession Agreement and the Autonomy of the EU Legal Order' (2011) 48 *Common Market Law Review* 1025, 1031f.

provisions is not, in principle, incompatible with European Union law.[14] However, an international court must not be called upon to interpret and apply EU law, nor to determine a dispute in the light of fundamental rights and general principles of Union law, or even to examine the validity of an EU act.[15]

Part III of this book consequently analyses the draft agreement on accession by those standards of legal autonomy which the CJEU itself has devised in its past case law. Of course, it is axiomatic that those agreements providing for the jurisdiction of a court outside the Union's legal order are most likely to clash with the autonomy principle.[16] Therefore, after a first general overview over the agreement in the subsequent sections, the main sections of Part III extensively scrutinise the procedures before the European Court of Human Rights (ECtHR) and how these procedures may interfere with the legal autonomy of the EU. Moreover, the approaches which aim to solve these autonomy issues contained in the draft Agreement are thoroughly examined.

II. THE NEED FOR AN ACCESSION AGREEMENT

A. Preserving the Convention System

In contrast to the abovementioned international agreements between the European Union and other actors on the international plane, the Union's accession to the Convention is quite an unusual step, since the Accession Agreement will not include a transfer of the *acquis communautaire* to third states (such as in the EEA agreements). It is actually the EU that will join an established treaty regime for the protection of human rights, a fact which will compel the Union towards a greater degree of adaptation and willingness to compromise than in the past.[17]

The negotiators therefore emphasised that the general characteristics of the Convention system should be maintained and the adaptations be limited to the sole necessities of accession.[18] First and foremost, the Convention regime should be preserved as it stands, which means that major amendments to the Convention itself should be avoided or, at least, kept to a minimum. This step includes not only technical amendments, but also modifications entailing more complex repercussions on the Convention system. But at the same time, the modalities of accession should be kept as simple as possible, since the guiding principle of accession was and still is to

---

[14] See Opinion 1/09 *European and Community Patents Court* (n 9), para 74.
[15] See ibid, para 78.
[16] See Lock, 'Tightrope' (n 13) 1033.
[17] See ibid.
[18] See Council of Europe, '1st Meeting of the CDDH Informal Working Group on the Accession of the European Union to the European Convention on Human Rights (CDDH-UE) with the European Commission' CDDH-UE(2010)01, para 4.

increase the protection of human rights for individuals.[19] Although both avenues to accession, namely an accession treaty or an amending Protocol to the Convention, may be pursued, the negotiators have already expressed a preference for the former.[20] There are two crucial reasons for this: On the one hand, the conclusion of an accession agreement allows the negotiators to better comply with the relevant provisions of the TEU, the TFEU and Protocol No 8, wherein some essential conditions and procedural requirements for the conclusion of the agreement and the preservation of the Union's legal autonomy are set forth.[21] Moreover, an accession agreement would allow for the Union to become a contracting party to the Convention upon its entry into force and, concurrently, for a comprehensive definition of the Union's status within the Convention, since the EU would be bound by all the provisions set forth therein, even those which do not affect the original version of the Convention.[22] On the other hand, as previously mentioned, adaptations to the Convention or even an amending Protocol should be limited to what is strictly necessary in order to preserve the current control mechanism of the Convention.[23] The adoption of an amending protocol would involve a cumbersome two-tiered procedure, namely the signature and ratification of all contracting parties to the Convention and, after that, accession by the Union to the amended Convention.[24] As the example of Protocol No 14 to the Convention has shown, political obstacles and a time consuming ratification process would most certainly not allow for a quick and rapid accession in this scenario. The most important reason, nevertheless, is the fact that an agreement will be flexible enough to take all characteristics of the EU and its specific legal system properly into account and to create a legal basis for accession without any major modifications to the Convention itself.

However, negotiations on the accession treaty have already demonstrated that potential amendments to the Convention cannot be avoided. The accession of the EU, as a non-state entity with a specific and autonomous legal system, requires certain modifications of Convention provisions; firstly, to guarantee its implementation with the Union's participation; secondly, to clarify legal terms via supplementary interpretative provisions; and thirdly, to adapt the procedures before the Strasbourg Court which will take into account the characteristics of

---

[19] See ibid, para 5.
[20] See Council of Europe, '6th Working Meeting of the CDDH Informal Working Group on the Accession of the European Union to the European Convention on Human Rights (CDDH-UE) with the European Commission' CDDH-UE(2011)05, paras 3ff, and Explanatory Report to Protocol No 14 to the Convention for the Protection of Human Rights and Fundamental Freedom, amending the control system of the Convention, CETS No 194, Agreement of Madrid, para 101. See also Di Federico (n 6) 46.
[21] See CDDH-UE(2011)05 (n 20), para 5.
[22] See Di Federico (n 6) 46. See also Philippe Manin, 'L'Adhésion de l'Union Européenne à la Convention de sauvegarde des droits de l'homme et des libertés fondamentales' in Lucia Serena Rossi (ed), *Vers une nouvelle architecture de l'Union européenne: Le Projet de Traité-Constitution* (Brussels, Emile Bruylant, 2004) 265.
[23] See CDDH-UE(2011)05 (n 20), para 9.
[24] See Di Federico (n 6) 46 and fn 168; see also Steering Committee for Human Rights (CDDH), 'Technical and Legal Issues of a Possible EC/EU Accession to the European Convention on Human Rights' CDDH(2002)010 Addendum 2, para 8.

the EU's autonomous legal order and the relationship between the EU and its Member States.[25] Nonetheless, it is beyond dispute that the general principles underlying the Accession Agreement intend to preserve 'the equal rights of all individuals under the Convention, the rights of the applicant in the procedure, and the equality of all High Contracting Parties'.[26] The EU should thence, as a matter of principle, accede to the Convention on 'equal footing' with the other contracting parties and should enjoy the same rights, but also assume the same duties. Nevertheless, the Union is, as abovementioned, unquestionably a non-state entity which necessitates certain adaptations, but without affecting the existing obligations of the high contracting parties and without interfering with the distribution of competences between the EU and its Member States, as well as between the EU institutions.[27]

The negotiators therefore decided that the ratification of the accession treaty by the 47 contracting parties to the Convention and by the Union, and the subsequent entry into force of this treaty, will have the simultaneous effect of both amending the Convention and including the EU among its parties, without requiring a further deposit of an instrument of accession to the Convention by the EU.[28]

As a consequence, the finalised Accession Agreement would become an integral part of the Convention system for the following reasons: Some of the provisions in the agreement would deploy their effect immediately at their entry into force. But other provisions would have more 'permanent' effects and would remain relevant for the functioning of the Convention regime even after accession (eg financial provisions). In contrast to usual amending protocols, the Accession Agreement would thus not 'cease to exist' but would continue to have a legal effect after its entry into force.[29]

B. Scope of Accession and Amendments to the Convention

Since there are two parties involved in the accession procedure, there are also two different aspects regarding the scope of accession. Firstly, this book therefore defines and examines the degree of control exercised within the protection system of the Convention and the Strasbourg Court. This means that the following sections also identify the norms and provisions binding the Union. Secondly, this book analyses what action by the Union may be challenged in Strasbourg.[30]

---

[25] See CDDH-UE(2011)009 (n 2) 15, para 3.
[26] See ibid 16, para 7.
[27] See ibid 16, para 7.
[28] See ibid 17, para 16.
[29] See Council of Europe, '5th Working Meeting of the CDDH Informal Working Group on the Accession of the European Union to the European Convention on Human Rights (CDDH-UE) with the European Commission' CDDH-UE(2011)01, para 4.
[30] See Jean-Paul Jacqué, 'The Accession of the European Union to the European Convention on Human Rights and Fundamental Freedoms' (2011) 48 *Common Market Law Review* 995, 1002f.

The first issue is dealt with hereinafter, whereas the second aspect is subsequently assessed in chapter eight.

i. Accession to the Additional Protocols

According to Article 1 (1) of the Draft Accession Agreement, the European Union will not only accede to the Convention itself, but also to the Protocol to the Convention[31] and to Protocol No 6 to the Convention. As abovementioned, the Accession Agreement will simultaneously amend the Convention and include the Union among its contracting parties, without requiring the EU to deposit a further instrument of accession. This also applies to the EU's accession to Protocol Nos 1 and 6. Future accession to other protocols, however, will prompt the Union to deposit separate accession instruments.[32]

As a consequence, the Union will be bound by the Convention itself and Protocols No 1 and No 6 upon accession. This path was chosen to retain the principle of neutrality of accession with special regard to the Member States, since it would not call into question the legal action of a Member State in the field of European Union law relating to a protocol which has not been ratified by a Member State. The negotiators therefore decided that the Union should only accede to those protocols to which all Member States are already contracting parties, among them Protocol No 1, guaranteeing the right to property, education and free elections, and Protocol No 6, abolishing the death penalty. Thus, accession to Protocol Nos 1 and 6 seem to be the lowest common denominator of human rights protection beyond the core Convention. The other protocols containing substantial rights (Protocols Nos 4,[33] 7,[34] 12[35] and 13[36]) have not been ratified by all EU Member States,[37] even though they contain rights that are also guaranteed by the European Union's own Charter of Fundamental Rights.[38] In other words, the minimalist approach proposed by some Member States has prevailed.[39]

---

[31] Commonly referred to as Protocol No. 1.

[32] See CDDH-UE(2011)009 (n 2) 17, para 16.

[33] Protocol No 4, guaranteeing the freedom of movement, prohibition of collective expulsion of aliens and the prohibition of imprisonment for debt, was not ratified by Greece and the United Kingdom.

[34] Protocol No 7, containing the procedural safeguards for expulsion of aliens, the right of appeal to a higher court, compensation for wrongful conviction, the principle of double jeopardy or *ne bis in idem* and the equality between spouses, was not ratified by Belgium, Germany and Poland.

[35] Protocol No 12, safeguarding the general prohibition of discrimination, was only ratified by Estonia, Finland, Romania and Spain.

[36] Protocol No 13, enshrining the abolition of the death penalty in all circumstances, was not ratified by Latvia and Poland.

[37] See Jacqué, 'Accession' (n 30) 1004.

[38] Charter of Fundamental Rights of the European Union, OJ C326/391, 26 October 2012.

[39] See Xavier Groussot, Tobias Lock and Laurent Pech, 'EU Accession to the European Convention on Human Rights: A Legal Assessment of the Draft Accession Agreement of 14th October 2011' [2011] *Fondation Robert Schuman—European Issues* No 218, 1, 9.

In this context, one may wonder how the Luxembourg Court will decide in cases where individuals rely on such rights set forth in the Charter which, in turn, refers back to the Convention in Article 52 (3) of the Charter of Fundamental Rights (ChFR) when the Charter 'contains rights which correspond to rights guaranteed by the Convention'. The CJEU may either follow the wording and purport of the Accession Agreement and interpret and apply only those provisions of protocols to which the EU has in fact acceded, or it might engage in judicial activism and consider that the other protocols are also covered by the corresponding Charter provisions.[40] Alternatively, when the provisions of a protocol to which the EU has not acceded are invoked by an individual, the CJEU could fall back on Article 6 (3) TEU and dynamically apply the provisions in question as general principles of law,[41] thereby avoiding differences of interpretation between the Charter and the Convention and achieving a greater degree of coherence between those two documents. Another question pertains to the attitude of the Strasbourg Court in cases where it is called upon to decide on an application against an EU Member State for having violated—when implementing Union law—a right laid down in a protocol to which the Union has not acceded, but which the Member State has ratified. Strasbourg may revive its *Bosphorus*[42] formula and determine whether the protection offered by the Union is manifestly deficient.[43]

ii. The Need for Further Internal Legal Rules

The Accession Agreement will amend Article 59 (2) ECHR and subsequently introduce a letter b) which foresees that the status of the Union as a high contracting party to the Convention shall be further defined in the Agreement itself. This explicit reference to the Accession Agreement allows for limits to the amendments necessary for accession made to the Convention. In other words, accession will mostly be governed by the final Accession Agreement, and not by amendments to the Convention. Furthermore, inasmuch as the Agreement will continue to have a legal effect after the EU's accession, its provisions will be subject to interpretation by the Strasbourg Court. However, in order to implement the Accession Agreement and to uphold its specific characteristics within an established international system of human rights protection, the EU will need to adopt internal legal rules to regulate various matters in relation to accession, most importantly rules for the functioning of the co-respondent mechanism and the prior involvement of the CJEU.[44] Consequently, the requirement to adopt further rules within the Union's legal system does not endanger its autonomy; quite the contrary, this step

---

[40] See Jacqué, 'Accession' (n 30) 1004f.

[41] See Schorkopf, 'Art 6 EUV' (n 3), para 52, and European Convention, 'Draft of Articles 1 to 16 of the Constitutional Treaty' CONV 528/03, 13.

[42] *Bosphorus v Ireland* App no 45036/98 (ECtHR, 30 June 2005).

[43] See Jacqué, 'Accession' (n 30) 1005.

[44] See CDDH-UE(2011)009 (n 2) 18, para 20. For more details on the adoption of further internal legal rules on the part of the European Union, see chs 9 and 11.

will facilitate the accession procedure by securing the autonomy of EU law and its distinctive features as a supranational organisation.

iii. Effects of Accession

Beyond that, the Accession Agreement will introduce a letter c) to Article 59 (2) ECHR which reflects two requirements already laid down in Article 2 of Protocol No 8 for the preservation of the Union's legal autonomy. Firstly, this provision clarifies that the Union's accession to the Convention imposes on the EU certain 'obligations with regard only to acts, measures or omissions of its institutions, bodies, offices or agencies, or of persons acting on their behalf'.[45] This means that, since the Strasbourg Court has the jurisdiction to settle disputes between individuals and the high contracting parties (under Art 34 ECHR) and between high contracting parties *inter se* (under Art 33 ECHR) and consequently to interpret the provisions enshrined in the Convention, its decisions will be binding on the Union and its institutions, including the CJEU, in all disputes to which the Union is party.[46] This view is consistent with Luxembourg's own approach in *Opinion 1/91*[47] and *Opinion 1/92*[48] and therefore, since Strasbourg will not interpret or apply Union law in a binding manner,[49] the autonomy of EU law will not be jeopardised.

Secondly, Article 1 (2) lit c of the Accession Agreement and the newly amended Article 59 (2) ECHR also assert that '[n]othing in the Convention or the Protocols thereto shall require the European Union to perform an act or adopt a measure for which it has no competence under European Union law'.[50] This provision reproduces Article 2 of Protocol No 8 almost verbatim and aims at preventing any allocation of competences at the expense of the Member States. It is, however, merely a clause that mirrors the Member States' concerns of losing sovereignty and competences to the Union. National governments are worried that, after accession, the CJEU might pressurise the Member States to abide by the Convention and the ECtHR's case law in a 'downwards' or vertical fashion,[51] mostly by expanding its competences in the field of fundamental rights at the expense of the Member States'

---

[45] Art 1 (2) lit c of the Draft Accession Agreement and Art 59 (2) lit c ECHR in its amended form; CDDH-UE(2011)009 (n 2) 6.

[46] See ibid 18, para 21.

[47] See Opinion 1/91 *EEA I* (n 7), paras 36 and 39.

[48] See Opinion 1/92 *EEA II (Draft agreement between the Community, on the one hand, and the countries of the European Free Trade Association, on the other, relating to the creation of the European Economic Area)* [1992] ECR I-2821, paras 22, 25 and 29.

[49] See ch 8 for more details.

[50] Art 1 (2) lit c of the Draft Accession Agreement and art 59 (2) lit c ECHR in its amended form; CDDH-UE(2011)009 (n 2) 6.

[51] See Julie Vondung, *Die Architektur des europäischen Grundrechtsschutzes nach dem Beitritt der EU zur EMRK* (Tübingen, Mohr Siebeck, 2012) 224.

powers.[52] Nevertheless, the Member States disregard the fact that an agreement under international law imposes certain duties upon the contracting parties, but it does not govern the internal or 'constitutional' rules of allocating competences and powers. Furthermore, if legal acts by the Union are being reviewed with respect to their accordance with fundamental rights under the first half of the first sentence of Article 51 (1) ChFR, the internal division of competences between the Union and the Member States will not be affected at all. In this context, conflicts may only arise from situations in which the Member States are (exceptionally) bound by the Union's fundamental rights, according to the second half of the first sentence of Article 51 (1) ChFR; in other words when they are implementing Union law.[53] This provision, however, creates neither new obligations for the Member States nor relocates any powers, as the Member States are already legally bound by the Convention *before* accession when implementing Union law.[54]

III. THE STATUS OF THE CONVENTION AND THE AGREEMENT IN EU LAW

A. The Status of International Agreements within Union Law

According to the general principles of international law,[55] specifically the principle of state sovereignty, it is entirely within the domestic jurisdiction of states (or state-like polities such as the Union) to govern the status of international law and international treaties in their legal order.[56] Consistently, both the Convention and the Accession Agreement remain silent as to what legal status or rank these two treaties will enjoy after accession. Nonetheless, the question of where these two international treaties will rank within the Union's legal order is of utmost importance with respect to the CJEU's further fundamental rights jurisdiction when referring to the Convention, its relationship with the Strasbourg Court and the supremacy of Union law over the domestic law of the Member States. Since the subsequent chapters of this book examine these pressing questions in relation to the European Union's legal autonomy, the following subsections must now build on the elementary clarifications of the chapter at hand concerning the post-accession

---

[52] See Sebastian Winkler, *Der Beitritt der Europäischen Gemeinschaften zur Europäischen Menschenrechtskonvention* (Baden-Baden, Nomos, 2000) 116f.

[53] See Thorsten Kingreen, 'Art 6 EUV' in Christian Calliess and Matthias Ruffert (eds), *EUV/AEUV. Kommentar*, 4th edn (Munich, Beck, 2011) para 29.

[54] See *Bosphorus v Ireland* App no 45036/98 (n 42); see also Christoph Grabenwarter, *Europäische Menschenrechtskonvention*, 4th edn (Munich, Beck, 2009) § 17, para 8.

[55] See also Paul Gragl, 'Der rechtliche Status der EMRK innerhalb des Unionsrechts—Zu den Auswirkungen auf die Rechtsautonomie der Europäischen Union nach ihrem Beitritt zur EMRK' (2011) 14 *Zeitschrift für Europarechtliche Studien* 409, 409ff.

[56] See eg, Ian Brownlie, *Principles of Public International Law*, 6th edn (Oxford, Oxford University Press, 2003) 31ff, and Malcolm N Shaw, *International Law*, 6th edn (Cambridge, Cambridge University Press, 2008) 129ff.

status of the Convention and the Agreement. However, as the Accession Agreement forms an integral part of the Convention,[57] only the legal status of the Convention within EU law will be explicitly analysed, thereby comprising the status of the Agreement as well.

Pursuant to the settled case law of the CJEU, international agreements form an integral part of the Union's legal order[58] and rank between primary and secondary EU law,[59] thereby binding the Union and its institutions both externally under international law[60] and internally by virtue of Article 216 (2) TFEU. This monistic interpretation of the international legal principle of *pacta sunt servanda* (codified in Article 26 of the Vienna Convention on the Law of Treaties) and of the internal effects of international law seems to be the 'external projection' of the supremacy of Union law. In light of *Costa v ENEL*,[61] it is consistent to grant international treaties, which play an integral part within the Union's legal order, the same supremacy over national law as 'genuinely' generated Union law.[62]

Furthermore, especially in the context of human rights law and the Convention, international agreements are self-executing and thereby directly applicable within the EU, when, regarding its wording and the purpose and nature of the international agreement itself, the provision in question contains 'a clear and precise obligation which is not subject, in its implementation or effects, to the adoption of any subsequent measure'.[63] Given the concept of legal autonomy and the provision in Article 19 (1) TEU, the CJEU ensures that the Treaties are uniformly interpreted and applied and that the law is observed. This provision is apparently very broad in concept, consequently rendering the term 'the law' very vague and putting it in dire need of further interpretation. Nevertheless, according to the CJEU's case law, this vague term also encompasses international law,[64] be it customary international law[65] or international treaties.[66] As the ultimate guardian of Union law, the jurisdiction of the CJEU consequently encompasses all EU law,[67] including international treaties in the form of 'unionised international law'.[68]

---

[57] See CDDH-UE(2011)01 (n 29), para 4.

[58] See Case 181/73 *Haegeman v Belgian State* [1974] ECR 449, para 5.

[59] See Case C-61/94 *Commission v Germany (International Dairy Arrangement)* [1996] ECR I-3989, para 52.

[60] See Case 104/81 *Kupferberg & Cie KG (Kupferberg I)* [1982] ECR 3641, para 14.

[61] Case 6/64 *Costa v ENEL* [1964] ECR 585.

[62] See Daniel Thym, 'Auswärtige Gewalt' in Armin von Bogdandy and Jürgen Bast (eds), *Europäisches Verfassungsrecht. Theoretische und dogmatische Grundzüge* (Berlin Heidelberg, Springer, 2009) 457.

[63] Case 12/86 *Demirel* [1987] ECR 3719, para 14.

[64] See Joined Cases 21/72–24/72 *International Fruit Company and Others v Produktschap voor Groenten en Fruit* [1972] ECR 1219, para 7, and Case C-286/90 *Poulsen* [1992] ECR I-6019, para 9.

[65] See Case C-162/96 *Racke GmbH v Hauptzollamt Mainz* [1998] ECR I-3655, para 45.

[66] See Case 181/73 *Haegeman* (n 58) para 5.

[67] Note, however, that by virtue of the last sentence of Art 24 (1) TEU, most of the Union's common foreign and security policy is exempt from the CJEU's jurisdiction.

[68] See eg, Case C-280/93 *Germany v Council (Bananas—Common Organisation of the Markets)* [1994] ECR I-4973, para 144; Case C-149/96 *Portugal v Council (Market Access in Textile Products)* [1999] ECR I-8395, paras 47ff.

Bearing in mind this argumentative point of departure, the Convention, as an international treaty, will consequently form an integral part of the Union's legal order after accession, ranking as a 'mezzanine'[69] between primary and secondary EU law and subsequently binding the Union and its organs. The most important reason for this status is to uphold and preserve the supremacy of EU law which, at this point of time, also includes the Convention and thus the Accession Agreement. Since the wording, purpose and nature of the Convention are precise and contain clearly understandable rights for individuals and obligations, which are not subject to the adoption of any subsequent measures, the Convention is directly applicable and unfolds self-executing effects for both the individual and governmental authorities. Beyond that, the Convention will be, after accession, part of '*the law*' mentioned in Article 19 (1) TEU. This will make it primarily the duty of the CJEU to interpret and apply the Convention as part of Union law and, according to the principle of subsidiarity under Article 35 (1) ECHR, to ensure an effective protection of human rights within the Union, before the Strasbourg Court may hear EU-related cases.

B. The Convention as Part of Primary Law?

Nevertheless, when looking at the provisions set forth in the three paragraphs of Article 6 TEU, all of them directly or indirectly referring to the Convention, it may be doubtful whether the Convention will adopt the aforementioned 'mezzanine' status within the EU's legal order, as it is prima facie equally reasonable to accept the Convention post-accession as part of primary Union law.[70] This status, however, would lead to an entirely different outcome in terms of certain jurisdictional and procedural issues, most notably with regard to the preservation of the legal autonomy of the EU. The following three sections therefore show that the argument of placing a Convention within the rank of primary law cannot be consistently corroborated.

i. Art 6 (1) TEU

Article 6 (1) TEU, in conjunction with Article 52 (3) ChFR,[71] states that the Charter is part of primary law and that the meaning and scope of those Charter rights corresponding to rights guaranteed by the Convention shall be the same as those laid down by the Convention. Therefore, one might argue that the

---

[69] See Andreas J Kumin, 'Die Verhandlungsvorbereitungen für den Beitritt der Europäischen Union zur Europäischen Menschenrechtskonvention—Ein Erfahrungsbericht' in Sigmar Stadlmeier (ed), *Von Lissabon zum Raumfahrzeug: Aktuelle Herausforderungen im Völkerrecht. Beiträge zum 35. Österreichischen Völkerrechtstag* (Vienna, NWV, 2011) 73.

[70] See ibid 73f.

[71] See also ch 5 for more details.

Convention will also form part of primary law after accession via corresponding Charter provisions.

There are, however, arguments against this opinion. The objective and purpose of Article 52 (3) ChFR is to ensure the greatest coherence between the Convention and the Charter, especially by 'parallel interpretation' of the two documents,[72] and to create consistency[73] and harmony between the Union's system of fundamental rights protection and that of the Convention. The Convention thus merely constitutes the bottom threshold of human rights protection in the EU, without adversely affecting the autonomy of Union law,[74] nor becoming primary law after accession. Moreover, as set forth in the second sentence of Article 52 (3) ChFR, it is within the discretion of Union legislation to provide a more extensive fundamental rights protection.[75] Thence, if both the Convention and the Charter ranked as primary law, this would inevitably result in judicial divergences in the CJEU's case law, a conflict of laws and, most importantly, in legal uncertainty, as the Union would be simultaneously bound by a higher and a lower standard, not knowing which one to apply. As a result, the Convention will not enter the stage of primary law in the guise of the Charter through Article 6 (1) TEU.

ii. Art 6 (2) TEU

Article 6 (2) TEU sets out the Union's legal obligation[76] to accede to the Convention: 'the Union *shall* accede to the European Convention of Human Rights'.[77] It might be argued that such an obligation, enshrined in a legal provision of primary law itself, which is crucial in relation to the Union's system of fundamental rights protection, might mean that the Convention is given a special status after accession; a rank on par with that of the Treaties.

Yet, this argument cannot be maintained for the following reasons: As a logical prerequisite, it must be noted that the inclusion of the Convention in primary EU law would constitute an amendment to the Treaties under Article 48 TEU. However, as the Union lacks any '*Kompetenz-Kompetenz*' to amend the Treaties and enjoys only those powers conferred on it by the Member States, primary law can only be amended by and with the collaboration of the Member States which are still the 'Masters of the Treaties'.[78]

---

[72] See Joint Communication from Presidents Costa and Skouris, 17 January 2011, 1.
[73] See Thomas von Danwitz, 'Art 52' in Peter J Tettinger and Klaus Stern (eds), *Kölner Gemeinschaftskommentar zur Europäischen Grundrechte-Charta* (Munich, Beck, 2006) para 51f.
[74] See Explanations relating to the Charter of Fundamental Rights [2007] OJ C303/33.
[75] See Martin Borowsky, 'Art 52' in Jürgen Meyer (ed), *Charta der Grundrechte der Europäischen Union* (Baden-Baden, Nomos, 2010) para 30b.
[76] See Schorkopf, 'Art 6 EUV' (n 3), para 37.
[77] Emphasis added.
[78] See Jens Budischowsky, 'Art 48 EUV' in Heinz Mayer (ed), *EUV/AEUV Kommentar* (Vienna, Manz, 2010) paras 3ff.

It is obvious, however, that the Member States do not play a decisive role in the accession procedure; not to mention that there is no reason why they would, even implicitly, intend to amend the treaties in the course of accession. The general procedure to conclude international agreements between the Union and third countries or international organisations is laid down in Article 218 TFEU, or more precisely, with special regard to the accession, in Article 218 (6) lit a (ii), and Article 218 (8) TFEU. Unless the agreement in question is a 'mixed agreement',[79] the participants in this procedure are the Council, the Commission and the Parliament, but not the Member States. However, since the Accession Agreement will be concluded between the Union on the one hand and the contracting parties of the Convention on the other hand without involving the Member States as another treaty partner on the part of the Union, the agreement cannot be qualified as a mixed agreement.[80] The Member States may only include themselves in the procedure by obtaining an opinion of the CJEU 'whether an agreement envisaged is compatible with the Treaties', according to Article 218 (11) TFEU. Consequently, since the Member States are not involved in the accession procedure as independent and sovereign parties, and the Union itself is not entitled to amend its primary law, the Treaties cannot be (implicitly) amended by the EU's accession to the Convention. Moreover, Article 218 TFEU is, most obviously, not a valid legal source for Treaty amendments. Furthermore, there is neither the need nor the intention of the Member States to amend the Treaties, nor does the obligation itself to accede to the Convention entail the inclusion of it into primary European Union law.

iii. Art 6 (3) TEU

The last provision to be analysed at this point, Article 6 (3) TEU, states that fundamental rights, as guaranteed by the Convention and as they result from the constitutional traditions common to the Member States, constitute general principles of EU law. This third dimension of fundamental rights protection besides the Charter and the Convention appears to be an anachronistic and now dispensable remnant of the CJEU's past protection system by case law.[81] This provision has nonetheless a dogmatic function as a source of law-determining principles to fill lacunae within the existing system of fundamental rights protection. The question remains whether the Convention is or will become, after accession, primary law

---

[79] See Khan, 'Art 218 AEUV' (n 5) para 17.

[80] See Hannes Kraemer, 'The Logistics and Technicalities of the Accession' Lecture at the UCL Institute for Human Rights Conference: 'Who Will be the Ultimate Guardian of Human Rights in Europe?', at the University College London, 20 May 2011. See also Susanne Stock, *Der Beitritt der Europäischen Union zur Europäischen Menschenrechtskonvention als Gemischtes Abkommen?* (Hamburg, Verlag Dr Kovac, 2010) 209ff, and Tobias Lock, *Das Verhältnis zwischen dem EuGH und internationalen Gerichten* (Tübingen, Mohr Siebeck, 2010) 292.

[81] See Schorkopf, 'Art 6 EUV' (n 3), para 52.

via these 'general principles of EU law'[82] which have been derived from both the Convention and ECtHR case law.

The answer is quite simple: Article 6 (3) TEU is, of course, part of primary law. This, however, does not make the Convention part of primary law, but merely those general principles derived by the CJEU from the Convention. In other words, the CJEU has taken these general principles from the Convention, has interpreted and applied them and has thus 'transformed' them into Union law, bestowing on them another legal quality. It is therefore obvious that the Convention will not become primary EU law via the provision enshrined in Article 6 (3) TEU.

C. Legal Consequences of the Convention's Mezzanine Status

After having disproved a possible primary law status of the Convention after accession, this legal analysis is now on safe ground to proceed with an assessment of the most prominent legal consequences of the future status of the Convention. Regarding the Union itself, these legal consequences are prima facie rather obvious and unproblematic. According to the aforementioned 'mezzanine' theory, the Convention will rank below primary, but above secondary Union law, thus making it a yardstick for the lawfulness of the latter.[83] This means that any secondary Union legislation or legal acts, as enumerated in Article 288 TFEU, must comply with both primary Union law,[84] including the Charter, and the Convention.[85] As the CJEU, by virtue of Article 19 (1) TEU, will have jurisdiction over the Convention as an integral part of Union law, it can be called upon under Article 263 TFEU to review and possibly annul Union legislation which is allegedly in violation of the Convention. The Luxembourg Court will therefore be able to adjust potential human rights violations within the EU and be part of the Convention's subsidiary protection machinery on the 'domestic' level. In the event of a divergence in interpreting or applying the Convention, the case may subsequently be brought before the Strasbourg Court which will render a judgment, either acquitting or convicting the European Union.

At this point, however, one might ask whether such a move could endanger the Union's legal autonomy. But even when Strasbourg rules on the Convention as part of EU law, the Union's legal autonomy is not jeopardised: It is the ECtHR's

---

[82] See eg, Kumin (n 69) 74.

[83] See Kirsten Schmalenbach, 'Struggle for Exclusiveness: The CJEU and Competing International Tribunals' in Isabelle Buffard, James Crawford, Alain Pellet and Stephan Wittich (eds), *International Law between Universalism and Fragmentation. Festschrift in Honour of Gerhard Hafner* (Leiden, Brill, 2008) 1066.

[84] See eg, Markus Kotzur, 'Art 288 AEUV' in Rudolf Geiger, Daniel-Erasmus Kahn and Markus Kotzur (eds), *EUV/AEUV. Kommentar*, 5th edn (Munich, Beck, 2010) para 4; Andreas von Arnauld, 'Normenhierarchien innerhalb des primären Gemeinschaftsrechts. Gedanken im Prozess der Konstitutionalisierung Europas' (2003) 38 *Europarecht* 191, 204.

[85] For more details, see ch 8.

very own duty to interpret and apply the Convention, regardless of its status in national or EU law. The Strasbourg Court merely declares whether the Convention as an international treaty has been violated, without challenging or even invalidating Union legislation. This role is exclusively reserved for the CJEU.[86]

Nonetheless, when taking a closer look, there are three scenarios where the inclusion of the Convention in EU law and, most importantly, the Convention's newly won supremacy over domestic law, might lead to major complications, including potential risks to the autonomy of EU law:

i. A Clash of Principles

The first scenario is related to the fact that the Member States may grant a higher level of protection than the Charter and the Convention or than the CJEU and the ECtHR, respectively.[87] This principle, which favours the legal regime providing the most extensive and highest fundamental rights protection is, on the part of the Convention, set forth in Article 53 ECHR and states that the Convention does not limit or derogate from any of the human rights that may be ensured under the national laws of the high contracting parties. In other words, this provision underlines the Convention's subsidiary character[88] ensuring a common minimum standard of protection, without prejudice to a more extensive level of protection by the parties to the Convention.[89] On the part of the Union, this principle is enshrined in Article 53 ChFR which reads that the provisions of the Charter shall not be interpreted as restricting or adversely affecting human rights and fundamental freedoms as recognised by, inter alia, Union law, international law and by the Member States' constitutions.[90] This provision thus allows the respective constitutional human rights catalogues of the Member States to grant a higher and more extensive scope of protection than the Charter.[91]

However, this concession of sovereignty to the Member States may clash with the principle of supremacy that now also encompasses the Convention in its mezzanine status, since the principle favouring the most extensive scope of protection

---

[86] See Case 314/85 *Foto-Frost v Hauptzollamt Lübeck-Ost* [1987] ECR 4199, para 15.

[87] See Aida Torres Pérez, *Conflicts of Rights in the European Union: A Theory of Supranational Adjudication* (Oxford, Oxford University Press, 2009) 37.

[88] See Helen Keller, Andreas Fischer and Daniel Kühne, 'Debating the Future of the European Court of Human Rights after the Interlaken Conference: Two Innovative Proposals' (2010) 21 *European Journal of International Law* 1025, 1031.

[89] See Oliver Klein, 'Straßburger Wolken am Karlsruher Himmel. Zum geänderten Verhältnis zwischen Bundesverfassungsgericht und Europäischem Gerichtshof für Menschenrechte seit 1998' (2010) 29 *Neue Zeitschrift für Verwaltungsrecht* 221, 223.

[90] See Martin Borowsky, 'Art 53' in Jürgen Meyer (ed), *Charta der Grundrechte der Europäischen Union* (Baden-Baden, Nomos, 2010) para 14; see also Olivier De Schutter, 'Art 53—Niveau de protection' in EU Network of Independent Experts on Fundamental Rights, *Commentary of the Charter of Fundamental Rights of the European Union* (2006) 409f.

[91] See Walter Frenz, *Handbuch Europarecht. Band 4: Europäische Grundrechte* (Berlin Heidelberg, Springer, 2009) para 547; see also Stefan Ibing, *Die Einschränkung der Europäischen Grundrechte durch Gemeinschaftsrecht* (Baden-Baden, Nomos, 2006) 340.

must not water down or even take precedence over the supremacy of EU law.[92] Assuming that there are, in certain cases, areas of overlapping fundamental rights, the more favourable legal regime of a Member State would then take precedence over the competing provisions in the Charter and the 'unionised' Convention, which principally guarantee a lower standard. This in fact may jeopardise the principle of supremacy and thence the Union's legal autonomy—Union law would not be uniformly applied in those areas where a higher and more extensive standard of protection is ensured by the Member States, thereby preventing the application of legal acts by the EU. Consequently, the principle favouring the highest standard of protection and the principle of supremacy cannot be upheld and complied with at the same time.[93] In cases where the protection of fundamental rights possibly clashes with EU fundamental freedoms,[94] these circumstances lead to the interesting and paradoxical situation where EU law claims to be both the floor (via the Convention) and the ceiling (via the principle of supremacy) which the Member States are required to respect.[95] In this situation, individuals would be refused the higher protection standard of their respective domestic legal regime for the price of the Convention's minimum standard, now enjoying supremacy as an integral part of Union law.

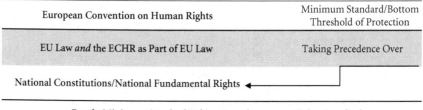

European Convention on Human Rights	Minimum Standard/Bottom Threshold of Protection
EU Law *and* the ECHR as Part of EU Law	Taking Precedence Over

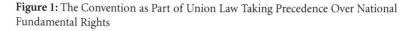

National Constitutions/National Fundamental Rights ⟵————————

Result: Minimum Standard Taking Precedence over Higher Standard
of Domestic Fundamental Rights Protection

Figure 1: The Convention as Part of Union Law Taking Precedence Over National Fundamental Rights

It is nonetheless obvious that such a post-accession situation, in which individuals enjoy a lesser degree of fundamental rights protection than the status quo, would lead the objective and purpose of the Union's accession to the Convention *ad absurdum*. However, the Charter itself demonstrates that neither the autonomy of Union law nor the standards of the European multi-level system of fundamental rights protection are in actual peril. The first sentence of Article 51 (1) ChFR

---

[92] See Thorsten Kingreen, 'Art 53 Charta' in Christian Calliess and Matthias Ruffert (eds), *EUV/ AEUV. Kommentar*, 4th edn (Munich, Beck, 2011) para 4.

[93] See ibid para 5; see also De Schutter, 'Art 53' (n 90) 411, mentioning 'un risque de remise en cause de la primauté du droit de l'Union sur les droits nationaux des Etats membres'.

[94] See eg, Case C-112/00 *Schmidberger v Austria* [2003] ECR I-5659, or Case C-438/05 *Viking Line* [2007] ECR I-10779.

[95] See Torres Pérez (n 87) 36.

sets out that the fundamental rights of the EU are addressed to the Member States 'only when they are implementing Union law'. This means that fundamental rights stemming from Union law, ie from both the Charter and the Convention, are only applied in cases where Member States implement EU law and thus a uniform application thereof is absolutely necessary.[96] At this point, it should be noted that the wording 'implementation of Union law' also encompasses the Member States' exercise of discretionary choices involving the interpretation or implementation of an EU act, and that, consequently, even discretionary actions taken by the Member States have to satisfy the EU's fundamental rights provisions.[97] In other words, the fundamental rights of the Union's legal order will be taken into consideration solely for the purposes of interpreting EU law, and there will be no involvement or assessment of national law in any such case.[98] Moreover, when examining the genesis of Article 53 ChFR, it is evident that this provision was never meant to call into question the supremacy of Union law and thus the very foundations of the EU's legal order.[99] Accordingly, the principle of supremacy remains unaffected by the principle of favouring the highest standard of fundamental rights protection[100]—one might even say that these two principles move in two different legal spheres without interfering with each other. Therefore, there is no clash of these two principles and thus no risk to the Union's legal autonomy.

ii. Duplicating the Convention

The second scenario, in which the Convention's newly acquired supremacy over domestic law might lead to substantive issues with respect to the Union's legal autonomy, concerns the status of the Convention within the legal order of the Union's Member States. Today, the Convention, as an international treaty, has been incorporated into the law of all the contracting parties,[101] but its status in the hierarchy of national laws varies considerably from one country to another.[102]

---

[96] See Paul Gragl, 'Anwendungsbereich und Tragweite der Europäischen Grundrechte' (2011/2012) 22 *Juristische Ausbildung und Praxisvorbereitung* 47, 47f.

[97] See eg, Joined Cases C-411/10 and C-493/10 *NS v Secretary of State for the Home Department and ME v Refugee Applications Commissioner* [2011] ECR I-0000, paras 66–68, and Case C-101/01 *Criminal Proceedings against Bodil Lindqvist* [2003] ECR I-12971, para 92.

[98] See Case C-400/10 PPU *McB v LE* [2010] ECR I-8965, para 52.

[99] See Borowsky, 'Art 53' (n 90) para 10; see also *Jonas Bering Liisberg*, 'Does the EU Charter of Fundamental Rights Threaten the Supremacy of Community Law? Article 53 of the Charter: A Fountain of Law or Just an Inkblot?' (2001) 38 *Common Market Law Review* 1171, 1172f.

[100] See Borowsky, 'Art 53' (n 90) para 10; De Schutter, 'Art 53' (n 90) 411; Ulrich Everling, 'Durch die Grundrechtecharta zurück zu Solange I?' (2003) 14 *Europäische Zeitschrift für Wirtschaftsrecht* 225, 225.

[101] See David Harris, Michael O'Boyle, Ed Bates and Carla Buckley (eds), *Law of the European Convention on Human Rights*, 2nd edn (Oxford, Oxford University Press, 2009) 23; Grabenwarter, *Europäische Menschenrechtskonvention* (n 54) § 3, para 1.

[102] See Jörg Polakiewicz, 'The Status of the Convention in National Law' in Robert Blackburn and Jörg Polakiewicz (eds), *Fundamental Rights in Europe. The ECHR and its Member States, 1950–2000* (Oxford, Oxford University Press, 2001) 36.

Basically, three types of status can be distinguished.[103] Firstly, the Convention may be on par with other ordinary legislation, ie non-constitutional laws and statutes;[104] secondly, the Convention may rank on a 'mezzanine' below the Constitution, but with superiority over domestic legislation;[105] and thirdly, the Convention may be part of the Constitution[106] or even enjoy a status superior to the Constitution.[107]

Yet, whatever status the Convention as an international treaty may have within the domestic legal order of the EU's Member States, it is unquestionable that Union law takes precedence over national law by virtue of its supremacy. Since the Convention will be an integral part of Union law after accession, it will also enjoy supremacy and thus supersede domestic law in cases of conflict. Under these circumstances, accession might lead to a paradoxical situation for the Member States—by incorporating the Convention both into the Member States' respective legal systems and into the legal order of the EU, the Convention is, in a manner of speaking, duplicated, and will therefore bind the Member States on two different legal planes.[108] More precisely, the Convention as part of Union law will take precedence over the Convention as part of domestic law. The case law of the Strasbourg Court will then take effect on the plane of national law on the basis of the Member States' obligations under international law; the case law of the Luxembourg Court, however, will take effect on a superior plane, namely on the plane of Union law. Consequently, the interpretation and application of the Convention by the CJEU will take precedence over that of the ECtHR. Principally, this scenario should not cause any problems, unless the CJEU deviates from Strasbourg's case law. In cases of judicial divergence, the Member States might face major legal issues,[109] which may also interfere with the Union's legal autonomy.

The following example may shed more light on the possible ramifications of divergences between Luxembourg and Strasbourg.[110] According to its obligations under the Convention Relating to the Status of Refugees, Austria officially recognises A, an asylum seeker, as a refugee. Thereafter, his brother, B, who has very close ties with A, enters the EU via Italy and continues to Austria, where he

---

[103] See Grabenwarter, *Europäische Menschenrechtskonvention* (n 54) § 3, paras 1–5.

[104] In Denmark, Finland, Germany, Ireland, Italy, Latvia, Lithuania, Poland, Sweden and the United Kingdom.

[105] In Belgium, Bulgaria, Cyprus, Czech Republic, Estonia, France, Greece, Hungary, Luxembourg, Malta, Portugal, Romania, Slovakia, Slovenia and Spain.

[106] In Austria.

[107] In the Netherlands.

[108] See Gregor Heißl, 'Happy End einer unendlichen Geschichte? Der Beitritt der EU zur EMRK und seine Auswirkungen auf Österreich' in Michael Holoubek, Andrea Martin and Stephan Schwarzer (eds), *Die Zukunft der Verfassung—Die Verfassung der Zukunft? Festschrift für Karl Korinek zum 70. Geburtstag* (Vienna New York, Springer, 2010) 141f, examining this paradoxical situation with particular respect to Austria's obligations under the Convention.

[109] See ibid 142.

[110] This example is taken from ibid 142f.

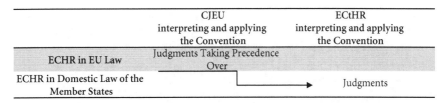

	CJEU interpreting and applying the Convention	ECtHR interpreting and applying the Convention
ECHR in EU Law	Judgments Taking Precedence Over	
ECHR in Domestic Law of the Member States		Judgments

Result: Interpretation and Application of the Convention by the CJEU Taking Precedence Over Interpretation and Application of the Convention by the ECtHR

Figure 2: The Duplication of the Convention

applies for asylum. A closer look at the EU's Dublin II-Regulation[111] will show whether Austria or Italy is now responsible for examining the asylum application of B. One criterion for that responsibility, set forth in Article 7 of the Regulation, is whether the asylum seeker in question has a family member who has been allowed to reside as a refugee in a Member State. In this case, this Member State, ie Austria, shall be responsible for examining the asylum application. However, according to Article 2 lit i of the Regulation, the term 'family member' only includes the so-called nuclear family, ie spouses or unmarried partners in stable relationships, minor children, and parents or guardians. No mention is made of siblings. Conversely, according to the settled case law of the ECtHR, the term 'family' in Article 8 ECHR is interpreted extensively, and therefore also includes members of the extended family, provided that those family members have close ties to each other.[112]

It now rests with the CJEU and its decision whether Austria or Italy is responsible for examining B's application for asylum. If the CJEU interprets the term 'family member' in a restrictive manner and according to the provisions of the Dublin II-Regulation, Italy is the Member State responsible for the examination. If, however, the CJEU complies with Strasbourg's settled case law and applies an extensive interpretation, ie the Convention, Austria is responsible for examining the asylum application.[113] In this case, the solution is quite simple—if the CJEU were to choose the first alternative, it would violate both the Convention and Union law. The violation of the Convention arises from the Union's obligations under international law after accession; the violation of Union law, by contrast, arises from the Convention's mezzanine status, giving it superiority over secondary law. Consequently, as laid down in Article 19 (1) TEU, the CJEU shall ensure that the law is observed and must correspondingly give priority to the

---

[111] Council Regulation (EC) No 343/2003 of 18 February 2003 establishing the criteria and mechanisms for determining the Member State responsible for examining an asylum application lodged in one of the Member States by a Third-Country National [2003] OJ L50/1.

[112] See *Marckx v Belgium* App no 6833/74 (ECtHR, 13 June 1979) para 45; *Elsholz v Germany* App no 25735/94 (ECtHR, 13 July 2000) para 43; *K and T v Finland* App no 25702/94 (ECtHR, 12 July 2001) paras 150–51.

[113] See Heißl (n 108) 142.

Convention's higher rank within the EU's legal hierarchy and apply its pertinent provisions and Strasbourg's case law, thereby ignoring the provisions of the lower ranking Regulation. This *modus operandi* would thence avoid any violation of the law.

iii. Conflicting Obligations

The third and last scenario in this context illustrates two interrelated legal problems; on the one hand the questions resulting from the Member States' concurrent and thus possibly conflicting obligations under the Convention and EU law; and on the other hand the relevance of cases where the CJEU does not comply with the Convention and the ECtHR's case law.

To demonstrate the impact of these potential conflicts on the system of European human rights protection and the autonomy of Union law better, the abovementioned brothers A and B will again set the scene.[114] B's application for asylum is eventually dismissed by the Austrian authorities. In the next stage, B brings the case before the Austrian Constitutional Court which does not request a preliminary ruling from the CJEU under Article 267 TFEU, as it considers the wording of the Dublin II-Regulation clear and unambiguous and hence does not raise a question concerning its validity or interpretation, thus pursuing the CJEU's 'acte claire-doctrine'.[115] Since B, as an individual, is not entitled to initiate a preliminary ruling procedure,[116] the Constitutional Court dismisses the case. The Strasbourg Court, however, holds that the restrictive interpretation of the term 'family member' in the Dublin II-Regulation constitutes a violation of Article 8 ECHR. As a result, the ECtHR thereby reviews the validity and conformity of secondary Union law with the Convention; a task which is exclusively reserved for the CJEU.[117] The national courts, however, are obliged under the Union Treaties to apply supreme EU law, *in concreto* the Dublin II-Regulation, and to violate the Convention by disregarding Strasbourg's decision.[118]

In an alternative scenario, the Austrian Constitutional Court requests a preliminary ruling from the CJEU on the interpretation of the term 'family member'. Yet, the CJEU deviates from Strasbourg's case law on Article 8 ECHR, adheres

---

[114] This example is again taken from ibid 143f.

[115] See Case 283/81 *CILFIT v Ministry of Health* [1982] ECR 3415, para 16, ruling that 'the correct application of Community Law may be so obvious as to leave no scope for any reasonable doubt as to the manner in which the question raised is to be resolved'. For more details, see David Edward, '*CILFIT* and *Foto-Frost* in their Historical and Procedural Context' in Miguel Poiares Maduro and Loïc Azoulai (eds), *The Past and Future of EU Law. The Classics of EU Law Revisited on the 50th Anniversary of the Rome Treaty* (Oxford, Hart Publishing, 2010) 173ff.

[116] See Bernhard W Wegener, 'Art 267 AEUV' in Christian Calliess and Matthias Ruffert (eds), *EUV/AEUV. Kommentar*, 4th edn (Munich, Beck, 2011) para 21.

[117] See Case 314/85 *Foto-Frost* (n 86) para 15. See, however, ch 8 for more details regarding the external review of secondary Union law, and ch 11 for the CJEU's prior involvement in EU-related cases before the ECtHR in order to preserve the Union's legal autonomy.

[118] See Heißl (n 108) 143.

to the unambiguous wording of the Regulation and does not apply the term 'family member' to A's brother B. The Constitutional Court is now bound by Luxembourg's legal opinion and has to dismiss the case, whereas the ECtHR subsequently holds that there has been a violation of Article 8 ECHR.[119] But again, the national court must primarily follow the CJEU's decision and disregard the findings of the ECtHR.

Both scenarios lead to similar results—due to the supremacy and direct applicability of Union law, domestic courts are obliged to abide by Luxembourg's rulings, thus infringing the Member States' international obligation to abide by the final judgment of the Strasbourg Court (Art 46 (1) ECHR), since primary Union law ranks above the Convention within the respective domestic legal orders. The national courts are thence not authorised to comply with the ECtHR's rulings until the CJEU applies Strasbourg's case law and entirely complies with it. Consequently, individuals remain fully dependent on national courts and their proneness to request preliminary rulings from the CJEU.[120] The final outcome of this problem is that a request for a preliminary reference procedure under Article 267 TFEU becomes a necessary precondition for the Member States in order to avoid conflicting obligations under international law and Union law, but only if the CJEU ultimately complies with Strasbourg's decision.

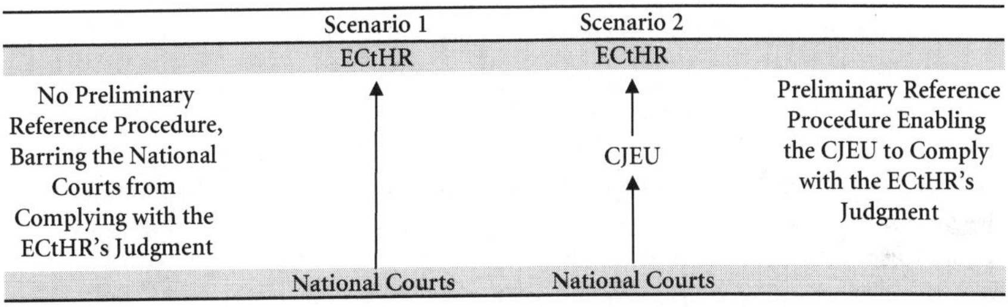

	Scenario 1	Scenario 2	
	ECtHR	ECtHR	
No Preliminary Reference Procedure, Barring the National Courts from Complying with the ECtHR's Judgment	↑	↑ CJEU ↑	Preliminary Reference Procedure Enabling the CJEU to Comply with the ECtHR's Judgment
	National Courts	National Courts	

Result: The Final Decision of Exposing Member States to Conflicts between International Law and Union Law Rests with the National Courts Themselves (Scenario 1) and the CJEU (Scenario 2)

Figure 3: Does Luxembourg Have the Last Say in Human Rights?

Nonetheless, these scenarios do not take into account that the Convention forms an integral part of Union law after accession, ranking above secondary EU legislation and thus above the Dublin II-Regulation. The solution to these problems is quite similar to that shown in the previous section ii and lies again in the Convention's newly-won supremacy and its legal status. In the first scenario, where the respective national court decides not to request a preliminary ruling from the CJEU, it must take into consideration both the Dublin II-Regulation

---

[119] See ibid.
[120] See ibid 144.

and the pertinent provisions of the Convention as EU law, including Strasbourg's case law. In case of contradiction, for example between Article 2 lit i of the Regulation and Article 8 ECHR concerning the term 'family member', the court must apply the higher-ranking Union law, which is the Convention on its mezzanine level. By applying these provisions, the domestic court would firstly avoid judicial divergences between its own decisions and those of the ECtHR; secondly, by following this *modus operandi*, the court would prevent conflicts between the Member States' obligations under international law and Union law; but thirdly, and most importantly, by applying the Convention as EU law, the decision lies with the national court itself not to put the Strasbourg Court into the awkward situation of deciding on the validity and conformity of secondary Union law with the Convention. This approach would also be in accordance with the duty of sincere cooperation by virtue of Article 4 (3) TEU, obligating the Member States to refrain from any measure which could jeopardise the attainment of the Union's objectives. As a result, the autonomy of Union law would be perfectly preserved in this scenario.

In the second scenario, where the respective national court decides to request a preliminary ruling, it is the CJEU itself that must take into account the pertinent provisions of the Convention as EU law, also including Strasbourg's case law. As set forth in Article 19 (1) TEU, it is the Luxembourg Court's duty to ensure that the law is observed in the interpretation and application of the Treaties. Correspondingly, it must give priority to the Convention's higher rank within the EU's legal hierarchy and apply its pertinent provisions, thereby disregarding the provisions of the lower ranking Dublin II-Regulation. This course of action would also prevent the abovementioned issues, namely the judicial divergences between the courts, conflicts between the Member States' different legal obligations and any risks for the EU's legal autonomy. It is therefore in the best interest of both national courts and the CJEU to adhere to the Convention and the ECtHR's case law as an integral part of Union law in order to avoid detrimental impacts on the autonomy of Union law and the new legal architecture of European human rights protection after accession.

IV. INTERIM CONCLUSIONS

The objective of the present chapter was to give an introduction to the questions regarding the accession procedure and to illustrate two interrelated topics which are of utmost relevance to this book's object of investigation. On the one hand, it examined why an accession agreement was preferable to any further Protocols amending the Convention; and on the other ascertained where this agreement, along with the Convention itself, would rank within the Union's legal order after accession. The clarifications made in this chapter are the theoretical foundation and the preliminary reference point for the discussion in the subsequent chapters.

Firstly, it is certain that accession will be carried out on the basis of an international agreement between the Union and the high contracting parties to the Convention. It was agreed that the EU's accession to the Convention is based on an agreement rather than on a Protocol amending the Convention in order to preserve the main feature of the Convention system, ie the effective protection of human rights, as far as possible and to keep the adaptations necessary for the EU's accession to a minimum. In other words, it is evident that the special characteristics of the Union must be taken into account, but not at the price of compromising the properly working Convention system. Nonetheless, it is precisely for this reason that an agreement is more favourable for the EU and its legal autonomy than an amendment to the Convention. The conclusion of an agreement allows the negotiating parties to be more flexible and to thoughtfully consider the provisions of EU law relevant to the conditions and procedural requirements for preserving the autonomy of EU law. Beyond that, the entry into force of the finalised Accession Agreement will in fact not only allow the EU to accede to the Convention, but also amend the Convention without any further legal complications. The Agreement will thus become an integral part of the Convention itself, since some of the provisions of the Agreement will have permanent effects and will remain relevant for the future functioning of the Convention system. Figuratively speaking, the life cycle of the Accession Agreement does not end with its entry into force and the subsequent accession, but continues to be an essential part of the Convention system in the future.

Secondly, this chapter clarified that both the Convention and the Accession Agreement will not become part of primary Union law after accession, neither through the accession procedure itself nor through the three paragraphs of Article 6 TEU, wherein explicit references to the Convention are made. It is through the CJEU's settled case law that international treaties, concluded between the EU and third parties, become an integral part of Union law, ranking on a 'mezzanine' level below primary, but above secondary Union law. As this specific status renders it part of EU law, the Convention will not only take precedence over secondary law in violation of the Convention, but also over the legal orders of the Member States. Moreover, as part of '*the law*' mentioned in Article 19 (1) TEU, the Convention will consequently be interpreted and applied by the CJEU, in order to guarantee an effective human rights protection mechanism on the 'domestic' plane.

Lastly, this chapter has made it clear that, despite serious doubts and concerns regarding this matter, the Convention's newly won supremacy over domestic law does not jeopardise the Union's legal autonomy. In the first scenario presented above, an impending clash between the principle which favours the legal regime providing the most extensive and highest standard of protection and the supremacy principle of Union law seemed very likely. In this case, the minimum standard of the Convention, as an integral part of Union law, would take precedence over domestic laws and their higher standard of protection, leaving individuals with a lesser degree of protection than before accession. However, this clash of principles can be easily avoided by taking into account a provision of the Charter. According to the first sentence of Article 51 (1) ChFR, the fundamental rights of the Union, ie both the Charter and the Convention as part of EU law, are only addressed to the Member States in cases 'when they are implementing Union law'. As a result, there is no clash between these two principles, as they are applied in different cases, and thence, there is no risk to the autonomy of EU law.

In the second scenario, it seemed that the Convention's duplication as part of supreme Union law and also domestic law, thus binding the Member States on two different legal levels, created an impending risk to the Union's legal autonomy. More precisely, Luxembourg's decisions would take precedence over those of Strasbourg, leading to major problems in cases where the CJEU deviates from the ECtHR's case law. The solution to this problem lies in the fact that the CJEU must comply with the Convention and Strasbourg's case law when secondary EU law is in violation of the Convention, since the Convention will rank, as part of Union law, on a higher plane than secondary law. A divergence from the Convention would thus not only lead to a violation of the Convention itself, but also to a violation of Union law. The CJEU is therefore advised to abide by the provisions of the Convention and by Strasbourg's case law in order to avoid legal complications in the future.

The last scenario showed that the potentially conflicting obligations of the Member States under both the Convention and EU law do not pose a risk for the autonomy of EU law. In the case of conflict between the Convention and secondary Union law, the national courts must also apply the Convention as higher ranking EU law. By applying the Convention in the first place, the courts of the Member States would not only avoid judicial divergences between Luxembourg and Strasbourg, but also circumvent a situation in which the Strasbourg Court would be put into the awkward position of deciding on the validity and conformity of secondary Union law with the Convention. Thereby, there would be no danger for the autonomy of EU law.

8

External Review by Strasbourg:
A Hierarchy of Courts?

I. EXTERNAL REVIEW VS AUTONOMY: THE LEGAL ISSUE SITUATED

O N THE BASIS of Article 6 (2) of the Treaty on European Union (TEU), this chapter examines which legal action by the European Union may be challenged before the Strasbourg Court.[1] It is the primary purpose and objective of the European Union's accession to the Convention to subject the Union and its institutions to the judicial review of an external court, namely the European Court of Human Rights (ECtHR) and its protection regime. The most desirable consequence of this step is to close the existing lacunae in the European system of human rights protection and thus remedy the ECtHR's lack of jurisdiction *ratione personae* over the EU.[2] After accession, the EU will be bound by the provisions enshrined in the Convention and individuals will accordingly be entitled to file applications for infringements of the Convention directly against the EU and its institutions, and not against the Member States for 'merely' implementing Union law. Such infringements of the Convention by EU law can be found in virtually every legal act of the Union—in primary law such as the Treaties themselves; in all legal acts of secondary law under Article 288 of the Treaty on the Functioning of the European Union (TFEU); in executive actions or omissions; and in the decisions of the Union courts.[3]

As aforementioned in previous parts of this book, it has repeatedly been assured that, firstly, the ECtHR 'could not be regarded as a superior Court but rather as a specialised Court exercising external control over the international law obligations of the Union resulting from the accession to the ECHR';[4] secondly,

---

[1] See also Jean-Paul Jacqué, 'The Accession of the European Union to the European Convention on Human Rights and Fundamental Freedoms' (2011) 48 *Common Market Law Review* 995, 1002f.

[2] See in this respect the cases examined in Part II eg, *Confédération Française Démocratique du Travail (CFDT) v The European Communities, alternatively: Their Member States a) jointly and b) severally* App no 8030/77 (Commission Decision, 10 July 1997) para 3; *Matthews v United Kingdom* App no 24833/94 (ECtHR, 18 February 1999) para 32; *Bosphorus v Ireland* App no 45036/98 (ECtHR, 30 June 2005) paras 149ff.

[3] See Tobias Lock, 'Walking on a Tightrope: The Draft Accession Agreement and the Autonomy of the EU Legal Order' (2011) 48 *Common Market Law Review* 1025, 1034.

[4] See European Convention, 'Final Report of Working Group II' CONV 354/02, WG II 16, 12; see also European Parliament, 'Resolution on the Institutional Aspects of Accession by the European

that 'accession shall not affect the Union's competences as defined in the Treaties';[5] and thirdly, that the accession agreement 'shall make provision for preserving the specific characteristics of the Union and Union law'.[6] By and large, this means that neither the procedures before nor the judgments of the Strasbourg Court may, in any way, encroach upon the autonomy of the EU's legal order. Thence, the question remains whether applications directly addressed against the Union, and the subsequent judgments of the Strasbourg Court, which the Union as a contracting party has to abide by under Article 46 of the European Convention on Human Rights (ECHR)[7] and its obligations under international law,[8] may nevertheless violate the Union's legal autonomy. Such a violation is most likely to happen in the subsequent two scenarios. The first issue to be examined is whether the Strasbourg Court would have to interpret Union law in a binding manner; the second issue is whether a judgment by the ECtHR, holding that Union legislation infringed the Convention, would be compatible with the EU's legal autonomy.[9]

The following sections now delve into more detail and examine whether these two problems truly pose any risk to the autonomy of the Union's legal system or whether these problems are simply unjustified concerns.

II. A BINDING INTERPRETATION OF UNION LAW BY STRASBOURG?

A. Assessing Domestic Law under the Convention

According to Article 1 ECHR, it is primarily the ECtHR's task to interpret and apply the Convention, the Convention being the basic document of Strasbourg's system of human rights protection and therefore of its jurisdiction *ratione materiae*.[10] The Strasbourg Court interprets the provisions of the Convention according to the international rules on the interpretation of treaties, namely the

---

Union to the European Convention for the Protection of Human Rights and Fundamental Freedoms' P7_TA-PROV(2010)0184, para 1; and Hans Christian Krüger, 'Reflections Concerning Accession of the European Communities to the European Convention on Human Rights' (2002) 21 *Penn State International Law Review* 89, 97.

[5] Art 6 (2) TEU.

[6] Art 1 of Protocol 8 relating to art 6, para 2 of the Treaty on European Union on the accession of the European Union to the European Convention on the Protection of Human Rights and Fundamental Freedoms.

[7] See Jens Meyer-Ladewig, *Europäische Menschenrechtskonvention. Handkommentar*, 3rd edn (Baden-Baden, Nomos, 2011) Einleitung, paras 32–34, and art 46, para 2; see also David Harris, Michael O'Boyle, Ed Bates and Carla Buckley (eds), *Law of the European Convention on Human Rights*, 2nd edn (Oxford, Oxford University Press, 2009) 862f.

[8] See Wolf Okresek, 'Die Umsetzung der EGMR-Urteile und ihre Überwachung' (2003) 30 *Europäische Grundrechte-Zeitschrift* 168, 168.

[9] See Lock, 'Tightrope' (n 3) 1034.

[10] See Harris, O'Boyle, Bates and Buckley (n 7) 800f; see also Chittharanjan F Amerasinghe, *Jurisdiction of International Tribunals* (Leiden, Brill, 2003) 755ff.

Vienna Convention on the Law of Treaties (VCLT),[11] and correspondingly applies them 'in the light of present-day conditions'.[12] Beyond that, however, the ECtHR must also consider pertinent domestic law in its judgments in order to ascertain whether there has in fact been a violation of the Convention. Of course, after accession, the term 'domestic law' will also comprise European Union law. Prima facie, according to *Opinion 1/91*, an international court interpreting EU law thus seems like a serious peril to the EU's legal autonomy. However, it is by no means unheard of for an international court or tribunal to take into account national law when dealing with issues of international law.[13] For instance, the ECtHR regards, like any other international court,[14] the domestic law of the parties involved as part of the facts.[15] The Strasbourg Court confirmed this *modus operandi* in a couple of its judgments, especially by ruling that 'it is primarily for the national authorities, notably the courts, to interpret and apply domestic law [...]. It is therefore not for the Court to express an opinion contrary to theirs [...].'[16]

Furthermore, Strasbourg also made it clear that it does not constitute a further court of appeal, namely a 'fourth instance' ('*quatrième instance*'), from the decisions of national courts applying and interpreting national law.[17] It held that 'it is not its function to deal with errors of fact or law allegedly committed by a national court unless and in so far as they may have infringed rights and freedoms protected by the Convention'.[18]

This means that an application merely claiming that a domestic court has made an error of fact or law in its decision, cannot be dealt with by the Strasbourg Court, 'as it is not competent to deal with an application alleging that errors of law or fact have been committed by domestic courts [...]',[19] and the application will accordingly be declared inadmissible *ratione materiae*. Moreover, in cases where an application alleges that domestic law is in violation of the Convention, the Strasbourg Court will in no way call into question the competence of the national courts and take their place in the interpretation of domestic law.[20] However, sometimes there are cases in which the ECtHR must pronounce a judgment on the provisions of domestic law and consequently on European Union law after accession. Although it is not Strasbourg's responsibility 'to review the observance of domestic

---

[11] See *Golder v United Kingdom* App no 4451/70 (ECtHR, 21 February 1975) para 29.

[12] See *Tyrer v United Kingdom* App no 5856/72 (ECtHR, 25 April 1978) para 31.

[13] See Ian Brownlie, *Principles of Public International Law*, 6th edn (Oxford, Oxford University Press, 2003) 36; see also Helmut Strebel, 'Erzwungener, verkappter Monismus des Ständigen Internationalen Gerichtshofs?' (1971) 31 *Zeitschrift für ausländisches öffentliches Recht und Völkerrecht* 855, 855ff.

[14] See *Certain German Interests in Polish Upper Silesia (Germany v Poland)* PCIJ Series A No 6, 19; see also Gernot Biehler, *Procedures in International Law* (Berlin Heidelberg, Springer, 2008) 312.

[15] See Lock, 'Tightrope' (n 3) 1034.

[16] See *Huvig v France* App no 11105/84 (ECtHR, 24 April 1990) para 28.

[17] See Harris, O'Boyle, Bates and Buckley (n 7) 14.

[18] See *García Ruiz v Spain* App no 30544/96 (ECtHR, 21 January 1999) para 28.

[19] *Reiss v Austria* App no 23953/94 (Commission Decision, 6 September 1995).

[20] See *X and Y v The Netherlands* App no 8978/80 (ECtHR, 26 March 1985) para 29.

law by the national authorities',[21] it is not entirely prevented from taking up a stance towards national law and its provisions. One of the ECtHR's duties is, for example, to take into consideration the specific interpretation of domestic law by a national Supreme or Constitutional Court and the pronouncements thereof by the respective national government in Strasbourg.[22] Beyond that, even if assessing the facts is a quite delicate matter, the ECtHR can in no way accept, at any rate, the national law of the respondent party as simple facts.[23] There are undoubtedly situations in which Strasbourg's assessment of an alleged violation of the Convention necessarily forces it to interpret provisions of domestic law.[24]

For instance, in cases where the right to liberty and security of the person under Article 5 ECHR has allegedly been violated, the Strasbourg Court maintains a supervisory role since compliance with the domestic law is inextricably related to legal justification for detention.[25] Therefore, as such a supervisory body, the Court must have the competence to retain a certain power of review to interpret and apply domestic law when the Convention refers directly back to national law, 'for, in such matters, disregard of the domestic law entails breach of the Convention [...]'.[26]

Certainly, this argument analogously applies to the question as to whether a national remedy is *effective*, as set forth in Article 13 ECHR. Cases filed under this provision usually compel the Court to scrutinise national laws in order to find out whether the applicant was provided with an effective remedy[27] at the domestic plane in the sense that this remedy, if reverted to, 'could have prevented the alleged violation occurring or continuing or could have afforded the applicant appropriate redress for any violation that had already occurred'.[28] But even though the best legal technique for a high contracting party to shield itself from infringing Article 13 ECHR in a case is to incorporate the Convention into national law, there is no requirement to do so;[29] parties to the Convention are rather 'afforded a margin of appreciation in conforming to their obligations under this provision'.[30] In a nutshell, this means that it is basically up to the contracting parties how they shape

---

[21] See *Winterwerp v The Netherlands* App no 6301/73 (ECtHR, 24 October 1979) para 46.

[22] See *Pine Valley Developments Ltd v Ireland* App no 12742/87 (ECtHR, 29 November 1991) para 52.

[23] See Olivier De Schutter, *L'adhésion de l'Union européenne à la Convention européenne des droits de l'homme: feuille de route de la négociation.* European Parliament, Committee on Constitutional Affairs, Hearing on the Institutional Aspects of the European Union's Accession to the European Convention on Human Rights, 18 March 2010, 11.

[24] See Lock, 'Tightrope' (n 3) 1035.

[25] See Harris, O'Boyle, Bates and Buckley (n 7) 134; see also Meyer-Ladewig (n 7) art 5, para 12.

[26] *Winterwerp v The Netherlands* App no 6301/73 (n 21) para 46.

[27] See *Martins Castro and Alves Correia de Castro v Portugal* App no 33729/06 (ECtHR, 10 June 2008) para 56.

[28] *Ramirez Sanchez v France* App no 59450/00 (ECtHR, 4 July 2006) para 160.

[29] See Harris, O'Boyle, Bates and Buckley (n 7) 558f.

[30] *Smith and Grady v United Kingdom* App nos 33985/96 and 33986/96 (ECtHR, 27 September 1999) para 135.

and flesh out remedies at the domestic level, but the ECtHR must nevertheless check their effectiveness by examining the corresponding national law.

Lastly, the Strasbourg Court also takes a probing look at domestic law in cases where rights under Articles 8 to 11 ECHR have allegedly been violated. These four articles share some common formal features, most prominently the second paragraph, setting up the conditions under which a state may interfere with these rights.[31] According to its consistent and settled case law, the ECtHR uses the following formula to determine whether an interference with the exercise of these specific rights violates the Convention—an interference with the rights under Articles 8 to 11 ECHR violates the Convention, unless the interference was '*prescribed by law or in accordance with the law*, pursued a legitimate aim and was necessary in a democratic society'.[32] In the context of the potential external review of domestic law, the wording '*prescribed by law*' and '*in accordance with the law*' deserves special consideration at this point. When the ECtHR assesses applications alleging violations of the aforementioned articles, it must scrutinise whether the interference was indeed in accordance with or prescribed by national law. The Court must thus firstly examine whether the interference in question has some basis in domestic law[33] and secondly, it must explicitly determine whether the law was adequately accessible for the citizen and whether the law in question was formulated with sufficient precision to enable the citizen to regulate his or her conduct.[34] Hence, despite the wide margin of appreciation the contracting parties are given in interfering with rights laid down in Articles 8 to 11 ECHR,[35] the Strasbourg Court usually has a closer look at domestic provisions, being the legal basis for potential interferences of Convention rights.

The legal consequences of this analysis for the Union after accession are perfectly obvious. Even though the Strasbourg Court considers the national courts the only authorities to interpret and apply national law under the subsidiarity principle, it cannot refrain from examining domestic laws in cases where the Convention itself refers to these national provisions as justifiable interferences. In the context of the EU's accession to the Convention, this means that the Court of Justice of the European Union (CJEU) will, of course, remain the ultimate arbiter of Union law. However, in cases involving claims under Articles 5, 8–11 and 13 ECHR, where the sphere of domestic law is eminently affected, the ECtHR must also take a closer look at 'domestic' law, ie Union law, in order to determine whether an interference

---

[31] See Colin Warbrick, 'The Structure of Article 8' [1998] EHRLR 32, 32ff; see also Harris, O'Boyle, Bates and Buckley (n 7) 341. See also Jochen Frowein, 'Vorbemerkungen zu Art 8-11' in Jochen Frowein and Wolfgang Peukert (eds), *EMRK-Kommentar* (Kehl am Rhein, NP Engel, 2009) paras 1ff.

[32] See eg, *Bladet Tromsø and Stensaas v Norway* App no 21980/93 (ECtHR, 20 May 1999) para 50 (emphasis added).

[33] See *Sunday Times v United Kingdom* App no 6538/74 (ECtHR, 26 April 1979) para 47, and *Silver v United Kingdom* App nos 5947/72; 6205/73; 7052/75; 7061/75; 7107/75; 7113/75; 7136/75 (ECtHR, 25 March 1983) para 86.

[34] See *Sunday Times v United Kingdom* App no 6538/74 (n 33) para 49.

[35] See *Handyside v United Kingdom* App no 5493/72 (ECtHR, 7 December 1976) paras 48 and 49.

was prescribed by or in accordance with the law or whether the remedies available under EU law are indeed effective.

B. European Union Law as 'Domestic Law'

Thus, in a manner of speaking, Articles 5, 8–11 and 13 ECHR could be considered to be those provisions of the Convention which will most likely 'invite' the Strasbourg Court to examine 'domestic' law, ie EU law, after accession. The following cases will further show scenarios in which a similar review by the ECtHR was made in the past on the basis of Union law[36] and what this approach entails for the future and thereby the autonomy of the Union's legal order after accession.

i. Connolly v 15 Member States of the European Union

In this case, Strasbourg had to determine whether the CJEU's decision not to accept any written statement by the applicant in response to the Opinion of the Advocate General violated the right to a fair trial under Article 6 EHCR. Bernard Connolly, a former official of the European Commission, had written a book criticising the European Union and its institutions and had published it without prior permission of his employers, ie the Commission. He was therefore removed from his post following a decision of the Disciplinary Board of the Commission. Mr Connolly subsequently brought an action for annulment of this decision that was eventually dismissed by the Court of First Instance,[37] as was the filing of the appeal against this judgment, by the Court of Justice.[38] Before the CJEU, however, he requested permission to file a written statement to respond to the Opinion of the Advocate General, which was nevertheless denied. Consequently, he filed an application against the then 15 Member States of the Union before the ECtHR and alleged that the CJEU's refusal to accept written statements constituted a violation of Articles 6 and 13 ECHR, respectively.[39] The Strasbourg Court then drew on the pertinent provisions of the Staff Regulation of EU Officials,[40] most notably on Article 17 of the Regulation which obliges officials to refrain from any unauthorised disclosure of information received in the line of duty. In the end, the Court concluded that Mr Connolly had actually contested the decisions of the Court of First Instance and the Court of Justice, but not an action conducted

---

[36] See also Lock, 'Tightrope' (n 3) 1035.

[37] See Case T-203/95 *Connolly v Commission* [1999] ECR II-443.

[38] See Case C-274/99 P *Connolly v Commission* [2001] ECR I-1611.

[39] For more details, see eg, Nikolaus Marsch and Anna-Catherina Sanders, 'Gibt es ein Recht der Parteien auf Stellungnahme zu den Schlussanträgen des Generalanwalts? Zur Vereinbarkeit des Verfahrens vor dem EuGH mit Art. 6 I EMRK' (2008) 43 *Europarecht* 345, 345ff.

[40] Regulation No 31 (EEC), 11 (EAEC), laying down the Staff Regulations of Officials and the Conditions of Employment of other servants of the European Economic Community and the European Atomic Energy Community [1962] OJ 45, 1385.

by one of the 15 Member States. Due to the lack of jurisdiction *ratione personae* over the Union, the ECtHR referred to its *Bosphorus*[41] judgment and subsequently dismissed the case.[42]

ii. *Kokkelvisserij v The Netherlands*

In a case similar to *Connolly*, the applicant, the *Kokkelvisserij* association, a company engaged in mechanical cockle fishing in the Wadden Sea, had applied for a fishing licence, which was subsequently granted by the Dutch authorities. The Wadden Sea Society, a non-governmental organisation for the protection of the environment, however, had lodged an objection against this licence. The Dutch Administrative Jurisdiction Division of the Council of State subsequently felt the need to seek a preliminary ruling under Article 267 TFEU and asked Luxembourg to interpret certain provisions of the Habitats Directive.[43] Like Mr Connolly, the applicant association asked to submit written remarks in response to the Opinion of the Advocate General. Since this request was denied,[44] the applicant association filed an application before the ECtHR and complained that its right to adversarial proceedings according to Article 6 (1) ECHR had been violated.[45] In the following procedure, the ECtHR took a very close look at 'domestic' Union law and examined several provisions thereof, namely the Treaties, the Rules of Procedure of the CJEU and CJEU case law.[46] However, in contrast to the abovementioned *Connolly* case, the ECtHR addressed the substantive question of this case[47] and accepted the CJEU's argument that, according to Article 61 of the Rules of Procedure of the CJEU, the Court may order the reopening of the oral procedure after hearing the Advocate General,[48] in case it still lacked sufficient information or needed to address an argument which had not been dealt with by the parties.[49] In terms of its *Bosphorus* judgment, the Strasbourg Court held that the procedure before the CJEU was therefore accompanied by guarantees which *ensured equivalent* protection

---

[41] *Bosphorus v Ireland* App no 45036/98 (n 2).

[42] See *Connolly v 15 Member States of the European Union* App no 73274/01 (ECtHR, 9 December 2008).

[43] Council Directive 92/43/EEC of 21 May 1992 on the conservation of natural habitats and of wild fauna and flora [1992] OJ L206/7.

[44] See Case C-127/02 *Landelijke Vereniging tot Behoud van de Waddenzee and Nederlandse Vereniging tot Bescherming van Vogels v Staatssecretaris van Landbouw, Natuurbeheer en Visserij* [2004] ECR I-7405, para 20.

[45] See Marco Borraccetti, 'Fair Trial, Due Process and Rights of Defence in the EU Legal Order' in Giacomo Di Federico (ed), *The EU Charter of Fundamental Rights. From Declaration to Binding Document* (Dordrecht, Springer, Netherlands 2011) 106.

[46] For more details, see Jessica Baumann, 'Auf dem Weg zu einem doppelten EMRK-Schutzstandard? Die Fortschreibung der Bosphorus-Rechtsprechung des EGMR im Fall Nederlandse Kokkelvisserij' (2011) 38 *Europäische Grundrechte-Zeitschrift* 1, 6.

[47] See Lock, 'Tightrope' (n 3) 1035.

[48] See *Cooperatieve Producentenorganisatie van de Nederlandse Kokkelvisserij v The Netherlands* App no 13645/05 (ECtHR, 20 January 2009).

[49] See Anthony Arnull, *The European Union and its Court of Justice*, 2nd edn (New York, McGraw-Hill Books, 2006) 18.

of the applicant's rights and thus emphasised that, particularly in light of the Opinion of Advocate General Sharpston in another case,[50] the possibility of reopening the oral proceedings, after the Advocate General has read out his or her opinion, must explicitly be accepted as realistic and not merely theoretical.

The ECtHR was thence, to a certain extent, compelled to take a closer look at Union law in order to determine whether it could apply its *Bosphorus* formula or not. Consequently, due to the equivalent protection of fundamental rights by the Union's legal system, the application was declared inadmissible.[51]

iii. MSS v Belgium and Greece

In this more recent case where Strasbourg referred to European Union law, the ECtHR had to analyse the Dublin II-Regulation[52] which determines the Member State responsible for examining asylum applications lodged on EU territory. The applicant, Mr MSS, an Afghan national, had entered the Union through Greece where he had not applied for asylum. He had then left the country and, after arriving in Belgium, had applied for asylum there. The Belgian authorities had expulsed him from Belgium to Greece on the grounds of Article 3 (1) in conjunction with Article 10 (1) of the Regulation, providing that the Member State first entered shall be responsible for examining the application for asylum. Given the location of Greece on the Union's external frontier, the Greek asylum system was already under particularly heavy pressure and the conditions in Greek detention camps consequently involved a high risk of ill-treatment. The applicant therefore alleged that an expulsion to Greece would constitute a violation of Articles 2 and 3 ECHR. The ECtHR examined the pertinent provisions in the Treaties and, of course, the Dublin II-Regulation itself,[53] and reiterated that the Convention did not prevent the contracting parties from transferring sovereign powers to an international organisation, ie the European Union, for the purposes of cooperation in certain fields of activity. However, according to the *Bosphorus* presumption, the states nevertheless remain responsible under the Convention for all actions and omissions of their bodies under their domestic law or under their international legal obligations. Conversely, a state would be entirely responsible under the Convention for all acts falling outside its strict international legal obligations vis-à-vis other organisations, most notably where it was permitted to exercise discretion.[54] The Court then scrutinised Article 3 (2) of the Regulation, the so-called

---

[50] See Case C-212/06 *Government of the French Community and Walloon Government v Flemish Government* [2008] ECR I-1683, Opinion of AG Sharpston, para 157.

[51] See *Cooperatieve Producentenorganisatie van de Nederlandse Kokkelvisserij v The Netherlands* App no 13645/05 (n 48).

[52] Council Regulation (EC) No 343/2003 of 18 February 2003 establishing the criteria and mechanisms for determining the Member State responsible for examining an asylum application lodged in one of the Member States by a Third-Country National [2003] OJ L50/1.

[53] See *MSS v Belgium and Greece* App no 30696/09 (ECtHR, 21 January 2011) paras 62–82.

[54] See ibid para 338.

'sovereignty clause' which sets forth that, when derogating from the general rules laid down in Article 3 (1) of the Regulation, each Member State may examine an application for asylum lodged in its territory, even in cases in which the Member State was not the one first entered into by the applicant, and may thence become responsible for the application under the criteria laid down in the Regulation. In such a case the state concerned, ie Belgium, will become the Member State responsible for the purposes of the Regulation and take on the obligations that are associated with that responsibility.[55] The Strasbourg Court consequently found a violation of Articles 2 and 3 ECHR by Belgium. In January 2012, the ECtHR confirmed its critical view of the Dublin II-Regulation and decided in another case to suspend the transfer of a Sudanese asylum seeker from Austria to Hungary on the basis of an interim measure.[56] This course of action not only underlines the fact that an increasing number of EU Member States do not comply with their obligations under the Convention,[57] but also supports the argument that the assessment of domestic law is part of Strasbourg's standard procedure.

In the *MSS* case, the analysis of 'domestic' EU law, in this case the Dublin II-Regulation, was essential for the ECtHR to conclude that Belgium could have refrained under the provisions of EU law from transferring the applicant to Greece and that the impugned measure taken by the Belgian authorities did not strictly fall within Belgium's international legal obligations.[58] Moreover, by respecting the discretionary provision of Article 3 (2) of the Regulation and opting in as the Member State responsible for the asylum procedure, Belgium would have also complied with its international obligations under the Convention at the same time.

C. Ramifications for the European Union's Legal Autonomy

These cases plainly show that Strasbourg is occasionally forced to take a closer look at the provisions of national law (and, after accession, also at Union law) in order to be able to determine alleged violations of the Convention; especially in cases where the Convention itself refers to domestic law. But still, examining national law and taking it as a basis for later decisions does not per se interfere with the domestic legal systems of the high contracting parties, let alone the legal autonomy of the European Union. However, this autonomy would only be adversely affected if such decisions by Strasbourg led to an internally binding determination of their content[59]—which would in no way be the case, since,

---

[55] See ibid para 339.
[56] See *Mohammed v Austria* App no 2283/12 (ECtHR, 11 January 2012).
[57] See also Nora Markard, 'Die "Rule 39" des Europäischen Gerichtshofs für Menschenrechte. Vorläufige Maßnahmen des EGMR bei drohenden Abschiebungen' [2012] *Asylmagazin* 3, 5.
[58] See *MSS v Belgium and Greece* App no 30696/09 (n 53) para 340.
[59] See Lock, 'Tightrope' (n 3) 1035.

according to Article 46 (1) ECHR, it is the contracting parties' duty to implement judgments by the ECtHR, as these judgments do not uncover any *self-executive* character.[60] Most importantly, it is an undeniable fact that Strasbourg is not entitled to quash domestic legal acts,[61] which means that it is not authorised to invalidate EU law either.[62] This principle is not explicitly laid down in the Convention, but follows from the wording of Article 41 ECHR, which authorises the Strasbourg Court to afford just satisfaction to the injured party, if national law only allows partial reparation to be made.[63] This consequence also underlines the importance of domestic law and its role in giving full effect to Strasbourg's decisions,[64] particularly by imposing on the respondent party the legal obligation to 'put an end to the breach and make reparation for its consequences in such a way as to restore as far as possible the situation existing before the breach'.[65] In discharging its legal obligations under Article 46 ECHR, the respondent party is additionally allowed a certain measure of discretion[66] in choosing the general or appropriate 'individual measures to be adopted in their domestic legal order to put an end to the violation found by the Court and to redress so far as possible the effects'.[67] Furthermore, Article 46 (1) ECHR does not set out a duty for national courts to disapply those domestic provisions the Strasbourg Court declared to be in violation of the Convention.[68] From an international law perspective, the judgments of the Strasbourg Court therefore address the respondent party as a subject of international law, hereby obliging it to fulfil its obligations under international law, *in concreto* under the Convention, and to implement the decisions of the ECtHR.[69] However, the obligation of a state under public international law does not automatically imply an obligation under domestic law.[70] Thus, the European

---

[60] See Walter Frenz, *Handbuch Europarecht. Band 4: Europäische Grundrechte* (Berlin Heidelberg, Springer, 2009) paras 83ff.

[61] See Jochen Frowein, 'Art 46' in Jochen Frowein and Wolfgang Peukert (eds), *EMRK-Kommentar* (Kehl am Rhein, NP Engel, 2009) para 3; Meyer-Ladewig (n 7) art 46, para 23.

[62] See Kyra Strasser, *Grundrechtsschutz in Europa und der Beitritt der Europäischen Gemeinschaften zur Europäischen Menschenrechtskonvention* (Frankfurt am Main, Peter Lang, 2001) 128; Gerhard Baumgartner, 'EMRK und Gemeinschaftsrecht' [1996] *Zeitschrift für Verwaltung* 319, 330.

[63] See Frowein, 'Art 46' (n 61) para 3.

[64] See Hans-Joachim Cremer, 'Entscheidung und Entscheidungswirkung' in Rainer Grote and Thilo Marauhn (eds), *EMRK/GG: Konkordanzkommentar zum europäischen und deutschen Grundrechtsschutz* (Tübingen, Mohr Siebeck, 2006) 1731ff.

[65] *The Former King of Greece v Greece* App no 25701/94 (ECtHR, 28 November 2002) para 72; see also *Iatridis v Greece* App no 31107/96 (ECtHR, 19 October 2000) para 32.

[66] See Meyer-Ladewig (n 7) art 46, para 25; see generally Yutaka Arai-Takahashi, *The Margin of Appreciation Doctrine and the Principle of Proportionality in the Jurisprudence of the ECHR* (Antwerp, Intersentia, 2002).

[67] *Görgülü v Germany* App no 74969/01 (ECtHR, 26 February 2004) para 64.

[68] See Meyer-Ladewig (n 7) art 46, para 25.

[69] See Kai Ambos, 'Der europäische Gerichtshof für Menschenrechte und die Verfahrensrechte: Waffengleichheit, partizipatorisches Vorverfahren und Art. 6 EMRK' (2003) 115 *Zeitschrift für die Gesamte Strafrechtswissenschaft* 583, 591.

[70] See Frank Czerner, 'Inter partes- versus erga omnes-Wirkung der EGMR-Judikate in den Konventionsstaaten gemäß Art. 46 EMRK' (2008) 46 *Archiv des Völkerrechts* 345, 354; Heiko Sauer, *Jurisdiktionskonflikte in Mehrebenensystemen* (Berlin Heidelberg, Springer, 2008) 263ff.

Union's obligation under international law to abide by Strasbourg's decision does not interfere with its legal autonomy.

More precisely, the Strasbourg Court only decides whether there is a violation of the Convention in a concrete case after all local remedies, ie proceedings under domestic law, have been exhausted. The ECtHR then considers the relevant provisions of domestic law and the practice of the courts in interpreting and applying these provisions.[71] In the *Kemmache v France (No 3)* case, for example, the ECtHR ruled that:

> the words 'in accordance with a procedure prescribed by law' essentially refer back to domestic law; they state the need for compliance with the relevant procedure under that law. However, the domestic law must itself be in conformity with the Convention, including the general principles expressed or implied therein [...].[72]

Beyond that, it held that:

> [a]lthough it is not normally the Court's task to review the observance of domestic law by the national authorities, it is otherwise in relation to matters where, as here, the Convention refers directly back to that law; for, in such matters, disregard of the domestic law entails breach of the Convention, with the consequence that the Court can and should exercise a certain power of review. However, the logic of the system of safeguard established by the Convention sets limits on the scope of this review. *It is in the first place for the national authorities, notably the courts, to interpret and apply the domestic law,* even in those fields where the Convention 'incorporates' the rules of that law: *the national authorities are, in the nature of things, particularly qualified to settle the issues arising in this connection* [...].[73]

In a nutshell, this means firstly that the regime of the ECHR builds upon the principle of subsidiarity found in Article 35 (1) ECHR and secondly that Strasbourg would not, in any case, be the Court to decide on the interpretation and application of domestic law in the first instance.[74] In proceedings relating to EU law, the CJEU would be—speaking in terms of the *Kemmache* case—the 'national' authority which interprets and applies 'domestic' law, ie EU law, and which is particularly qualified to settle the dispute. In the *Bosphorus* case, Strasbourg compared the CJEU's position with the role of national authorities and held that the 'Community's judicial organs are better placed to interpret and apply Community law'.[75] The CJEU would therefore have the chance to rule on the interpretation and application of Union law before a case is submitted to the ECtHR,[76] thereby enabling it to simultaneously exercise its right to declare secondary Union law invalid and thus to preserve the Union's legal autonomy.

---

[71] See Lock, 'Tightrope' (n 3) 1035.
[72] *Kemmache v France (No 3)* App no 17621/91 (ECtHR, 24 November 1994) para 37.
[73] Ibid para 37 (emphasis added).
[74] See Lock, 'Tightrope' (n 3) 1036.
[75] *Bosphorus v Ireland* App no 45036/98 (n 2) para 143.
[76] See ch 11, which analyses the legal issues with respect to the prior involvement of the CJEU in EU-related cases before the ECtHR.

This *modus operandi* is completely consistent with both the Convention system in particular and international law in general, as the rule of exhausting local remedies is a basic principle of international law.[77] It must be the duty of the contracting parties first and foremost to prevent or to put right the violations alleged against them, before those allegations are submitted to the ECtHR. As a result, the European Union is principally exempt from answering for its acts in Strasbourg before the EU authorities, most notably the CJEU, have had the opportunity to remedy alleged violations through the Union's legal system.[78] The primary responsibility for implementing and enforcing the rights guaranteed by the Convention after accession is therefore given to the Union's institutions and the courts of the other contracting parties,[79] rendering the protection machinery of the Court subsidiary to those protection systems. This, in particular, is set forth in Articles 13 and 35 (1) ECHR, ensuring the right to an effective remedy.[80]

Moreover, the decisions of the Strasbourg Court cannot prejudice the interpretation of Union law by the CJEU, since the ECtHR's decision-making powers are limited to two possible results. On the one hand, Strasbourg may consider the interpretative practice of a domestic provision by a domestic court as compliant with the Convention. In this case, the ECtHR would not need to interpret the national law itself but simply take it into account as a fact.[81] As a result, the interpretation of the provision in question and thus the autonomy of EU law would not be affected by Strasbourg's course of action,[82] as it would interpret and apply the Convention after national courts and the CJEU have interpreted and applied their respective laws.[83]

On the other hand, the Strasbourg Court may not regard the practice of the national authorities as sufficient. It might conclude that a specific measure was not prescribed by domestic law,[84] as laid down in Articles 8 to 11 ECHR, or that there was no effective remedy,[85] as ensured by Article 13 ECHR. In cases which resulted from a malfunctioning of legislation, the respondent party would then have to implement general measures[86] in the form of new legislation conforming to the Convention in order to put an end to the violation. But the Strasbourg Court would neither have to perform an original interpretation of national or Union law in such cases nor determine the interpretation of existing domestic

---

[77] See Council of Europe, *Collected edition of the* 'Travaux préparatoires' *of the European Convention on Human Rights*, Vol 3. Committee of Experts (2 February–10 March 1950) (Leiden, Brill, 1976) 38ff, and *Interhandel Case (Switzerland v United States of America)* ICJ Rep [1959] 6, 27.

[78] See *Selmouni v France* App no 25803/94 (ECtHR, 28 July 1999) para 74.

[79] See generally Frenz, *Europäische Grundrechte* (n 60) para 727.

[80] See *Kudla v Poland* App no 30210/96 (ECtHR, 26 October 2000) para 152; *Van Oosterwijck v Belgium* App no 7654/76 (ECtHR, 6 November 1980) para 34.

[81] See *Certain German Interests in Polish Upper Silesia* (n 14) 19.

[82] See Lock, 'Tightrope' (n 3) 1036.

[83] See *Cardot v France* App no 11069/84 (ECtHR, 19 March 1991) para 34.

[84] See *Sunday Times v United Kingdom* App no 6538/74 (n 33) para 49.

[85] See *Airey v Ireland* App no 6289/73 (ECtHR, 9 October 1979) para 19.

[86] See *Broniowski v Poland* App no 31443/96 (ECtHR, 22 June 2004) paras 189 and 193.

law in an internally binding manner. It can thus be concluded that external review of EU legal acts by the ECtHR will not jeopardise the legal autonomy of the Union.[87]

III. EUROPEAN UNION LAW IN VIOLATION OF THE CONVENTION

A. The EU's 'Constitutional' Foundation: Primary Law

i. An Exclusion of Primary Law from Strasbourg's Jurisdiction?

Before and during the actual negotiations on accession, proposals were made that the Union's primary law, comprised of the Treaties, the Charter, Protocols and Annexes, should be excluded from Strasbourg's external review.[88] In particular, the French Government argued that subjecting the EU's primary law to the ECtHR's control would not be without difficulty,[89] especially when considering the statement in *Matthews v United Kingdom* that certain acts of Union law could not be challenged before the CJEU[90] and could therefore not be 'domestically' remedied. This line of reasoning stems from the fact that the Union itself lacks any '*Kompetenz-Kompetenz*' to amend its primary law which is in fact its own constitutional basis. According to the principle of conferral laid down in Article 5 (1) and (2) TEU, the European Union shall act only within the limits of the competences conferred upon it by the Member States in the Treaties. Conversely, those competences not conferred upon the EU in the Treaties remain exclusively with the Member States.[91] Since the Treaties can only be amended by virtue of Article 48 TEU which requires an amending treaty to be concluded and ratified by all the Member States, which remain the 'Masters of the Treaties',[92] the Union should accordingly not be held responsible for the Treaties and potential violations of the Convention within them.[93] According to Strasbourg's findings in the *Matthews* case,[94] this would mean that the European Union will not be responsible for any violations rooted in primary law after accession. In fact, the Member States, as the 'legislators' of the EU's 'constitutional' law, would remain liable

---

[87] See Lock, 'Tightrope' (n 3) 1036.

[88] See ibid 1038.

[89] See Sénat Français, 'Adhésion de l'Union Européenne à la Convention européenne de sauvegarde des droits de l'homme, Communication de M. Robert Badinter sur le mandat de négociation' (E 5248), 25 May 2010, <www.senat.fr/europe/r25052010.html#toc1> accessed 1 November 2012.

[90] See *Matthews v United Kingdom* App no 24833/94 (n 2) para 33.

[91] See Rudolf Geiger, 'Art 5 EUV' in Rudolf Geiger, Daniel-Erasmus Kahn and Markus Kotzur (eds), *EUV/AEUV. Kommentar*, 5th edn (Munich, Beck, 2010) para 3.

[92] See 2 BvE 2/08, 2 BvE 5/08, 2 BvR 1010/08, 2 BvR 1022/08, 2 BvR 1259/08, 2 BvR 182/09 *Lissabon-Urteil* BVerfGE 123, 267 para 231.

[93] See Matthias Köngeter, 'Völkerrechtliche und innerstaatliche Probleme eines Beitritts der Europäischen Union zur EMRK' in Jürgen Bast (ed), *Die Europäische Verfassung—Verfassungen in Europa* (Baden-Baden, Nomos, 2005) 245.

[94] See *Matthews v United Kingdom* App no 24833/94 (n 2) paras 26–35.

for any infringements of the Convention resulting from the application of this specific layer of Union law.

The solution to this legal problem is of principal relevance to the EU's standing to be sued in cases where the EU's primary law is allegedly in violation of the Convention or where Union institutions or domestic courts cannot help infringing the Convention due to peremptory obligations under primary law, thus placing them in inevitable legal conflicts of contradicting provisions. In any case, if the Strasbourg Court held that a provision of primary law was indeed in violation of the Convention, the consequence would be a mandatory Treaty revision by the Member States on the basis of Article 48 TEU.[95]

ii. Luxembourg's Restricted Jurisdiction on Primary Law

Another argument for excluding primary Union law from Strasbourg's review is the fact that the Luxembourg Court itself is not authorised to invalidate primary law. When a domestic court requests a preliminary ruling from the CJEU according to Article 267 TFEU, the CJEU has the jurisdiction to rule on the *interpretation* of the Treaties (lit a) or the *validity* and *interpretation* of acts of the institutions or other organs of the Union (lit b).[96] Due to the restrictive and unambiguous wording of this provision,[97] the CJEU is consequently permitted to interpret primary law on the one hand[98] and to interpret and to rule on the validity of secondary Union law on the other,[99] but not to invalidate or quash any provisions of primary law. Therefore, the CJEU's competence of judicial review is restricted to ruling on the validity of secondary law—questions relating to the validity of primary law as the constitutional basis of all Union acts[100] are beyond Luxembourg's judicial reach.[101]

In the absence of explicit provisions allowing the CJEU to rule on the validity of primary law, one may ask whether the Court might be awarded such a competence via systematic or teleological interpretation. Within the context of the CJEU's establishment as a judicial supervisory body for the then-Community, however, it is very unlikely to assume that the Member States as the 'Masters of

---

[95] See Andreas J Kumin, 'Die Verhandlungsvorbereitungen für den Beitritt der Europäischen Union zur Europäischen Menschenrechtskonvention—Ein Erfahrungsbericht' in Sigmar Stadlmeier (ed), *Von Lissabon zum Raumfahrzeug: Aktuelle Herausforderungen im Völkerrecht. Beiträge zum 35. Österreichischen Völkerrechtstag* (Vienna, NWV, 2011) 75.

[96] Emphasis added.

[97] See Ulrich Ehricke, 'Art 234 EGV' in Rudolf Streinz (ed), *EUV/EGV. Vertrag über die Europäische Union und Vertrag zur Gründung der Europäischen Gemeinschaft* (Munich, Beck, 2003) para 11.

[98] See Bernhard W Wegener, 'Art 267 AEUV' in Christian Calliess and Matthias Ruffert (eds), *EUV/AEUV. Kommentar*, 4th edn (Munich, Beck, 2011) para 8.

[99] See ibid para 9.

[100] See Markus Kotzur, 'Art 267 AEUV' in Rudolf Geiger, Daniel-Erasmus Kahn and Markus Kotzur (eds), *EUV/AEUV. Kommentar*, 5th edn (Munich, Beck, 2010) para 11.

[101] See Patricia Thomy, *Individualrechtsschutz durch das Vorabentscheidungsverfahren* (Baden-Baden, Nomos, 2009) 60; Lukas Bauer, *Der Europäische Gerichtshof als Verfassungsgericht?* (Vienna, Facultas, 2008) 128.

the Treaties' intended to create an organ which would in turn annul or invalidate the international treaties concluded and ratified by the Member States themselves. A teleological approach to this issue is of no avail either—neither Article 19 (1) TEU or any other provision of Union law, for example the action for annulment under Article 263 TFEU, includes a reference or provision that would authorise the Luxembourg Court to rule on the validity of primary law.[102] As a result, the Union's primary law is in no way subject to the CJEU's judicial review.[103]

Regarding the Union's other policy areas, one may also call into question whether *intergovernmental* policies such as the Union's Common Foreign and Security Policy (CFSP) or the Common Security and Defence Policy (CSDP) should be subject to Strasbourg's review to the same extent as the Union's *supranational* policies.[104] According to Article 24 (1) TEU, the CFSP is subject to 'special rules and procedures', which means that these policies are in fact defined and implemented by the European Council and the Council—two Union bodies that are effectively dominated by the Member States. Furthermore, whereas the CFSP shall be put into effect by both the Union's High Representative for Foreign Affairs and Security Policy and the Member States, the competences of the Union's supranational organs such as the Parliament are restricted to consultative tasks (Article 36 TEU). The most distinctive evidence of the CFSP's intergovernmental nature, however, lies in the fact that the CJEU shall not have jurisdiction with respect to these provisions, with minor exceptions regarding the delineation of intergovernmental and supranational competences within the Union's external policies (Article 40 TEU) and reviewing the legality of decisions providing for restrictive measures against natural or legal persons (Article 275 (2) TFEU).[105]

As a result, most of the legal acts and measures enacted within the framework of the CFSP/CSDP are beyond Luxembourg's judicial reach, excluding the CJEU from reviewing these provisions on the grounds of an action for annulment (Article 263 TFEU), infringement proceedings (Articles 258 and 259 TFEU) or a preliminary reference procedure (Article 267 TFEU). This means that in these specific situations the CJEU is incapable of autonomously and independently applying the standards demanded by the Convention and Strasbourg's case law and thus of preventing violations of the Convention on the 'domestic' plane.[106] As a consequence, since the European Union is unable to redress human rights violations rooted in primary law, this specific layer of EU law should arguably not be covered by the ECtHR's jurisdiction.

---

[102] See Bauer (n 101) 128.

[103] See Waltraud Hakenberg and Christine Stix-Hackl, *Handbuch zum Verfahren vor dem Europäischen Gerichtshof* (Vienna, Verlag Österreich, 2005) 66.

[104] See Kumin (n 95) 76.

[105] See Rudolf Geiger, 'Art 24 EUV' in Rudolf Geiger, Daniel-Erasmus Kahn and Markus Kotzur (eds), *EUV/AEUV. Kommentar*, 5th edn (Munich, Beck, 2010) para 4.

[106] See Kumin (n 95) 76.

iii. Again: A Question of Legal Autonomy

In light of the abovementioned arguments, it seems justifiable to exclude the Union's primary law from Strasbourg's review. However, when looking at the bigger picture of European human rights protection, it would be a profound mistake[107] to take this step for the following reasons. There is no other contracting party to the Convention whose constitution or constitutional provisions are excluded from Strasbourg's external review. The mere fact that the Union is not legally able to independently amend its own 'constitution', ie primary law, is not a sufficiently convincing reason to entirely exclude this area of its legal order from the Convention's protection machinery.[108] This is especially true when taking Strasbourg's case law into consideration; it does not make any sense to apply the '*equivalent protection*' of the *Bosphorus* formula[109] and to grant the Union any judicial privileges after accession. In comparable cases in the future, individuals will presumably not apply against Member States merely implementing Union acts that leave them no room for discretion, but directly against the European Union itself for passing legislation in violation of the Convention. Under these circumstances, there is no reason to uphold Strasbourg's *Bosphorus* presumption and to treat the Union and its organs differently from the other contracting parties.[110]

Beyond that, even though the Luxembourg Court is not entitled to annul or invalidate provisions of primary law, it has proved to be perfectly capable of handling legal conflicts between primary law and fundamental rights; namely by interpreting primary law *in conformity* with the Charter[111] and in particular the Convention,[112] for example by applying Article 6 (3) TEU and thereby establishing a '*practical concordance*'[113] between the fundamental right in question and

---

[107] See Françoise Tulkens, *Les aspects institutionnels de l'adhésion de l'Union européenne à la Convention européenne de sauvegarde des droits de l'homme et des libertés fondamentales.* L'audition du 18 mars 2010. European Parliament, Committee on Constitutional Affairs, Hearing on the Institutional Aspects of the European Union's Accession to the European Convention on Human Rights, 18 March 2010, 4.

[108] See Tobias Lock, 'EU Accession to the ECHR: Implications for Judicial Review in Strasbourg' (2010) 35 *European Law Review* 777, 783.

[109] See *Bosphorus v Ireland* App no 45036/98 (n 2) para 156.

[110] See Jean-Paul Jacqué, *L'adhésion à la Convention européenne des droits de l'homme. Note à l'attention de la Commission institutionnelle en vue de l'audition du 18 mars 2010.* European Parliament, Committee on Constitutional Affairs, Hearing on the Institutional Aspects of the European Union's Accession to the European Convention on Human Rights, 18 March 2010, 3.

[111] See Jean-Paul Jacqué, 'L'adhésion de l'Union européenne à la Convention européenne des droits de l'homme et des libertés fondamentales' in Wolfgang Benedek, Florence Benoît-Rohmer, Wolfram Karl and Manfred Nowak (eds), *European Yearbook on Human Rights 2011* (Vienna, NWV, 2011) 150.

[112] See Christiaan Timmermans, *L'adhésion de l'Union Européenne à la Convention européenne des Droits de l'homme,* Audition organisée par la Commission des affaires constitutionnelles du 18 mars 2010. European Parliament, Committee on Constitutional Affairs, Hearing on the Institutional Aspects of the European Union's Accession to the European Convention on Human Rights, 18 March 2010, 5.

[113] See eg, 1 BvR 1257/84 *Herrnburger Bericht* BVerfGE 77, 240, and Conseil Constitutionnel, No. 94-352 DC.

European Union law. One example of such a course of action can be found in the *Defrenne II* judgment, where the CJEU departed from retroactively applying the principle of equal employment conditions and payment for men and women under Article 157 TFEU[114] for the sake of preserving legal certainty.[115] Other examples are the CJEU's decisions in *Schmidberger v Austria*[116] and *Omega Spielhallen*[117] where Luxembourg managed to reconcile the application of a Treaty provision, namely the free movement of goods, with the application of fundamental rights. Even in cases where a conflict between a provision of primary law and a fundamental right could not be solved by interpreting the provisions in question concerning conformity with each other, for example in cases such as *Matthews*, the CJEU would be able to examine and assess this special circumstance. From this moment forth, it is incumbent upon the Member States, the 'Masters of the Treaties', to solve this conflict.[118]

Most significantly, however, the proposal to exclude the Union's primary law from Strasbourg's review was not included in the Draft Accession Agreement. In its Article 2 (2), the Draft Accession Agreement provides for an amendment to Article 57 (1) ECHR which will allow the EU to only

> make a reservation in respect of any particular provision of the Convention to the extent that *any law of the European Union* then in force is not in conformity with the provision. *Reservations of a general character shall not be permitted under this Article.*[119]

The question remains whether this article allows for a general reservation excluding the EU's primary law from the ECtHR's review. The *Explanatory Report to the Draft Accession Agreement* states that the aforementioned

> expression 'law of the European Union' is meant to cover the Treaty on European Union, the Treaty on the Functioning of the European Union, or any other provision having the same legal value pursuant to those instruments (the EU 'primary law') [...].[120]

This, of course, would speak in favour of such a reservation on behalf of the Union.

The Explanatory Report, however, also stresses that the EU should accede to the Convention on an equal footing with the other high contracting parties and that any reservation should be consistent with the relevant rules of international law.[121] In order to be on an equal footing with the other contracting parties to the Convention, the European Union should consequently not be allowed to make a reservation which

---

[114] Then art 119 of the EEC Treaty.
[115] See Case 43/75 *Defrenne II* [1976] ECR 455, para 74.
[116] See Case C-112/00 *Schmidberger v Austria* [2003] ECR I-5659, para 77.
[117] See Case C-36/02 *Omega Spielhallen* [2004] ECR I-9609, para 33.
[118] See Timmermans (n 112) 5.
[119] Council of Europe, 'Steering Committee for Human Rights—Report to the Committee of Ministers on the Elaboration of Legal Instruments for the Accession of the European Union to the European Convention on Human Rights' CDDH(2011)009, 7 (emphasis added).
[120] Ibid 20, para 28.
[121] Ibid 19, para 27.

would allow the exclusion of its own 'constitutional law'; this would be tantamount to a privilege similar to that granted by the Strasbourg Court in the *Bosphorus* case which, after accession, cannot be reasonably endorsed. Moreover, if any reservation by the EU should be consistent with the relevant rules of international law, Article 2 (2) of the Draft Accession Agreement (the second sentence in particular) would make a reservation with respect to the entire primary law of the Union impermissible,[122] especially when taking into account the identical Article 19 lit b VCLT and Article 19 lit b of the Vienna Convention on the Law of Treaties between States and International Organizations or Between International Organizations (VCLTIO) which lay down that a state or an international organisation may, when acceding to a treaty, formulate a reservation unless the treaty provides that only specified reservations, not including the reservation in question, may be made. This view is supported by the International Court of Justice's (ICJ) judgment in the *Aegean Sea Continental Shelf (Greece v Turkey)* case where the ICJ presumed that

> [w]hen a multilateral treaty [...] provides in advance for the making only of particular, designated categories of reservations, there is clearly a high probability, if not an actual presumption, that reservations made in terms used in the treaty are intended to relate to the corresponding categories in the treaty.[123]

From this presumption, it can be deduced *e contrario* that a reservation to exclude primary EU law in its entirety from Strasbourg's jurisdiction would be an unauthorised reservation within the meaning of Article 19 lit b VCLT,[124] especially given the wording of Article 2 (2) of the Draft Accession Agreement.

Alternatively, one may also argue that according to Article 19 lit c VCLT and Article 19 lit c VCLTIO, a reservation made to exclude the entire 'constitutional' layer of a contracting party's legal order is incompatible with the object and purpose of the Convention. In Strasbourg's own words:

> the existence of such a restrictive clause governing reservations suggests that States could not qualify their acceptance of the optional clauses thereby effectively excluding areas of their law and practice within their 'jurisdiction' from supervision by the Convention institutions. The inequality between Contracting States which the permissibility of such qualified acceptances might create would, moreover, run counter to the aim, as expressed in the Preamble to the Convention, to achieve greater unity in the maintenance and further realisation of human rights.[125]

The exact legal effects of a reservation impermissible under Article 19 lit c VCLT are controversial[126]—if the European Union formulated an impermissible

---

[122] But see Lock, 'Tightrope' (n 3) 1038, who argues that this provision would make it possible to make a reservation as regards primary law.

[123] See *Aegean Sea Continental Shelf (Greece v Turkey)* ICJ Rep [1978] 3, 55.

[124] See Christian Walter, 'Art 19' in Oliver Dörr and Kirsten Schmalenbach (eds), *Vienna Convention on the Law of Treaties. A Commentary* (Berlin Heidelberg, Springer, 2012) para 65.

[125] See *Loizidou v Turkey (Preliminary Objections)* App no 15318/89 (ECtHR, 23 March 1995) para 77.

[126] See Christian Walter, 'Art 19' (n 124) para 114.

reservation, one could argue, on the one hand, that both reservation and ratification were invalid and that the EU did not accede to the Convention at all;[127] or, on the other hand, that the impermissible reservation was to be severed from the ratification, which would lead to the EU's accession without a valid reservation. Given Strasbourg's case law in this respect,[128] an impermissible reservation formulated by the EU would have led to the severability of the impermissible reservation from the ratification, thus leaving the latter intact.[129] In this case, the European Union would accede to the Convention without the benefit of a permissible and thus valid reservation.

In addition, Article 3 of the Draft Accession Agreement, covering the procedural details of the so-called co-respondent mechanism,[130] suggests that such exclusion by means of a reservation is not intended.[131] Article 3 (3) states that when an application is directed against the Union, a Member State may become a co-respondent to the proceedings,[132]

> if it appears that such allegation calls into question the compatibility with the Convention rights at issue of a provision of the Treaty on European Union, the Treaty on the Functioning of the European Union or any other provision having the same legal value [...].[133]

This explicit mention of the European Union's primary law as a legal basis for future applications makes it clear that an exclusion of this specific kind of law is not part of the Draft Accession Agreement.[134]

In conclusion, the most convincing and—in the context of this book—most important argument against the exclusion of the EU's primary law from Strasbourg's review is the potential danger to the autonomy of EU law. Such exclusion could even prove counter-productive since it may compel the ECtHR to delineate violations of the Convention found in primary law (as it did in the *Matthews* case) from violations rooted in secondary law or other executive or judicial acts. This assessment would require the Strasbourg Court to interpret EU law and to make decisions on the basis of the Treaties, thereby forcing it to identify which entity—either the European Union or one or more Member States—is in fact responsible for an alleged violation. This *modus operandi* would endanger the Union's legal autonomy and of course Luxembourg's jurisdictional monopoly as

---

[127] See *Reservations to the Convention on the Prevention and Punishment of the Crime of Genocide* (Advisory Opinion) ICJ Rep [1951] 15, 21.
[128] See *Belilos v Switzerland* App no 10328/83 (ECtHR, 29 April 1988) para 60.
[129] See Christian Walter, 'Art 19' (n 124) para 117.
[130] For more details on the co-respondent mechanism, see ch 9.
[131] See Lock, 'Tightrope' (n 3) 1038.
[132] See Kumin (n 95) 75, and Olivier De Schutter, *L'adhésion de l'Union européenne à la Convention européenne des droits de l'homme: feuille de route de la négociation*. European Parliament, Committee on Constitutional Affairs, Hearing on the Institutional Aspects of the European Union's Accession to the European Convention on Human Rights, 10 April 2010, 12.
[133] CDDH-UE(2011)009 (n 119) 7 (emphasis added).
[134] See Lock, 'Tightrope' (n 3) 1038.

the ECtHR would have to interpret the Treaties in a binding fashion. Moreover, the Union should not be held responsible for its own primary law when its Member States are already accountable for Union acts which they merely implemented without having any margin of discretion. Correspondingly, it is not possible to exclude the Union's primary law from the ECtHR's review.[135]

B. European Union Legislation: Secondary Law

i. Responsibility for Secondary Law

In contrast to its 'constitutional law' (ie primary law), secondary Union law is not created or enacted by the Member States, but by the European Union itself. As set forth in Article 289 TFEU in conjunction with Article 294 TFEU, it rests with the Union organs, namely the Commission, the Council and the Parliament, to pass legislation and legal acts as enumerated in Article 288 TFEU and thus to guarantee its subsequent conformity with fundamental rights in general and the Convention in particular. As aforementioned,[136] after accession both primary law and the Convention will rank above secondary law, which makes them the yardstick for the lawfulness of the latter.[137] Eventually, in cases where the Convention has been violated, the CJEU may be called upon to remedy these violations by interpreting secondary law in conformity with primary law, including the Charter,[138] or by annulling the legal acts in question. There is consequently no reason to argue for an exclusion of the Union's secondary law from Strasbourg's review as it was stipulated with respect to primary law. Furthermore, in the *NS v Secretary of State for the Home Department and ME v Refugee Applications Commissioner* case,[139] the Luxembourg Court proved that it is fully capable of interpreting EU law in accordance with the Convention. In this judgment, the CJEU gave full effect to Strasbourg's *MSS* judgment and held that the Member States may not transfer asylum seekers to the Member State responsible for examining the asylum application under the Dublin II-Regulation, if systemic deficiencies in that Member State amount to real risks of inhuman or degrading treatment within the meaning

---

[135] See ibid 1038, and Lock, 'Implications for Judicial Review' (n 108) 783.

[136] See ch 7.

[137] See Matthias Ruffert, 'Art 288 AEUV' in Christian Calliess and Matthias Ruffert (eds), *EUV/AEUV. Kommentar*, 4th edn (Munich, Beck, 2011) paras 8–9; Markus Kotzur, 'Art 288 AEUV' in Rudolf Geiger, Daniel-Erasmus Kahn and Markus Kotzur (eds), *EUV/AEUV. Kommentar*, 5th edn (Munich, Beck, 2010) para 4; Walter Frenz, *Handbuch Europarecht. Band 5: Wirkungen und Rechtsschutz* (Berlin Heidelberg, Springer, 2010) paras 813ff.

[138] See the CJEU's settled case law in eg, Case 218/82 *Commission v Council (Lomé Convention)* [1983] ECR 4063, para 15; Joined Cases 201/85 and 202/85 *Klensch v Secrétaire d'État* [1986] ECR 3477, para 21; Case C-314/89 *Rauh v Hauptzollamt* [1991] ECR I-1647, para 17; Case C-98/91 *Herbrink v Minister van Landbouw* [1994] ECR I-223, para 9; Case C-1/02 *Borgmann v Hauptzollamt* [2004] ECR I-3219, para 30.

[139] See Joined Cases C-411/10 and C-493/10 *NS v Secretary of State for the Home Department and ME v Refugee Applications Commissioner* [2011] ECR I-0000.

of Article 3 ECHR or Article 4 ChFR.[140] In other words, Luxembourg veers towards a legal status *post-accession*, where it will review the Member States' obligation under the Convention in accordance with the subsidiarity principle of Article 35 (1) ECHR, which affords the European Union the opportunity of preventing or redressing alleged violations before those allegations are submitted to Strasbourg.[141] Thus, the CJEU ensured that, after accession, it would have the opportunity to deal with cases involving alleged fundamental rights violations and to remedy them before any application reaches Strasbourg. One might also argue that through this course of action, the Luxembourg Court also assumes full responsibility for interpreting and applying secondary law in accordance with the Convention.

ii. Luxembourg's Exclusive Jurisdiction over Secondary Law

The legal question of utmost importance is, however, whether a finding of the Strasbourg Court that a specific piece of secondary law has violated the Convention would infringe the autonomy of Union law.[142] According to Article 19 (1) TEU and its settled case law, the Luxembourg Court has the exclusive jurisdiction, or virtually the monopoly, on annulling or declaring EU law invalid in order to ensure that Union law is applied uniformly. This requirement is especially crucial in cases where the validity of an EU act is called into question and divergences between the domestic courts regarding the validity of Union acts would thus jeopardise the very unity of the Union's legal order.[143] Since the entry into force of the Lisbon Treaty, the CJEU has shown increased readiness to annul EU legislation,[144] to declare national acts inapplicable[145] or to heed the ECtHR's opinion[146] when it found them in conflict with fundamental rights protected by the Charter or the Convention. Some cases also demonstrate how the Luxembourg Court discharges its obligations under Article 52 (3) ChFR regarding a harmonious and coherent interpretation of the Charter with the Convention.[147]

As a result, any declaration on the invalidity of European Union law by a domestic or international court would be incompatible with the autonomy of the Union's legal order.[148] Nevertheless, the Strasbourg Court does not decide on the validity of domestic law in practice. Even in cases where the phrase 'in accordance

---

[140] See ibid, para 94.
[141] See *Selmouni v France* App no 25803/94 (n 78) para 74.
[142] See Lock, 'Tightrope' (n 3) 1036.
[143] See Case 314/85 *Foto-Frost v Hauptzollamt Lübeck-Ost* [1987] ECR 4199, para 15.
[144] See eg, Joined Cases C-92/09 and C-93/09 *Schecke und Eifert* [2010] ECR I-11063, paras 89ff.
[145] See eg, Case C-555/07 *Kücükdeveci* [2010] ECR I-365, paras 52 and 54.
[146] See eg, Joined Cases C-411/10 and C-493/10 *NS v Secretary of State for the Home Department and ME and Others v Refugee Applications Commissioner* (n 139).
[147] See Wolfgang Benedek, 'EU Action on Human and Fundamental Rights in 2010' in Wolfgang Benedek, Florence Benoît-Rohmer, Wolfram Karl and Manfred Nowak (eds), *European Yearbook on Human Rights 2011* (Vienna, NWV, 2011) 100f.
[148] See Lock, 'Tightrope' (n 3) 1036.

with the law'[149] requires that the impugned measure or legal act should have some basis in national law,

> [t]he Court reiterates that it is primarily for the national authorities, notably the courts, to interpret and apply domestic law. More specifically, it is not for the Court to rule on the validity of national laws in the hierarchy of domestic legislation.[150]

Strasbourg's decisions do not have any '*self executing*' or direct effect within the legal orders of the Convention's contracting parties,[151] since Article 46 (1) ECHR states that '[t]he High Contracting Parties undertake to abide by the final judgment of the Court in any case to which they are parties'. Strasbourg is not authorised to quash domestic legal acts, thus making its judgments declaratory in nature and only binding under the obligations imposed by the contracting parties on themselves under international law.[152] But even though the legal impact of these judgments, *in concreto* the parties' obligation to either put an end to violations of the Convention or to pass conforming legislation,[153] solely depends on the parties and their respective legal orders, the CJEU's own case law in *Opinion 1/91* insinuates that the decisions of an international court, ie the ECtHR, might become directly applicable within the Union's legal order:

> Where, however, an international agreement provides for its own system of courts, including a court with jurisdiction to settle disputes between the Contracting Parties to the agreement, and, as a result, to interpret its provisions, *the decisions of that court will be binding on the Community institutions, including the Court of Justice*. Those decisions *will also be binding* in the event that the Court of Justice is called upon to rule, by way of preliminary ruling or in a direct action, on the interpretation of the international agreement, *in so far as that agreement is an integral part of the Community legal order*.[154]

Of course, this does not imply that a piece of secondary legislation considered to be in violation of the Convention would be automatically invalid at the precise moment of Strasbourg's judgment. The quoted paragraph from *Opinion 1/91* rather demonstrates that an applicant would still need to file an action for annulment under Article 263 (4) TFEU in order to receive a declaration of invalidity by the CJEU. This declaration, however, would be bound by the precedent judgment of the Strasbourg Court. The Union's other institutions could amend or annul the provisions found to be in violation of the Convention by passing conforming legislation. Moreover, they would be obliged to do so pursuant to their obligations under international law in general and Article 46 ECHR in particular. This

---

[149] For example in arts 8–11 ECHR.

[150] *W v The Netherlands* App no 20689/08 (ECtHR, 20 January 2009); see also *Kruslin v France* App no 11801/85 (ECtHR, 24 April 1990) para 29.

[151] See Lock, 'Tightrope' (n 3) 1037.

[152] See Frowein, 'Art 46' (n 61) para 3.

[153] See Meyer-Ladewig (n 7) art 46, paras 22ff.

[154] See Opinion 1/91 *EEA I (Draft agreement between the Community, on the one hand, and the countries of the European Free Trade Association, on the other, relating to the creation of the European Economic Area)* [1991] ECR I-6079, para 39 (emphasis added).

step, however, cannot lead to incompatibility with or risks to the Union's legal autonomy, since the reason for the aforementioned receptiveness towards the decisions of the Strasbourg Court can be found in the Union's own 'constitutional' foundations as interpreted by Luxembourg. This means that this quasi-monistic open-mindedness towards international law would not be imposed upon the EU by accession or the Accession Agreement, but by the Union's own legal order.[155]

iii. A Convincing Argument

This leads to a further and even more convincing argument that a finding by Strasbourg that certain Union actions or omissions are in violation of the Convention would not jeopardise the autonomy of EU law. When Article 6 (2) TEU, which provides the legal basis of accession, was drafted by the Member States, it was their primary intention that by acceding to the Convention, the Union and its institutions would subject themselves to the jurisdiction of the Strasbourg Court in order to close existing lacunae in the field of fundamental rights protection and to enable an external court to review the EU's legal acts.[156] Therefore, since the legal autonomy of the Union stems from the Treaties and the CJEU's interpretation of them, explicit provisions in the Treaties cannot be in contradiction to it.[157]

IV. INTERIM CONCLUSIONS

This chapter has examined how Strasbourg's external review of European Union law may interfere with the autonomy of the EU's legal order. The preceding analysis clarified that such a violation of autonomy is principally interrelated with two core questions—on the one hand it must be asked whether the ECtHR would interpret Union law in a binding manner, and, on the other hand, whether a judgment by Strasbourg, finding that legal acts of the Union violated the Convention, would be compatible with the concept of the EU's legal autonomy. Regarding the first question, this chapter made it clear that the ECtHR primarily regards the national authorities and courts as the competent institutions to interpret and apply domestic law. It is therefore the ECtHR's constitutive task to interpret and apply the Convention, not national law. Sometimes, however, Strasbourg must also take domestic law into account in order to scrutinise whether there has been a violation of the Convention. This means that after accession the ECtHR will also take a closer look at Union law in certain proceedings. This is particularly the case when an applicant alleges that a provision was violated which refers back to domestic law, for instance Articles 5, 8–11 and 13 ECHR. Of course, according to

---

[155] See Lock, 'Tightrope' (n 3) 1037.
[156] See eg, European Convention, 'Final Report of Working Group II' CONV 354/02, WG II 16, 11f.
[157] See Lock, 'Tightrope' (n 3) 1037.

the CJEU's own decision in *Opinion 1/91*, an international court like the ECtHR interpreting Union law could seriously endanger the EU's legal autonomy.

Nevertheless, the ECtHR does not interpret domestic law in an internally binding manner, since, pursuant to their obligations under international law, it is up to the contracting parties to implement Strasbourg's decisions. According to Article 41 ECHR in conjunction with Article 46 (1) ECHR, these decisions are not directly applicable and, most importantly, they cannot take precedence over or even quash domestic legal acts, since the contracting parties' obligations under international law do not automatically entail an obligation under domestic law. Moreover, by virtue of the subsidiarity principle set forth in Article 35 (1) ECHR, Strasbourg would not, in any case, decide on the interpretation and application of domestic law in the first instance—in EU cases, the CJEU would be the relevant authority to interpret and apply Union law in the first place and thus settle the dispute. The principal responsibility for implementing and enforcing the rights enshrined by the Convention after accession therefore lies with the Union's institutions and the courts of the other contracting parties, before Strasbourg can be called upon. As a consequence, the interpretation of the provisions in question and thence the Union's legal autonomy would not be affected by Strasbourg's decisions, since it would only interpret and apply the Convention *after* the CJEU has interpreted and applied European Union law. It is therefore apparent that an external review of EU acts by the ECtHR does in no way endanger the legal autonomy of the Union.

In regards to the second question, an external review by the Strasbourg Court will cover all of the European Union's activities as well as its legal acts. There have been arguments to exclude the Union's primary law from Strasbourg's scope of control, especially because the Union itself is not entitled to amend its own 'constitutional' basis and the Luxembourg Court's jurisdiction is restricted in some areas of primary law (eg the CFSP). This means that the EU and its institutions are not able to remedy any violations of the Convention found in primary law, neither through legislative nor through judicial avenues. However, it would be a major mistake to exclude the EU's primary law from the ECtHR's external review for the following reasons. Firstly, such exclusion is tantamount to a disproportionate privilege granted solely to the EU, but not to the other contracting parties. However, it is futile to uphold the *Bosphorus* presumption in the future, as individuals in comparable cases will no longer apply against Member States implementing Union acts that leave them no room for discretion, but instead will apply directly against the Union itself for passing legislation in violation of the Convention. Secondly, the Luxembourg Court is highly qualified and perfectly capable of reconciling legal conflicts between primary law and fundamental rights, by interpreting the former in accordance with the EU's own Charter of Fundamental Rights on the one hand and the Convention on the other. The CJEU will therefore also be able to handle conflicts between those provisions that are beyond its judicial reach and fundamental rights. After that, it would be up to the Member States to solve this conflict by amending the Union's primary law.

Lastly, and most importantly, the exclusion of primary law was not included in the Draft Accession Agreement. Article 3 of the Draft Accession Agreement governs the details of the co-respondent mechanism and explicitly mentions the Union's primary law as a legal basis for future applications, thus making it clear that such exclusion is not intended. Yet, the most convincing argument against exclusion is the fact that it might force the Strasbourg Court to delineate violations of the Convention found in primary law from those found in secondary law. This would necessitate the ECtHR to interpret EU law in a binding manner and to decide upon the division of competences between the EU itself and the Member States. This course of action would in fact jeopardise the autonomy of the European Union's legal order and must thence be avoided.

9

Individual Applications after Accession: Introducing the Co-Respondent Mechanism

I. INDIVIDUAL APPLICATIONS: CORE OF THE CONVENTION

WHEN CONSIDERING THE state-centred Westphalian approach of international law over the past centuries, the individual complaint procedure under Article 34 of the European Convention on Human Rights (ECHR) is undoubtedly the most innovative element the Convention has introduced in order to take action against human rights violations on a regional plane. Within an international legal order based on nation-states and inter-state relations, an individual right to sue states for human rights violations was a ground-breaking and pioneering step. After abolishing the European Commission on Human Rights via Protocol No 11 to the Convention,[1] applicants have been able to bring their cases directly before the Strasbourg Court without any restrictions whatsoever.[2] Today, Article 34 ECHR sets forth that

> [t]he Court may receive applications from any person, non-governmental organisation or group of individuals claiming to be the victim of a violation by one of the High Contracting Parties of the rights set forth in the Convention or the protocols thereto. The High Contracting Parties undertake not to hinder in any way the effective exercise of this right.

This instrument of individual applications gave the Convention system its specific distinction and invigorated it with the efficacy[3] necessary for a functioning regime of human rights protection. The Convention is thus sometimes referred to as a 'European Fundamental Rights Constitution',[4] while the Strasbourg

---

[1] Protocol No 11 to the Convention for the Protection of Human Rights and Fundamental Freedoms, E.T.S. 155, entered into force on 1 November 1998.

[2] See Andrew Drzemczewski, 'The European Human Rights Convention: Protocol No. 11— Entry into Force and First Year of Application' 226 <www.gddc.pt/actividade-editorial/pdfs-publicacoes/7980-a.pdf> accessed 1 November 2012.

[3] See Jens Meyer-Ladewig, *Europäische Menschenrechtskonvention. Handkommentar*, 3rd edn (Baden-Baden, Nomos, 2011) art 34, para 1.

[4] See eg, Christian Walter, 'Die Europäische Menschenrechtskonvention als Konstitutionalisierungsprozess' (1999) 59 *Zeitschrift für ausländisches öffentliches Recht und Völkerrecht* 961, 962f.

Court coined it the 'constitutional instrument of European Public Order'.[5] But even though the Convention also envisages a more 'traditional' instrument of international dispute settlement, namely inter-state complaints under Article 33 ECHR, this instrument is rarely used, mainly due to its negative political ramifications among the European states.[6] The majority of complaints before the Strasbourg Court consequently consist of individual applications.[7] This fact emphasises the significance of this special procedure in contrast to inter-state complaints. Due to this particular and important position of individual applications within the Convention's regime of human rights protection, the chapter at hand therefore thoroughly examines how the individual complaint procedure will be legally organised after accession and what perils the embedding of new procedures and mechanisms may pose for the autonomy of European Union law.

II. IDENTIFYING THE RIGHT RESPONDENT AFTER ACCESSION

A. The Problem Located: Who is the Appropriate Addressee?

From the outset of discussions in 1979, the main argument in favour of the European Union's accession to the Convention has been that this step would close the existing gaps and lacunae in the field of European human rights protection. Primarily, accession would enable individuals to directly apply against legal acts by the Union and restore the legal position in which individuals found themselves before the Member States transferred certain competences to the Union.[8] The most convincing reason for accession is, nonetheless, the simplification of remedies for individuals. In the current situation before accession, an applicant must follow intricate procedures and should, advantageously, possess profound legal knowledge of European Union law and the law of the ECHR. According to Article 35 (1) ECHR, applicants must exhaust domestic and EU remedies, after which they must lodge an application before the Strasbourg Court, however, not against the actual perpetrator of the contentious act, which is the Union, but against a Member

---

[5] See *Loizidou v Turkey (Preliminary Objections)* App no 15318/89 (ECtHR, 23 March 1995) para 75. See also Carl Lebeck, 'The European Court of Human Rights on the Relation between ECHR and EC-Law: The Limits of Constitutionalisation of Public International Law' (2007) 62 *Zeitschrift für Öffentliches Recht* 195, 202f.

[6] So far, only a couple of inter-state complaints have been brought before the Strasbourg Court since its establishment in 1959. See European Court of Human Rights, 'Inter-State Applications' <www .echr.coe.int/NR/rdonlyres/5D5BA416-1FE0-4414-95A1-AD6C1D77CB90/0/Requ%C3%AAtes_inter%C3%A9tatiques_EN.pdf> accessed 1 November 2012.

[7] See Tobias Lock, 'EU Accession to the ECHR: Implications for Judicial Review in Strasbourg' (2010) 35 *European Law Review* 777, 779.

[8] See Commission of the European Communities, 'Memorandum on the Accession of the European Communities to the Convention for the Protection of Human Rights and Fundamental Freedoms' Bulletin Supplement 2/79, COM (79) 210 final, paras 14 and 15.

State that merely implemented Union law.[9] This situation will not change until the European Union accedes to the Convention, as Strasbourg currently has no jurisdiction *ratione materiae* over the EU. As a result, the European Court of Human Rights (ECtHR) in its current situation cannot convict the Union of any alleged fundamental rights violations,[10] but rather the Member State in question. Yet, in this case, there is no guarantee that the applicant's situation will be remedied, as such a remedy depends on the European Union and its institutions.[11] An example of such an action can be found in the aforementioned judgment of the Strasbourg Court in *Matthews v United Kingdom*[12] and particularly in the consecutive infringement proceedings between Spain and the United Kingdom before the Court of Justice of the European Union (CJEU).[13]

Beyond that, according to Strasbourg's *Bosphorus* formula, the applicant must at present delve into subtle legal investigations in order to find out whether the fundamental rights protection provided for by the Union is equivalent to that guaranteed by the provisions of the Convention.[14] Certainly, there are several unknown factors in these analyses which may prevent the applicant from lodging an application. This would hardly be conducive to ensuring an effective judicial human rights protection in Europe. Lastly, it is rather illogical and even unfair for a Member State to be accused of a legal act for which it is not responsible, whilst the EU, which is in fact the polity responsible, cannot be party to the proceedings.[15]

In all past cases in which EU law was involved in proceedings before the ECtHR—most notably the cases *CFTD*,[16] *M & Co*,[17] *Cantoni*,[18] *Matthews*[19] and *Bosphorus v Ireland*[20]—the results would have been different if, at that point of time, the Union had already acceded to the Convention.

---

[9] See Florence Benoît-Rohmer in Council of Europe—Parliamentary Assembly, *The Accession of the European Union/European Community to the European Convention on Human Rights*, Doc 11533 (Committee on Legal Affairs and Human Rights) 19.

[10] See Paul Gragl, 'Accession Revisited: Will Fundamental Rights Protection Trump the European Union's Legal Autonomy' in Wolfgang Benedek, Florence Benoît-Rohmer, Wolfram Karl and Manfred Nowak (eds), *European Yearbook on Human Rights 2011* (Vienna, NWV, 2011) 165.

[11] See Benoît-Rohmer, 'Accession' (n 9) 19.

[12] See *Matthews v United Kingdom* App no 24833/94 (ECtHR, 18 February 1999).

[13] See Case C-145/04 *Spain v United Kingdom* [2006] ECR I-7917, para 13.

[14] See *Bosphorus v Ireland* App no 45036/98 (ECtHR, 30 June 2005) para 155.

[15] See Benoît-Rohmer, 'Accession' (n 9) 20; Christiaan Timmermans, *L'adhésion de l'Union Européenne à la Convention européenne des Droits de l'homme*, Audition organisée par la Commission des affaires constitutionnelles du 18 mars 2010. European Parliament, Committee on Constitutional Affairs, Hearing on the Institutional Aspects of the European Union's Accession to the European Convention on Human Rights, 18 March 2010, 3.

[16] See *Confédération Française Démocratique du Travail (CFDT) v The European Communities*, alternatively: *Their Member States a) jointly and b) severally* App no 8030/77 (Commission Decision, 10 July 1978).

[17] See *M & Co v Federal Republic of Germany* App no 13258/87 (Commission Decision, 9 February 1990).

[18] See *Cantoni v France* App no 17862/91 (ECtHR, 15 November 1996.

[19] See *Matthews v United Kingdom* App no 24833/94 (n 12).

[20] See ch 5 for more details on these cases.

Likewise, accession will have an enormous impact on the outcomes of similar cases in the future, since the European Union will be subject to Strasbourg's personal jurisdiction after accession, which means that individual claimants are entitled to file direct applications against the EU. It will therefore be of utmost importance for an individual applicant to know which entity they should apply against and whom to hold responsible in Strasbourg for violations originating in EU law. Individuals are then confronted with the fact that the Member States usually implement Union law, thus making the applicant believe that the Member State acted on its own. In such a situation, the applicant will most likely hold the Member State in question responsible even when this Member State enjoyed no discretion in implementing Union law, such as in *Bosphorus*. But even after accession, an applicant without profound legal education will be in a similar situation and might not be aware of the complexities of Union law and the exact implementation rules of EU law. Thus, the applicant may lodge an application against the Member State responsible, since they had only ever been in contact with the Member State's authorities and not with the Union.[21] This, however, will constitute the majority of cases, since individuals seldom engage in a direct legal relationship with the Union and its organs, with the notable exceptions of entrepreneurs under competition or antitrust law,[22] for example.

It seems that the drafters of the failed Constitutional Treaty[23] anticipated these difficulties[24] within the context of accession and therefore arranged for a provision that would address this issue. This provision was adopted verbatim by the Treaty of Lisbon in Article 1 lit b of Protocol No 8 to the Treaties and reads that

[t]he agreement relating to the accession of the Union to the European Convention on the Protection of Human Rights and Fundamental Freedoms [...] provided for in Article 6 (2) of the Treaty on European Union shall make provision for preserving the specific characteristics of the Union and Union law, in particular with regard to [...] the mechanisms necessary to ensure that proceedings by non-Member States and individual applications *are correctly addressed to Member States and/or the Union as appropriate.*[25]

This provision is without doubt a declaration of intention with high legal value; however, it merely states that individual applications under Article 34 ECHR should be correctly addressed to the appropriate respondent, which may be a Member State and/or the Union. In other words, it should guarantee that all proceedings

---

[21] See Tobias Lock, 'Walking on a Tightrope: The Draft Accession Agreement and the Autonomy of the EU Legal Order' (2011) 48 *Common Market Law Review* 1025, 1038f.

[22] See arts 101 and 102 TFEU.

[23] In the Treaty Establishing a Constitution for Europe, the provision in question was laid down in Protocol No 32 relating to Article I-9 (2) of the Constitution on the Accession of the Union to the European Convention on the Protection of Human Rights and Fundamental Freedoms [2004] OJ C310/378.

[24] See Lock, 'Implications for Judicial Review' (n 7) 780.

[25] Protocol No 8 Relating to Article 6 (2) of the Treaty on European Union on the Accession of the Union to the European Convention on the Protection of Human Rights and Fundamental Freedoms (emphasis added).

are made against the entity actually responsible for the alleged violation of the Convention.[26] This provision in its succinct form, however, remains silent on the precise legal method of identifying this appropriate addressee. The establishment of such an identification mechanism is exceedingly vital for the proper functioning of individual applications after accession, since the responsibility of Member States and the Union is frequently intertwined[27] and the indirect implementation of EU law by the Member States represents the exception rather than the rule.[28] This specific characteristic of European Union law must necessarily be taken into consideration in order to prevent lacunae in the future protection regime. The application could be, for instance, declared inadmissible if the applicant did not designate the correct respondent—which would force the applicant to start proceedings all over again, depending on whether this option would still be available to the applicant at all.[29]

One may hence ask whether the Member State should remain responsible alone or alongside the European Union, and whether the Union should be the sole respondent in such a situation, as the alleged violations of the Convention in both cases stem from acts by the Union's organs. Nevertheless, it is beyond dispute that two basic assumptions can be agreed upon beforehand. Firstly, any solution must take into account the applicant's difficult situation and guarantee an effective protection of their human rights; and secondly, this solution must preserve the autonomy of the Union's legal order as well.[30]

B. The Applicant: An Average Person without Legal Education

Given the abovementioned legal entanglement of the Member States and the European Union, the main concern after accession is that the applicant may be left in a sort of legal limbo in cases where it is difficult to distinguish which entity is actually responsible for an alleged violation of the Convention. This situation is all the more aggravated by the fact that pursuant to Article 47 (1) lit c Rules of Court, the designation of the respondent party rests with the applicant, but usually, as the heading of this section suggests,[31] they do not have the legal education

---

[26] See Florence Benoît-Rohmer, 'Completing the Transformation: Values and Fundamental Rights in the Treaty of Lisbon' in Wolfgang Benedek, Florence Benoît-Rohmer, Wolfram Karl and Manfred Nowak (eds), *European Yearbook on Human Rights 2010* (Vienna, NWV, 2010) 61.

[27] See Jean-Paul Jacqué, 'The Accession of the European Union to the European Convention on Human Rights and Fundamental Freedoms' (2011) 48 *Common Market Law Review* 995, 1014.

[28] See Thomas von Danwitz, *Europäisches Verwaltungsrecht* (Berlin Heidelberg, Springer, 2008) 315ff.

[29] See Jacqué, 'Accession' (n 27) 1014.

[30] See Lock, 'Implications for Judicial Review' (n 7) 780.

[31] The reader is therefore advised not to interpret the heading as condescending or derogatory; quite the contrary, it is intended to convey the fact that any citizen without legal education might end up in such a complex and difficult situation.

necessary to identify the responsible party in the first place.[32] In addition, as laid down in Article 36 (1) Rules of the Court, representation by a counsel is not mandatory in submitting applications to the Strasbourg Court,[33] which would leave the applicant on their own. When considering cases such as *Bosphorus*, an applicant without legal education will most likely not be able to distinguish between the responsibilities of the Member State and that of the EU, especially when the Member State is left no discretion in implementing Union law. Either way, in the eyes of the applicant, only the respective Member States' authorities act vis-à-vis the applicant, resulting in an alleged violation of the Convention. To make a proper assessment as to whether the legal act in question stems from an obligation under Union law or an obligation under national law, it is necessary for the applicant to conduct extensive legal research into the background of the case, which is almost impossible without a lawyer. As a result, it would be best to introduce a mechanism which would not require the applicant to distinguish between Member State action under its obligations of Union law and action in other situations.[34]

C. Designating the Right Respondent: Risks to the Union's Autonomy

Given this complex situation, mostly due to the intricate division of competences between the Union and the Member States, it is accordingly of utmost importance to guarantee that applications are lodged against the party actually responsible for an alleged violation. This decision, however, is not easy in cases where Member States are granted a margin of discretion in implementing Union law. In these cases, it must be determined whether or not an alleged violation took place within this scope of discretion granted to the Member States[35]—such as in the aforementioned *MSS v Belgium and Greece* case.[36]

At this point, the question remains who or what institution should determine whether the alleged violation stems from domestic law or from legal acts performed within the Member States' margin of discretion, respectively, or whether it is rooted in European Union law. Sometimes these lines of division are not clearly defined, mostly due to the fact that firstly, the rules on attribution under international law are not clear either, and secondly, that the distinction between the states' strict international obligations and the states' discretion within the scope of these obligations is very vague. It was therefore argued that in cases where the EU and a Member State are subject to the same complaint and the line of division is

---

[32] See Lock, 'Implications for Judicial Review' (n 7) 780.

[33] See Wolfgang Peukert, 'Art 34' in Jochen Frowein and Wolfgang Peukert (eds), *EMRK-Kommentar* (Kehl am Rhein, NP Engel, 2009) para 66.

[34] See Lock, 'Implications for Judicial Review' (n 7) 780f.

[35] See Benoît-Rohmer, 'Accession' (n 9) 20.

[36] See *MSS v Belgium and Greece* App no 30696/09 (ECtHR, 21 January 2011), analysed in more detail in ch 8.

not clear, the Strasbourg Court should decide whether the state and/or the Union shall be held responsible for the alleged violation of the Convention.[37]

Prima facie, it seems obvious to leave such a determination to the ECtHR which will, at the end of the day, decide on the case and the violation. This decision, however, would fatally undermine the Union's legal autonomy, in particular when taking into account Article 1 of Protocol No 8 to the Treaties which highlights that the '*specific characteristics of the Union and Union law*'[38] must be preserved. If Strasbourg indeed had the last say on the determination of responsibility, this would be tantamount to allowing it to decide on the allocation and internal distribution of competences between the Union and its Member States. This situation would not be acceptable, as it would be entirely incompatible with the autonomy of Union law,[39] especially in light of Article 19 (1) of the Treaty on European Union (TEU) and *Opinion 1/91*.[40] The rules regarding internal distribution of competences were created by the drafters of the Treaties, and consequently, any external interference or review on these rules would be a grave encroachment on the autonomy of EU law.[41] It is thence evident that no external institution, such as the Strasbourg Court, must decide on this matter. Yet, this approach does not answer the last question, namely who or what organ should decide in lieu thereof and on what legal grounds this decision can be based upon.

D. Solutions Based on the Present Convention System

Before the Draft Accession Agreement was negotiated and agreed upon in 2011, there had been various solutions to solve the problem of determining the responsibility shared between the European Union and its Member States. All these approaches were based on the Convention system prior to accession. Although these proposals have been rejected and thence seem outdated in light of the solution found in Article 3 of the Draft Accession Agreement, they are briefly presented in order to contrast them with the solution eventually adopted.

---

[37] See Jonas Christoffersen, *Institutional Aspects of the EU's Accession to the ECHR*. European Parliament, Committee on Constitutional Affairs, Hearing on the Institutional Aspects of the European Union's Accession to the European Convention on Human Rights, 18 March 2010, 7.

[38] Emphasis added.

[39] See Jean-Paul Jacqué, *L'adhésion à la Convention européenne des droits de l'homme. Note à l'attention de la Commission institutionnelle en vue de l'audition du 18 mars 2010.* European Parliament, Committee on Constitutional Affairs, Hearing on the Institutional Aspects of the European Union's Accession to the European Convention on Human Rights, 18 March 2010, 2; Benoît-Rohmer, 'Accession' (n 9) 20, and Lock, 'Implications for Judicial Review' (n 7) 782f.

[40] See Opinion 1/91 *EEA I (Draft agreement between the Community, on the one hand, and the countries of the European Free Trade Association, on the other, relating to the creation of the European Economic Area)* [1991] ECR I-6079.

[41] See Jacqué, 'Accession' (n 27) 1012f.

i. Joint Liability

The first solution to preserve the Union's legal autonomy is a joint liability model which is often included in mixed agreements,[42] wherein the EU and the Member States 'are jointly liable unless the provisions of the agreement point to the opposite'.[43] When disregarding the simple fact that the final Accession Agreement does not qualify as a mixed agreement, such a model of liability would have the advantage that both the Union and the Member State in question would be bound by Strasbourg's decision finding a violation of the Convention. Moreover, they would both be obligated to remove this violation. But most notably, there would be no need for the Strasbourg Court to scrutinise Union law and to delineate the competences between the Member States and the Union,[44] as the internal rules of the EU would appear to be irrelevant. The main focus in this context is rather on the stability of treaties entered into in good faith under Article 27 of the Vienna Convention on the Law of Treaties (VCLT)[45] and thence the generally accepted principle of international law that the provisions of national law cannot prevail over those of the international treaty in question.[46]

The substantial disadvantage in this model, however, lies in the fact that in cases which are entirely unrelated to Union law, an applicant would file claims against both the Member State and the EU. In such cases, the European Union has a legitimate interest in not being involved as a party to such a dispute, since any conviction by Strasbourg entails a condemnation of that party's legal order, which failed to remove the violation itself in the first place.[47] It is therefore both legally and politically unacceptable for the Union to be held responsible for violations committed by a Member State in a field of law that has no connection to Union law whatsoever.

ii. Joint and Several Liability

As an alternative, the introduction of a joint and several liability model was suggested. This model allows the applicant to file an application against either the

---

[42] For more details, see Martin Björklund, 'Responsibility in the EC for Mixed Agreements—Should Non-Member Parties Care?' (2001) 70 *Nordic Journal of International Law* 373, 373f.

[43] Case C-316/91 *European Parliament v Council (Lomé Convention)* [1994] ECR I-625, Opinion of AG Jacobs, para 69.

[44] See Tobias Lock, 'Accession of the EU to the ECHR: Who Would be Responsible in Strasbourg?' Working Paper Series, 3 October 2010, 18 <http://papers.ssrn.com/sol3/papers.cfm?abstract_id=1685785> accessed 1 November 2012.

[45] See Björklund (n 42) 388.

[46] See *Alabama Claims Arbritration (United States v United Kingdom)*, Decision and Award Made by the Tribunal of Arbitration constituted by virtue of the First Article of the Treaty Concluded at Washington the 8th of May, 1871, between the United States of America and Her Majesty the Queen of the United Kingdom of Great Britain and Ireland, in John Bassett Moore (ed), *History and Digest of the International Arbitrations to which the United States has been a Party—Vol. 1* (Washington, 1898) 653ff.; *The Greco-Bulgarian Communities* (Advisory Opinion) PCIJ Series B No 17, 32.

[47] See Lock, 'Responsible in Strasbourg' (n 44) 18.

Member State or the European Union or against both at the same time regardless of what entity is actually responsible for the alleged violation. This would avoid any external interference and thence any danger to the autonomy of EU law by leaving the attribution of liability to an internal organ, namely the CJEU.[48] A similar solution is provided for in Article 6 (2) of Annex IX to the United Nations Convention on the Law of the Sea (UNCLOS),[49] which reads:

> Any State Party may request an international organisation or its member States which are States Parties for information *as to who has responsibility in respect of any specific matter.* The organisation and the member States concerned shall provide this information. Failure to provide this information within a reasonable time or the provision of contradictory information shall result in *joint and several liability.*[50]

Under such a legal regime adapted to the specific characteristics of the Convention system, the Strasbourg Court could request the European Union or its Member States to deliver relevant information on the internal allocation of competences. Unless these two parties comply with this request, both entities could then be held responsible for the alleged violation. Moreover, the EU could issue a declaration concerning the division of competences between the Union itself and its Member States, as it has already done with regard to matters governed by UNCLOS:

> With regard to the provisions on maritime transport, safety of shipping and the prevention of marine pollution [...] the Community has exclusive competence only to the extent that such provisions of the Convention or legal instruments adopted in implementation thereof affect common rules established by the Community. When Community rules exist but are not affected, in particular in cases of Community provisions establishing only minimum standards, the Member States have competence, without prejudice to the competence of the Community to act in this field. Otherwise competence rests with the Members States.[51]

Most certainly, from the applicant's point of view, this solution would be very effective and straightforward, since the chosen respondent would be fully responsible for the alleged violation of the Convention. The negative aspects, though, outweigh the benefits since in cases which have no connection to Union law at all, the joint and several liability model must also envisage a solution politically acceptable to the EU which ensures that such cases are not directed against the Union. As a consequence, there would have to be some substantial and concrete criterion that would enable the applicant to determine whether

---

[48] See ibid 18f.

[49] See Gragl, 'Accession Revisited' (n 10) 167; Benoît-Rohmer, 'Completing the Transformation' (n 26) 61f; Jacqué, *L'adhésion à la Convention européenne* (n 39) 2.

[50] Emphasis added.

[51] Declaration concerning the competence of the European Community with regard to matters governed by the United Nations Convention on the Law of the Sea of 10 December 1982 and the Agreement of 28 July 1994 relating to the implementation of Part XI of the Convention [1998] OJ L179/130. For more details, see Natalie Klein, *Dispute Settlement in the UN Convention on the Law of the Sea* (Cambridge, Cambridge University Press, 2005) 49ff.

to file the complaint against both the Union and the Member State or solely against the Member State.[52] But even in cases where the Union has issued a declaration concerning the internal distribution of competences between the EU and its Member States, such a criterion remains vague and difficult to grasp for an applicant without any legal education and legal counsel. Even though the Treaty of Lisbon has gone some way towards greater clarity in terms of the division of competences, the difficulty in determining this allocation of powers between different levels of government is an endemic issue within any non-unitary polity.[53] This is especially true of the individual applicant wishing to understand the division between EU competence and that of the Member States, who would again be compelled to engage in subtle legal research on the specific Treaty provisions governing this issue, namely Article 5 TEU and Articles 2–6 TFEU),[54] in order to correctly determine the respondent actually responsible for the alleged violation. Accordingly, the abovementioned problems would arise in the simple joint liability model as well as the joint and several liability model, if they were adopted within the course of accession.[55]

iii. The Needs of the Applicant

In order to avoid huge legal burdens for the applicant, it was suggested that the individual alleging human rights violations should file the application against the party which acted vis-à-vis the applicant *in concreto*. Where the European Union's organs or institutions have acted—most importantly in competition law or anti-trust law cases—the applicant must direct its complaint against the Union; where a Member State has acted by implementing EU law or, more generally, under any obligation stemming from EU law, the application must be directly lodged against the Member State in question,[56] although this Member State was obliged to act under Union law and the actual violation is caused by a provision of EU law. In contrast to the models presented above, the benefits of this solution are strikingly clear, since it would make it easy to both identify the correct addressee of an application and thus the right domestic remedy. This would allow domestic courts to request a preliminary ruling from the CJEU, pursuant to Article 267 TFEU, or, in cases where there is no further judicial remedy, oblige them to do so. Luxembourg would then have the opportunity to determine whether the alleged violation of the Convention is rooted in European Union law or not.[57] Beyond that, this solution would, on the one hand, preserve the Union's legal autonomy,

---

[52]   See Lock, 'Responsible in Strasbourg' (n 44) 19.
[53]   See Paul Craig, *The Lisbon Treaty. Law, Politics, and Treaty Reform* (Oxford, Oxford University Press, 2010) 187; Ernest Young, 'Protecting Member State Autonomy in the European Union: Some Cautionary Tales from American Federalism' (2002) 77 *New York University Law Review* 1612, 1712.
[54]   See Craig, *The Lisbon Treaty* (n 53) 188.
[55]   See Lock, 'Responsible in Strasbourg' (n 44) 19.
[56]   See Lock, 'Implications for Judicial Review' (n 7) 784.
[57]   See Gragl, 'Accession Revisited' (n 10) 168.

since Strasbourg would not be put into the awkward position of deciding on the internal distribution of competences between the EU and the Member States, and on the other hand, avoid the disadvantages of the aforementioned models.[58] This solution was also suggested by the European Parliament's Committee on Constitutional Affairs albeit with a notable difference:

> [A]ny application by a natural or legal person concerning an act or failure to act by an institution or body of the Union should be directed solely against the latter and that similarly any application concerning a measure by means of which a Member State implements the law of the Union should be directed solely against the Member State, without prejudice to the principle that, *where there might be any doubt about the way in which responsibility is shared, an application may be brought simultaneously against the Union and the Member State.*[59]

The last clause, highlighted in italics in order to underline the differences from previous models, indicates that an application may be filed against both the European Union and the Member State in all cases where the delineation of the shared responsibility of the parties involved is doubtful. This model, however, would neither yield any additional value nor unburden the applicant. On the contrary, this proposal could prove counterproductive and make matters worse as it is uncertain what domestic remedies must be exhausted under Article 35 (1) ECHR[60] which remains silent on this matter.[61] In this context, one must ask whether the wording 'exhaustion of all local remedies' requires the applicant to exhaust (a) the remedies before the courts of the Member State in question; or (b) those before the CJEU; or (c) those before both judicial systems. Due to the lack of legal clarity and potential further complications for the applicant, this solution must also be rejected.

E. The Co-Respondent Model

i. Preliminary Remarks on the Co-Respondent Model

In light of these abovementioned proposals and their respective downsides, another approach was taken in the form of the so-called 'co-respondent model'. It was first mentioned by the Steering Committee on Human Rights in 2002

---

[58]   See Lock, 'Implications for Judicial Review' (n 7) 784.

[59]   European Parliament, 'Resolution on the Institutional Aspects of Accession by the European Union to the European Convention for the Protection of Human Rights and Fundamental Freedoms' P7_TA-PROV(2010)0184, para 9 (emphasis added).

[60]   See Lock, 'Responsible in Strasbourg' (n 44) 22.

[61]   Art 35 (1) ECHR itself does not contain any concrete or detailed presets for the exhaustion of local remedies. In its settled case law, the ECtHR has further clarified the meaning of this provision by holding that domestic remedies must be available to the applicant and effective within the meaning of art 13 ECHR (see eg, *Kudla v Poland* App no 30210/96 (ECtHR, 26 October 2000) para 158). Due to obvious reasons, however, the ECtHR could not decide so far on the purport of art 35 (1) ECHR within the context of the European Union's accession to the Convention.

which recommended that the EU should be given ample opportunity to defend itself in cases where Union law was at stake before the Strasbourg Court.[62] Such an opportunity could be achieved by introducing a mechanism under which the Union could be invited or even obliged to join the case as a co-respondent, alongside the Member State against which the application was initially lodged.[63] This proposal was also seized by the European Parliament's Committee on Constitutional Affairs which considered it appropriate for the Union to intervene as a co-respondent in cases brought before the Strasbourg Court raising issues with regard to EU law. Vice versa, any Member State may be permitted to intervene as co-respondent in cases brought against the Union subject to the same conditions.[64]

The negotiators eventually agreed that such a mechanism was indispensable for the future functioning of the Convention system and set up the necessary provisions for its future implementation. Article 3 of the Draft Accession Agreement will therefore introduce the co-respondent mechanism by amending Article 36 ECHR, especially through changing the heading of this very article[65] and adding the following paragraph to this provision:

> The European Union or a member State of the European Union may become a co-respondent to proceedings by decision of the Court in the circumstances set out in the Agreement on the Accession of the European Union to the Convention for the Protection of Human Rights and Fundamental Freedoms. A co-respondent is a party to the case. The admissibility of an application shall be assessed without regard to the participation of a co-respondent in the proceedings.[66]

This solution will implement a system of 'shared responsibility' which will enable the Union or a Member State to join the proceedings as co-respondent alongside the original addressee of the application. If Strasbourg finds a violation of the Convention, the co-respondent will be equally bound by its judgment, and it is then exclusively for the Union to determine the actual perpetrator of the violation.[67] Thereby, it becomes futile for the Member States to make excuses by arguing that their hands were tied due to their obligations under Union law. In cases such as *Matthews*, giving the EU the opportunity to join the proceedings as

---

[62] See Steering Committee for Human Rights (CDDH), 'Technical and Legal Issues of a Possible EC/EU Accession to the European Convention on Human Rights' CDDH(2002)010 Addendum 2, para 57.

[63] See ibid, para 59.

[64] See European Parliament, 'Resolution on the Institutional Aspects of the Accession (n 59) para 12.

[65] Now reading as: 'Third Party Intervention and Co-Respondent Mechanism'.

[66] Art 3 (1) lit b of the Draft Accession Agreement; Council of Europe, 'Steering Committee for Human Rights—Report to the Committee of Ministers on the Elaboration of Legal Instruments for the Accession of the European Union to the European Convention on Human Rights' CDDH-UE(2011)009, 7.

[67] See Jacqué, 'Accession' (n 27) 1014.

co-respondent would at least involve the party which could actually redress the alleged human rights violation.[68]

The introduction of the co-respondent mechanism was considered essential by the negotiators in order to accommodate the particular situation of the European Union as a non-state entity with an autonomous legal system to the Convention system.[69] Furthermore, this mechanism also takes into account that there are significant differences between the situation of 'multiple respondents' and of 'co-respondents', since the latter would be specific to the Union's legal system and characterised by the involvement of two or more respondents whose legal orders are intertwined and thus not entirely autonomous from each other as far as shared responsibility for a legal act is concerned.[70] Beyond that, the co-respondent mechanism will exonerate individual applicants from venturing into the legal sophistries of the intricate division of competences between the Union and the Member States, since it will merely require that the domestic remedies of either the Union *or* the Member State be exhausted.[71] The main reason for introducing this mechanism, nonetheless, is to avoid lacunae in the participation, accountability and enforceability of the Convention system, which fully corresponds to the very purpose of accession and serves the proper administration of justice and the protection of human rights.[72] For example, there are currently two situations in which the practical need for adjustments emerge—on the one hand, in cases where the applicant has lodged a complaint against the wrong entity (for instance against a Member State instead of the Union), the application would currently be dismissed due to the lack of jurisdiction *ratione personae*; and on the other hand, in cases where an applicant has failed to lodge a complaint against the relevant entity (for instance only against a Member State, but not against the Union), the party not subject to the application will go free without any conviction by the Strasbourg Court.[73] By introducing the co-respondent mechanism via the final Accession Agreement, such cumbersome situations will expectably cease to arise for individual applicants in the future.

Most importantly in the context of this book, however, the negotiators opine that the introduction of the co-respondent mechanism is entirely in line with art 1 lit b of Protocol No 8 to the Treaties, which ensures that 'individual applications are correctly addressed to Member States and/or the

---

[68] See Noreen O'Meara, '"A More Secure Europe of Rights?" The European Court of Human Rights, the Court of Justice of the European Union and EU Accession to the ECHR' (2011) 12 *German Law Journal* 1813, 1820.

[69] See CDDH-UE(2011)009 (n 66) 20, para 32.

[70] See Council of Europe, '3rd Working Meeting of the CDDH Informal Working Group on the Accession of the European Union to the European Convention on Human Rights (CDDH-UE) with the European Commission' Meeting Report, CDDH-UE(2010)14, para 9.

[71] See CDDH-UE(2011)009 (n 66) 20f, para 34, and 22f paras 46–50.

[72] See ibid 20, para 33.

[73] See Christoffersen (n 37) 7.

Union, as appropriate', and thus with the autonomy of European Union law.[74] Nevertheless, at this point it is appropriate to exercise due care and some scepticism vis-à-vis the co-respondent mechanism and its potential ramifications for the legal system of the European Union. One may ask whether this new mechanism does in fact comply with the prerequisites which the accession of a supranational polity such as the Union necessitates or whether it will be as effective as expected with regard to the protection of the individual's human rights. The subsequent sections consequently analyse whether this new mechanism is indeed compatible with the Union's legal autonomy, firstly by illustrating the relevant provisions of the Draft Accession Agreement (in particular Art 3 of the Agreement), and secondly, by scrutinising the advantages and possible risks of this mechanism to the autonomy of the Union's legal order and the situation of the individual applicant.

ii. Differences between Third Party Interventions and the Co-Respondent Mechanism

There are substantial differences between third party interventions as set forth in Article 36 ECHR and the co-respondent mechanism. Whereas the third party intervener is, a fortiori of Article 44 (3) lit a Rules of Court, not considered as a party to the proceedings,[75] a co-respondent will become a full party to the case and will accordingly be bound by Strasbourg's judgment.[76] However, in cases where an application is directed against a contracting party which is not an EU Member State but associated to parts of the Union's legal order through separate international agreements (for instance, the Schengen Agreement,[77] the Dublin Convention,[78] the EEA Agreement[79] or any association agreement with a third country), a third party intervention may be the most appropriate and sometimes the only way to involve the European Union in the proceedings. The co-respondent mechanism should thence not be regarded as precluding the Union from partaking in proceedings as a third party intervener, where the essential preconditions for becoming a full party as a co-respondent are not met.[80]

---

[74] See CDDH-UE(2011)009 (n 66) 21, para 35.
[75] See David Harris, Michael O'Boyle, Ed Bates and Carla Buckley (eds), *Law of the European Convention on Human Rights*, 2nd edn, Oxford, Oxford University Press, 2009) 855.
[76] See CDDH-UE(2011)009 (n 66) 21, para 39.
[77] Iceland, Norway and Switzerland.
[78] Although the Dublin Convention has effectively been replaced by the Dublin II-Regulation for European Union Member States, the Convention's scope of application has been extended to the non-member states Iceland, Norway and Switzerland.
[79] Iceland, Liechtenstein and Norway.
[80] See CDDH-UE(2011)009 (n 66) 21, para 40.

iii. Situations in Which the Co-Respondent Mechanism May Be Applied

a. The Legal Framework of the Accession Agreement

First, it must be determined in which situations or scenarios the co-respondent mechanism may be applied after accession. It is therefore worthwhile to take a closer look at the provisions in Article 3 of the Draft Accession Agreement:

Article 3 (2) governs the scenario in which the European Union joins the proceedings as a co-respondent against a Member State as the original respondent:

> Where an application is *directed against one or more member States of the European Union, the European Union may become a co-respondent* to the proceedings in respect of an alleged violation notified by the Court if it appears that such allegation calls into question the compatibility with the Convention rights at issue of a provision of European Union law, notably where that violation could have been avoided only by disregarding an obligation under European Union law.[81]

Article 3 (3) of the Draft Accession Agreement, on the other hand, regulates the conditions under which the EU Member States may join the proceedings as co-respondents against the Union as the original respondent:

> Where an application is *directed against the European Union, the European Union member States may become co-respondents* to the proceedings in respect of an alleged violation notified by the Court if it appears that such allegation calls into question the compatibility with the Convention rights at issue of a provision of the Treaty on European Union, the Treaty on the Functioning of the European Union or any other provision having the same legal value pursuant to those instruments, notably where that violation could have been avoided only by disregarding an obligation under those instruments.[82]

Lastly, Article 3 (4) of the Draft Accession Agreement sets forth that applications may also be directed against both a Member State and the Union:

> Where an application is directed against and notified to *both the European Union and one or more of its member States*, the status of any respondent may be changed to that of a correspondent if the conditions in paragraph 2 or paragraph 3 of this Article are met.[83]

As a consequence, there are basically two ways in which the co-respondent mechanism may be triggered—firstly, the mechanism may be invoked in cases where either the European Union or one or more Member states are designated as the original respondents and a co-respondent later joins the proceedings (art 3 (2) and (3) of the Draft Accession Agreement). In such a scenario, the mechanism would allow the Union to become a co-respondent to disputes in which the claimant has filed an application against only one or more Member States. Moreover, the mechanism would equally allow the Member States to become co-respondents

---

[81] Emphasis added.
[82] Emphasis added.
[83] Emphasis added.

to cases where the individual has filed an application solely against the Union.[84] Secondly, the mechanism may be applied in situations in which *both* the Union and one or more Member States are held responsible for the same alleged violation right from the initiation of the proceedings (Art 3 (4) of the Accession Agreement). This means that the mechanism will be initiated in cases where the EU or the respective Member State was not the party that actually acted or omitted to act with regard to the applicant, but was instead the party which provided the legal basis for the said act or omission. In such a situation, the co-respondent mechanism would prevent the dismissal of an application in respect of that party on the grounds that this application was incompatible *ratione personae*.[85] The co-respondent mechanism will, however, not be applied in cases in which the individual applicant alleges different violations of the Convention and files separate complaints against both the Union and a Member State.[86]

b. Designating the Co-Respondent

At this point, one must ask how the co-respondent mechanism should be initiated or, more precisely, by whom the co-respondent should be designated. In the past, three options have been put forward to answer these questions. This decision could be either made by the Strasbourg Court; or by the original respondent; or alternatively, by the future co-respondent.[87]

Regarding the first option, the Steering Committee concluded that it would be difficult to give Strasbourg the power to designate a co-respondent *proprio motu* and to oblige the Union to join the proceedings as a co-respondent, as this step might prejudge some legal questions in relation to the respective responsibilities of the contracting parties[88] and thus jeopardise the Union's legal autonomy. It is thence obvious that Strasbourg must not be given the right to designate the co-respondent.

With respect to the second approach, there are various arguments for giving the original respondent the right to designate the European Union as the co-respondent. In most cases, the original respondent will be a Member State implementing Union law. Therefore, the Member States will be initially responsible for responding to complaints alleging violations of the Convention.[89] This scenario could nonetheless lead to some undesirable results for the Member States. For example, due to qualified majority voting in the Council according to Article 16 (3)

---

[84] See CDDH-UE(2011)009 (n 66) 21, para 36.
[85] See ibid 21, para 37.
[86] See ibid 21, para 38.
[87] See Lock, 'Implications for Judicial Review' (n 7) 786.
[88] See CDDH(2002)010 Addendum 2 (n 62) para 59.
[89] See Lock, 'Implications for Judicial Review' (n 7) 786.

TEU[90] and Article 238 (2) and (3) TFEU,[91] a situation may arise in which a Member State is held responsible before the Strasbourg Court for EU legislation allegedly in violation of the Convention which was not voted for by the Member State in question. Accordingly, there is a policy argument that in cases where the respondent Member State is falsely accused and it therefore presumes that the alleged violation could indeed stem from Union law, it should consequently be authorised to nominate the Union as its co-respondent. The concerns that this mechanism is susceptible to abuse by the Member States, ie a designation of the Union by the respective Member State in cases which bear no relation to EU law, are clearly unfounded, since such a course of action would most likely violate the Member State's duty of loyalty,[92] pursuant to Article 4 (3) TEU, and subsequently trigger infringement procedures. It would be contrary to the nature of the Union's legal system to allow Member States to introduce or retain measures which are capable of prejudicing the practical effectiveness of EU law[93] or which are likely to interfere with the internal functioning of the Union's institutions.[94] By and large, such a course of action by a Member State, which would virtually thwart the effectiveness and enforcement of Union law, would be tantamount to abusive litigation,[95] which is of course incompatible with Article 4 (3) TEU.

In the context of the third option, the question is whether the EU should be entitled to designate itself as a co-respondent in such cases. One may argue that such cases could also be covered by a third party intervention under Article 36 ECHR. This, however, will prove detrimental to non-EU citizens filing an application before the Strasbourg Court, as no right to a third party intervention exists in such cases. Accordingly, there is good reason to enable the European Union to nominate itself as a co-respondent alongside a Member State.[96]

The drafters of the Accession Agreement apparently took into account these preliminary considerations and included a provision stating that '[a] High

[90]   See Christian Calliess, 'Art 16 EUV' in Christian Calliess and Matthias Ruffert (eds), *EUV/AEUV. Kommentar*, 4th edn (Munich, Beck, 2011) paras 10ff; Christina Ziegenhorn, 'Art 16 EUV' in Eberhard Grabitz, Meinhard Hilf and Martin Nettesheim (eds), *Das Recht der Europäischen Union. Band I* (Munich, Beck, 2010) paras 38ff.

[91]   See Matthias Ruffert, 'Art 238 AEUV' in Christian Calliess and Matthias Ruffert (eds), *EUV/ AEUV. Kommentar*, 4th edn (Munich, Beck, 2011) para 4; Markus Kotzur, 'Art 238 AEUV' in Rudolf Geiger, Daniel-Erasmus Kahn and Markus Kotzur (eds), *EUV/AEUV. Kommentar*, 5th edn (Munich, Beck, 2010) paras 15–22.

[92]   See Lock, 'Implications for Judicial Review' (n 7) 786.

[93]   See Case 14/68 *Wilhelm v Bundeskartellamt* [1969] ECR 1, para 6.

[94]   See Case 208/80 *Lord Bruce of Donington* [1981] ECR 2205, para 14; Case 230/81 *Luxembourg v European Parliament* [1983] ECR 255, para 37; Case C-293/03 *Gregorio My v Office national des pensions* [2004] ECR I-12013, paras 48–49.

[95]   See Armin von Bogdandy and Stephan Schill, 'Art 4 EUV' in Christian Calliess and Matthias Ruffert (eds), *EUV/AEUV. Kommentar*, 4th edn (Munich, Beck, 2011) para 65.

[96]   See Lock, 'Implications for Judicial Review' (n 7) 786f.

Contracting Party shall become a co-respondent *only at its own request* and *by decision of the Court*.'[97]

This means that there are two basic definitional elements involved in designating a co-respondent. The first element is that, in cases that have been directed against either one (or more) Member States *or* the Union, the potential co-respondent can only assume this role *at its own request*, if it considers that the criteria set out in Article 3 (2)[98] or (3)[99] of the Draft Accession Agreement are fulfilled. In addition, any such request should be reasoned and well-founded.[100] In cases that have been directed against *both* the European Union and one (or more) Member States in respect of an alleged violation, either of these respondents might, if it considers that the criteria set out in Article 3(2) or (3) of the Draft Accession Agreement are fulfilled, *ask* the Strasbourg Court to change its status into that of a co-respondent.[101]

The second element, on the other hand, is that *the Strasbourg Court ultimately decides* whether a high contracting party may partake in the proceedings as a co-respondent, if the application is lodged against either the European Union or a Member State,[102] or whether its status is changed into that of a co-respondent, if the application is directed against both the Union and a Member State. In the latter case, the high contracting party becoming a co-respondent would be the party not actually responsible for the act or omission which allegedly caused the violation, but only for the legal basis of such an act or omission.[103] As a consequence, a request by the said high contracting party is a necessary precondition for it to become co-respondent.[104] Such a decision by Strasbourg will most certainly prompt the sceptics to fear for the autonomy of the Union's legal order, as the ECtHR might interpret EU law in a binding manner when deciding on the admission of a potential co-respondent. This, however, will not be the case. The Strasbourg Court must limit itself in these decisions to simply assessing whether the reasons stated by the high contracting parties requesting to join the proceedings as co-respondents are plausible in light of the criteria set out in Article 3 (2) and (3) of the Draft Accession Agreement, as appropriate, and, most notably, without prejudice to its assessment of the merits of the case.[105]

This means that, pursuant to the wording of the first sentence of Article 3 (5) of the Draft Accession Agreement and the Explanatory Report, a high contracting

---

[97] First sentence of art 3 (5) of the Draft Accession Agreement; CDDH-UE(2011)009 (n 66) 8 (emphasis added).

[98] Art 3 (2) is applicable in cases where the application is directed against one (or more) Member State(s) of the EU, but not against the EU itself.

[99] Art 3 (3) is applicable in cases where the application is directed against the EU, but not against one (or more) of its Member States.

[100] See CDDH-UE(2011)009 (n 66) 22, para 46.

[101] See ibid 23, para 49.

[102] See ibid 23, para 47.

[103] See ibid 23, para 49.

[104] See ibid 23, paras 47 and 49.

[105] See ibid 23, paras 48 and 50.

party can join the proceedings as a co-respondent only at its own request. In other words, no contracting party to the Convention can be compelled against its will to become a co-respondent. But even though it is argued in the Explanatory Report that the voluntary nature of the co-respondent mechanism reflects the fact that the original application was directed against another party and not against the potential co-respondent and that no high contracting party can therefore be forced to become a party to a concrete case where it was not named in the original application,[106] it is not entirely clear why a potential co-respondent should not be forced to join the proceedings. It is also beyond doubt that in cases where an application is directed against both the Union and a Member State and both respondents are therefore parties to the case from the outset of the proceedings, they have no choice but to participate in these proceedings in Strasbourg. Most convincingly, such a situation will not differ when these parties are joined as co-respondents by a decision of the Strasbourg Court in a later stage of the proceedings.[107] This is nonetheless a weakness of the Draft Accession Agreement which may easily be overcome by introducing an obligation on the European Union to join proceedings as co-respondent when the compatibility of EU law with a Convention right is called into question.[108]

c. Preliminary Analysis

The preceding description of the legal framework governing the co-respondent mechanism demonstrates that, prima facie, this new mechanism does not pose any serious risks to the autonomy of European Union law. This is especially true of the provision that Strasbourg's decision to join the Union and a Member State as co-respondents is limited to assessing whether the reasons stated by the high contracting parties are plausible in light of specific criteria (which will be described and examined below), as it does not necessitate the ECtHR to determine the division of competences between the Union and the Member States and to interpret the Treaties in a binding fashion.[109] In fact, the primary intent of introducing a co-respondent mechanism was, firstly, to avoid situations in which Strasbourg would be compelled to decide upon the internal distribution of powers between the Union and the Member States,[110] which is in effect an internal matter of Union law,[111] and secondly, to avoid situations in which a Member State would claim

---

[106] See ibid 23, para 47.

[107] See Lock, 'Tightrope' (n 21) 1044f.

[108] See O'Meara (n 68) 1821.

[109] See Lock, 'Tightrope' (n 21) 1040.

[110] See Benoît-Rohmer, 'Completing the Transformation' (n 26) 61; Olivier De Schutter, *L'adhésion de l'Union européenne à la Convention européenne des droits de l'homme: feuille de route de la négociation*. European Parliament, Committee on Constitutional Affairs, Hearing on the Institutional Aspects of the European Union's Accession to the European Convention on Human Rights, 10 April 2010, 7.

[111] See Giacomo Di Federico, 'Fundamental Rights in the EU: Legal Pluralism and Multi-Level Protection after the Lisbon Treaty' in Giacomo Di Federico (ed), *The EU Charter of Fundamental Rights. From Declaration to Binding Document* (Dordrecht, Springer Netherlands, 2011) 48.

not to be responsible for an alleged violation by arguing that the said violation was within the responsibility of the Union, or vice versa.[112] The co-respondent mechanism is thence the perfect instrument in preventing potential pitfalls for the Union's legal autonomy in the form of external interferences by Strasbourg.

Nevertheless, the preservation of the autonomy of EU law via the co-respondent mechanism only works if the respondents in such proceedings are not entitled to invoke the aforementioned defence, ie more precisely, claiming that an alleged violation was entirely the responsibility of the other respondent. In this respect, the *Bosphorus* case sets an ostensive example, in which the Irish Government asserted that the regulation in question had left no room for the independent exercise of discretion by the Member State.[113] If, in a similar case after accession, the European Union refuses to join the proceedings as co-respondent alongside the respondent Member State, this very Member State should not be able to counter that the responsibility for the alleged violation lies in fact with the Union. As a result, the Member States' responsibility for violations of the Convention in cases such as *Matthews*[114] would principally have to continue. Otherwise, Strasbourg would end up in the problematic situation of deciding which entity is indeed responsible for a violation of the Convention under Union law[115]—a course of action which would necessitate an interpretation of the Treaties in a binding fashion and thus a grave infringement of the Union's legal autonomy.[116]

iv. Substantial Questions: Tests for Triggering the Co-Respondent Mechanism

a. A Viable Criterion: Normative Conflict, Substantive Link or Compatibility?

The preceding section merely touched on the crucial subject of how the Member States' discretion in implementing EU law and the intricate division of competences between the Union and the Member States will impinge on the responsibilities of the respondents before the Strasbourg Court. These questions now lead to the next legal issue in this context, namely by what substantive criterion the ECtHR will make its decision to join the parties involved as co-respondents.[117]

In the very first draft agreement of February 2011, it was suggested that the Strasbourg Court may join the European Union and one or more Member States as co-respondents when an alleged violation of the Convention 'appears to have a *substantive link* with European Union legal acts or measures [...].'[118] At the

---

[112] See Lock, 'Tightrope' (n 21) 1040.
[113] See *Bosphorus v Ireland* App no 45036/98 (n 14) para 110.
[114] See *Matthews v United Kingdom* App no 24833/94 (n 12) paras 32 and 34.
[115] See Lock, 'Tightrope' (n 21) 1041.
[116] See Opinion 1/91 *EEA I* (n 40) para 39.
[117] See Jacqué, 'Accession' (n 27) 1015.
[118] Art 4 (1); Council of Europe, '6th Working Meeting of the CDDH Informal Working Group on the Accession of the European Union to the European Convention on Human Rights (CDDH-UE) with the European Commission' CDDH-UE(2011)04, 5 (emphasis added).

outset, the drafters obviously deemed this criterion wide enough to avoid any problems in the future, as the wording 'substantive link' would be sufficient[119] and could be extensively interpreted in order to retrace any legal nexus between the European Union and a Member State. However, the second draft agreement of March 2011 stated that the co-respondent mechanism would be initiated in situations of *normative conflicts*[120] between the obligations of the Member States under the Convention and European Union law. More precisely, a high contracting party may become a co-respondent in cases where it appears 'that an act or omission underlying an alleged violation notified could only have been avoided *by disregarding an obligation under European Union law* [...].'[121] This wording was considered less satisfactory, since, for the EU to become a co-respondent, it had to appear that the respondent Member State could not have prevented the alleged violation of the Convention without disregarding an obligation under EU law.[122] Moreover, this would only be the case in situations where the respective Member State had no discretion in implementing its obligations under Union law (for example, in implementing or enforcing the provisions of a regulation). But if the Member State had some discretion, for example in transposing a directive, this would inevitably lead to a normative conflict with the party's obligations as an EU Member State.[123] When taking Strasbourg's past case law into consideration, this version is reminiscent of the requirements for applying the '*equivalent protection*'formula,[124] as set forth in the *Bosphorus* judgment. But, more importantly, this wording would also compel the Strasbourg Court to assess whether it appears that the respondent state could have only avoided a violation of the Convention by concurrently violating an obligation under Union law. For this assessment, Strasbourg has to define what the obligations of the respondent Member State under Union law are beforehand and whether Union law granted the Member State a margin of discretion, which would have allowed the Member State to avoid the normative conflict in the first place. Such a definition of the obligations would necessarily include a detailed interpretation of European Union law and is consequently in conflict with the legal autonomy of the EU,[125] especially when considering Luxembourg's own words in *Opinion 1/91*[126] on this specific matter.

---

[119] See Jacqué, 'Accession' (n 27) 1015.

[120] See Lock, 'Tightrope' (n 21) 1041.

[121] Art 4 (1); Council of Europe, '6th Working Meeting of the CDDH Informal Working Group on the Accession of the European Union to the European Convention on Human Rights (CDDH-UE) with the European Commission' CDDH-UE(2011)06, 11 (emphasis added).

[122] See Jacqué, 'Accession' (n 27) 1015.

[123] See Lock, 'Tightrope' (n 21) 1041.

[124] See *Bosphorus v Ireland* App no 45036/98 (n 14) para 155.

[125] See Lock, 'Tightrope' (n 21) 1042.

[126] See Opinion 1/91 *EEA I* (n 40) para 35.

In the third version of the draft agreement of May 2011, the drafters dropped the term 'substantive link' and any other requirement of a normative link and stated that the co-respondent status may be granted in a case

> if it *appears* that such allegation calls into question the *compatibility* with the Convention rights at issue of a provision of European Union law [...] or of a provision of the Treaty on European Union, the Treaty on the Functioning of the European Union or any other provision having the same legal value pursuant to those instruments.[127]

The verb 'appears' again indicates that the ECtHR is not expected or even allowed to delve into a comprehensive and meticulous examination of the situation and must accept the co-respondent as such when an acceptance is prima facie obvious.[128] This version does not necessitate the existence of a normative conflict and resembles much more the draft agreement of February 2011 which required a 'substantive link'. In this version, Strasbourg's role is reduced to reviewing whether it merely *appears* that a provision of EU law is indeed compatible with the Convention. The Strasbourg Court could then suppose such appearance to exist whenever one of the parties involved brings forward an argument to that very effect.[129]

b. The Final Version: Compatibility, Plausibility and Normative Conflicts

In the final version of the Draft Accession Agreement of October 2011, however, the negotiators agreed to include the following paragraphs. Firstly, with regard to the designation of the European Union as co-respondent, they stated that

> [w]here an application is directed against one or more member States of the European Union, the European Union may become a co-respondent to the proceedings in respect of an alleged violation notified by the Court if it *appears* that such allegation calls into question *the compatibility with the Convention rights at issue of a provision of European Union law, notably where that violation could have been avoided only by disregarding an obligation under European Union law*.[130]

In terms of the nomination of a Member State as co-respondent, the agreement sets forth that

> [w]here an application is directed against the European Union, the European Union member States may become co-respondents to the proceedings in respect of an alleged violation notified by the Court if it *appears* that such allegation calls into question *the compatibility with the Convention rights at issue of a provision of the Treaty on European Union, the Treaty on the Functioning of the European Union or any other provision having*

---

[127] Art 4 (2) and (3); Council of Europe, '7th Working Meeting of the CDDH Informal Working Group on the Accession of the European Union to the European Convention on Human Rights (CDDH-UE) with the European Commission' CDDH-UE(2011)10, 13 (emphasis added).

[128] See Jacqué, 'Accession' (n 27) 1015.

[129] See Lock, 'Tightrope' (n 21) 1043f.

[130] Art 3 (2) of the Draft Accession Agreement; CDDH-UE(2011)009 (n 66) 7 (emphasis added).

the same legal value pursuant to those instruments, notably where that violation could have been avoided only by disregarding an obligation under those instruments.[131]

Lastly, the final version states that, after the Strasbourg Court has received the parties' request to become co-respondents, '[it] shall assess whether, in the light of the reasons given by the High Contracting Party concerned, it is *plausible* that the conditions in paragraph 2 or paragraph 3 of this Article are met'.[132]

The conditions for becoming a co-respondent in cases where an application is directed against *both* the EU and one or more of its Member States, are almost identical with those in the preceding provision (Art 3 (5) of the Draft Accession Agreement) and will therefore not be scrutinised separately. The ECtHR may, in these cases, also change the status to that of a co-respondent if the conditions in paragraphs 2 or 3 are met. The most striking difference is, however, the absence of the word '*plausible*' in Article 3 (4) of the Draft Accession Agreement.[133]

It is in fact very intriguing that the drafters chose an option which would ultimately combine three of the aforementioned versions. Yet, whereas the first two elements are plainly unproblematic for the autonomy of Union law, the last one might prove rather intricate or even detrimental. Firstly, the drafters again included the word '*appear*' which indicates the marginal role the ECtHR is expected to play in designating the co-respondent. This means that the Strasbourg Court must accept a party as a co-respondent at the slightest hint of compatibility issues between provisions of Union law and the Convention. Therefore, Strasbourg would not thoroughly examine the situation, but rather cursorily analyse whether the conditions for joining the parties as co-respondents in a concrete case are fulfilled.

Secondly, the ECtHR shall only assess—in due consideration of the arguments brought forward by the high contracting parties—whether it is *plausible* that the conditions for joining the parties as co-respondents are met. '*Plausible*' is not a very persuasive or powerful word and will consequently not prompt the ECtHR to immerse itself into the delicacies of European Union law and the internal division of competences between the Union and its Member States. It will most likely content itself with the assessment whether there is an evident and comprehensive nexus between domestic law and Union law or that an alleged violation of the Convention is rooted in the interaction of those two legal orders, without specifying any legal details on this matter.

Thirdly, however, both Article 3 (2) and (3) of the Draft Accession Agreement apparently readopt the precondition that a *normative conflict* between EU law and the Convention must exist in order to initiate the co-respondent mechanism, most prominently by stating that the alleged violation of the Convention '*could have been avoided only by disregarding an obligation under European Union law*'.

---

[131] Art 3 (3) of the Draft Accession Agreement; CDDH-UE(2011)009 (n 66) 7 (emphasis added).
[132] Art 3 (5) of the Draft Accession Agreement; CDDH-UE(2011)009 (n 66) 8 (emphasis added).
[133] Art 3 (4) of the Draft Accession Agreement; CDDH-UE(2011)009 (n 66) 8.

This clearly reintroduces the proposal found in the second draft agreement of March 2011. Of course, one may argue at this point, when examining the two paragraphs in their entirety that the word '*notably*' at the beginning of this last contentious clause may insinuate that the element of a normative conflict is simply one of several such elements which are not included in this non-exhaustive enumeration.

Nonetheless, this assumption can be easily disproved by taking a closer look at the Explanatory Report to the last version of the Draft Accession Agreement. When the ECtHR is called upon to decide whether a case involving Union law is in fact suitable for applying the co-respondent mechanism, it must take into account the tests set out in Article 3 (2) and (3) of the Draft Accession Agreement, respectively.[134] In the first scenario, when an application is lodged against one or more Member States of the EU, but not against the Union itself, the test is fulfilled if it appears that the alleged violation of the Convention calls into question the compatibility of a provision of European Union law, either primary or secondary law, with the Convention rights at issue.[135] The existence of a normative conflict is then explicitly mentioned as the most distinctive example of such an incompatibility. Moreover, the Explanatory Report states that a violation of the Convention, which could only have been avoided by a Member State by disregarding an obligation under Union law, is most likely to emerge when a provision of EU law 'leaves *no discretion* to a member state as to its implementation at the national level'.[136] Conversely, the test for applying the co-respondent mechanism fails in cases where it would be inappropriate to include the Union as a co-respondent, for example, when EU law does not force a Member State to act in a way contrary to the Convention.[137]

In the second scenario, in which an application is lodged against the European Union, but not against one or more Member States, the test is fulfilled if it appears that the alleged violation of the Convention calls into question the compatibility of a provision of primary EU law (ie the Treaties or any other provision having the same legal value) with the Convention rights at issue.[138] Again, as in the first scenario, the existence of a normative conflict is mentioned at the end of the respective provision, namely in Article 3 (3) of the Draft Accession Agreement.

Yet, even though the Explanatory Report states that these tests would take account of the provisions of European Union law as interpreted by the competent

---

[134] See CDDH-UE(2011)009 (n 66) 22, para 41.
[135] See ibid 22, para 42.
[136] Ibid 22, para 42 (emphasis added).
[137] See Submission by the AIRE Centre and Amnesty International, Informal Working Group on the Accession of the European Union to the European Convention on Human Rights (CDDH-UE), AI Index: IOR 61/003/2011, 14 March 2011, para 6. The document lists the following real-life cases as examples for an inappropriate inclusion of the European Union as a co-respondent: *MSS v Belgium and Greece* App no 30696/09 (n 36); *Rantsev v Cyprus and Russia* App no 25965/04 (ECtHR, 7 January 2010); Case C-497/10 PPU *Mercredi v Chaffe* [2010] ECR I–14309.
[138] See CDDH-UE(2011)009 (n 66) 22, para 43.

courts,[139] thus including the interpretation of the CJEU, it must be examined whether dangers remain in regards to the autonomy of the Union's legal order via the co-respondent mechanism. Despite the clause that the Strasbourg Court will only apply the co-respondent mechanism in cases where it appears that an alleged violation calls into question the compatibility of Union law with the Convention, the fact remains that it will have a margin of discretion that might permit—should the situation arise—an interpretation of EU law and the internal distribution of competences. At this point in time it is unclear as to whether the ECtHR will cross this legal Rubicon or whether it will settle for the interpretation of mere 'appearance'.[140] The following two sections thence examine these issues and investigate whether the European Union's legal autonomy faces problems and where these might be situated.

c. Test One: The Member States—Discretion, Defence and Omissions

The first scenario to be analysed is the case in which an application is lodged against one or more Member States (ie as the original respondent(s)), which means that the European Union may request to join the proceedings at a later stage as a co-respondent. As aforementioned, the Explanatory Report points out that a normative conflict between Union law and the Convention may arise when an EU law provision leaves no discretion to a Member State as to its implementation at the national level.[141] The drafters clearly based this first test on the *Bosphorus* case,[142] which provides an excellent example for the subsequent reasoning.

The legal situation in *Bosphorus* was—at least for lawyers and experts in this specific field of law—comparatively clear and uncomplicated. The decision of the Irish Government and authorities to impound the aircraft was based on one legal foundation, which was, by virtue of Article 288 (2) TFEU, a directly applicable EU regulation.[143] In a similar case, the Strasbourg Court would not have any serious legal problems in identifying the roots of the alleged violation, since it would not be forced to delve into the intricate interpretations of Union law.[144] It could easily determine that, according to Article 3 (2) of the Draft Accession Agreement, the

---

[139] See ibid 22, para 41.

[140] See Jacqué, 'Accession' (n 27) 1015.

[141] See CDDH-UE(2011)009 (n 66) 22, para 42.

[142] See Council of Europe, '8th Meeting of the CDDH Informal Working Group on the Accession of the European Union to the European Convention on Human Rights (CDDH-UE) with the European Commission' CDDH-UE(2011)16, 17, para 44 and fn 18, which states that '[d]uring the negotiations, the view was expressed that in recent years, the only cases which might have certainly required the application of the co-respondent mechanism would have been *Matthews v United Kingdom*, *Bosphorus Hava Yollari Turizm Ve Ticaret Anonim Sirketi v Ireland* and *Cooperatieve Producentenorganisatie van de Nederlandse Kokkelvisserij U.A. v the Netherlands*.'

[143] For the criteria of direct applicability, see eg, Case 43/71 *Politi v Ministry for Finance* [1971] ECR 1039, para 9; Case 93/71 *Leonesio v Ministero dell'agricoltura* [1972] ECR 287, paras 5–6; Case 94/77 *Zerbone v Amministrazione delle finanze* [1978] ECR 99, paras 22–24.

[144] See Lock, 'Tightrope' (n 21) 1041.

alleged violation by the Member State could have only been avoided by disregarding an obligation under European Union law, or, *in concreto*, by disapplying the said Regulation and not impounding the aircraft. In the words of the Agreement and the Explanatory Report, the appearance of an incompatibility between the Convention rights at issue and a provision of EU law seems very plausible in such a case, and the ECtHR would most likely join the respective Member State and the Union as co-respondents, but without prejudice to its assessment of the merits of the case.[145]

Another more topical example of a normative conflict between European Union law and the Convention may arise in the context of the EU's anti-piracy '*Operation Atalanta*' conducted off the coast of Somalia. This naval operation is based on Council Joint Action 2008/851[146] and Council Decision 2008/918[147] which, in turn, were enacted in support of several Resolutions of the United Nations Security Council adopted under Chapter VII of the UN Charter.[148] If military personnel were to arrest persons suspected of piracy under Article 2 lit e in conjunction with Article 12 of Council Joint Action 2008/851, Strasbourg could effortlessly conclude that any alleged violation of the Convention (in this case, supposedly a breach of Article 5 ECHR) could have only been circumvented by disregarding an obligation under EU law, namely by disapplying the above-mentioned legal acts and not arresting any suspects. The Strasbourg Court would again join the respective Member State(s) and the Union as co-respondents, but without assessing the merits of the case or ruling on the internal division of competences. It therefore seems that those legal acts especially, which have been adopted in support of anti-terrorism or anti-piracy resolutions of the United Nations Security Council, may open unprecedented doors for the development of Strasbourg's future case law on the question of dual attribution and the co-respondent mechanism.[149]

There are, however, cases in which the assessment of such a normative conflict might prove more difficult than in the examples above, and, most notably, possibly detrimental to the autonomy of Union law, for example in cases where an EU directive that has been transposed into domestic law is allegedly in violation of the Convention. Notwithstanding the fact that the Member States usually have some discretion in transposing and implementing the provisions of a directive

---

[145] See CDDH-UE(2011)009 (n 66) 23, para 48.

[146] Council Joint Action 2008/851/CFSP on a European Union military operation to contribute to the deterrence, prevention and repression of acts of piracy and armed robbery off the Somali Coast [2008] OJ L301/33.

[147] Council Decision 2008/918/CFSP on the launch of a European Union military operation to contribute to the deterrence, prevention and repression of acts of piracy and armed robbery off the Somali Coast (Atalanta) [2008] OJ L330/19.

[148] UNSC Res 1814 (15 May 2008) UN Doc S/RES/1814; UNSC Res 1816 (2 June 2008) UN Doc S/RES/1816; UNSC Res 1838 (7 October 2008) UN Doc S/RES/1838; UNSC Res 1846 (2 December 2008) UN Doc S/RES/1846.

[149] See Stefano Piedimonte Bodini, 'Fighting Maritime Piracy under the European Convention on Human Rights' (2011) 22 *European Journal of International Law* 829, 846.

under Article 288 (3) TFEU[150] (particularly the discretion to choose the most appropriate forms and methods to ensure the effective functioning of directives[151]), the legislative und judicative organs of the EU tend to regard and deploy directives as a '*loi uniforme*'[152] which then considerably curtails or even entirely annuls this margin of discretion.[153] Thus, a Member State may raise the defence that the alleged violation of the Convention occurred due to this lack of discretion in transposing and implementing the relevant provisions of the directive in question. If Strasbourg assessed such a situation, it would necessarily be compelled to interpret the directive as to how much discretion was actually left to the Member State, which would most certainly be irreconcilable with the autonomy of Union law. In order not to transgress in this legal minefield and to meddle in the internal affairs of the EU and its Member States, the Strasbourg Court should uphold its cooperative attitude towards Luxembourg and declare such a defence—if raised by a Member State in a concrete case—inadmissible in any event.[154]

Another risk to the autonomy of the Union's legal order might arise in relation to alleged violations of the Convention by omission of a positive obligation.[155] A decision by Strasbourg in such a case may involve a determination of the entity under an obligation to act in the case at hand, either the European Union or a Member State. By assessing such a case, the ECtHR would necessarily take recourse to the internal allocation of competences within the Union and thus violate the autonomy of EU law. In proceedings where both the European Union and one or more Member States are joined as co-respondents, this situation could be avoided if it were inadmissible to submit the defence of not being internally responsible. Nonetheless, the amendment of Article 59 ECHR via Article 1 (2) lit c of the Draft Accession Agreement may cause some grave legal concerns in this context.[156] It sets forth that

> [a]ccession to the Convention and the Protocols thereto shall impose on the European Union obligations with regard only to acts, measures or omissions of its institutions, bodies, offices or agencies, or of persons acting on their behalf. *Nothing in the Convention*

---

[150] See the wording of art 288 (3) TFEU reading that '[a] directive shall be binding, as to the result to be achieved, upon each Member State to which it is addressed, *but shall leave to the national authorities the choice of form and methods*' (emphasis added).

[151] See Case 48/75 *Royer* [1976] ECR 497, para 73.

[152] See Walter Frenz, *Handbuch Europarecht. Band 5: Wirkungen und Rechtsschutz* (Berlin Heidelberg, Springer, 2010) para 912; Jürgen Bast, 'Handlungsformen und Rechtsschutz' in Armin von Bogdandy and Jürgen Bast (eds), *Europäisches Verfassungsrecht. Theoretische und dogmatische Grundzüge* (Berlin Heidelberg, Springer, 2009) 504f; Armin von Bogdandy, Jürgen Bast and Felix Arndt, 'Handlungsformen im Unionsrecht. Empirische Analysen und dogmatische Strukturen in einem vermeintlichen Dschungel' (2002) 62 *Zeitschrift für ausländisches öffentliches Recht und Völkerrecht* 77, 92.

[153] See Case 38/77 *Enka v Inspecteur der Invoerrechten* [1977] ECR 2203, paras 11–12.

[154] See Lock, 'Tightrope' (n 21) 1041.

[155] See generally on '*positive obligations*' under the Convention, Harris, O'Boyle, Bates and Buckley (n 75) 18ff, and Christoph Grabenwarter, *Europäische Menschenrechtskonvention*, 4th edn (Munich, Beck, 2009) § 19, paras 1ff.

[156] See Lock, 'Tightrope' (n 21) 1042.

or the Protocols thereto shall require the European Union to perform an act or adopt a measure for which it has no competence under European Union law.[157]

The according paragraph of the Explanatory Report states that this provision reflects the requirements of Article 6 (2) TEU and Article 2 of Protocol No 8 to the Treaties which demand that the Union's accession to the Convention shall not affect its competences or the powers of its institutions.[158] Moreover, it expounds that an alleged violation possibly arising from the omission of a positive obligation deriving from the Convention will not affect the application of the tests laid down in Articles 3 (2) and (3) of the Draft Accession Agreement to trigger the co-respondent mechanism.[159] Again, the risk to the EU's legal autonomy lies in the fact that this provision may be invoked as a defence in proceedings before the Strasbourg Court, which would then be forced to decide on the division of competences based on EU law. It would therefore be of paramount importance that in cases of an omission, no such defence could be proffered and that the ECtHR would—in cases in which the respondent entity would in fact raise such a defence—consequently declare it inadmissible, in order to leave it to the Union and the Luxembourg Court to resolve these questions internally.[160] Strasbourg is therefore again advised to perpetuate its judicial comity vis-à-vis Luxembourg so as not to interfere with the autonomy of European Union law.

d. Test Two: The European Union as Original Respondent and Primary Law

The second scenario to be examined is where an application is filed against the European Union itself, but not against a Member State, which means that the latter may request to join the proceedings at a later stage as a co-respondent. Again, the Explanatory Report emphasises that the Strasbourg Court can decide to join the two parties as respondent and co-respondent, if it appears that there has been a normative conflict between Union law and the Convention. More precisely, it may decide to do so if it appears that the alleged violation of the Convention calls into question the compatibility of a provision of *primary Union law* with the Convention rights at issue.[161] It is therefore apparent that the drafters based the second test for triggering the co-respondent mechanism on Strasbourg's *Matthews* judgment.[162]

When comparing the different versions of the Draft Accession Agreement, notable risks to the Union's legal autonomy may arise in cases in which the

---

[157] Art 1 (2) lit c of the Draft Accession Agreement; CDDH-UE(2011)009 (n 66) 6 (emphasis added).

[158] See CDDH-UE(2011)009 (n 66) 18, para 21.

[159] See CDDH-UE(2011)16 (n 142) 17, para 43.

[160] See Lock, 'Tightrope' (n 21) 1042f.

[161] See CDDH-UE(2011)009 (n 66) 22, para 43 (emphasis added).

[162] See n 142.

EU is the original respondent. The draft agreement of March 2011 stated that the test for triggering the co-respondent mechanism is fulfilled if an 'alleged violation could only have been avoided by the European Union disregarding an obligation upon it under European Union law which cannot be modified by its institutions alone'.[163] In other words, the obligation in question derives from the primary law of the Union which can only be modified by an agreement concluded by the Member States.[164] In the second draft agreement of May 2011, most of the content of this provision has been retained, but the reference to the exclusive powers of the Member States in terms of amending the Union's primary law has been struck out.[165] The key difference between the two drafts lies in Strasbourg's competence in scrutinising the conditions for applying the co-respondent mechanism. Whereas the first draft would have required the ECtHR to interpret Union law and assess which rank within the internal hierarchy of norms the provision in question has—which would most likely interfere with the autonomy of Union law—the second draft agreement only required Strasbourg to assess whether 'it *appears* that such allegation calls into question the compatibility with the Convention rights at issue of a provision of the [primary law of the European Union]'.[166] The ECtHR would, again, carry out this assessment in a quite superficial manner, without interpreting Union law in an internally binding fashion.[167]

The final version of the Draft Accession Agreement of October 2011, however, included again, in Article 3 (3), the element of a normative conflict between primary Union law and the Convention in order to allow for the application of the co-respondent mechanism. The detrimental effects of this element which would arise if Strasbourg carried out an exhaustive assessment and interpretation of Union law have been mitigated by the fact that the ECtHR can base its decision on the mere appearance of such an incompatibility between the Convention and the Union's primary law. Consequently, the only assessment Strasbourg is required to conduct is to look at the legal basis of the alleged violation in order to find out whether this legal basis is enshrined in the Treaties or not. Moreover, the autonomy of EU law is preserved as the Court does not engage in a profound legal analysis of the legal roots of the alleged violation, but simply contents itself with its appearance in primary law. The ECtHR does not, therefore, examine the exact rank the provision in question has within the hierarchy of Union law, which leaves the autonomy of the Union's legal order perfectly intact.

---

[163] Art 4 (3); CDDH-UE(2011)06, (n 121), 11.

[164] See Council of Europe, '7th Working Meeting of the CDDH Informal Working Group on the Accession of the European Union to the European Convention on Human Rights (CDDH-UE) with the European Commission' CDDH-UE(2011)08, para 37. See also ch 8 for more details.

[165] Art 4 (3); CDDH-UE(2011)10 (n 127) 13.

[166] Ibid 13.

[167] See Lock, 'Tightrope' (n 21) 1044.

e. Analysis: A Cooperative Approach

The preceding discussion demonstrated that the relevant provisions of the Draft Accession Agreement are appropriate in shielding the EU from any external interference, but that the Agreement—in a manner of speaking—is also stuck halfway on its road from Luxembourg to Strasbourg. In order to fully comply with the requirements of the European Union's legal autonomy, the current situation in which a Member State is held principally responsible for all actions and omissions in violation of the Convention and associated with the discharge of its obligations under Union law would have to be maintained. This means that the Agreement relies on the ECtHR's willingness to cooperate and to dismiss any defence raised by a Member State claiming that it had only acted in strict compliance with its obligations as an EU Member State and accordingly was not responsible for the alleged violation of the Convention. Moreover, the drafters of the Agreement managed to take into account the EU's specific legal situation as a non-state federal entity, where the 'federation' (EU) legislates and the 'states' (Member States) implement such legislation,[168] which may lead to divergent responsibilities for human rights violations. In this context, the final version of the Draft Accession Agreement and the trust in the Strasbourg Court, based on its past case law, seem to be a viable solution to circumvent any problems and to uphold the EU's legal autonomy in the future.[169]

Beyond that, the two tests guarantee equal terms with other high contracting parties and increase the likelihood that the Union may apply to join proceedings as co-respondent in such situations. Yet, of course, it remains to be seen how eagerly the EU will choose to involve itself as co-respondent where the conditions of Articles 3 (2) and (3) of the Draft Accession Agreement are fulfilled. With respect to the Member States, joining proceedings as co-respondents may be attractive in cases where a supremacy-based argument could be made regarding the obligations under EU law which allegedly violates the Convention.[170] However, as shown above, Strasbourg should maintain a strict attitude towards such a course of action and accordingly dismiss any defence that a Member State had only acted in strict compliance with its obligations under European Union law.

---

[168] See Xavier Groussot, Tobias Lock and Laurent Pech, 'EU Accession to the European Convention on Human Rights: A Legal Assessment of the Draft Accession Agreement of 14th October 2011' [2011] *Fondation Robert Schuman—European Issues* No 218, 1, 13.

[169] See Lock, 'Tightrope' (n 21) 1045.

[170] See O'Meara (n 68) 1821f.

v. Effects of the Co-Respondent Mechanism

a. The Need for Further Union-Internal Rules

The analysis above has shown that the Strasbourg Court will only assess the conditions under which the co-respondent mechanism may be applied. Conversely, it must not assess the division of competences between the Union and its Member States since this step would encroach upon the EU's legal autonomy. Consequently, in its judgments, Strasbourg will hold the respondent and the co-respondent *jointly* responsible for the alleged violation of the Convention for which a high contracting party has become a co-respondent. Should the ECtHR in fact find a violation, it must generally do so jointly against the original respondent and the co-respondent, for if it attributed which entity is responsible and to what extent, the Strasbourg Court would assess the internal allocation of powers between the European Union and its Member States.[171] Nevertheless, this solution does not preclude the respondent or co-respondent from making submissions disclaiming any responsibility for the alleged human rights violations. It will be very interesting to see how Strasbourg will handle such a scenario.[172]

Although there will presumably be an interest in indicating the origin of the violation exactly and the precise share of blame in order to guarantee that such a violation does not occur again[173] or that the payment of just satisfaction is divided proportionally according to each party's responsibility,[174] such a demand is irreconcilable with the autonomy of European Union law. This means that after accession, the Union must develop internal rules to determine the procedure for implementing and activating the co-respondent mechanism and to enforce Strasbourg's judgments in accordance with the division of competence.[175] It may be assumed that in most cases, a conviction by the ECtHR will be accepted without further ado by both the original respondent and the co-respondent and they will henceforth cooperate to remove the violation of the Convention. However, due to political reasons in particular, there may be situations in which a Member State would not be willing to accept a joint conviction for a violation of the Convention, for instance in a high profile case where internal political pressure is exercised within the respective Member State to not be officially blamed. But more importantly, there may be monetary interests involved in cases where the applicant was awarded pecuniary compensation under Article 41 ECHR.[176] It would

---

[171] See CDDH-UE(2011)009 (n 66) 24, para 54.

[172] See O'Meara (n 68) 1822.

[173] See Council of Europe, '4th Working Meeting of the CDDH Informal Working Group on the Accession of the European Union to the European Convention on Human Rights (CDDH-UE) with the European Commission' CDDH-UE(2010)17, para 14.

[174] See Response of the European Group of National Human Rights Institutions, 'EU Accession to the ECHR' CDDH-UE, 15-18 March 2011, 11.

[175] See Jacqué, 'Accession' (n 27) 1016.

[176] See Lock, 'Implications for Judicial Review' (n 7) 787.

thence be very sensible to establish an internal Union mechanism to attribute the joint responsibility for violations of the Convention (which the Strasbourg Court has determined in the joint proceedings) ex post between the Union and its Member States. In cases where the Member State implementing or enforcing EU law was left no discretion in doing so, it may be argued that the Union should bear the costs for the compensation awarded. In contrast, such an assumption of costs should be impermissible in cases in which the courts of the Member States—in breach of their obligations under Article 267 (3) TFEU—omitted to request a preliminary ruling from the CJEU to review the compatibility of the respective legal act with the Charter of Fundamental Rights. Usually, if the affirmations of the Luxembourg Court are believed to be true, such a review should not lead to a different result than a subsidiary judgment of the Strasbourg Court.[177]

b. Models for Attributing Responsibility

Two models for the internal attribution of responsibility for violations of the Convention have been proposed in the past. Firstly, the European Union may establish a committee or any other permanent body which would be made up of representatives from the Member States and the EU (to ensure independence from the national governments, it would be preferable to have representatives from the European Commission) who would then decide, on the basis of Union law, how the internal responsibility should be allocated. Secondly, however, the Luxembourg Court may also be given jurisdiction to assign the responsibility.[178] This would, of course, entail the introduction of a new procedure before the CJEU, since no existing procedure entirely fits the requirements of this special form of action.[179] The introduction of a new procedure to internally distribute the responsibility determined by the ECtHR would therefore necessitate an amendment to the Treaties which is—given the political real-life facts—unlikely to succeed. Such an amendment could only be conducted through a legal back-door, for instance by including the relevant provisions in a future treaty providing for the accession of a new Member State under Article 49 TEU.[180] An argument against such an internal attribution of responsibility is the fact that such a procedure before the CJEU would be time-consuming. This should nevertheless not affect the individual applicant who was awarded a pecuniary compensation by the Strasbourg Court, since both respondents should pay their respective share of the said compensation to the applicant beforehand and only then initiate the procedure before the CJEU. By and large, the introduction of such a procedure

---

[177] See Sebastian Winkler, *Der Beitritt der Europäischen Gemeinschaften zur Europäischen Menschenrechtskonvention* (Baden-Baden, Nomos, 2000) 56.

[178] See Lock, 'Implications for Judicial Review' (n 7) 787.

[179] See eg, the different preconditions necessary for initiating actions for contractual and non-contractual liability under arts 268 and 340 TFEU, respectively.

[180] See Hans-Joachim Cremer, 'Art 49 EUV' in Christian Calliess and Matthias Ruffert (eds), *EUV/ AEUV. Kommentar*, 4th edn (Munich, Beck, 2011) para 7.

before the Luxembourg Court would also benefit the development and further clarification of European Union law, as it would result in an authoritative and binding interpretation of the Union-internal distribution of competences and thus responsibilities.[181]

c. Potential Yardsticks for the Internal Attribution of Responsibility

It is, of course, a highly complex task for the Luxembourg Court to determine whether the Union or a Member State is in fact responsible for an alleged violation. Accordingly, it may be argued that the legislative organs of the European Union would be held responsible for directly applicable regulations in violation of the Convention, as the Member States are firstly obligated to comply with their provisions and they secondly have, in the majority of cases, no discretion in doing so. In most of the cases, however, European Union law is indirectly implemented and enforced by the Member States,[182] which leaves the Luxembourg Court with two options. It could either decide that the legal act in violation of the Convention fell within the Member States' scope of application, since their organs have acted in the first place, or that the Union remains responsible as the Member States ultimately act in lieu and support of the European Union.[183]

The internal attribution of responsibility for legal acts in violation of the Convention is even more complex with regard to directives, for they require legislative transposition into the legal system of the Member States. If the directive in question is transposed verbatim or synonymously into domestic law, or if the Member State is not left any discretion in doing so, the Union may be held responsible for the violation. This yardstick would of course analogously apply in cases where the transposition into domestic law remains within the boundaries of a certain 'structural congruence'[184] or general legal context which the CJEU requires the Member State to respect.[185] In other words, if the Member State remains within the limits of the discretion conferred on it, the responsibility lies with the Union; if the Member State chooses to implement provisions which go beyond these limits, the respective Member State may be held responsible.[186]

---

[181] See Lock, 'Implications for Judicial Review' (n 7) 787.

[182] See eg, von Danwitz, *Europäisches Verwaltungsrecht* (n 28) 315ff.

[183] See Gregor Heißl, 'Happy End einer unendlichen Geschichte? Der Beitritt der EU zur EMRK und seine Auswirkungen auf Österreich' in Michael Holoubek, Andrea Martin and Stephan Schwarzer (eds), *Die Zukunft der Verfassung—Die Verfassung der Zukunft? Festschrift für Karl Korinek zum 70. Geburtstag* (Vienna New York, Springer, 2010) 146.

[184] See Frenz, *Wirkungen und Rechtsschutz* (n 152) para 923.

[185] See Case C-131/88 *Commission v Germany (Groundwater Directive)* [1991] ECR I-825, para 6.

[186] See Heißl (n 183) 146.

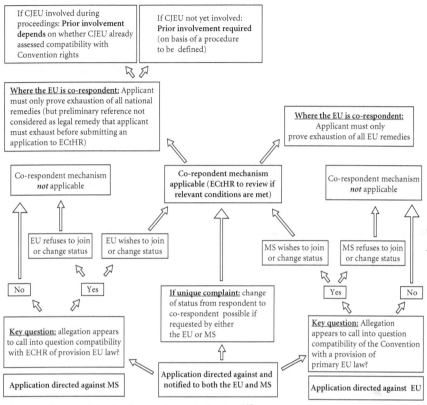

Figure 4: Stages of the Co-Respondent Mechanism[187]

III. INTERIM CONCLUSIONS

Within the legal protection regime provided for by the Convention, individual applications under Article 34 ECHR account for the majority of cases lodged against the high contracting parties—a fact that underscores their outstanding significance both in the present form and in the new European system of human rights protection after the European Union's accession to the Convention. The preceding chapter consequently examined how the individual complaint procedure will be arranged after accession in order to take into consideration the specific features of the Union's legal order, and the risks the introduction of this new procedure may evoke for the EU's legal autonomy.

---

[187] See Groussot, Lock and Pech (n 168), 13.

The main reason for accession is Strasbourg's current lack of jurisdiction *ratione personae* over the Union and its organs. In other words, after accession, individuals will be entitled to lodge applications not just against one or more Member States, but also against the EU in order to hold it responsible for alleged violations of the Convention. The principal downside in this deliberation is, however, that since most of the European Union's legal acts are in fact implemented by the Member States or transposed into domestic law, individual applicants will not know for certain which entity they should ultimately hold responsible for violations of the Convention stemming from Union law. Their situation is further aggravated by the fact that, in most cases, individual applicants do not have any legal education or any particular knowledge about the complexities of Union law, and that the involvement of legal counsel is not compulsory in lodging applications to the ECtHR. It was thence clear that a mechanism had to be devised to hold both the Member States and the Union responsible for EU-related cases and to avoid situations where an application was only declared inadmissible because the applicant had directed it against the wrong respondent.

After numerous models (such as the joint liability and the joint and several liability models) had been proposed to solve this issue, it became clear that the designation of the right respondent should not be left to the Strasbourg Court, as it would, by explicitly designating the respondent and its respective responsibility, implicitly decide on the division of competences between the Union and its Member States. This course of action would interfere with Luxembourg's exclusive jurisdiction and the Union's legal autonomy. The final version of the Draft Accession Agreement therefore introduces the so-called co-respondent mechanism which will allow the European Union to join cases as a co-respondent, alongside the Member State against which the application was initially lodged (Art 3 (2) of the Draft Accession Agreement), and Member States to join cases as co-respondents, alongside the Union as original respondent (Art 3 (3)). Moreover, applicants may also direct applications against both the EU and a Member State from the outset of the proceedings (Art 3 (4)). The main difference between third party interventions under Article 36 ECHR and the new co-respondent procedure lies in the fact that under the latter both respondents become parties to the proceedings and are therefore fully bound by Strasbourg's judgment.

Most importantly, Article 3 (5) of the Draft Accession Agreement clarifies that a high contracting party shall become a co-respondent only at its own request and by the subsequent decision of the Strasbourg Court. This means that on the one hand, a party may not be compelled to become a co-respondent, and, on the other hand, that the decision to join the proceedings in this role rests with the respective high contracting party. Accordingly, the autonomy of EU law is preserved, as the ECtHR is not given any right or power to designate a party as co-respondent *proprio motu*. In its decision whether or not to apply the co-respondent mechanism, the Strasbourg Court is in fact limited to assessing whether the reasons stated by a high contracting party in its request are plausible in light of the following criteria. In cases where an application is filed against one or more Member States, but not against the EU, Strasbourg may decide to join the parties as respondent and co-respondent if it appears that the alleged violation can only be ascribed to a normative conflict between the Convention and primary or secondary European Union law, notably where that violation could have only been avoided by the respective Member State by disregarding an obligation under EU law (Art 3 (2) of the Draft Accession Agreement). Vice versa, in cases in which an application is filed against the European Union, but not against a Member State, the ECtHR may decide to join the parties as co-respondents if it appears that the alleged violation can only be ascribed to a normative conflict between the Convention and primary European Union law, notably where that violation could have only been avoided by the Union by disregarding an obligation under primary law (Art 3 (3) of the Draft Accession Agreement). The same conditions and criteria apply in the scenario where an application is lodged against both the Union and a Member State (Art 3 (4) of the Draft Accession Agreement).

The Strasbourg Court will thus only examine the plausibility and the mere appearance of a normative conflict between the provisions of the Convention and Union law, but—particularly in the context of preserving the autonomy of the EU's legal order—without delving into the details of European Union law or without interpreting it in a binding manner. The ECtHR can consequently avoid determining the exact internal allocation of powers within the Union's legal system and can limit itself to assessing the joint responsibility of the respondent and the co-respondent. Furthermore, Strasbourg must show a certain degree of willingness to cooperate, particularly by dismissing any defence raised by a Member State which claims that it had only acted in strict compliance with its obligations under European Union law or that it enjoyed no discretion in implementing EU law.

Lastly, the above chapter demonstrated that the provisions of the Draft Accession Agreement will not suffice to effectively implement the co-respondent mechanism in the future. In accordance with the autonomy of the Union's legal order, the Agreement remains silent on the issue of how the joint responsibility of the original respondent and the co-respondent should be internally attributed. The Union and the Member States, however, may have a certain interest in attributing this responsibility exactly, especially due to political and monetary reasons. The most appropriate organ to decide on this matter would undoubtedly be the CJEU, but to this end, new provisions regarding the exact procedure would have to be introduced in the Treaties—which could prove problematic. The Member States should therefore quickly make up their minds about how this issue could be tackled without any further complications.

10

Inter-Party Cases after Accession

I. INTER-STATE CASES: A REMINISCENCE OF WESTPHALIA

IN COMPARISON TO individual applications, inter-state cases under Article 33 of the European Convention on Human Rights (ECHR) represent classic instruments for the peaceful settlement of disputes under international law, for this provision allows that '*[a]ny High Contracting Party* may refer to the Court any alleged breach of the provisions of the Convention and the protocols thereto *by another High Contracting Party*.'[1]

The objective of Article 33 of the ECHR is to assign to the contracting parties the role of a collective 'watchdog' who permanently observes the compliance of the other parties with the provisions of the Convention. There are basically two scenarios in which a contracting party may refer an alleged violation of the Convention to the Strasbourg Court. Firstly, a contracting party may lodge an application against another party to secure and guard the interests of its own citizens with regard to alleged human rights violations,[2] thereby taking the effect of an individual application.[3] The most vivid examples for this practice are the three complaints by Cyprus against Turkey to protect its citizens in the occupied northern parts of Cyprus[4] and the three complaints by Georgia against Russia to protect the human rights of its citizens in Russian detention.[5] Secondly, a complaint may assume the character of an *actio popularis*[6] whereby a state does not file a complaint for the purpose of enforcing its own rights or the rights of its citizens,

---

[1] Emphasis added.

[2] See Christoph Grabenwarter, *Europäische Menschenrechtskonvention*, 4th edn (Munich, Beck, 2009) § 10, para 2.

[3] See *Ireland v United Kingdom* App no 5310/71 (ECtHR, 18 January 1978); *Denmark v Turkey* App no 34382/97 (ECtHR, 5 April 2000); *Cyprus v Turkey (IV)* App no 25781/94 (ECtHR, 10 May 2001).

[4] See *Cyprus v Turkey (I)* App no 6780/74 (Commission Report, 10 July 1976); *Cyprus v Turkey (II)* App no 6950/75, Joined with *Cyprus v Turkey (I)*; *Cyprus v Turkey (III)* App no 8007/77 (Commission Reports, 12 July 1980 and 4 October 1983).

[5] See *Georgia v Russia (I)* App no 13255/07 (ECtHR, 30 June 2009); *Georgia v Russia (II)* App no 38263/08 (ECtHR, 13 December 2011); *Georgia v Russia (III)* App no 61186/09 (ECtHR, 16 March 2010).

[6] See Leo Zwaak, 'General Survey of the European Convention' in Pieter van Dijk, Fried van Hoof, Arjen van Rijn and Leo Zwaak (eds), *Theory and Practice of the European Convention on Human Rights*, 4th edn (Antwerp Oxford, Intersentia, 2006) 47.

'but rather as bringing before the [Court] an alleged violation of the public order of Europe'.[7] This collective enforcement of human rights was chosen by Denmark, Norway, Sweden and the Netherlands in their applications against Greece and its military junta in the late 1960s and early 1970s.[8]

As aforementioned,[9] the high contracting parties rarely use the inter-state complaint under Article 33 ECHR to enforce human rights enshrined in the Convention, primarily due to its negative political consequences within the European neighbourhood, as it may be considered an unfriendly act.[10] Given the low number of inter-state cases compared to the overwhelming success of individual applications, it is obvious that the inter-state complaint procedure only plays a minor role in Strasbourg's protection machinery. Beyond that, since the creation of the European Union, there have been no inter-state complaints between EU Member States.[11] There are nevertheless two facets which are worth exploring in this context. The subsequent sections will thus illustrate whether Luxembourg's exclusive jurisdiction, particularly its jurisdiction under Article 344 of the Treaty on the Functioning of the European Union (TFEU) and thus the Union's legal autonomy, may be endangered by accession on the one hand, in the hypothetical situation where one EU Member State brings an application against another EU Member State or against the Union itself before the Strasbourg Court; and, on the other hand, in cases where the European Union may use the future inter-party complaint procedure against non-EU Member States to enforce human rights in its external relations.

II. THE INTERNAL DIMENSION: LUXEMBOURG VERSUS STRASBOURG

The first question relates to the 'internal' problems between the European Union and its Member States within the Convention system, namely the future relationship between the Luxembourg and Strasbourg courts after accession and how their respective 'exclusive jurisdiction' clauses (namely Article 344 TFEU and Article 55 ECHR) for settling disputes might endanger both the effective protection of human rights within the Convention's regime and autonomy of European Union law. Therefore, these two provisions are subsequently presented and comprehensively analysed in order to understand the legal framework which the drafters have chosen in the Draft Accession Agreement to address this particular matter.

---

[7] *Austria v Italy* App no 788/60 (Commission Report, 30 March 1963).

[8] See *Denmark, Norway, Sweden and the Netherlands v Greece (I)* App nos 3321/67, 3322/67, 3323/67, 3344/67 (Commission Decision, 5 November 1969); *Denmark, Norway, Sweden and the Netherlands v Greece (II)* App no 4448/70 (Commission Decisions, 5 October 1970 and 4 October 1976).

[9] See ch 9.

[10] See European Court of Human Rights, 'Inter-State Applications' <www.echr.coe.int/NR/rdonlyres/5D5BA416-1FE0-4414-95A1-AD6C1D77CB90/0/Requ%C3%AAtes_inter%C3%A9tatiques_EN.pdf> accessed 1 November 2012.

[11] See Sebastian Winkler, *Der Beitritt der Europäischen Gemeinschaften zur Europäischen Menschenrechtskonvention* (Baden-Baden, Nomos, 2000) 84.

A. An Encounter of Exclusive Jurisdiction

i. Luxembourg's Exclusive Jurisdiction: Article 344 TFEU

As early as 1979, when the European Union's accession to the Convention was first brought into play, the potential risks of disrupting the Union's judicial system in the context of inter-state applications between Member States and the future relationship between Article 33 ECHR and Article 344 TFEU caused great anxiety.[12] The question remains whether this concern is justified or not. The object and purpose of Article 344 TFEU is to guarantee that European Union law (as mentioned in Article 19 (1) TEU) is interpreted in a consistent and coherent manner which can most efficiently be accomplished by designating the Union courts as the only courts competent to decide problems of EU law.[13] Moreover, the reference to '*the Treaties*' in Article 344 TFEU does not only refer to primary law, but it also encompasses secondary Union law[14] and thus, a fortiori, international agreements on their mezzanine rank between primary and secondary law.[15] This approach was also confirmed in *Opinion 1/91*, in which the Court of Justice of the European Union (CJEU) held that conferring to an external court the power of deciding what entity was to be regarded as the party to a dispute, was incompatible with Article 344 TFEU and the exclusive jurisdiction of the CJEU.[16] Furthermore, as illustrated in a preceding chapter,[17] Luxembourg ruled in the *Commission v Ireland (MOX Plant)* case that Article 344 TFEU precludes Member States from initiating proceedings before another court for the settlement of disputes within the scope of Union law.[18] After accession, the Convention and the final Accession Agreement will become an integral part of the Union's legal order,[19] which means that the CJEU will have the corresponding jurisdiction, under Article 19 (1) TEU, to interpret and apply the provisions of the Convention. Most importantly, this jurisdiction is exclusive as the Member States are prohibited under Article 344 TFEU from submitting 'a dispute concerning the interpretation or application of the Treaties *to any method of settlement other than those provided for therein.*'[20]

---

[12] See Commission of the European Communities, 'Memorandum on the Accession of the European Communities to the Convention for the Protection of Human Rights and Fundamental Freedoms' Bulletin Supplement 2/79, COM (79) 210 final, para 27.

[13] See Tobias Lock, 'The ECJ and the ECtHR: The Future Relationship between the Two European Courts' (2009) 8 *The Law and Practice of International Courts and Tribunals* 375, 389.

[14] See Bernhard W Wegener, 'Art 344 AEUV' in Christian Calliess and Matthias Ruffert (eds), *EUV/ AEUV. Kommentar*, 4th edn (Munich, Beck, 2011) para 1.

[15] See ch 7 for more details.

[16] See Opinion 1/91 *EEA I (Draft agreement between the Community, on the one hand, and the countries of the European Free Trade Association, on the other, relating to the creation of the European Economic Area)* [1991] ECR I-6079, paras 34–35.

[17] See ch 4 for more details.

[18] See Case C-459/03 *Commission v Ireland (MOX Plant)* [2006] I-4635, paras 133 and 135.

[19] See Case 181/73 *Haegeman v Belgian State* [1974] ECR 449, para 5.

[20] Emphasis added.

As a consequence, Luxembourg's exclusive jurisdiction to interpret and apply the Convention will—pursuant to Article 344 TFEU—bar the EU Member States from bringing inter-state complaints against each other before the Strasbourg Court.[21] According to the CJEU, this obligation imposed upon the Member States is a specific expression of the principle of sincere and loyal cooperation resulting from Article 4 (3) TEU,[22] which also prohibits the Union organs from submitting a dispute concerning the interpretation or application of EU law to other courts or tribunals.[23] The Member States and the Union organs are subsequently left with the internal Union dispute settlement mechanisms provided for by the Treaties, namely infringement proceedings under Articles 258 and 259 TFEU, the action for annulment under Article 263 TFEU and the action for failure to act under Article 265 TFEU. Prima facie, these procedures constitute the sole conflict resolution mechanisms available to the Member States and the Union organs for the settlement of disputes between them,[24] whereas complaints by the Member States against each other under Article 33 ECHR would be incompatible with Article 344 TFEU.[25] This argument was also emphasised in Article 3 of Protocol No 8 to the Treaties which reads that '[n]othing in the [Accession Agreement] [...] shall affect Article 344 of the Treaty on the Functioning of the European Union'. It is thence clear that this requirement on accession was particularly designed to preserve the role of the Luxembourg Court and to retain its exclusive jurisdiction.[26]

It is still debatable, however, whether all applications concerning an alleged violation of the Convention must be exclusively submitted to the CJEU after accession. The answer to this question lies in the fact that the Accession Agreement cannot be qualified as a mixed agreement,[27] where, due to their shared competences, neither the Member States nor the Union alone could be members of the Agreement. In other words, the competences shared between the Union and its Member States for the protection of human rights cannot be exactly delineated from one another to the effect that certain provisions of the Convention are within the Union's competences and thus part of Luxembourg's exclusive jurisdiction, whereas the other provisions of the Convention remain within the competences of the Member

---

[21] See Tobias Lock, *Das Verhältnis zwischen dem EuGH und internationalen Gerichten* (Tübingen, Mohr Siebeck, 2010) 292, and Thorsten Kingreen, 'Art 6 EUV' in Christian Calliess and Matthias Ruffert (eds), *EUV/AEUV. Kommentar*, 4th edn (Munich, Beck, 2011) para 33.

[22] See Case C-459/03 *Commission v Ireland (MOX Plant)* (n 18) para 169.

[23] See Lock, *Verhältnis* (n 21) 292.

[24] See Markus Schott, 'Die Auswirkungen eines Beitritts der EU zur EMRK auf die Durchsetzung des Grundrechtsschutzes in Europa' *Jusletter* (22 March 2010) 4.

[25] See European Convention, 'Modalities and consequences of incorporation into the Treaties of the Charter of Fundamental Rights and accession of the Community/Union to the ECHR' CONV 116/02, WG II 1, fn 2.

[26] See Florence Benoît-Rohmer in Council of Europe—Parliamentary Assembly, *The Accession of the European Union/European Community to the European Convention on Human Rights*, Doc 11533 (Committee on Legal Affairs and Human Rights) 21.

[27] See ch 7.

States.[28] The decisive factor for the CJEU's jurisdiction regarding the Convention cannot be whether the relevant provision is part of the exclusive jurisdiction of the Member States or not; it is rather crucial whether genuinely created European Union law, not the Convention as an international treaty on its mezzanine rank, is applicable in the case at hand. Only in the former case does the Luxembourg Court have exclusive jurisdiction to settle the dispute. As a result, it will not be able to claim jurisdiction in situations related to wholly domestic fields of law, for example family law or criminal procedure.[29] Even though a sceptic might argue that the EU now has explicit competence over criminal procedure under Article 82 (2) TFEU, the terms of this specific competence are nevertheless circumspectly defined and basically restricted to facilitating mutual recognition of judgments, judicial decisions and police and judicial cooperation in criminal matters with a cross-border aspect.[30] Proceedings between Member States before the CJEU are therefore only conceivable in cases where Member States have constrained fundamental freedoms or where they have implemented Union law.[31] The CJEU also confirmed this view in several cases where it held that it had no jurisdiction with regard to domestic legislation falling outside the scope of European Union law.[32]

ii. Strasbourg's Exclusive Jurisdiction: Art 55 ECHR

Luxembourg's exclusive jurisdiction might possibly clash with its counterpart in Strasbourg, namely in regards to Article 55 ECHR which grants the European Court of Human Rights (ECtHR) exclusive jurisdiction and priority[33] in settling inter-state complaints between the contracting parties to the Convention under Article 33 ECHR. This provision states that

> [t]he High Contracting Parties agree that, *except by special agreement*, they will not avail themselves of treaties, conventions or declarations in force between them for the purpose of submitting, by way of petition, a dispute arising out of the interpretation or application of this Convention *to a means of settlement other than those provided for in this Convention*.[34]

---

[28] See Lock, *Verhältnis* (n 21) 292f.

[29] See Lock, 'Future Relationship' (n 13) 391. But see AG Toth, 'The European Union and Human Rights: The Way Forward' (1997) 34 *Common Market Law Review* 491, 509, who opines that the CJEU would have jurisdiction over any inter-state complaint between the Member States, even for alleged violations of the Convention outside the ambit of European Union law.

[30] See Paul Craig, *The Lisbon Treaty. Law, Politics, and Treaty Reform* (Oxford, Oxford University Press, 2010) 366.

[31] See Werner Schaller, 'Das Verhältnis von EMRK und deutscher Rechtsordnung vor und nach dem Beitritt der EU zur EMRK' (2006) 41 *Europarecht* 656, 663f.

[32] See eg, Case C-299/95 *Kremzow v Republik Österreich* [1997] ECR I-2629, para 15; Case C-291/96 *Criminal Proceedings against Martino Grado and Shahid Bashir* [1997] ECR I-5531, paras 12 and 17; C-309/96 *Annibaldi v Sindaco del Comune di Guidonia* [1997] ECR I-7493, para 13; Case C-333/09 *Noël v SCP Brouard Daude* [2009] ECR I-205.

[33] See Jens Meyer-Ladewig, *Europäische Menschenrechtskonvention. Handkommentar*, 3rd edn (Baden-Baden, Nomos, 2011) art 55.

[34] Emphasis added.

At first glance, it is obvious that Article 55 ECHR and Article 344 TFEU are diametrically opposed provisions, for both entitle the respective courts to exert exclusive jurisdiction over the same source of law, which is the Convention. This means that after accession, cases between the EU Member States or between a Member State and the Union could be adjudicated on by the CJEU *and* the ECtHR. Since both courts consider their jurisdiction as exclusive, it must be decided which of these courts, at the end of the day, shall be competent in deciding on such cases—otherwise, a conflict of jurisdictions might arise[35] due to the normative overlap of the Convention provisions in the Convention itself as an international treaty and in its manifestation as incorporated Union law.

Contrary to Article 344 TFEU, Article 55 ECHR is a flexible exclusive jurisdiction clause which explicitly acknowledges that the contracting parties to the Convention may, by special agreement, choose to waive Strasbourg's jurisdiction and to settle their disputes before another court or tribunal. This provision thus represents a preference for greater freedom of action to the parties involved, admittedly at the expense of legal coherence, but nonetheless via a provision that obliges the parties to settle their disputes within the respective subsystem.[36] The arising jurisdictional conflict between Luxembourg and Strasbourg may be solved by taking into account the CJEU's jurisdictional foundation, ie Article 19 (1) TEU and Article 344 TFEU, as a 'special agreement' between the Member States and the European Union within the meaning of this term contained in Article 55 ECHR.[37] However, it remains unclear whether these provisions truly fulfil the requirements of a special agreement, since sceptics may argue that firstly, Article 55 ECHR requires the special agreement to be concluded between all the contracting parties to the Convention; and that secondly, this special agreement must explicitly refer to the Convention. None of these conditions are met by Article 19 (1) TEU and Article 344 TFEU, since the EU Treaties have only been concluded between 27 of the contracting parties to the Convention and the said articles are worded in a very general manner,[38] without explicit reference to the Convention or its dispute settlement machinery.

a. The Treaties as an Agreement Concluded only between the European Union and the Member States

In order to answer the question of whether the Treaties qualify as a special agreement within the meaning of Article 55 ECHR, one must turn to the interpretation of this specific provision. The main obstacle in this undertaking is, however, that the precise scope of this provision is unclear and that it does not state to

---

[35] See Lock, 'Future Relationship' (n 13) 391f.

[36] See Yuval Shany, *The Competing Jurisdictions of International Courts and Tribunals* (Oxford, Oxford University Press, 2003) 188.

[37] See Winkler (n 11) 85.

[38] See Lock, 'Future Relationship' (n 13) 392.

what extent the contracting parties can invoke before other fora the provisions enshrined in the Convention.[39] On the one hand, it may be argued that this specific agreement has to be concluded between all contracting parties to the Convention,[40] but on the other hand, it may also be sufficient if all the parties to the proceedings have consented to submit the case at hand to another dispute settlement mechanism.[41] This position of the European Commission on Human Rights is backed by the *travaux préparatoires* to the Convention in which the Swedish delegation proposed that the decision whether or not to submit a dispute to another judicial or arbitral tribunal should be left to the parties concerned and the conclusion of an agreement expressly relating to the dispute at hand.[42] Moreover, this specific interpretation of Article 55 ECHR is also supported by the legal nature of the Convention system which is, in contrast to the European Union, not an autonomous legal order, since its purpose and objective is to protect human rights.[43] It thus seems that the drafters of the Convention were not concerned at all with the preservation of its legal nature, but rather with protecting the autonomy of the high contracting parties and not forcing states to appear before an international court against their will.[44] This is, of course, a reminiscence of the original version of the Convention before Protocol No 11 entered into force in 1998, as ex-Article 48 ECHR allowed the contracting parties to agree to the jurisdiction of the Strasbourg Court. Consequently, a historical interpretation of Article 55 ECHR demonstrates that there is no need for the conclusion of a special agreement between all the parties to the Convention. To fulfil the requirements of this provision, it rather suffices to have concluded a special agreement between *some* of the parties (for example, between the European Union Member States).[45]

b. Explicit Reference to the Convention in the Special Agreement

The second question addresses the matter of whether a special agreement, as set forth in Article 55 ECHR, must contain an explicit reference to the Convention or whether it is sufficient, by virtue of this agreement, to confer the jurisdiction over disputes in relation to Convention rights to another judicial body other than the ECtHR,[46] for instance via the Optional Clause under Article 36 (2) of the

---

[39] See Shany, *Competing Jurisdictions* (n 36) 188.

[40] See Jochen Frowein, 'Art 55' in Jochen Frowein and Wolfgang Peukert (eds), *EMRK-Kommentar* (Kehl am Rhein, NP Engel, 2009) paras 1ff.

[41] See *Cyprus v Turkey (IV)* App no 25781/94 (Commission Decision, 28 June 1996).

[42] See Council of Europe, *Collected edition of the* 'Travaux préparatoires' *of the European Convention on Human Rights*, Vol 5. Legal Committee, Ad hoc Joint Committee, Committee of Ministers, Consultative Assembly (23 June–28 August 1950) (Leiden, Brill, 1979) 58.

[43] See Lock, *Verhältnis* (n 21) 295.

[44] See Shany, *Competing Jurisdictions* (n 36) 191 and Council of Europe, *Collected edition of the* 'Travaux préparatoires', Vol 5 (n 42) 58.

[45] See Lock, 'Future Relationship' (n 13) 393.

[46] See ibid.

Statute of the International Court of Justice (ICJ) in which both parties declare that they accept the jurisdiction of the ICJ as compulsory in reciprocal relation to any other state accepting the same obligation.[47] Only if the latter scenario were the case, Article 19 (1) TEU and Article 344 TFEU would qualify as a special agreement within the meaning of Article 55 ECHR.[48] However, the drafters of the Convention intended to preclude court proceedings based on general juris- diction clauses and particularly construed Article 55 ECHR with special regard to declarations such as the Optional Clause in Article 36 (2) Statute of the ICJ, with which a state may generally accept *ipso facto* the jurisdiction of the ICJ. The purpose of Article 55 ECHR thence was to prevent jurisdictional conflicts, most importantly by stipulating the exclusive jurisdiction of the Strasbourg Court. It may accordingly be concluded that general provisions such as Article 19 (1) TEU and Article 344 TFEU do not represent sufficient ground to trump Strasbourg's exclusive jurisdiction and to establish that of the Luxembourg Court.[49]

Again, there is a substantial argument against this conclusion. When taking into consideration the effects of Protocol No 11 to the Convention—which is, most importantly, the obligatory jurisdiction of the ECtHR—the original intent enshrined in Article 55 ECHR is no longer reasonably applicable and the contract- ing parties do not require any protection from being subjected to procedures for the alleged violation of the Convention, since they cannot escape Strasbourg's jurisdiction.[50]

At this point, a sceptic will presumably ask why Article 55 ECHR is still included in the Convention and why it was not entirely abolished with the entry into force of Protocol No 11 that empowered the Strasbourg Court by discontinuing the Commission on Human Rights.[51] It seems that Article 55 ECHR, as an exclusive jurisdiction clause, generally excludes other courts and tribunals from deciding cases based on the Convention, in order to guarantee its coherent application and interpretation by the Strasbourg Court. Given the fact that the ECtHR is the only court deciding on individual applications (which are de facto more frequent and thus more important for the protection of human rights in Europe), it is consis- tent to grant the ECtHR the same exclusive jurisdiction in relation to inter-state

---

[47] See *Case Concerning Right of Passage over Indian Territory (Portugal v India)* ICJ Rep [1957] 125, 146.

[48] See Opinion 2/94 *Accession by the Community to the European Convention for the Protection of Human Rights and Fundamental Freedoms* [1996] ECR I-1759, c VI.1, para 7, where the Belgian Government states that '[i]n accordance with the possibility provided in Article [55] of the Convention, any action between the Community and its Member States [before the European Court of Human Rights] would be excluded, which would respect Article [344 TFEU]'.

[49] See Lock, 'Future Relationship' (n 13) 393f.

[50] See ibid 394.

[51] See Volker Schlette, 'Das neue Rechtsschutzsystem der Europäischen Menschenrechtskonvention. Zur Reform des Kontrollmechanismus durch das 11. Protokoll' (1996) 56 *Zeitschrift für ausländisches öffentliches Recht und Völkerrecht* 905, 941; Ingrid Siess-Scherz, 'Das neue Rechtsschutzsystem nach dem Protokoll Nr. 11 zur EMRK über die Umgestaltung des durch die Konvention eingeführten Kontrollmechanismus' in Christoph Grabenwarter and Rudolf Thienel (eds), *Kontinuität und Wandel der EMRK. Studien zur Europäischen Menschenrechtskonvention* (Kehl am Rhein, NP Engel, 1998) 1ff.

cases. Yet, since the Convention system is not a self-contained or autonomous legal regime such as the European Union where the CJEU enjoys exclusive jurisdiction in reviewing EU law,[52] the contracting parties are given the right to refer their dispute to another forum. Article 55 ECHR can thus be seen as a default rule giving the Strasbourg Court the general competence to decide on inter-state cases. The exception to the rule, however, must be interpreted narrowly, which means that an agreement conferring jurisdiction to another court or tribunal will have to refer explicitly to the Convention. Thence, Luxembourg's general exclusive jurisdiction by virtue of Article 19 (1) TEU and Article 344 TFEU does not represent an explicit reference to the Convention. Consequently, these provisions do not suffice to satisfy the requirements of Article 55 ECHR and both the ECtHR and the CJEU will have the jurisdiction to accept and decide inter-state cases.[53]

This leaves the two courts with a veritable and unfavourable jurisdictional conflict. Moreover, if Luxembourg is forced to concede a certain degree of its jurisdiction to Strasbourg, the Union's legal autonomy may again be in danger. In order to preserve the EU's autonomy, it might also be concluded from the foregoing analysis that it would be helpful to completely exclude inter-party applications between Member States and between the Member States and the Union after accession.

B. Exclusion of Inter-State Cases?

Given this apparent irreconcilability between Article 33 ECHR and the autonomy of Union law after accession, the question remains whether these complications could be avoided altogether, if inter-state complaints between Union Member States and between Member States and the Union were excluded in the first place, for example by a reservation under Article 57 ECHR or by a corresponding provision in the Accession Agreement. It was therefore argued that the European Union may have a legitimate interest in excluding inter-state applications,[54] for such a course of action would be hardly conceivable[55] within the Union's specific legal system and would run contrary to the principle of sincere and loyal cooperation under Article 4 (3) TEU. Furthermore, it was suggested that disputes between European Union Member States in particular should be excluded after accession, most importantly due to the internal prohibition of such applications

---

[52] See Joined Cases C-402/05 P and C-415/05 P *Kadi and Al Barakaat v Council and Commission* [2008] ECR I- 6351, para 317.

[53] See Lock, *Verhältnis* (n 21) 296f.

[54] See eg, Hans Christian Krüger and Jörg Polakiewicz, 'Vorschläge für ein kohärentes System des Menschenrechtsschutzes in Europa' (2001) 28 *Europäische Grundrechte-Zeitschrift* 92, 104; Benoît-Rohmer, 'Accession' (n 26) 21; Matthias Ruffert, 'Anmerkung zu Gutachten 2/94' [1996] JZ 624, 627; Opinion 2/94 *Accession to the ECHR* (n 48) c VI.2, para 2, where the Spanish Government argues that 'it would be necessary to exclude disputes between the Member States *inter se* or with the Community'.

[55] See Commission of the European Communities, 'Memorandum on the Accession' (n 12) para 27.

to Strasbourg under Article 344 TFEU.[56] A somewhat mitigated approach was taken by the Steering Committee for Human Rights in 2002, which proposed that the exclusion of inter-state complaints between Member States would probably not be necessary, as the issue is in fact one of European Union law and both EU Member States and the European Union might in practice only be expected to use Article 33 ECHR to the degree that such use is in accordance with their obligations under the Treaties. It would thus be for the Union and the Member States to decide whether or not this specific matter should be governed in an *inter-se* agreement.[57]

Yet, even though the exclusion of inter-state complaints under Article 33 ECHR after accession may resolve the imminent jurisdictional conflict between Strasbourg and Luxembourg and thereby preserve the autonomy of European Union law, there are both political and legal arguments as to why the Union should not be treated favourably in this respect. Primarily, the Union's accession to the Convention must not be reduced to a mere tokenism of concurrently accepting *and* curtailing Strasbourg's jurisdiction.[58] To exempt the EU from accountability under the Convention's enforcement machinery of human rights runs counter to the collective guarantee of human rights protection[59] and thus to the entire idea of the Convention. Moreover, when remembering the origins of the Convention in international law, it must be taken into account that originally it was not the individual complaint mechanism, but the inter-state complaint procedure which held the contracting parties responsible for alleged human rights violations.[60] As there is limited access to individual remedies under Article 263 (4) TFEU against the EU's violations of the Convention, the alternative remedy of inter-state applications represents a symbolic importance at the very least. Therefore, the only reason why inter-state cases should be excluded after accession is either based on the presumption that the EU would avoid accountability or that the Union's internal annulment procedures should prevail over the mechanism enshrined in Article 33 ECHR. Taking into account Article 27 of the Vienna Convention on the Law of Treaties (VCLT) and the principle that on the international level international

---

[56] See Jean-Paul Jacqué, 'The Accession of the European Union to the European Convention on Human Rights and Fundamental Freedoms' (2011) 48 *Common Market Law Review* 995, 1008.

[57] See Steering Committee for Human Rights (CDDH), 'Technical and Legal Issues of a Possible EC/EU Accession to the European Convention on Human Rights' CDDH(2002)010 Addendum 2, para 65.

[58] See Rudolf Bernhardt, 'Probleme eines Beitritts der Europäischen Gemeinschaft zur Europäischen Menschenrechts-Konvention' in Ole Due, Marcus Lutter and Jürgen Schwarze (eds), *Festschrift für Ulrich Everling. Band I* (Baden-Baden, Nomos, 1995) 111.

[59] See Franz Matscher, 'Kollektive Garantie der Grundrechte und die Staatenbeschwerde nach der EMRK' in Bernd-Christian Funk (ed), *Der Rechtsstaat vor neuen Herausforderungen: Festschrift für Ludwig Adamovich zum 70. Geburtstag* (Vienna, Verlag Österreich, 2002) 417.

[60] See Jonas Christoffersen, *Institutional Aspects of the EU's Accession to the ECHR* (European Parliament, Committee on Constitutional Affairs, Hearing on the Institutional Aspects of the European Union's Accession to the European Convention on Human Rights, 18 March 2010) 6.

law is supreme,[61] these arguments must of course be rejected, for it would defeat the objective and purpose of the Convention system if the internal rules of one contracting party prevailed over those of the Convention. Since no other contracting party is entitled to this privileged treatment, the EU should not be exempted either. Even if the Member States are bound by the duty of loyalty under Article 4 (3) TEU, European Union law must not prevail over the Convention. It is thence evident that, after accession, the European Union and its Member States must be subjected to the same obligations as other contracting parties to the Convention.[62]

C. The Legal Framework: Articles 4 and 5 of the Draft Accession Agreement

As the final version of the Draft Accession Agreement shows, the drafters of the Agreement deemed the potential exclusion of inter-state complaints between the Member States *inter se* and between the Member States and the Union to be an undue privilege, which would not fit into a system of equally obligated parties, and explicitly included two provisions on this specific topic in the Agreement (Articles 4 and 5). Similarly, no reservation under Article 57 ECHR by the Union is to be expected, as Article 11 of the Draft Accession Agreement sets forth that no reservations may be made in respect of the provisions of this Agreement. The drafters correspondingly agreed to solve the arising jurisdictional conflict between Luxembourg and Strasbourg by concluding a 'special agreement' within the meaning of Article 55 ECHR which will *expressis verbis* refer to the Convention and state that the Convention will be interpreted and applied by the CJEU in proceedings between the Member States or between a Member State and the European Union.

i. Art 4 of the Draft Accession Agreement: Inter-Party Cases

Article 4 (2) of the Draft Accession Agreement explicitly amends the heading of Article 33 ECHR and changes it to 'Inter-*Party* cases'[63] in order to make it correspond with the substance of Article 33 ECHR after accession[64] and to take into consideration the supranational character of the EU as a non-state polity.[65] Moreover, the Explanatory Report clarifies once and for all that after accession,

---

[61] See Mark E Villiger, *Commentary on the 1969 Vienna Convention on the Law of Treaties* (Leiden, Brill Academic Publishers, 2009) 375, para 12.

[62] See Christoffersen (n 60) 6.

[63] Emphasis added.

[64] See Council of Europe, 'Steering Committee for Human Rights—Report to the Committee of Ministers on the Elaboration of Legal Instruments for the Accession of the European Union to the European Convention on Human Rights' CDDH-UE(2011)009, 25, para 63.

[65] See also the interpretation clause of Art 1 (2) and (3) of the Draft Accession Agreement, amending Art 59 ECHR; CDDH-UE(2011)009 (n 64) 5f.

when the European Union has become a high contracting party to the Convention, all states parties to the Convention will be able to bring a case against the Union and vice versa under Article 33 ECHR.[66] In other words, neither the Union nor its Member States will in any way be exempt from the regular inter-party procedures under Article 33 ECHR, at least from the legal vantage point of international law in general and the Convention in particular.

From the internal EU point of view, however, things are quite different. In order not to infringe the autonomy of EU law and its legal sovereignty, the Draft Accession Agreement does not govern the question of whether Union law permits inter-party complaints to the Strasbourg Court involving issues of European Union law between the Member States *inter se* or between the Union and one or more of its Member States. The Explanatory Report expressly mentions that Article 344 TFEU—to which Article 3 of Protocol No 8 to the Treaties refers— bars the Member States from submitting disputes concerning the interpretation or application of the Treaties to another court or tribunal other than the CJEU.[67] Bearing in mind the CJEU's past case law, especially the judgments in the *MOX Plant* and *Kadi and Al Barakaat v Council and Commission*[68] cases, it is expected that Luxembourg will construe Article 19 (1) TEU in conjunction with Article 344 TFEU and thus its exclusive jurisdiction over cases falling within the ambit of EU law in a broad and extensive manner. Consequently, despite the fact that the Convention and the Accession Agreement allow for inter-party applications between the Member States and between the Member States and the Union, the Luxembourg Court has the last say in matters regarding European Union law and may determine that a Member State has failed to fulfil its obligations under Article 4 (3) TEU and Article 344 TFEU, if the said Member State had first lodged an inter-party application before the Strasbourg Court. It thence seems that the autonomy of the Union's legal order has mainly been preserved at the expense of Strasbourg's jurisdiction over the Convention in cases where applications are directed against EU Member States.

ii. Art 5 of the Draft Accession Agreement: Interpretation of Art 55 ECHR

Apparently, Article 5 of the Draft Accession Agreement pursues the same direction as Article 4 of the Draft Accession Agreement. It reads that '[p]roceedings before the Court of Justice of the European Union shall [not] be understood as constituting [...] *means of dispute settlement within the meaning of Article 55 of the Convention*'.[69]

---

[66] See CDDH-UE(2011)009 (n 64) 25, para 62.
[67] See ibid 25, para 64.
[68] See Joined Cases C-402/05 P and C-415/05 P *Kadi and Al Barakaat v Council and Commission* [2008] ECR I-6351.
[69] Art 5 of the Draft Accession Agreement; CDDH-UE(2011)009 (n 64) 8 (emphasis added).

In other words, article 5 of the Draft Accession Agreement safeguards the Union's legal autonomy and contains the 'special agreement' and the explicit reference to the Convention which are necessary to satisfy the requirements of Article 55 ECHR and to uphold Luxembourg's exclusive jurisdiction over EU-related inter-party applications. This provision solves the looming jurisdictional conflict between Strasbourg and Luxembourg and arranges, with regard to Union Member States, that proceedings before the CJEU do not represent a 'means of dispute settlement' within the meaning of Article 55 ECHR. Accordingly, this provision does not prevent the operation of the rule laid down in Article 344 TFEU.[70] Again, the aforementioned prediction regarding Luxembourg's reaction to inter-party cases after accession applies mutis mutandis—being given the exclusive jurisdiction in adjudicating on inter-party cases within the scope of European Union law, the CJEU will undoubtedly seize the chance to extensively apply Article 344 TFEU and to coerce the Member States into using the internal Union dispute settlement mechanism in order to solve legal conflicts between them. In cases of non-compliance, the European Commission may initiate infringement proceedings under Article 258 TFEU whereupon the Luxembourg Court will again resort to the standards found in its *MOX Plant* judgment. The question remains whether the Union's legal autonomy has been upheld largely at the expense of Strasbourg's jurisdiction and the effective protection of human rights at the international level. Of course, the drafters of the agreement set out to take into account the specific nature and thus the autonomy of the EU's legal system, but it is doubtful whether accession is still meaningful if the external review body, ie the Strasbourg Court, is precluded from adjudicating on disputes between the high contracting parties. The next section therefore closely analyses whether these assumptions are true or not and investigates whether the Union's legal autonomy and the effective protection of human rights within the legal framework of inter-party cases are in fact irreconcilable.

iii. Art 5 of the Draft Accession Agreement: Interpretation of Art 35 ECHR

Surprisingly, the solution to these problems can be found within the same provision that enables the Luxembourg Court, by virtue of Article 344 TFEU, to exercise its exclusive jurisdiction in disputes between Member States, namely Article 5 of the Draft Accession Agreement. This provision contains a clause which has deliberately been omitted in the preceding analysis in order to conduct a proper line of reasoning, and which reads in its entirety as follows:

> Proceedings before the Court of Justice of the European Union shall be understood as constituting neither *procedures of international investigation or settlement within the meaning of Article 35, paragraph 2.b., of the Convention*, nor means of dispute settlement within the meaning of Article 55 of the Convention.[71]

---

[70] See CDDH-UE(2011)009 (n 64) 26, para 66.
[71] Art 5 of the Draft Accession Agreement; CDDH-UE(2011)009 (n 64) 8 (emphasis added).

Principally, the italicised clause of Article 5 of the Draft Accession Agreement clarifies that, as a necessary corollary of the European Union's accession to the Convention, proceedings before the European Commission or the Luxembourg Court shall not be understood as constituting procedures of international investigation or international settlement, submission to which would make an application to the ECtHR inadmissible, pursuant to Article 35 (2) lit b ECHR.[72]

However, let us expound this situation in a clear and concise manner with respect to the EU's accession. According to the generally recognised rules of international law, Article 35 (1) ECHR requires the applicants to exhaust all domestic remedies before the ECtHR can deal with a case. This requirement mirrors the principle of subsidiarity which the Convention builds upon and affords the contracting parties the opportunity to prevent or put right violations alleged against them.[73] However, according to the wording of Article 35 (2) ECHR, this admissibility criterion only applies in the case of individual applications under Article 34 ECHR, which means that they will be declared inadmissible if the applicant has not exhausted all local remedies beforehand. Yet, Article 46 lit d Rules of Court requires a contracting party intending to bring a case before the ECtHR under Article 33 ECHR to set out a statement to show whether all local remedies have already been exhausted. Beyond that, the Convention organs have also applied this criterion in inter-party cases where a contracting party directed an application against another party in the interests of its own citizens, which means that the concerned individuals must have availed themselves of effective remedies to secure redress before a contracting party may submit the corresponding inter-party complaint.[74] On the other hand, the rule does not apply when the applicant party complains of general legislation or administrative practice allegedly in violation of the Convention in the form of an *actio popularis*, with the aim of preventing its continuation or recurrence.[75]

Moreover, Article 5 of the Draft Accession Agreement mentions paragraph 2 lit b of Article 35 ECHR, which states that the ECtHR shall not deal with any application that has 'already been submitted to *another procedure of international investigation or settlement* and contains no relevant new information'.[76] This *electa una via* provision bars multiple submissions of the same claim[77] and thus aims at avoiding parallel proceedings between the Strasbourg Court and any other international court or tribunal.[78] In this context, the different organs of the United Nations may come under deliberation, for example the United Nations

---

[72] See CDDH-UE(2011)009 (n 64) 26, para 65.
[73] See *Cardot v France* App no 11069/84 (ECtHR, 19 March 1991) para 36.
[74] See *Cyprus v Turkey (IV)* App no 25781/94 (n 3) para 99.
[75] See *Ireland v United Kingdom* App no 5310/71 (n 3) para 159.
[76] Emphasis added.
[77] See Shany, *Competing Jurisdictions* (n 36) 213.
[78] See Geir Ulfstein, 'The International Judiciary' in Jan Klabbers, Anne Peters and Geir Ulfstein (eds), *The Constitutionalization of International Law* (Oxford, Oxford University Press, 2011) 137.

Human Rights Committee which was established[79] to monitor the compliance of the Member States with the International Covenant on Civil and Political Rights (ICCPR).[80] It is, however, questionable how this provision is related to internal Union proceedings before the CJEU. Since the Union's judicial bodies are *stricto sensu* not domestic, but supranational courts, proceedings before the Luxembourg Court may principally be regarded as procedures of international investigation or settlement. This consideration is nonetheless irrelevant in light of Article 5 of the Draft Accession Agreement, which states that internal EU proceedings shall not be understood as constituting procedures of international investigation or settlement within the meaning of Article 35 (2) lit b ECHR. Beyond that, the ECtHR most recently held that the European Commission does not constitute an international body of investigation or settlement under Article 35 (2) lit b ECHR, since the Commission is given a margin of discretion as to whether to initiate infringement proceedings under Article 258 TFEU or not.[81] The same applies mutis mutandis to the Luxembourg Court. This means that an application will not be declared inadmissible by Strasbourg if substantially the same application has already been brought before the Union courts.

This last argument perfectly segues into the last section of this subchapter and thereby presents the solution to any potential jurisdictional conflict between Luxembourg and Strasbourg in adjudicating on inter-party cases. According to Article 35 (1) ECHR and the requirement that all local remedies be exhausted (which, as aforementioned, also applies to inter-party cases), the ECtHR's role is restricted to the *subsidiary* judicial review of alleged violations of the Convention. Consequently, the domestic courts—including the CJEU after accession—must be given ample opportunity to remedy these violations themselves before an external body may decide on them. This means that Strasbourg has no *complementary* jurisdiction alongside Luxembourg to adjudicate on inter-party complaints, but rather a *subsidiary* jurisdiction, which can only be triggered after all local remedies have been exhausted by virtue of Article 35 (1) ECHR. Disputes between EU Member States *inter se* or between the Member States and the Union where a party acts in the interests of its citizens must therefore be brought before the CJEU, on the one hand, due to the internal Union provision of Article 344 TFEU, and, more importantly, on the other hand, due to the international obligations under the Convention itself, namely Article 35 (1) ECHR.[82] Thence, Article 5 of the Draft Accession Agreement not only succeeds in balancing the respective provisions of the Convention and the European Union Treaties, but also in reconciling the Union's legal autonomy with the Convention's procedural mechanisms.

---

[79] See art 28 ICCPR.

[80] See *Pauger v Austria* App no 24872/94 (Commission Decision, 9 January 1995) holding that 'the applicant's communication to the Human Rights Committee and his present application concern essentially the same issue, [...]. It follows that the Commission is prevented from dealing with the present application by virtue of Article [35 (2) lit b] of the Convention.'

[81] See *Karoussiotis v Portugal* App no 23205/08 (ECtHR, 1 February 2011) paras 69 and 76.

[82] See Kingreen, 'Art 6 EUV' (n 21) para 33, and Winkler (n 11) 84f.

D. The Locus Standi of the Parties after Accession

The foregoing analysis represents a firm theoretical foundation for further investigation on the question of how inter-party cases between the Member States *inter se* and between the Member States and the Union will proceed after accession. The subsequent section examines the legal grounds the *locus standi* of the parties will be based on and under what circumstances the Member States or the European Union may direct an inter-party case against one another, particularly in view of the provisions scrutinised above in Article 344 TFEU and Article 35 (1) ECHR.

i. Art 5 of the Draft Accession Agreement: A Disconnection Clause?

As abovementioned, Article 5 of the Draft Accession Agreement, in conjunction with Articles 35 (1) and 55 of the ECHR, does not prevent the operation of the provision set out in Article 344 TFEU[83] since the functioning and autonomy of European Union law remains unaffected by inter-party applications after accession. One might argue that this provision may qualify as a so-called '*disconnection clause*' (or '*clause de déconnexion*')[84] which can generally be found in treaties drafted and concluded by the Council of Europe and which usually provides that if the parties to a treaty are EU Member States, they shall continue to apply European Union law between themselves. The treaty in question shall only be applied by Member States in their external relations, which means it can only be applied when dealing with parties that are not EU Member States, not between Member States *inter se*.[85]

The object and purpose of disconnection clauses is to ensure legal certainty and clarity and to guarantee the consistency of domestic measures taken on the basis of the treaty with European Union law which will in turn help avoid the fragmentation of the Union's legal order.[86] Most importantly, however, the disconnection clause upholds the supremacy of Union law and thus its autonomy.[87] This is exactly what Article 5 of the Draft Accession Agreement does—it permits the EU and its Member States to apply internal Union rules in order to meet Luxembourg's standards of preserving the Union's legal autonomy. The CJEU can apply Article 19 (1) TEU and Article 344 TFEU in order to settle internal Union disputes whereupon the subsidiary dispute settlement mechanism of the Convention, according to the rules of Article 35 (1) ECHR, will be applied. The

---

[83] See CDDH-UE(2011)009 (n 64) 26, para 66.

[84] See Constantin Economidès and Alexandros Kolliopoulos, 'La clause de déconnexion en faveur du droit communautaire: Une pratique critiquable' (2006) 110 *Revue Générale de Droit International Public* 273, 273ff.

[85] See Jan Klabbers, *Treaty Conflict and the European Union* (Cambridge, Cambridge University Press, 2009) 220.

[86] See Commission of the European Communities, 'Commission Staff Working Paper. Council of Europe Draft Convention on Cybercrime—Accession of the EC and Disconnection Clause' SEC(2001) 315.

[87] See Klabbers, *Treaty Conflict* (n 85) 221.

following sections take these provisions into consideration and illustrate the interaction between European Union law and the respective Convention provisions, in particular the procedural steps before the CJEU and the ECtHR.

ii. The Locus Standi of the Member States

a. Legal Actions between the Member States

Given the abovementioned provisions set forth in the Treaties, the Convention and the Draft Accession Agreement, the Member States are not left with a plethora of alternatives in settling disputes between them before they can lodge an inter-party complaint before the Strasbourg Court. Within the European Union's legal system, the only option at their disposal is the action for failure to fulfil obligations (or infringement proceedings) under Article 259 TFEU. Although infringement proceedings between Member States are as practically irrelevant as inter-party applications under the Convention,[88] this special form of proceedings will be illustrated at this point for the sake of completeness. Generally, this action is objective in nature and the only question raised is whether or not the respondent Member State has infringed Union law.[89] The most relevant fact in the context of this legal analysis is, however, that after accession Member States may also initiate this kind of proceeding for alleged violations of Convention rights, as the wording 'an obligation under the Treaties' covers not only primary and secondary law, but also international agreements concluded by the Union,[90] encompassing the Convention and the final Accession Agreement. Subsequently, this special procedure is briefly illustrated with the help of a concrete case.

A colourful example can be found in the case of *Matthews v United Kingdom*[91] and the subsequent proceedings between Spain and the United Kingdom before the Luxembourg Court,[92] but the scenario will be changed slightly to fit the requirements of the legal situation after accession. If the United Kingdom denies the citizens of Gibraltar their right to vote and to stand as a candidate in elections to the European Parliament, another Member State (such as Spain in the real life case) may file a complaint on the grounds that the United Kingdom has violated the fundamental right to vote and to stand as a candidate under Article 3 of Protocol No 1 to the Convention. However, unlike in the *Matthews* case,[93]

---

[88] So far, only four infringement proceedings between two Member States have been instigated before the Luxembourg Court; see Case 141/78 *French Republic v United Kingdom* [1979] ECR 2923; Case C-388/95 *Belgium v Spain* [2000] ECR I-3123; Case C-145/04 *Spain v United Kingdom* [2006] ECR I-7917; and Case C-364/10 *Hungary v Slovakia* [2012] ECR I-0000.

[89] See eg, Case C-140/00 *Commission v United Kingdom (Fisheries)* [2002] ECR I-10379, para 34.

[90] See eg, Case 104/81 *Kupferberg & Cie KG (Kupferberg I)* [1982] ECR 3641, para 11.

[91] See *Matthews v United Kingdom* App no 24833/94 (ECtHR, 18 February 1999).

[92] See Case C-145/04 *Spain v United Kingdom* (n 88).

[93] The author is well aware of the fact that this very case was lodged by an individual in real-life, namely Mrs Matthews, and not by a contracting party to the Convention. This special circumstance will be ignored at this point in order to illustrate the example.

the applicant would be barred from submitting the application to the ECtHR, since the Convention after accession forms part of Union law and the CJEU has exclusive jurisdiction to interpret and apply this law in all disputes between its Member States. Thus, Spain may initiate infringement proceedings before the Luxembourg Court on the grounds that the United Kingdom violated the fundamental right to vote and to stand as a candidate, as laid down in Article 39 of the Charter of Fundamental Rights of the European Union (ChFR) in conjunction with Articles 22 (2) and 223 (1) TFEU, and, most certainly, in Article 3 of Protocol No 1 to the Convention.

In a case where the CJEU found that the United Kingdom had not infringed the fundamental right in question, a thorough look at Article 5 of the Draft Accession Agreement will answer the question as to whether Spain should decide to file an inter-party complaint before the ECtHR. Since proceedings before the CJEU do not constitute procedures of international investigation or settlement within the meaning of Article 35 ECHR, nor means of dispute settlement within the meaning of Article 55 ECHR (which would prevent the application of Article 344 TFEU), the aforementioned *modus operandi* would fully comply with the requirements of the Treaties, the Convention and the Accession Agreement. The infringement proceedings would fulfil the demands of Article 344 TFEU and thus preserve Luxembourg's exclusive jurisdiction and the Union's legal autonomy, for the CJEU would be given the chance to interpret and apply EU law before the ECtHR does so. Thereby, Strasbourg must accept Luxembourg's interpretation of EU law as factual and is not compelled to encroach upon the autonomy of the European Union's legal system. Moreover, these proceedings would constitute the local remedy Spain has to exhaust before it can lodge an application before the ECtHR.

b. Legal Actions by the Member States against the European Union

If the Member States choose to take action against the European Union for allegedly violating the Convention, the abovementioned conditions also apply. Before they can submit an application against the European Union to the Strasbourg Court, the Member States must first choose a form of legal action provided for by the Treaties and bring their case before the Luxembourg Court. Suitable choices for this course of action are the action for annulment under Article 263 (2) TFEU and the action for failure to act under Article 265 (1) TFEU.

The first option, the action for annulment, enables Member States to bring actions on the grounds of infringement of the Treaties before the CJEU, which in turn will review the legality of legislative acts and acts of the Union's institutions and their conformity with superior law. This means that the Member States may contest the conformity of secondary law with primary law or with the Convention which will, as an integral part of Union law, rank above secondary law.[94] In other

---

[94] See Case 181/73 *Haegeman* (n 19) para 5.

words, the infringement of European Union law for which annulment is sought may consist of an *active* misapplication of the law,[95] for example by enacting secondary legislation in violation of fundamental rights—either those enshrined in the Charter (primary law) or those of the Convention (mezzanine status above secondary law). Furthermore, Member States are privileged applicants, which mean that they may bring an action for annulment before the CJEU without proving that they have a particular interest in the action.[96]

After accession, the same conditions as for infringement proceedings under Article 259 TFEU apply. *In concreto*, a Member State presuming that certain secondary legislation might be in violation of the Convention, must first bring an action for annulment of the legal act in question before the Luxembourg Court. Only then may it direct an inter-party complaint to Strasbourg. Article 5 of the Draft Accession Agreement acknowledges both Luxembourg's exclusive jurisdiction under Article 344 TFEU and the Convention's requirements under Article 35 (1) of the ECHR which will require Member States seeking to annul secondary law in alleged violation of the Convention to first bring their case before the CJEU, in order to exhaust all domestic remedies and to give the CJEU the chance to interpret and apply Union law. In a case where the CJEU does not annul the respective legal act, the Member State may file an inter-party complaint to the ECtHR which will then consider the CJEU's interpretation as facts, but without interfering with the Union's legal order. Thus, the autonomy of the European Union will also be perfectly upheld in actions for annulment between a Member State and the Union.

The second option, the action for failure to act under Article 265 (1) TFEU, entitles the Member States to bring an action before the Luxembourg Court, if the institutions of the Union, in infringement of the Treaties, failed to act in a concrete situation. In contrast to the action for annulment, the action for failure to act consequently requests judicial review on the EU's *passivity* or *inaction* in a specific field of legislation.[97] In other words, the applicant Member State seeks a declaration that the respondent Union institution acted unlawfully by failing to take a decision or to enact secondary legislation,[98] even though this institution was obliged to take action in order to comply with Union law and, after accession, the Convention. In short, the Union's inaction is allegedly in violation of fundamental rights and in breach of the Convention in particularly. Similarly to the action for annulment, Member States are privileged applicants. This situation

---

[95] See eg, Case 18/62 *Barge v High Authority* [1963] ECR 259; see also Koen Lenaerts, Dirk Arts, Ignace Maselis and Robert Bray, *Procedural Law of the European Union*, 2nd edn (London, Sweet & Maxwell, 2006) 307.

[96] See Case 230/81 *Luxembourg v European Parliament* [1983] ECR 255, para 23.

[97] See Lenaerts, Arts, Maselis and Bray (n 95) 329.

[98] See eg, Case 346/85 *United Kingdom v Commission* [1987] ECR 5179, para 1.

unburdens them from proving that they have a particular interest in bringing an action for failure to act before the Luxembourg Court.[99]

Nevertheless, the preconditions for submitting an action for failure to act for not complying with the Convention are quite different and more intricate than those filing an action for annulment for actively violating human rights, as the former is directed against an inaction which in turn presupposes an actual competence or positive obligation to act on the part of the Union. As *Opinion 2/94* has confirmed, however, there is no treaty provision that confers on the EU institutions any general power to enact human rights legislation.[100] In addition, explicit and implicit competence in this field has intentionally been kept under rigid control and has effectively been confined to individual acts of secondary law, usually on the grounds of specific primary law provisions.[101] Since the European Union has no genuine competence in the field of human rights,[102] a Member State would thus have to investigate whether the Union was in any way obliged to act on a specific legal basis. This undertaking could prove difficult[103] as positive obligations are generally associated with economic, social and cultural rights,[104] for which the Union has only limited or even no competence.

However, within the field of free movement of workers (Article 45 TFEU), freedom of establishment (Article 49 TFEU) and freedom to provide services (Article 56 TFEU), the Union actually possesses a potent human rights tool in the form of Article 19 TFEU. This provision provides the EU with the competence to take appropriate action to combat discrimination based on sex, racial or ethnic origin, religion or belief, disability, age or sexual orientation. Since the European Union has already enacted legislation on this subject matter, *inter alia*, the Racial Equality Directive,[105] the Framework Employment Directive[106] and the Self-Employment Directive,[107] an applicant may also construe that the Union failed to enact

---

[99] See Wolfram Cremer, 'Art 265 AEUV' in Christian Calliess and Matthias Ruffert (eds), *EUV/AEUV. Kommentar*, 4th edn (Munich, Beck, 2011) paras 12–13; Markus Kotzur, 'Art 265 AEUV' in Rudolf Geiger, Daniel-Erasmus Kahn and Markus Kotzur (eds), *EUV/AEUV. Kommentar*, 5th edn (Munich, Beck, 2010) para 8.

[100] See Opinion 2/94 *Accession to the ECHR* (n 48) para 27.

[101] See Andrew Williams, *EU Human Rights Policies. A Study in Irony* (Oxford, Oxford University Press, 2005) 114.

[102] On this issue, see generally JHH Weiler and Sybilla C Fries, 'A Human Rights Policy for the European Community and Union: The Question of Competences' in Philipp Alston, Mara Bustelo and James Heenan (eds), *The EU and Human Rights* (Oxford, Oxford University Press, 1999) 147ff.

[103] See Walter Frenz, *Handbuch Europarecht. Band 4: Europäische Grundrechte* (Berlin Heidelberg, Springer, 2009) paras 773–75.

[104] See GJH van Hoof, 'The Legal Nature of Economic, Social and Cultural Rights: A Rebuttal of Some Traditional Views' in Philipp Alston and Katarina Tomaševski (eds), *The Right to Food* (The Hague, Kluwer Law, 1984) 97.

[105] Council Directive 2000/43/EC of 29 June 2000 implementing the principle of equal treatment between persons irrespective of racial or ethnic origin [2000] OJ L180/22.

[106] Council Directive 2000/78/EC of 27 November 2000 establishing a general framework for equal treatment in employment and occupation [2000] OJ L303/16.

[107] Directive 2010/41/EU of the European Parliament and of the Council of 7 July 2010 on the application of the principle of equal treatment between men and women engaged in an activity in a self-employed capacity and repealing Council Directive 86/613/EEC [2010] OJ L180/1.

secondary legislation and thereby violated Article 14 ECHR as the respective EU institution was obliged to take action in order to comply with Union law and the Convention.

Still, positive obligations can also be imposed with regard to civil and political rights[108] such as the right to a fair trial under Article 6 ECHR and the right to an effective remedy under Article 13 ECHR. In this context, the limited access of individuals to the Union courts under Article 263 (4) TFEU may qualify as a suitable example for the Union's failure to act. The problem with this example nonetheless lies in the fact that Article 263 (4) TFEU is part of primary law and cannot be independently amended by the European Union in order to conform to the respective provisions of the Convention.[109]

A less intricate example might shed more light on this issue. After the entry into force of the Maastricht Treaty, the Union initiated the transition from national arrangements to the common organisation of the markets. The Commission, however, has failed to take into consideration the situation of the traders who have taken action without having been able to foresee the legal ramifications of this transition. Without laying down concrete rules catering for cases of hardship arising from this transition, a Member State thence may suppose that the European Union failed to act accordingly, for example by passing secondary legislation, and intend to correct the concrete human rights violation stemming from this failure to act, namely the right to property under Article 1 of Protocol No 1 to the Convention.[110] Again, a Member State seeking a corresponding declaration must comply with Article 344 TFEU and Article 5 of the Draft Accession Agreement and must first bring the case before the Luxembourg Court before it can direct an application to Strasbourg, in order to exhaust all domestic remedies (according to Art 35 (1) ECHR) and to give the CJEU the chance to interpret and apply Union law. In a case where the CJEU does not find a failure to act, the Member State may file an inter-party complaint to the ECtHR which will then consider the CJEU's interpretations as facts, but without interfering with the Union's legal order. Prima facie, this *modus operandi* preserves the autonomy of EU law.

Most importantly in the context of the EU's accession, however, Article 6 (2) TEU and Article 2 of Protocol No 8 prescribe that accession shall neither affect the competences of the Union or the power of its institutions, nor the situation of the Member States in relation to the Convention.[111] Accordingly, positive obligations of the European Union to take action in order to comply with the Convention would only arise to the extent to which EU competences permitting such action exist under primary law.[112] At this point, sceptics will indicate one scenario in

---

[108] See David Harris, Michael O'Boyle, Ed Bates and Carla Buckley (eds), *Law of the European Convention on Human Rights*, 2nd edn (Oxford, Oxford University Press, 2009) 18ff.

[109] For more details on this specific problem, see ch 11.

[110] See Case C-68/95 *T Port GmbH & Co KG v Bundesanstalt für Landwirtschaft und Ernährung* [1996] ECR I-6065.

[111] See also Craig, *The Lisbon Treaty* (n 30) 214f.

[112] See European Convention, 'Final Report of Working Group II' CONV 354/02, WG II 16, 13.

which the Union's legal autonomy might be in serious jeopardy. In cases where the Strasbourg Court determines that the Union has violated the Convention by not enacting a particular piece of legislation, which in fact does not fall into the EU's competence, the competence for legislating in this field of law might implicitly shift to the European Union at the expense of the Member States. Such a judgment by Strasbourg would dramatically interfere with the internal division of competences between the Union and its Member States and thus its legal autonomy. Yet again, there is a practical solution to this issue—according to Article 3 (3) of the Draft Accession Agreement, the Member States may become co-respondents in this situation, as the application is directed against the European Union and the alleged violation calls into question the compatibility of primary law with the Convention. Subsequently, the Strasbourg Court would hold both the Union and the Member States responsible and would not adjudicate on the allocation of powers. The respondents may then decide how to remedy the violation of the Convention on the basis of EU law and the ECtHR would not encroach upon the autonomy of the EU's legal order.

iii. The Locus Standi of the European Union

a. Legal Actions against the Member States When Implementing EU Law

The Union is given one form of action to settle disputes with the Member States before it may submit an inter-party complaint to the Strasbourg Court. According to the Treaties, the Union's only option is the action for failure to fulfil obligations (or infringement proceedings) under Article 258 of the TFEU, which is—due to the increasing numbers of infringement proceedings initiated by the Commission—of utmost importance for the development, coherence and effective enforcement of European Union law.[113] In contrast to infringement proceedings between the Member States, the applicant under Article 258 TFEU is not a Member State but the European Commission which may bring an action against a Member State for failing to fulfil an obligation under the Treaties. This competence is consistent with Article 17 (1) TEU which entrusts the Commission with ensuring and overseeing the application of the Treaties under the control of the Luxembourg Court, whereby it is not necessary for the Commission to have a specific interest in bringing an action in order to commence with the infringement proceedings.[114] After accession, the Commission may also initiate this kind of proceeding for alleged violations of the Convention by the Member States when implementing Union law, since the wording 'an obligation under the Treaties' also

---

[113] See European Commission, '28th Annual Report on Monitoring the Application of EU Law (2010)' COM(2011) 588 final, 9.

[114] See Case C-422/92 *Commission v Germany (Toxic and Dangerous Waste Directives)* [1995] ECR I-1097, para 16.

covers international agreements concluded by the Union,[115] thus encompassing the Convention and the Accession Agreement. Again, a concrete example might help one to understand the legal ramifications of the accession. In a recent case, the Commission requested that the CJEU declare that national authorities outside the public sector must not be made responsible for monitoring the processing of personal data. The CJEU held that by doing so, Germany had incorrectly trans-posed the Directive on the Protection of Individuals with regard to the processing of personal data and on the free movement of such data[116] and, most impor-tantly, interfered with the individual right to privacy under Article 8 ECHR.[117] After accession, the Commission is obliged to act in the same way—Article 5 of the Draft Accession Agreement acknowledges the CJEU's right under Article 344 TFEU to settle internal Union disputes before the Strasbourg Court may be called upon. Moreover, the Commission has to exhaust all domestic remedies under Article 35 (1) ECHR before directing an application to the ECtHR. This means that all actions for failure to fulfil obligations under the Treaties initiated by the Commission must first be brought before the CJEU before the Commission can lodge an inter-party application against a Member State for allegedly violating the Convention when implementing Union law to Strasbourg. Assuming that the aforementioned concrete case takes place after accession, the CJEU may also determine that Germany has not failed to fulfil its obligations under Union law, which means that it has correctly transposed the Directive in question, and has thus not violated the Convention and the right to privacy. In this case, the Commission may content itself with this decision or take the case to Strasbourg in order to remedy the alleged violation of Article 8 ECHR.

b. Legal Actions against the Member States When Not Implementing EU Law

At this point, however, another and more intricate question arises, namely whether the European Union is also entitled to file an inter-party complaint against the Member States in cases in which the respondent Member State has allegedly violated the Convention, but has *not* implemented Union law. One might argue that, since the Convention and the Accession Agreement have become an integral part of EU law upon accession, every violation of the Convention concurrently constitutes a failure to fulfil an obligation under the Treaties.

There are several arguments against this point of view. As abovementioned in cases regarding actions for failure to act by a Member State against the Union, Article 6 (2) TEU and Article 2 of Protocol No 8 to the Treaties set forth that

---

[115] See eg, Case 22/70 *Commission v Council (AETR)* [1971] ECR 263, paras 15 and 19; Case 104/81 *Kupferberg I* (n 90) para 11.

[116] Directive 95/46/EC of the European Parliament and of the Council of 24 October 1995 on the protection of individuals with regard to the processing of personal data and on the free movement of such data [1995] OJ L281/31.

[117] See Case C-518/07 *Commission v Germany (Personal Data)* [2010] ECR I-1885, para 21.

accession shall not affect the division of competences between the Union and the Member States. Therefore, accession must not lead to any extension of the Union's competences, let alone to the creation of a general competence on legislating and enforcing fundamental rights. Correspondingly, the Commission's right to initiate infringement proceedings under Article 258 TFEU would only arise to the extent to which competences of the Union allowing for such action exist under primary law.[118] Luxembourg's exclusive jurisdiction is thus only relevant if genuine EU law is applicable in the case at hand. In situations where the alleged violation lies outside the ambit and scope of EU law, for example in entirely domestic fields of law, the CJEU cannot claim jurisdiction, even though the Convention forms part of Union law.[119] This view is also corroborated by the wording of the first sentence of Article 51 (1) ChFR, according to which the fundamental rights of the EU are only addressed to the Member States when they are implementing Union law. The purport of this provision has been interpreted as prompting the Luxembourg Court to exercise due caution and judicial restraint in the future.[120] This means that the CJEU is not entitled to hold the Member States responsible for alleged violations of the Convention in those fields of law which lie outside the Union's competences and in cases where they are not implementing Union law.[121]

III. THE EXTERNAL DIMENSION: THE EUROPEAN UNION AS A HUMAN RIGHTS LITIGATOR IN EUROPE?

A. The European Union's External Human Rights Policy and Accession

The European Union's accession to the Convention is not confined to the internal functioning of the Union. Quite the contrary, the EU is a powerful and representative actor on the international plane, which means that it also has the capacity and responsibility to positively influence the human rights policies of third states, as well as those of international organisations. The EU has recognised this responsibility and therefore insists that non-Member States seeking accession to the Union must meet and fulfil strict human rights criteria.[122] These criteria are enshrined in Article 49 TEU which requires candidate states to respect the values referred to in Article 2 TEU, namely human dignity, freedom, democracy, equality, human rights, including the rights of persons belonging to minorities and the rule of law. In other words, candidate states must first accede to the ECHR before they

---

[118] See European Convention, 'Final Report of Working Group II' CONV 354/02 (n 112) 13.
[119] See Lock, 'Future Relationship' (n 13) 391.
[120] See Martin Borowsky, 'Art 51', in Jürgen Meyer (ed), *Charta der Grundrechte der Europäischen Union* (Baden-Baden, Nomos, 2010) paras 24ff.
[121] See Schott (n 24) 5.
[122] See Philip Alston and JHH Weiler, 'An 'Ever Closer Union' in Need of a Human Rights Policy: The European Union and Human Rights' in Philipp Alston, Mara Bustelo and James Heenan (eds), *The EU and Human Rights* (Oxford, Oxford University Press, 1999) 7.

can become Member States of the European Union.[123] The values laid down in the Convention represent the first batch of the so-called Copenhagen Criteria[124] which every state aspiring membership must respect and enforce.[125]

Despite the fact that the European Union's human rights policies are afflicted with various paradoxes and a lack of coherence[126]—problems which will be ignored at this point for the sake of argumentative straightforwardness and the lack of space—the EU's accession to the Convention may have a stimulating effect on its external human rights policies and open up new ways of enforcing human rights in the European neighbourhood, particularly with the objective of putting candidates on the right track towards EU membership. These may be sound political arguments, but the following sections will of course concentrate on the legal questions with respect to the Union as a human rights litigator in Europe, namely by the means of directing inter-party applications against non-Member States—an ambitious option in terms of the Union's human rights policy.[127] More precisely, notwithstanding the fact that neither the Convention nor the Accession Agreement preclude the Union from bringing inter-party complaints against a third country under Article 33 ECHR, the subsequent sections will investigate whether the European Union actually has the necessary competence to do so under EU law and whether such a course of action is therefore compatible and reconcilable with the Union's legal autonomy.

B. A Question of Competence

i. The Importance of Competence and the Union's Legal Autonomy

The European Union's competence in lodging inter-party complaints against third countries after accession is not a self-evident fact, in particular with regard

---

[123] See eg, Meinhard Hilf and Frank Schorkopf, 'Art 2 EUV' in Eberhard Grabitz, Meinhard Hilf and Martin Nettesheim (eds), *Das Recht der Europäischen Union. Band I* (Munich, Beck, 2010) paras 15–17.

[124] See European Council in Copenhagen, 21–22 June 1993, Conclusions of the Presidency, SN 180/1/93 REV 1, 13.

[125] See Hans-Joachim Cremer, 'Art 2 EUV' in Christian Calliess and Matthias Ruffert (eds), *EUV/ AEUV. Kommentar*, 4th edn (Munich, Beck, 2011) para 10.

[126] For a detailed analysis of the Union's coherence problems in its human rights policies, see for instance Kirsten Siems, *Das Kohärenzgebot in der Europäischen Union und seine Justitiabilität* (Baden-Baden, Nomos, 1999); Sacha Prechal and Bert Van Roermund (eds), *The Coherence of EU Law. The Search for Unity in Divergent Concepts* (Oxford, Oxford University Press, 2008); Philipp Alston, Mara Bustelo and James Heenan (eds), *The EU and Human Rights* (Oxford, Oxford University Press, 1999).

[127] See Davide Zaru, 'EU Reactions to Violations of Human Rights Norms by Third States' in Wolfgang Benedek, Florence Benoît-Rohmer, Wolfram Karl and Manfred Nowak (eds), *European Yearbook on Human Rights 2011* (Vienna, NWV, 2011) 240f; Andrew Clapham, 'Where is the EU's Human Rights Common Foreign Policy, and How is it Manifested in Multilateral Fora?' in Philipp Alston, Mara Bustelo and James Heenan (eds), *The EU and Human Rights* (Oxford, Oxford University Press, 1999) 675ff.

to the protection of human rights *outside* the ambit of Union law. Sceptics may also argue that an inter-party complaint initiated by the EU against a non-Member State would have an effect contrary to the original object and purpose of accession, namely to improve the protection of individuals against legal acts by the Union which are allegedly in violation of the Convention. It was, however, not intended to expand the Union's competences at the expense of the Member States or vis-à-vis third countries in the course of accession,[128] as the establishment of such a new competence may jeopardise the Union's legal autonomy. In *Opinion 1/91*, Luxembourg ruled that an international agreement concluded by the Union may certainly bestow new functions or competences on the Union's institutions, but it must not change the nature of their function.[129] The same point can be made on the European Union's new power to direct inter-party complaints against third countries after accession. If this competence is in fact likely to alter the functional nature of the EU's institutions, the Union must be precluded from directing inter-party applications against third countries in order to uphold its own legal autonomy.

From the outset, there are two different situations which must be distinguished from one another, namely whether this new competence arises from the Accession Agreement or the Union Treaties. If the Accession Agreement were to provide the European Union and its institutions with new powers which would change the nature of their function under the Treaties, its conclusion would be incompatible with the autonomy of Union law. There is, however, no provision in the Agreement which confers any new power to the EU or its institutions as regards inter-party complaints. It can therefore be concluded that this competence is firstly not a new one arising from the entry into force of the Accession Agreement, but rather that this competence can be found in Union law itself. As a consequence, if this competence already forms part of EU law, it is not capable of changing the functional nature of the Union's institutions and thus of jeopardising the autonomy of European Union law.

The following sections will thus investigate whether the EU's legal order does in fact authorise the Union to bring inter-party complaints before the Strasbourg Court, and where this competence may be found in Union law. Yet, the quest for such an explicit competence seems to be a futile one. A thorough search of the Treaties does not yield a usable solution in this respect, as the EU's primary law neither contains an instrument comparable to the Convention's inter-party complaints nor the explicit competence to take legal action against non-Member States for the violation of human rights. The closest thing there is to inter-party applications against third countries is the Union's competence in concluding agreements with third countries. But still, the relevant provisions remain silent on whether the Union has basic competence in the field of international human

---

[128] See Winkler (n 11) 87.
[129] See Opinion 1/91 *EEA I* (n 16) paras 59 and 61.

rights protection, for example by concluding corresponding agreements to promote human rights vis-à-vis third countries. In the case where the Union has indeed competence to conclude international agreements for the protection of human rights, it is only logical in the sense of an *argumentum a maiori ad minus* that it also has competence to enforce its external human rights policy through inter-party complaints against third countries under Article 33 ECHR.

ii. Pre-Lisbon: Luxembourg's Case Law in Opinion 2/94 and the AETR Case

In this context, it is crucial to distinguish between two different kinds of external action by the European Union in the sphere of human rights. Firstly, the Union can conclude agreements which do not have human rights as their principal objective, but which are based on the respect for human rights or contain provisions or even human rights clauses in this field—for instance all bilateral cooperation, partnership and association agreements between the European Union and third countries such as the Cotonou Agreement.[130] Secondly, however, it is doubtful whether the Union has the competence to conclude agreements which explicitly contain human rights provisions in the sense of laying down rules and standards of human rights protection for the contracting parties involved. Moreover, as regards the first category of agreements, there is substantial practice, based on express provisions in the Treaties such as Article 21 (2) lit b TEU[131] and Article 212 TFEU,[132] which was also recognised by the Luxembourg Court.[133] By contrast, the second category of agreements is more problematic, as it has not been exercised in the past.[134]

Consequently, when referring to the accession to the Convention, the CJEU held in *Opinion 2/94* that '[n]o Treaty provision confers on the Community institutions any general power to enact rules on human rights or to conclude international conventions in this field'.[135] Yet, since the Union has always been under the obligation to respect and protect fundamental rights on the internal plane, mostly due to the CJEU's past case law on this matter, it may also be necessary for the Union to commit itself on the international parquet. The European Union has, for example, enacted secondary law[136] based on Article 19 TFEU in order to expand

---

[130] See art 9 of the Cotonou Agreement between the European Union and the African, Caribbean and Pacific states which emphasises human rights as an essential element of the Agreement and reiterates that serious violations of human rights constitute a breach of this Agreement.

[131] Ex-art 177 (2) Treaty establishing the European Community (TEC).

[132] Ex-art 181a TEC.

[133] See Case C-268/94 *Portugal v Council (Cooperation Agreement with India)* [1996] ECR I-6177.

[134] See Piet Eeckhout, *External Relations of the European Union. Legal and Constitutional Foundations* (Oxford, Oxford University Press, 2005) 470.

[135] See Opinion 2/94 *Accession to the ECHR* (n 48) para 27.

[136] See Council Directive 2000/43/EC of 29 June 2000 implementing the principle of equal treatment between persons irrespective of racial or ethnic origin [2000] OJ L180/22; Council Directive 2000/78/EC of 27 November 2000 establishing a general framework for equal treatment in employment and occupation [2000] OJ L303/16.

its non-discrimination policies. Analogously, the CJEU's famous *implied powers* doctrine,[137] introduced in its *Commission v Council (AETR)* judgment, may be applied to the conclusion of international agreements in this field. In this case, the Luxembourg Court held that

[...] each time the Community, with a view to implementing a common policy envisaged by the Treaty, adopts provisions laying down common rules, [...] the Member States no longer have the right [...] to undertake obligations with third countries which affect those rules. [...]

With regard to the implementation of the provisions of the Treaty the system of internal Community measures may not therefore be separated from that of external relations.[138]

In other words, Luxembourg asserted that the Union automatically acquires exclusive external competence in an internal policy field in which it has already enacted legislation. This approach supports the principle of parallelism in powers or, more elegantly put, '*in foro interno, in foro externo*'.[139] This is not mere theory, for it may be argued that Article 19 TFEU gives the Union exclusive competence for the conclusion of Protocol No 12 to the Convention insofar as the provisions contained in the Protocol affect Union legislation.[140]

In a nutshell, the Union's legal foundation pre-Lisbon provided for—at least to a certain extent—competence in the field of international human rights protection which is still relevant today. However, as will be shown below, the Treaty of Lisbon expanded this competence dramatically.

iii. Post-Lisbon: A New Human Rights Dimension

Again, another look at the abovementioned argument will help shed more light on the research questions of this chapter. If the European Union has the competence to conclude agreements in the field of human rights protection, it must also have the competence to bring inter-party complaints under Article 33 ECHR before the Strasbourg Court. Currently, following the entry into force of the Treaty of Lisbon, there are two main arguments in favour of a broad EU human rights policy and thence for the Union's competence to lodge inter-party complaints against third countries.

---

[137] See Christophe Hillion, '*ERTA, ECHR* and *Open Skies*: Laying the Grounds of the EU System of External Relations' in Miguel Poiares Maduro and Loïc Azoulai (eds), *The Past and Future of EU Law. The Classics of EU Law Revisited on the 50th Anniversary of the Rome Treaty* (Oxford, Hart Publishing, 2010) 225.

[138] See Case 22/70 *Commission v Council (AETR)* (n 115) paras 17 and 19.

[139] See Line Holdgaard and Rass Holdgaard, 'The External Powers of the European Community' [2001] *Retsvidenskabeligt Tidsskrift Publications* 108, 114 <http://law.au.dk/fileadmin/site_files/filer_jura/dokumenter/forskning/rettid/artikler/20010108.pdf> accessed 1 November 2012.

[140] See Eeckhout, *External Relations* (n 134) 471.

a. Art 216 (1) TFEU

The first argument is based on the fact that the legal principles resulting from Luxembourg's settled case law (especially the aforementioned *Opinion 2/94* and the *AETR* case) are now enshrined in two Treaty provisions, namely Articles 3 (2) and 216 TFEU. The first paragraph of Article 216, which is relevant in the context of this chapter, mentions the following options to conclude international agreements:

> The Union may conclude an agreement with one or more third countries or international organisations [1] *where the Treaties so provide* or [2] *where the conclusion of an agreement is necessary in order to achieve, within the framework of the Union's policies, one of the objectives referred to in the Treaties,* or [3] *is provided for in a legally binding Union act* or [4] *is likely to affect common rules or alter their scope.*[141]

Although Article 216 (1) TFEU accords the Union's treaty-making powers in four principal types or categories, the reality following the entry into force of the Lisbon Treaty is that the EU will in any case have the competence necessary to conclude an international agreement,[142] even in the field of human rights protection which is not part of the Union's exclusive competences under Article 3 (1) TFEU.[143] Of course, in theory, it is possible to picture cases which do not fit into the four categories set out in Article 216 (1) TFEU, but in practice, one or more of these categories will always legitimate and entitle the Union to conclude an international treaty. The second category in particular—the competence to conclude an agreement where such conclusion is necessary in order to achieve, within the framework of the Union's policies, one of the objectives referred to in the Treaties—is worth emphasising in this context.[144] This category has been introduced and confirmed by the Luxembourg Court[145] which also ruled that whenever European Union law created powers for its institutions within its internal system for the purpose of accomplishing a specific objective, the Union had the competence to take on international commitments necessary for the attainment of that very objective.[146] There are, however, well-founded reasons that the second category of the EU's treaty-making powers under Article 216 (1) TFEU is not applicable in the context of inter-party complaints against third countries.

The Union's accession to the Convention and the corresponding conclusion of the Accession Agreement are laid down in Article 6 (2) TEU and Article 218 (6)

---

[141] Emphasis added; numbers in brackets included by the author.
[142] See Craig, *The Lisbon Treaty* (n 30) 165 and 399.
[143] The Union's exclusive competences according to art 3 (1) TFEU include the establishment of a customs union, the enactment of the competition rules necessary for the functioning of the internal market; a monetary policy for the Member States whose currency is the Euro; the conservation of marine biological resources under the common fisheries policy; and the common commercial policy; but obviously no competence in the field of (international) human rights.
[144] See Craig, *The Lisbon Treaty* (n 30) 399.
[145] See Joined Cases 3/76, 4/76 and 6/76 *Kramer (Biological Resources of the Sea)* [1976] ECR 1279, para 30/33; Opinion 1/76 *Draft Agreement Establishing a European Laying-up Fund for Inland Waterway Vessels* [1977] ECR 741, para 4.
[146] See Opinion 1/03 *Lugano Convention* [2006] ECR I-1145, para 114.

lit a (ii) TFEU, which are undoubtedly primary law provisions. Consequently, the first category of Article 216 (1) TFEU is applicable, which means that the Union may conclude an agreement in which the Treaties so provide.[147] This option is self-evident or simply a redundant truism as the Treaties provide that the Union may conclude an international agreement if the Treaties so provide.[148] Therefore, the Union would even have the competence to conclude the agreement on accession to the Convention, if there was no explicit reference to this competence in Article 216 (1) TFEU.[149]

b. Art 3 (2) TFEU

Nonetheless, there is another provision which is worth analysing at this point to emphasise the Union's competence in concluding international agreements in the field of human rights, in particular the Accession Agreement. There is a significant link between Article 216 TFEU and Article 3 (2) TFEU, for the former provision is concerned with whether the Union has the competence to conclude an international agreement and the latter covers the related issue regarding whether this very competence is exclusive or not.[150] Article 3 (2) TFEU states that

> [t]he Union shall also have exclusive competence for the conclusion of an international agreement when its conclusion is provided for in a legislative act of the Union or is necessary to enable the Union to exercise its internal competence, or insofar as its conclusion may affect common rules or alter their scope.

When read together with Article 216 (1) TFEU, Article 3 (2) TFEU is by no means easy to interpret,[151] especially because these two provisions cover an overlapping scope, but are not identical.[152] This fact will most likely lead to major issues regarding the proper interpretation of Article 216 (1) TFEU in conjunction with Article 3 (2) TFEU.[153] It is, however, apparent that Article 3 (2) puts Article 216 (1) in more concrete terms,[154] since it states that where the conclusion of an international agreement is provided for in a legislative Union act (ie secondary law), the

---

[147] See Kirsten Schmalenbach, 'Art 216 AEUV' in Christian Calliess and Matthias Ruffert (eds), *EUV/AEUV. Kommentar*, 4th edn (Munich, Beck, 2011) para 9.

[148] See Bardo Fassbender, 'Die Völkerrechtssubjektivität der Europäischen Union nach dem Entwurf des Verfassungsvertrages' (2004) 42 *Archiv des Völkerrechts* 26, 37.

[149] See Daniel-Erasmus Khan, 'Art 216 AEUV' in Rudolf Geiger, Daniel-Erasmus Kahn and Markus Kotzur (eds), *EUV/AEUV. Kommentar*, 5th edn (Munich, Beck, 2010) para 8.

[150] See Craig, *The Lisbon Treaty* (n 30) 399.

[151] See Marise Cremona, 'The Draft Constitutional Treaty: External Relations and External Action' (2003) 40 *Common Market Law Review* 1347, 1347.

[152] See Christoph Vedder, 'Art I-13' in Christoph Vedder and Wolff Heintschel von Heinegg (eds), *Europäischer Verfassungsvertrag. Handkommentar* (Baden-Baden, Nomos, 2007) para 5.

[153] See Martin Nettesheim, 'Die Kompetenzordnung im Vertrag über eine Verfassung für Europa' (2004) 39 *Europarecht* 511, 532f; Markus Ludwigs, 'Die Kompetenzordnung der Europäischen Union im Vertragsentwurf über eine Verfassung für Europa' (2004) 7 *Zeitschrift für Europarechtliche Studien* 211, 228.

[154] See Christian Calliess, 'Art 3 AEUV' in Christian Calliess and Matthias Ruffert (eds), *EUV/AEUV. Kommentar*, 4th edn (Munich, Beck, 2011) para 17.

Union consequently has exclusive external competence in this regard. Of course, the same reasoning applies a fortiori where a Treaty provision, ie primary law,[155] bestows upon the EU the power to conclude an international agreement, unless there is some explicit provision in the Treaties to the contrary,[156] which Article 3 (2) TFEU, however, does not mention.[157] As aforementioned, the conclusion of the Accession Agreement is provided for in Article 6 (2) TEU and Article 218 (6) lit a (ii) TFEU which are both primary law provisions. Thus, the Union indisputably has exclusive competence to conclude the Accession Agreement without any restrictions on behalf of the Member States.

c. Art 24 (1) TEU

The second argument in favour of a broad EU human rights policy and thus for the Union's competence in lodging inter-party complaints against third countries, is based on another provision of utmost importance at this point in the discussion, namely Article 24 (1) TEU and the Union's competence to act in its Common Foreign and Security Policy (CFSP) field. Despite the deconstruction of the European Union's pillar structure via the Treaty of Lisbon, distinct rules continue to apply to the CFSP. The provisions concerning the CFSP have been enshrined in the TEU, whereas the remainder of the provisions on external action have been laid down in the TFEU. Nevertheless, this spatial distance cannot hide the fact that some architectural link between those two provision bodies exists, since the general principles governing the Union's external actions are included within the CFSP rules.[158]

Correspondingly, the EU's competence in lodging inter-party complaints against third countries may also be based on the provisions regarding the CFSP. According to Article 24 (1) of the TEU, the European Union is being provided with comprehensive competence in CFSP matters which shall cover *all areas* of foreign policy. Due to the wording and thus the broad meaning of this provision, it can be easily argued that the Union has the competence within the legal framework of its CFSP to refer any breach of the Convention by a third country to the Strasbourg Court and that a wide-ranging role of the European Union to perform forms of control on the implementation of human rights norms could be framed under the CFSP.[159] As a result, this provision may serve as the legal foundation to authorise the EU to bring an inter-party case against a third country before the ECtHR.[160] This also means that the EU may use this newly available legal action as an instrument to promote its human rights policy, particularly in cases where there is no other legal or political instrument to do so.

---

[155] See ibid para 16.
[156] See, inter alia, art 209 (2) TFEU.
[157] See Craig, *The Lisbon Treaty* (n 30) 166.
[158] See ibid 408f.
[159] See Zaru (n 127) 232.
[160] See Schott (n 24) 5.

C. Conclusion

The preceding analysis has demonstrated that the European Union's potential competence to direct inter-party complaints against third countries can be found in Union law itself. Inter alia, both Articles 3 (2) and 216 (1) TFEU entitle the European Union to conclude international agreements with third countries or international organisations and, most importantly, the agreement to allow for the Union's accession to the Convention. Consequently, if the EU has the necessary power to conclude such agreements and especially the Accession Agreement, it is only logical that it must also have the competence to submit inter-party complaints under Article 33 ECHR as a means of its external human rights policy. Alternatively, one may also argue that the Union's explicit competence to accede to the Convention also encompasses its competence to lodge inter-party applications against third countries without any restrictions. In addition, Article 24 (1) TEU gives the Union a broad spectrum of competences in CFSP matters, which shall cover all areas of foreign policy. There is no logical reasoning why this specific competence should not encompass the power to lodge inter-party complaints against third countries.

With respect to the autonomy of the EU's legal order, the sceptics may also be reminded of the fact that Article 344 TFEU is not applicable in disputes between the European Union and third countries, ie non-Member States.[161] Correspondingly, the Luxembourg Court has no say in such cases, which further means that its involvement is not necessary to preserve the autonomy of EU law. Moreover, in inter-party cases between the Union and a third country, the EU will assume the role of the applicant party. As a result, there will be no need for Strasbourg to take EU law into account, but rather the relevant provisions of the respondent state which will leave the Union's autonomous legal order completely unharmed from external interference.

Another crucial argument is the fact that the Accession Agreement neither explicitly excludes inter-party cases lodged by the EU against a third country nor does it alter or restrict the functional nature of the Union's institutions within the meaning of *Opinion 1/91*. Accordingly, the competence to submit inter-party complaints against a third country does not involve any substantial risk to the autonomy of EU law. Beyond that, the hurdles set by Luxembourg in *Opinion 2/94* for the Union's accession to the Convention—namely the fundamental institutional implications of constitutional significance[162]—have been overcome by the Treaty of Lisbon's entry into force and the subsequent negotiations of the Draft Accession Agreement. The Explanatory Report also states that once the European Union is a party to the Convention, all contracting parties will be able to bring a case against the EU and vice versa under Article 33 ECHR.[163] *Ergo*, there are no obstacles within the legal order of the European Union for the future submission of inter-party complaints

---

[161] See Winkler (n 11) 86.
[162] See Opinion 2/94 *Accession to the ECHR* (n 48) para 35.
[163] See CDDH-UE(2011)009 (n 64) 25, para 62.

against third countries and the EU will be explicitly entitled to lodge cases against non-Member States after accession without risk to the Union's legal autonomy.

IV. INTERIM CONCLUSIONS

Although inter-state cases (or inter-*party* cases, as they will be called after accession) under Article 33 ECHR are practically irrelevant and thus almost negligible within the Convention regime, they constitute a classic dispute settlement mechanism of international law and the original judicial mechanism for the protection of human rights in Europe. Furthermore, inter-party complaints after accession may involve several risks to the legal autonomy of the European Union, in particular with respect to the exclusive jurisdiction over such disputes claimed by both the Luxembourg and the Strasbourg Court, and to the question of whether the European Union has the competence to lodge such complaints against third countries. These problems made it necessary to examine the future organisation of inter-party cases and their potential impact on the EU's legal system, although it is highly unlikely that such a situation will actually occur in practice.

The first part of this chapter dealt with the potential 'internal' problems between the Union and its Member States within the Convention system, the future relationship between the Luxembourg and the Strasbourg courts after accession and how their respective 'exclusive jurisdiction' clauses (namely Article 344 TFEU and Article 55 ECHR) for settling disputes might endanger both the effective protection of human rights within the Convention's regime and the autonomy of EU law. On the part of the Union, Article 344 TFEU ensures that Union law (within the meaning of Article 19 (1) TEU, ie primary and secondary law and 'unionised' international agreements) is uniformly interpreted and applied by the CJEU, which means that Luxembourg has the exclusive jurisdiction to adjudicate on all legal disputes between the Member States which involve EU law. However, as the Convention will become an integral part of the Union's legal order, the CJEU will have the corresponding jurisdiction to interpret and apply the provisions of the Convention. Thus, the EU Member States will be barred from bringing inter-state complaints against each other before the ECtHR. The Member States and the Union organs are consequently left with the internal Union dispute settlement mechanisms provided for by the Treaties. It is nevertheless evident that not all inter-party applications concerning an alleged violation of the Convention must be exclusively submitted to the CJEU after accession. The decisive factor for Luxembourg's exclusive jurisdiction is whether genuine EU law is applicable. As a consequence, the CJEU will not be able to claim jurisdiction in situations related to wholly domestic fields of law, for example criminal or family law. Proceedings between Member States before the CJEU are therefore only possible in cases where Member States have limited fundamental freedoms or where they have implemented Union law.

On the part of the Convention system, Article 55 ECHR grants Strasbourg exclusive jurisdiction in settling inter-party complaints. Yet, since both the CJEU and the ECtHR consider their respective jurisdiction as exclusive, jurisdictional conflicts after accession are imminent. The solution to this problem lies in the fact that Article 55 ECHR allows the contracting parties, by special agreement, to waive Strasbourg's jurisdiction and to settle their disputes before another court or tribunal. It was shown that the specific provisions of the Treaties, namely Article 19 (1) TEU and Article 344 TFEU, may qualify as a special agreement which would entitle the CJEU to settle inter-party disputes between the Member States and thus prevent jurisdictional conflicts. Luxembourg's exclusive jurisdiction by virtue of Article 19 (1) TEU and Article 344 TFEU, however, does not represent an explicit reference to the Convention. As a result, these provisions do not suffice to satisfy the requirements of Article 55 ECHR and both the ECtHR and the CJEU will have the jurisdiction to accept and decide inter-state cases, which may again lead to conflicts between those two courts.

These legal issues could be solved by simply excluding inter-party cases between Union Member States and between Member States and the Union. But as the EU should accede to the Convention on an equal footing, it must be subjected to the same obligations as other contracting parties to the Convention, which means that an exclusion of inter-party cases is not a viable option.

Article 4 of the Draft Accession Agreement clarifies that all state parties to the Convention will be able to bring a case against the Union and vice versa. But the Luxembourg Court nonetheless has the last say in matters regarding Union law and may determine that a Member State has failed to fulfil its obligations under Article 344 TFEU, if the said Member State first lodged an inter-party application before the Strasbourg Court. Article 5 of the Draft Accession Agreement, however, safeguards the Union's legal autonomy and contains the 'special agreement' and the explicit reference to the Convention which are necessary to satisfy the requirements of Article 55 ECHR and to uphold Luxembourg's exclusive jurisdiction over EU-related inter-party applications. In addition, according to Article 35 (1) ECHR, the CJEU must be given a chance to remedy alleged violations of the Convention before the ECtHR may adjudicate on any applications. Therefore, the Convention itself enables Luxembourg to interpret and apply Union law in order to preserve its well-guarded autonomy. The Member States and the Union are thence obliged to settle their disputes via the internal Union mechanisms (namely infringement proceedings, the action for annulment and the action for failure to act) before they can take their applications to Strasbourg.

The second part of the preceding chapter examined the problem of whether the EU has the competence to direct inter-party applications against third countries, ie non-Member States, in order to promote human rights in its external relations. It is, however, of paramount importance that such a competence, included in an international agreement concluded by the Union, must not change the functional nature of the Union's institutions and thus interfere with the autonomy of EU law. It was then clarified that if the EU has the competence to conclude international agreements for the protection of human rights with third countries, it must a fortiori also have the competence to protect human rights via inter-party complaints. Following the entry into force of the Lisbon Treaty, the Union may base such agreements on Article 216 (1) TFEU in conjunction with Article 3 (2) TFEU or take action within the legal framework of its CFSP under Article 24 (1) TEU. Moreover, the Accession Agreement neither explicitly excludes inter-party cases lodged by the EU against a third country nor does it alter or restrict the functional nature of the Union's institutions within the meaning of *Opinion 1/91*. The competence to submit inter-party complaints against a third country does consequently not involve any substantial risk to the autonomy of EU law. Beyond that, the Explanatory Report also states that once the European Union is a high contracting party to the Convention, all contracting parties will be able to bring a case against the EU and vice versa under Article 33 ECHR, without any risk to the Union's legal autonomy.

11

The Exhaustion of Domestic Remedies and the Prior Involvement of the Luxembourg Court

I. THE 'EXHAUSTION RULE' AFTER ACCESSION

THIS LAST CHAPTER explores another problem related to the European Union's accession to the Convention and to individual applications under Article 34 of the European Convention on Human Rights (ECHR), namely the interplay between the exhaustion of domestic remedies under Article 35 (1) ECHR and the prior involvement of the Luxembourg Court in EU-related cases. More precisely, as the Luxembourg Court stated in a Discussion Document, the specific characteristics of the EU's legal order include the prominent feature that legal acts by the Union usually take effect vis-à-vis individuals through the intermediary of national measures of implementation, transposition or application. According to the Convention's principle of subsidiarity, individuals alleging violations of their fundamental rights must therefore first approach the domestic authorities and courts before they can submit an application to the Strasbourg Court. In view of the Union's accession to the Convention, the European Union must now ensure that an external review by the Strasbourg Court can be preceded by an effective internal review by both the courts of the Member States and the courts of the EU,[1] in order to satisfy the requirements set out in of Article 35 (1) ECHR and to avoid any external interference with the EU's autonomous legal order. This view not only demonstrates that the exhaustion rule under Article 35 (1) ECHR and the prior involvement of the Court of Justice of the European Union (CJEU) are two closely intertwined principles, but it also reveals that the former must be taken into account to solve the legal issues of the latter.

In other words, it is the CJEU's objective to guarantee that cases relating to EU law do not reach Strasbourg before Luxembourg itself has had the opportunity to adjudicate on them. The chief concern for the Union's legal autonomy in this respect is that the exhaustion of local remedies under Article 35 (1) ECHR

---

[1] See Court of Justice of the European Union, 'Discussion Document of the Court of Justice of the European Union on certain aspects of the accession of the European Union to the European Convention for the Protection of Human Rights and Fundamental Freedoms' paras 57.

would be inadequate or insufficient to guarantee the Luxembourg Court's prior involvement in such a situation.[2] Some sceptics also fear that Luxembourg might be sidelined in proceedings which would result in a situation where Strasbourg would interpret a provision of EU law without the prior involvement of the CJEU, thereby undermining the jurisdictional monopoly of Luxembourg and thus the autonomy of EU law.[3] Apparently, from the view of European Union law, it would be enormously frustrating if Strasbourg found a violation of human rights with respect to the application of EU law without any prior participation of the Luxembourg Court which could have possibly prevented or remedied this violation. Beyond that, the 'exhaustion rule' under Article 35 (1) ECHR guarantees that a case is properly investigated on the national plane before it reaches Strasbourg and its external human rights enforcement machinery. This also includes the definite resolution of all questions of domestic law.[4] For instance, the Luxembourg Court has already demonstrated in the *Kadi and Al Barakaat v Council and Commission* case that it is perfectly apt to protect fundamental rights at the Union-internal level and that the internal review of such cases is capable of redressing fundamental rights violations.[5] But nonetheless, as long as questions of EU law have not yet been clarified and decided by the CJEU, it is possible that the case in Strasbourg is based on an erroneous understanding of the applicable law.[6]

It can therefore be assumed that Luxembourg's prior involvement is only ensured in those Union-internal proceedings which must be exhausted under the premise of Article 35 (1) ECHR in order to be declared admissible in Strasbourg. All other internal Union proceedings which do not qualify as domestic remedies and thus do not fulfil the requirement of Article 35 (1) ECHR, may lead to a situation in which the Luxembourg Court is simply bypassed by applicants and where Strasbourg adjudicates on a case without the CJEU's prior involvement. This means, in a nutshell, that contrary to the issue whether the ECtHR may be a superior court[7] or whether it would have the last say in the matter of human

---

[2] See Andreas J Kumin, 'Die Verhandlungsvorbereitungen für den Beitritt der Europäischen Union zur Europäischen Menschenrechtskonvention—Ein Erfahrungsbericht' in Sigmar Stadlmeier (ed), *Von Lissabon zum Raumfahrzeug: Aktuelle Herausforderungen im Völkerrecht. Beiträge zum 35. Österreichischen Völkerrechtstag* (Vienna, NWV, 2011) 82.

[3] See Jean-Paul Jacqué, 'The Accession of the European Union to the European Convention on Human Rights and Fundamental Freedoms' (2011) 48 *Common Market Law Review* 995, 1016.

[4] See Juliane Kokott and Christoph Sobotta, 'The Charter of Fundamental Rights of the EU after Lisbon' [2010] *EUI Working Papers, Academy of European Law* 1, 5.

[5] See Joined Cases C-402/05 P and C-415/05 P *Kadi and Al Barakaat v Council and Commission* [2008] ECR I- 6351. See Christiaan Timmermans, *L'adhésion de l'Union Européenne à la Convention européenne des Droits de l'homme*, Audition organisée par la Commission des affaires constitutionnelles du 18 mars 2010. European Parliament, Committee on Constitutional Affairs, Hearing on the Institutional Aspects of the European Union's Accession to the European Convention on Human Rights, 18 March 2010, 4.

[6] See Kokott and Sobotta, 'Charter of Fundamental Rights after Lisbon' (n 4) 4.

[7] See Hans Christian Krüger, 'Reflections Concerning Accession of the European Communities to the European Convention on Human Rights' (2002) 21 *Penn State International Law Review* 89, 96;

rights protection after accession, the legal problem at this point is what court will have the *first say* in such proceedings. Thus, the prior involvement of the Luxembourg Court seems to become *the* defining feature of the relationship between Luxembourg and Strasbourg after accession, which makes it crucial to arrange the procedural settlement of this judicial relationship in a correct and accurate fashion.[8] One might thence ask when and under what circumstances the requirements under Article 35 (1) ECHR are fulfilled in cases where European Union law is involved.[9] To answer these questions, one must take into consideration the relevant domestic remedies which are contained in the respondent party's legal system. This examination will, however, prompt a distinction to be drawn between cases which are directed against the European Union itself ('direct actions'; the action for annulment), and those cases which are directed against a Member State ('indirect actions'; the preliminary reference procedure)[10] in order to challenge EU acts. This chapter will therefore not deal with direct actions instigated against Member States or indirect actions contesting national measures and their compatibility with Union law. This distinction will help discover what internal Union proceedings fulfil the requirements of Article 35 (1) ECHR and thus guarantee Luxembourg's prior involvement, and what EU proceedings fail to do so. It is thus the latter category which urges the establishment of a specific mechanism to include the Luxembourg Court in all EU-related cases in Strasbourg.

II. DIRECT AND INDIRECT ACTIONS

In the context of the following sections, the Latin legal maxim '*ubi ius, ibi remedium*' is of utmost significance. It may be a truism that 'fundamental rights are only truly respected when the legal order concerned makes them enforceable against those who have breached them',[11] but it does not render this ancient proverb less important. Individuals seeking redress for alleged violations of human rights by EU acts before the Strasbourg Court must first consider the domestic remedies they have to exhaust beforehand.[12] At the Union level, the

---

Siegbert Alber and Ulrich Widmaier, 'Die EU-Charta der Grundrechte und ihre Auswirkungen auf die Rechtsprechung' (2000) 27 *Europäische Grundrechte-Zeitschrift* 497, 506.

[8] See Noreen O'Meara, '"A More Secure Europe of Rights?" The European Court of Human Rights, the Court of Justice of the European Union and EU Accession to the ECHR' (2011) 12 *German Law Journal* 1813, 1822.

[9] See Maria Berger, 'Der Beitritt der Europäischen Union zur EMRK' in Österreichische Juristenkommission (ed), *Grundrechte im Europa der Zukunft* (Vienna, Linde, 2010) 54.

[10] See Tobias Lock, 'EU Accession to the ECHR: Implications for Judicial Review in Strasbourg' (2010) 35 *European Law Review* 777, 787. See also Joint Communication from Presidents Costa and Skouris, 17 January 2011, 1f and Sebastian Winkler, *Der Beitritt der Europäischen Gemeinschaften zur Europäischen Menschenrechtskonvention* (Baden-Baden, Nomos, 2000) 63.

[11] Walter Van Gerven, 'Remedies for Infringements of Fundamental Rights' (2004) 10 *European Public Law* 261, 261.

[12] See Paul Craig, *The Lisbon Treaty. Law, Politics, and Treaty Reform* (Oxford, Oxford University Press, 2010) 240.

principal remedies for this course of action are the (direct) action for annulment and the (indirect) request for a preliminary ruling by the CJEU. The fact that the Charter and, after accession, the Convention are legally binding on the European Union and its institutions may dramatically alter the landscape of judicial review within the EU's legal system, and may, of course, pose new challenges and risks for its legal autonomy as well. During the last couple of years, the function of fundamental rights-based claims before the Luxembourg Court (albeit not a human rights court per se)[13] has expanded spectacularly which has forced the CJEU to decide on a rising number of cases[14] relating to both Union and domestic fundamental rights.[15]

In concreto, the subsequent analysis therefore scrutinises whether direct and indirect actions aimed at challenging EU law satisfy the requirements of Article 35 (1) ECHR (and thus the parameters of the 'exhaustion rule') and whether one of these procedures is accordingly prone to sidelining the CJEU by allowing applicants to submit complaints directly to the Strasbourg Court. Beyond that, the risk, but also the potential for the protection of human rights after accession, is subsequently explored and critically analysed in light of the autonomy of European Union law.

A. Direct Actions against EU Acts: The European Union as Respondent

i. *Actions for Annulment under Art 263 (4) TFEU*

a. Union-Internal Stages of Appeal under Art 263 (4) TFEU

In the first part of the discussion, direct actions against the European Union and the corresponding domestic remedies will be examined. As presented above,[16] procedures in Luxembourg will not be considered as international procedures under Article 35 (2) lit b ECHR after accession, as the CJEU will be seen rather as a domestic Supreme or Constitutional Court.[17] As a result, complaints will not be declared inadmissible just because they have already been submitted to 'another procedure of international investigation or settlement'.[18]

---

[13] See Dinah Shelton, *Remedies in International Human Rights Law* (Oxford, Oxford University Press, 2005) 203.

[14] See eg, European Commission, '2011 Report on the Application of the EU Charter of Fundamental Rights' COM(2012) 169 final, 6; see also Wolfgang Benedek, 'EU Action on Human and Fundamental Rights in 2010' in Wolfgang Benedek, Florence Benoît-Rohmer, Wolfram Karl and Manfred Nowak (eds), *European Yearbook on Human Rights 2011* (Vienna, NWV, 2011) 100ff.

[15] See Craig, *The Lisbon Treaty* (n 12) 243.

[16] See ch 10 for more details.

[17] See Steering Committee for Human Rights (CDDH), 'Technical and Legal Issues of a Possible EC/EU Accession to the European Convention on Human Rights' CDDH(2002)010 Addendum 2, paras 48–49 and European Convention, 'Final Report of Working Group II' CONV 354/02, WG II 16, 12.

[18] See also Lock, 'Implications for Judicial Review' (n 10) 788.

Therefore, prima facie, no major intricacies arise with respect to applications directed against legal acts of the Union, since individuals may contest these acts via direct actions for annulment under Article 263 (4) of the Treaty on the Functioning of the European Union (TFEU) before the CJEU.[19] In situations where the Union is held responsible as the sole respondent, the action for annulment is the only domestic remedy within the meaning of Article 35 (1) ECHR which is available to an individual at Union level.[20] In its amended form following the entry into force of the Treaty of Lisbon, Article 263 (4) TFEU states that

> [a]ny natural or legal person may [...] institute proceedings against an act addressed to that person or which is of direct and individual concern to them, and against a regulatory act which is of direct concern to them and does not entail implementing measures.

The 'exhaustion' rule under Article 35 (1) ECHR will therefore require the applicant to file an action for annulment in Luxembourg before they take the road to Strasbourg. In such a scenario, the European Court of Human Rights (ECtHR) will have the CJEU's interpretation at its disposal, and, according to its settled case law, it will not be up to the ECtHR to rule on the validity of national laws in the hierarchy of domestic legislation, which also applies to international treaties.[21] Strasbourg would thence consider the interpretation given by Luxembourg to be factual which will be expounded, where necessary, by means of the co-respondent mechanism.[22]

Beyond that, the now defunct European Commission for Human Rights explicitly stated in the *Dufay* case that remedies under Union law constituted *domestic* remedies in terms of Article 35 (1) ECHR. The application in *Dufay* was declared inadmissible not only due to the Commission's lack of jurisdiction *ratione personae* over the Union, but more importantly because the applicant had refrained from exhausting the domestic remedies before the CJEU within the proper time limit for instituting legal proceedings.[23] The applicant's claim had therefore expired[24] and the requirements under Article 35 (1) ECHR could not be properly satisfied.[25] It is therefore certain that, after accession, Strasbourg will all the more scrutinise whether an applicant has indeed exhausted all domestic remedies available under EU law. To this end, it must also have a closer look at the Union-internal stages of appeal as there are scenarios in which the applicant has to make use of more than one remedy in order to satisfy the requirements of Article 35 (1) ECHR.

---

[19] See Jacqué, 'Accession' (n 3) 1016.

[20] See Tobias Lock, 'Walking on a Tightrope: The Draft Accession Agreement and the Autonomy of the EU Legal Order' (2011) 48 *Common Market Law Review* 1025, 1045.

[21] See *W v The Netherlands* App no 20689/08 (ECtHR, 20 January 2009).

[22] See Jacqué, 'Accession' (n 3) 1017.

[23] See *Dufay v The European Communities, alternatively: Their Member States a) jointly and b) severally* App no 13539/88 (Commission Decision, 19 January 1989).

[24] See Case 257/85 *Dufay v European Parliament* [1987] ECR 1561, para 23.

[25] See Wolfgang Peukert, 'Art 35' in Jochen Frowein and Wolfgang Peukert (eds), *EMRK-Kommentar* (Kehl am Rhein, NP Engel, 2009) para 22.

The subsequent procedure exemplifies the European Union's domestic stages of appeal which an applicant must exhaust before lodging a complaint before the ECtHR. The European Commission, for instance, may take action under Article 105 TFEU[26] to ensure the application of the Union's anti-trust law under Articles 101 and 102 TFEU, and initiate investigations which might include the search of business premises. The addressee of the Commission's decision must then contest this decision and any alleged human rights violations—most likely the violation of the right to privacy under Article 7 of the Charter of Fundamental Rights of the European Union (ChFR) and Article 8 ECHR—before the Union courts. To be exact, the applicant must submit its action for annulment against an EU act to the General Court which has, by virtue of Article 256 (1), subparagraph 1 TFEU and *e contrario* Article 51 CJEU Statute,[27] jurisdiction to hear and determine actions for annulment submitted by individuals in the first instance. In case the General Court rules that such investigations do not constitute a breach of the right to privacy, the applicant has to linger in Luxembourg for a bit longer, as they must then seek an appeal to the Court of Justice, pursuant to Article 256 (1), subparagraph 2 TFEU and Article 56 CJEU Statute. Only then and only if the applicant's submissions have been unsuccessful in Luxembourg, the requirements of Article 35 (1) ECHR are satisfied and they may take the case to Strasbourg. Moreover, by taking this course of action pursuant to the Convention's principle of subsidiarity, the European Union's legal autonomy is safeguarded as the review exercised by the ECtHR will be preceded by the internal review exercised by the Union courts.[28]

b. The Constituent Elements of Art 263 (4) TFEU

As expected, the above statement that prima facie there would be no grave intricacies or legal issues in relation to actions for annulment was, of course, a *caveat* that there are nonetheless considerable exceptions to the aforementioned rule. A closer look at the constituent elements of Article 263 (4) TFEU will reveal that there are certain scenarios which might prove problematic in light of the requirements under Article 35 (1) ECHR. More precisely, Article 263 (4) TFEU lays down three alternatives which entitle individuals to file an action for annulment before the Union courts, whereof the first is generally unproblematic in the context of this analysis; the last two, however, deserve a thorough examination in order to dispel any doubts about their compatibility with the Union's accession to the Convention.

---

[26] See in particular Recital 14 of Council Regulation (EC) No 1/2003 of 16 December 2002 on the implementation of the rules on competition laid down in Articles 81 and 82 of the Treaty [2003] OJ L1/1.

[27] Protocol No 3 on the Statute of the Court of Justice of the European Union [2010] OJ C83/210.

[28] See Joint Communication from Presidents Costa and Skouris (n 10) 2.

In the first scenario, an EU institution addresses a legal act to a natural or legal person who, in turn, intends to institute proceedings against this act. In this respect, the term 'act' encompasses any legal act by the Union which unfolds legal effects vis-à-vis the individual addressee[29] and is, in most cases, a decision within the meaning of Article 288 (4) TFEU.[30] This scenario is generally unproblematic and the complaint brought under Article 263 (4) TFEU would usually be admissible under these preconditions.[31]

By contrast, the second scenario seems to be more complex than the first. In this case, a natural or legal person submits a complaint against an act that is actually *not* addressed to them. Pursuant to Article 263 (4) TFEU, a complaint against an act which is not addressed to the applicant can only be challenged if it is of direct and individual concern to them. '*Concern*' means that the applicant must show a vested and present interest in the annulment of the contested act,[32] whereas the term '*direct*' is used to exclude those applicants who are not in the precise legal position of the actual addressee of a decision.[33] '*Direct*' concern mainly exists when either the national authorities are left no discretion in implementing measures, which means that implementation is entirely automatic,[34] or if they are given discretion in implementing EU measures, the possibility of it being exercised is purely theoretical.[35] This, of course, is often the case with secondary law, with regulations in particular.[36] Most importantly, via the amendments brought about by the Treaty of Lisbon, the restrictive criteria for standing for non-privileged applicants—namely the requirement of 'individual' concern—was dropped for cases where the complaint is directed against a regulatory act of direct concern which does not entail implementing measures.[37] These changes were met with a warm response as they went some way to overcome the difficulties found in the existing case law of the CJEU which compelled the applicant to prove that they were 'directly' and 'individually' concerned in all cases where such an act was not addressed to them.[38] Nevertheless, it will be illustrated below that the term 'regulatory act' is difficult to grasp and may lead to unexpected problems which the drafters of the Lisbon Treaty and the Draft Accession Agreement could not foresee.

---

[29] See Ines Härtel, *Handbuch Europäische Rechtsetzung* (Berlin Heidelberg, Springer, 2006) 147.

[30] See Wolfram Cremer, 'Art 263 AEUV' in Christian Calliess and Matthias Ruffert (eds), *EUV/AEUV. Kommentar*, 4th edn (Munich, Beck, 2011) para 32.

[31] See Lock, 'Implications for Judicial Review' (n 10) 788.

[32] See Case 62/70 *Bock v Comission* [1971] ECR 897, para 10; Case T-138/89 *Nederlandse Bankiersvereniging and Nederlandse Vereniging van Banken v Commission* [1992] ECR II-2181, para 33.

[33] See Case 246/81 *Lord Bethell v Commission* [1982] ECR 2277, para 16.

[34] See Case 113/77 *NTN Toyo Bearing Company Ltd v Council* [1979] ECR 1185, para 2.

[35] See Case 11/82 *Piraiki-Patraiki v Commission* [1985] ECR 207, para 9.

[36] See Lock, 'Implications for Judicial Review' (n 10) 788.

[37] See Walter Frenz, *Handbuch Europarecht. Band 5: Wirkungen und Rechtsschutz* (Berlin Heidelberg, Springer, 2010) para 2929, and Cremer, 'Art 263 AEUV' (n 30) para 54.

[38] See Craig, *The Lisbon Treaty* (n 12) 129f.

The third scenario is even more intricate for the applicant. In this situation, they contest Union legislation or an act addressed to a *third party* and *not to them* directly and individually, and which is—in the terms of the Treaty of Lisbon amendments—*not* a regulatory act. Again, the same definitions of the terms '*direct*' and '*concern*' apply, but the decisive point for any applicant, however, is in fact to argue for their '*individual*' concern[39] which still represents a very strict criterion for individual applicants to bring actions for annulment against acts not directly and individually addressed to them. The CJEU defined this term in its famous and often criticised *Plaumann* judgment, by stating that

> [...] persons other than those to whom a decision is addressed may only claim to be individually concerned if that decision affects them by reason of certain attributes which are peculiar to them or by reason of circumstances in which they are differentiated from all other persons and by virtue of these factors distinguishes them individually just as in the case of the person addressed.[40]

Even though the Court of First Instance deviated from this restrictive view and held that an individual applicant 'is to be regarded as individually concerned [...] if the measure in question affects his legal position, in a manner which is both definite and immediate, by restricting his rights or by imposing obligations on him',[41] the Court of Justice confirmed its *Plaumann* formula in a later case by arguing that the explicit wording of the provision in question would not allow the Court to go beyond the jurisdiction conferred to it by the Treaties.[42] Luxembourg thereby emphasised the importance of national remedies available within the legal systems of the Member States.[43]

Given this case law, the question for the individual applicant after accession would be whether the remedy provided by Article 263 (4) TFEU was in fact effective. According to the ECtHR's judgment in the *De Wilde, Ooms and Versyp* ('*Vagrancy*') v Belgium cases, the Strasbourg Court would not require an applicant to lodge a clearly inadmissible complaint to the Luxembourg Court. To be exact, Strasbourg ruled that Article 35 (1) ECHR does not necessitate an applicant to make use of remedies which are inadmissible according to the domestic laws or settled legal opinions of the respondent state.[44] When applied to Luxembourg's case law regarding Article 263 (4) TFEU, it may therefore be assumed that an applicant would not have to make a fruitless and ineffective attempt to contest an EU act allegedly in violation of the Convention.[45]

---

[39] See Lock, 'Implications for Judicial Review' (n 10) 788.

[40] Case 25/62 *Plaumann v Commission* [1962] ECR 95, para 8. See also Case C-309/89 *Codorníu v Council* [1994] ECR I-1853, para 20.

[41] Case T-177/01 *Jégo-Quéré v Commission* [2002] ECR II-2365, para 51.

[42] See Case C-50/00 P *Unión de Pequeños Agricultores v Council* [2002] ECR I-6677, para 44.

[43] See Frenz, *Wirkungen und Rechtsschutz* (n 37) para 2919.

[44] See *De Wilde, Ooms and Versyp* ('*Vagrancy*') v Belgium App nos 2832/66; 2835/66; 2899/66 (ECtHR, 18 June 1971, para 62). See also Peukert, 'Art 35' (n 25) paras 25ff.

[45] See Lock, 'Implications for Judicial Review' (n 10) 788f.

This is the perfect time to revisit the second scenario and the legal issues relating to the vague meaning of the term 'regulatory act' within Article 263 (4) TFEU. Even though the introduction of this new element was suggested during the Constitutional Treaty negotiations[46] and later welcomed as 'the end of *Plaumann*'[47] and thus an effective expansion in the field of individual remedies,[48] it is now far less certain whether the Strasbourg Court will apply the standards found in *Vagrancy* in cases involving actions directed against regulatory acts after accession.[49] The term 'regulatory act' was introduced in Article III-365 (4) Constitutional Treaty which nonetheless does not easily fit with the Lisbon categorisation of legal acts, since it is a legal residue of the language used in the failed Constitutional Treaty in which it was understood to be a non-legislative measure.[50] The drafters of the Lisbon Treaty adopted this term in unmodified form, while the overall reference framework of the Treaties has been changed dramatically.[51] In other words, Article I-33 (1) Constitutional Treaty differentiated between European laws, European framework laws, European regulations etc, whereas the Lisbon Treaty kept the old terminology of the Community Treaty. This leads to the problematic fact that the term 'regulatory act' within the meaning of the Constitutional Treaty describes a non-legislative act, while the term 'regulatory act' in the context of the Lisbon Treaty refers to 'regulation' and thus a legislative act.[52] Accordingly, the wording 'regulatory act' could be construed broadly to cover all forms of secondary law, including regulations,[53] directives (when having direct effect)[54] and decisions,[55] provided that this piece of legislation does not entail implementation. Conversely, it could also be narrowly interpreted to cover any legislative, delegated or implementing act, given that it is a regulation or decision that does not entail implementing measures.[56] In 2011, the General Court had the chance to elucidate these definition problems in the

---

[46] See European Convention, 'Final Report of Working Group II' CONV 354/02 (n 17) 15f.

[47] See Stephan Balthasar, 'Locus Standi Rules for Challenges to Regulatory Acts by Private Applicants: The New Article 263 (4) TFEU' (2010) 35 *European Law Review* 542, 548.

[48] See Wolfram Cremer, 'Der Rechtsschutz des Einzelnen gegen Sekundärrechtsakte der Union gem. Art. III-270 IV Konventsentwurf des Vertrags über eine Verfassung für Europa' (2004) 31 *Europäische Grundrechte-Zeitschrift* 577, 577f.

[49] See Lock, 'Implications for Judicial Review' (n 10) 789.

[50] See European Convention, 'Articles on the Court of Justice and the High Court' CONV 734/03, 20, and Art III-365 (4) Constitutional Treaty.

[51] See Ulrich Everling, 'Lissabon-Vertrag regelt Dauerstreit über Nichtigkeitsklage Privater' (2010) 21 *Europäische Zeitschrift für Wirtschaftsrecht* 572, 574.

[52] See Lock, 'Implications for Judicial Review' (n 10) 789.

[53] See Hans-Jürgen Rabe, 'Zur Metamorphose des Europäischen Verfassungsvertrages' (2007) 60 *Neue Juristische Wochenschrift* 3153, 3157.

[54] See Juliane Kokott, Ioanna Dervisopoulos and Thomas Henze, 'Aktuelle Fragen des effektiven Rechtsschutzes durch die Gemeinschaftsgerichte' (2008) 35 *Europäische Grundrechte-Zeitschrift* 10, 14.

[55] See Hans Arno Petzold, *Individualrechtsschutz an der Schnittstelle zwischen deutschem und Gemeinschaftsrecht. Zugleich ein Beitrag zur Interpretation von Art. III-365 Abs. 4 VerfV* (Baden-Baden, Nomos, 2008) 77.

[56] See Craig, *The Lisbon Treaty* (n 12) 131.

Inuit case in which it held that the meaning of the term 'regulatory act' must be understood as

> covering all acts of general application apart from legislative acts. Consequently, a legislative act may form the subject-matter of an action for annulment brought by a natural or legal person only if it is of direct and individual concern to them.[57]

Nevertheless, since the applicants brought an appeal against the Court's order, claiming that the General Court's interpretation was erroneous,[58] the Court of Justice will have the final say on this matter and may overthrow the definition of 'regulatory act' given by the General Court.

This situation leaves the applicant with a certain amount of legal uncertainty. Luxembourg's final interpretation of Article 263 (4) TFEU will undoubtedly affect the impact of this provision and clarify whether the individuals' glass of remedies is 'half empty rather than half full' or vice versa.[59] Moreover, the Member States are also obliged to provide individuals with domestic remedies sufficient to ensure effective legal protection in the fields covered by Union law, pursuant to Aarticle 47 ChFR and Article 19 (1), subparagraph 2 TEU).[60] Until the CJEU fully answers this question, individual applicants alleging a violation of the Convention by a legislative act of the Union are therefore highly advised to first seek a ruling by the Union's courts via an action for annulment.[61] If individual claimants do not act accordingly, they are at high risk of their application being declared inadmissible due to failing to exhaust all domestic remedies as prescribed by Article 35 (1) ECHR.

Still, there is more to this finding than that. Given the fact that the 'exhaustion principle' obliges applicants to first submit an action for annulment under Article 263 (4) TFEU to Luxembourg, it is guaranteed that the CJEU has ample opportunity to review the alleged violation of the Convention before the applicant can take the case to Strasbourg. In conclusion, it is not necessary to include separate provisions in the Draft Accession Agreement to ensure Luxembourg's prior involvement in annulment proceedings, as they would be immune to these provisions.[62] The final outcome of the preceding analysis therefore is rather straightforward—applicants intending to directly challenge an EU act must pursue annulment proceedings under Article 263 (4) TFEU in order to exhaust all local remedies, as laid down in Article 35 (1) ECHR. Such proceedings necessarily

---

[57] See Case T-18/10 *Inuit Tapiriit Kanatami v European Parliament and Council* [2011] ECR II-0000, para 56.

[58] See Case C-583/11 P *Inuit Tapiriit Kanatami v the Order of the General Court*, OJ C58/3. 25 February 2012. The case was still pending at the time of writing.

[59] See Craig, *The Lisbon Treaty* (n 12) 130f.

[60] See Wolfram Cremer, 'Gemeinschaftsrecht und Deutsches Verwaltungsprozessrecht—Zum dezentralen Rechtsschutz gegenüber EG-Sekundärrecht' (2004) 37 *Die Verwaltung* 165, 165.

[61] See Lock, 'Implications for Judicial Review' (n 10) 789.

[62] See O'Meara (n 8) 1823.

involve the CJEU and thus give the Court sufficient opportunity to review and redress an alleged fundamental rights violation.

ii. 'Constitutional' Barriers: Violations Found in Primary Law

The delicate subject of 'primary EU law' leads to the next crucial issue in this context. Besides complaints directed against alleged violations of the Convention found in secondary law, an applicant may intend to claim a violation stemming from primary law for which there is, however, no remedy under Union law. To satisfy the preconditions of Article 35 (1) ECHR and to guarantee the CJEU's prior involvement, applicants could consider bringing complaints against EU acts to their national Constitutional or Supreme Court, provided that this domestic court of last resort actually offers a remedy against the violation of fundamental rights by the EU's primary law.[63] There are several examples[64] of such a *modus operandi* which would indicate that the applicant has to take a detour via the respective domestic courts to challenge primary law. The case law of the highest courts of the Member States seems to be unanimous in this regard.[65]

Alternatively, it can be argued that, where a case is brought against a Union act, the respective domestic remedy must also be found in Union law itself—even though Strasbourg's judgment in the *Demopoulos* case contradicts this very argument.[66] In these proceedings, the applicants were all Cypriot nationals of Greek-Cypriot origin who complained that the Turkish military operations in northern Cyprus and the continuing division of the territory of Cyprus led to the proclamation of the internationally unrecognised Turkish Republic of Northern Cyprus (TRNC) which, in turn, dispossessed them of their property located in the occupied territories. In 2005, the TRNC legislative enacted a law which provided that all natural and legal persons claiming rights to immovable property might bring a claim before the Immovable Property Commission.[67] It was argued that the 'exhaustion rule' only required the applicants to exhaust Turkish remedies, whereas the newly created Commission constituted a 'TRNC' remedy.[68] The Strasbourg Court considered this to be an artificial argument, as Turkey has been

---

[63] See Lock, 'Implications for Judicial Review' (n 10) 790.

[64] See, inter alia, for Germany: 2 BvE 2/08, 2 BvE 5/08, 2 BvR 1010/08, 2 BvR 1022/08, 2 BvR 1259/08, 2 BvR 182/09 *Lissabon-Urteil* BVerfGE 123, 267; for the Czech Republic: Ústavní soud eské republiky, Pl ÚS 19/08 *Lisabonská smlouva I (Lisbon Treaty I)*; for France: Conseil Constitutionnel, No 2004-496 DC; for Italy: Corte Costituzionale 232/1989 *FRAGD*; for Poland: Trybunał Konstytucyjny K 18/04 *Poland's Membership in the European Union (The Accession Treaty)*; for Spain: Tribunal Constitucional DTC 1/2004 *La constitucionalidad de los artículos I-6, II-111 y II-112 del Tratado por el que se establece una Constitución para Europa.*

[65] See Christian Tomuschat, 'Lisbon—Terminal of the European Integration Process? The Judgment of the German Constitutional Court of 30 June 2009' (2010) 70 *Zeitschrift für ausländisches öffentliches Recht und Völkerrecht* 251, 280.

[66] See Lock, 'Implications for Judicial Review' (n 10) 790.

[67] See *Demopoulos v Turkey* App nos 46113/99, 3843/02, 13751/02, 13466/03, 10200/04, 14163/04, 19993/04, 21819/04 (ECtHR, 1 March 2010) para 35.

[68] See ibid para 64.

held responsible for the acts and omissions of the authorities within the 'TRNC' entity in numerous cases in the past.[69] Furthermore, the procedure before the Immovable Property Commission may be regarded as 'domestic remedies' of the respondent state. No ground for exemption for the application of Article 35 (1) ECHR has therefore been established[70] which led the ECtHR to reject the afore-mentioned argument.

The most urgent question in this context remains whether Strasbourg may take a similar approach with respect to an application directed against the Union's primary law.[71] In *Demopoulos*, the Strasbourg Court again highlighted the fact that the machinery of protection established by the Convention is subsidiary to the domestic legal orders safeguarding human rights and that it is not a court of last instance. Thence, since it cannot and must not usurp the role of the con-tracting parties whose responsibility it is to guarantee that fundamental rights are respected and protected on the domestic level,[72] it does not seem entirely unlikely that the ECtHR might pursue a similar *modus operandi* after accession. Conversely, the legal situation in Northern Cyprus is indeed very special and a major international issue. Compared to the European Union, the TRNC is not recognised as having international legal personality, whereas the EU expressly enjoys such personality pursuant to Article 47 TEU. Beyond that, the EU will be directly bound by the Convention after accession, to which the TRNC has never become a contracting party.[73]

More generally, constitutional courts do not usually have the jurisdiction to review the validity and legality of provisions enshrined in the respective constitu-tion itself.[74] Likewise, Luxembourg does not have the jurisdiction to review the validity of primary law and its compatibility with the Convention.[75] This means that in cases where domestic constitutional provisions are the issue of the com-plaint brought before the Strasbourg Court, it will commonly be the first court to hear and examine the case. Since primary law fulfils a comparable function to the European Union's constitutional law, this may be another argument why Strasbourg might be very prone to decide that domestic remedies need not be exhausted in cases where the applicant challenges primary Union law.[76] Moreover,

---

[69] See ibid para 89.

[70] See ibid para 103.

[71] See Lock, 'Implications for Judicial Review' (n 10) 790.

[72] See *Demopoulos v Turkey* App nos 46113/99, 3843/02, 13751/02, 13466/03, 10200/04, 14163/04, 19993/04, 21819/04 (n 67) para 69.

[73] See Lock, 'Implications for Judicial Review' (n 10) 790.

[74] But see the so-called 'Eternity Clause' in Art 79 (3) of the German Basic Law and the judgment of the Austrian Constitutional Court in VfGH G 12/00, VfSlg 16327, where it ruled that there is such a thing as 'unconstitutional constitutional law'.

[75] See Patricia Thomy, *Individualrechtsschutz durch das Vorabentscheidungsverfahren* (Baden-Baden, Nomos, 2009) 60; Lukas Bauer, *Der Europäische Gerichtshof als Verfassungsgericht?* (Vienna, Facultas, 2008) 128.

[76] See Lock, 'Implications for Judicial Review' (n 10) 790.

given its judgments such as *Schmidberger v Austria*[77] and *Omega Spielhallen*,[78] the Luxembourg Court has clearly proven in the past that it is perfectly capable of balancing and reconciling fundamental rights and provisions laid down in primary Union law. There is no evidence to suggest that this cooperative approach vis-à-vis the Convention and the Strasbourg Court should end after accession.

iii. The European Ombudsman

Besides the 'classic' judicial remedy of annulment proceedings under Article 263 (4) TFEU, it must also be analysed whether other non-judicial complaint procedures must be invoked in order to guarantee Luxembourg's prior involvement and the exhaustion of local remedies under Article 35 (1) ECHR before an application can be directed to the Strasbourg Court. One of these alternative procedures is the right of every Union citizen under Article 24 (3) TFEU, in conjunction with Article 43 ChFR, to submit complaints to the European Ombudsman regarding instances of maladministration in the activities of the EU institutions, bodies, offices or agencies, with the exception of the CJEU.[79] However, in contrast to the CJEU, the Ombudsman cannot annul or quash any legal acts in violation of the Convention. Pursuant to Article 228 TFEU, the Ombudsman is only authorised to conduct inquiries within the scope of administrative acts of the Union[80] and, in the case where the Ombudsman establishes an instance of maladministration, the Ombudsman shall refer the matter to the institution concerned and submit a report to the European Parliament. Moreover, the Ombudsman is not entitled to submit complaints to the CJEU, which means that the Luxembourg Court cannot be involved in proceedings via the Ombudsman, thus rendering this specific complaint mechanism futile in light of the CJEU's desired prior involvement.

On the one hand, in the context of effective human rights protection, this approach is unsatisfactory as the Ombudsman's limited mandate does not cover potential fundamental rights violations stemming from Union legislation or its domestic implementation, from its intergovernmental policies (such as the Common Foreign and Security Policy) and the application of its financial instruments, without involving instances of maladministration.[81] On the other hand, the Convention

---

[77] See Case C-112/00 *Schmidberger v Austria* [2003] ECR I-5659.

[78] See Case C-36/02 *Omega Spielhallen* [2004] ECR I-9609.

[79] See Case T-209/00 *Lamberts v European Ombudsman* [2002] ECR II-2203, para 65 and Case T-193/04 *Tillack v Commission* [2006] ECR II-3995, para 128, where the Court held that '*in the institution of the Ombudsman, the Treaty has given citizens of the Union, and more particularly officials and other servants of the Community, an alternative remedy to that of an action before the Community Court in order to protect their interests.*'

[80] See Annette Guckelberger, 'Das Petitionsrecht zum Europäischen Parlament sowie das Recht zur Anrufung des Europäischen Bürgerbeauftragten im Europa der Bürger' (2003) 56 *Die öffentliche Verwaltung* 829, 835.

[81] See Office of the United Nations High Commissioner for Human Rights, 'The European Union and International Human Rights Law' 2011, 27 <www.europe.ohchr.org/Documents/Publications/EU_and_International_Law.pdf> accessed 1 November 2012, 40.

organs and the Strasbourg Court have repeatedly held in the past that a petition to an Ombudsman cannot be regarded as an adequate and effective remedy within the meaning of the generally recognised rules of international law and as required by Article 35 (1) ECHR.[82] It is consequently obvious that, after accession, the European Ombudsman will not qualify as a domestic remedy under European Union law which will be required to be exhausted according to Article 35 (1) ECHR.[83]

B. Indirect Actions against EU Acts: The Member States as Respondents

i. *The Preliminary Ruling Procedure under Art 267 TFEU and Accession*

a. Introductory Remarks and Preliminary Questions

In contrast to situations in which individual applicants decide to direct a complaint against the European Union via an action for annulment, the situation is made even more complex if they choose to lodge an application against a Member State implementing EU law allegedly in violation of the Convention. In this case, the remedies to be exhausted are found in the respective Member State's legal system[84] and before the domestic courts which have, as a result of the decentralised nature of the Union's judicial system, general jurisdiction in respect of EU law.[85] Moreover, there are three substantial reasons why an applicant will generally decide to take legal action against a Member State and not the Union itself. Firstly, EU law is not implemented principally by the European Union, but indirectly by the Member States, mostly by enforcing directly applicable Union law through national authorities or by transposing directives.[86] Secondly, it must again be assumed that the applicant may have no legal education and is therefore not aware of the fact that the Member State's action was based on EU legislation.[87] Lastly, it may be a prudent and tactical move to hold the respective Member State responsible for an alleged violation of the Convention, as the domestic courts and the Strasbourg Court would then review whether the implementing (administrative and legislative) actions of the Member State's authorities were compatible with the Convention. In this scenario, Strasbourg would not be solely restricted in reviewing the Union's legislative basis, which would be the case if the application were only directed against the European Union.[88]

---

[82] See *Leander v Sweden* App no 9248/81 (ECtHR, 26 March 1987) paras 80–84; *Montion v France* App no 11192/84 (Commission Decision, 14 May 1987); *Lehtinen v Finland* App no 39076/97 (ECtHR, 14 October 1999).

[83] See Lock, 'Implications for Judicial Review' (n 10) 789.

[84] See Lock, 'Tightrope' (n 20) 1046.

[85] See Court of Justice of the European Union, 'Discussion Document of the Court of Justice of the European Union' (n 1) para 10.

[86] See Thomas von Danwitz, *Europäisches Verwaltungsrecht* (Berlin Heidelberg, Springer, 2008) 315ff.

[87] See also ch 9.

[88] See Lock, 'Tightrope' (n 20) 1046.

Sceptics, however, might argue at this point that in such a scenario the Luxembourg Court would not have a chance to adjudicate on the compatibility of the Union's legal act with the Convention. Thence, both the principle of subsidiarity and the Union's legal autonomy would be infringed if the Union's own courts did not have ample opportunity to remedy the alleged violation themselves.[89] In this context, one may ask whether a preliminary ruling by the Luxembourg Court under Article 267 TFEU is a necessary precondition to involve the CJEU in fundamental rights proceedings and to satisfy the requirements of Article 35 (1) ECHR. Beyond that, it must also be examined—in case such a reference for a preliminary ruling is not made—whether Strasbourg's ruling on an application calling into question provisions of European Union law without the prior involvement of Luxembourg and thus without opportunity to review the consistency of that law with the fundamental rights enshrined in the Charter,[90] is in direct violation of the European Union's legal autonomy.

b. Strasbourg's Past Case-Law on the Preliminary Ruling Procedure

In order to answer the question as to whether the preliminary ruling procedure under Article 267 TFEU is a necessary requirement under Article 35 (1) ECHR, which must be exhausted before an application may be declared admissible by the ECtHR, a short analysis of Strasbourg's past case law might help shed more light on this issue. The abovementioned question was already put before the Strasbourg organs in the past, but not in relation to the European Union's potential accession to the Convention.[91]

In the *Divagsa* case, the European Commission on Human Rights held that the refusal by a national court to request a preliminary ruling from the CJEU may infringe the fairness of proceedings under Article 6 ECHR,[92] which means that preliminary ruling proceedings constitute an integral part of domestic remedies and that the CJEU represents an independent and impartial tribunal established by law.[93] Nevertheless, no complaint regarding the alleged violation of Article 6 ECHR by the refusal to request a preliminary ruling has yielded any noteworthy results so far, regardless of the fact whether the proceedings affected the freedom of goods,[94] the milk quota system,[95] the expulsion of a Union citizen,[96] the freedom of movement and residence,[97] or the fact that no relevant question of EU

---

[89] See Kumin (n 2) 82, and Berger (n 9) 54f.

[90] See Joint Communication from Presidents Costa and Skouris (n 10) 2.

[91] See Winkler (n 10) 64.

[92] See *Divagsa Company v Spain* App no 20631/92 (Commission Decision, 12 May 1993).

[93] See 2 BvR 197/83 *Solange II* BVerfGE 73, 339; 2 BvR 687/85 *Kloppenburg* BVerfGE 75, 223.

[94] See *FS and NS v France* App no 15669/89 (Commission Decision, 28 June 1993).

[95] See *Jansen and Verschueren-Jansen v The Netherlands* App no 17239/90 (Commission Decision, 31 March 1993).

[96] See *Brighina v Germany* App no 15271/89 (Commission Decision, 2 July 1990).

[97] See *Adams and Benn v United Kingdom* App nos 28979/95 and 30343/96 (Commission Decision, 13 January 1997).

law had been raised by the applicant.[98] The Strasbourg Court ruled, however, that there may be certain circumstances in which such a refusal by a domestic court might violate Article 6 (1) ECHR, particularly when it appears to be arbitrary.[99]

In conclusion, it is obvious that Strasbourg has not yet determined the scope and meaning of Article 267 TFEU and how it may coherently adjudicate on this matter, particularly in relation to Article 6 ECHR.[100] This leaves the individual applicant in an ambiguous and doubtful situation and does not answer the question of whether the preliminary ruling procedure under Article 267 TFEU is a necessary requirement under the 'exhaustion rule' of Article 35 (1) ECHR.

c. Foto-Frost, CILFIT and the Risks of Sidelining Luxembourg

Since the analysis of Strasbourg's past case law on the preliminary ruling procedure did not provide the individual applicants with any further help, a thorough examination of Luxembourg's case law and the interpretation of the provision in question—namely Article 267 TFEU—may take them a considerable step closer to the solution.

A quick glance at Article 267 TFEU reveals that this provision displays a two-tiered structure which deserves systematic inspection. By and large, Article 267 (1) TFEU enables the CJEU to give preliminary rulings concerning the interpretation of the Treaties and the validity and interpretation of secondary Union legislation. According to Article 267 (2) TFEU, a national court or tribunal *may*, if it considers that a decision on the question is necessary to enable it to give judgment, request that the CJEU gives a ruling thereon. This means that the national courts have the right to request a preliminary ruling from Luxembourg. Article 267 (3) TFEU, on the other hand, states that where any such question is raised in a case pending before a national court or tribunal against whose decisions there is no judicial remedy under national law, that court or tribunal *shall* bring the matter before the CJEU. This means that national courts of last resort are obliged to request a preliminary ruling from the Luxembourg Court.

Moreover, in its seminal *Foto-Frost v Hauptzollamt Lübeck-Ost* judgment, Luxembourg ruled that the national courts may consider the validity of a Union act and, in case they deem that the grounds put forward before them in support of invalidity are unfounded, then they are free to reject them and to conclude that the measure is completely valid. Conversely, domestic courts do not and must not have the power to declare Union legislation invalid.[101] In other words, the CJEU interpreted Article 267 TFEU to the effect that where the validity of Union legislation is contested before a national court, the power to declare the act in question invalid must be exclusively reserved for the CJEU. The national courts

---

[98] See *Moosbrugger v Austria* App no 44861/98 (ECtHR, 25 January 2000).
[99] See ibid para 2.
[100] See Winkler (n 10) 64f.
[101] See Case 314/85 *Foto-Frost v Hauptzollamt Lübeck-Ost* [1987] ECR 4199, paras 14-15.

are consequently obliged to request a preliminary ruling in case there are doubts concerning the validity of secondary legislation.[102] This approach is backed up by the analogous interpretation of Articles 263 and 267 TFEU. As Article 263 TFEU gives the CJEU exclusive jurisdiction to declare EU legislation null and void in a direct action, the coherence of the Union's judicial system requires that where the validity of a Union act was contested indirectly by means of Article 267 TFEU before a domestic court, the power to declare the legal act invalid should also be reserved for Luxembourg.[103]

The *Bosphorus* case perfectly illustrates the necessity of a reference after accession. Since the aircraft was impounded on the grounds of an EU regulation, its compatibility with fundamental rights was first contested before the Irish courts. After that, the Irish Supreme Court requested a preliminary ruling from the CJEU and thereby gave the Court ample opportunity to review the regulation as to its conformity with the fundamental rights set forth in European Union law.[104]

At this point, however, a major legal problem arises. One might ask whether a similar complaint to the Strasbourg Court would be admissible after accession, if the national court did not request a preliminary ruling from Luxembourg. In the CJEU's *Discussion Document* and in the *Joint Communication from Presidents Costa and Skouris*, it was already argued that it is not certain that a reference for a preliminary ruling will be made in every case in which the compatibility of an EU act with fundamental rights is contested. Moreover, in case such a reference is not made, it would be necessary for Strasbourg to adjudicate on an application involving EU law, but without the Luxembourg Court having had the opportunity to review the compatibility of the provision in question with the Union's own set of fundamental rights beforehand, namely the Charter.[105] Prima facie, such a procedure is highly detrimental to the European Union's legal autonomy, as Luxembourg's monopoly in declaring EU acts null and void would be completely undermined, if Strasbourg were in the position to adjudicate on a case without the prior involvement of the CJEU.[106] But nonetheless, as demonstrated above,[107] the ECtHR does not have the power to annul or quash any domestic legal acts,

---

[102] See Paul Gragl, 'Accession Revisited: Will Fundamental Rights Protection Trump the European Union's Legal Autonomy' in Wolfgang Benedek, Florence Benoît-Rohmer, Wolfram Karl and Manfred Nowak (eds), *European Yearbook on Human Rights 2011* (Vienna, NWV 2011) 168.

[103] See Case 314/85 *Foto-Frost* (n 101) para 15, and Paul Craig, 'The Classics of EU Law Revisited: *CILFIT* and *Foto-Frost*' in Miguel Poiares Maduro/Loïc Azoulai (eds), *The Past and Future of EU Law. The Classics of EU Law Revisited on the 50th Anniversary of the Rome Treaty* (Oxford, Hart Publishing, 2010) 190.

[104] See Lock, 'Implications for Judicial Review' (n 10) 791.

[105] See Court of Justice of the European Union, 'Discussion Document of the Court of Justice of the European Union' (n 1) para 10, and Joint Communication from Presidents Costa and Skouris (n 10) 2. See also Olivier De Schutter, *L'adhésion de l'Union européenne à la Convention européenne des droits de l'homme: feuille de route de la négociation*. European Parliament, Committee on Institutional Affairs, Hearing on the Institutional Aspects of the European Union's Accession to the European Convention on Human Rights, 10 April 2010, 16f.

[106] See Lock, 'Implications for Judicial Review' (n 10) 791.

[107] See ch 8 for more details.

which means that after accession it is neither entitled to declare any EU act null and void nor to effectively remove it. As a court established by an international treaty, Strasbourg would simply declare that a particular legal act was in violation of the Convention[108] which would in turn obligate the European Union, as a high contracting party to the Convention, under Article 46 ECHR, to remove or remedy the said violation rooted in an EU act.

Still, there are other problems to consider at this point, especially the situation of the applicant in the context of the 'exhaustion rule' under Article 35 (1) ECHR. Pursuant to Article 267 (3) TFEU, the courts of the Member States against whose decisions there is no judicial remedy under national law (usually the courts of last resort),[109] have the duty to request a preliminary ruling from the CJEU when the interpretation or validity of Union law is concerned. But in a case where such a court considers that the provisions of EU law involved in the proceedings are clear and do not require any further interpretation, it may decide not to make a reference. A domestic court might refuse to request a preliminary ruling, for example, if it erroneously assumes that there is no duty to do so in a concrete case or because it opines that one or more of the exceptions to Article 267 (3) TFEU applies, in particular those found in the CJEU's *CILFIT* judgment.[110] In this judgment, Luxembourg basically stressed the discretion of the domestic courts, including courts of last resort, to determine whether a decision on the question of EU law is necessary to enable them to actually adjudicate on this matter.[111] According to *CILFIT*, a domestic court of last resort is exonerated from its duty to make a reference to Luxembourg if the question raised is irrelevant, the EU provision has already been interpreted by the CJEU ('*acte eclairé*') or the correct application of Union law is so obvious as to leave no scope for any reasonable doubt ('*acte clair*').[112]

Individual applicants, however, still do not know whether a preliminary ruling procedure under Article 267 TFEU does indeed satisfy the requirements of Article 35 (1) ECHR or not. Beyond that, applicants alleging a violation of the Convention can neither initiate a reference to Luxembourg nor enforce the Member State's obligation to do so.[113] If the applicant then lodges an application to the ECtHR, the Strasbourg Court may either review the compatibility of an EU act with the Convention, but without the prior involvement of Luxembourg

---

[108] See Georg Ress, 'The Effect of Decisions and Judgments of the European Court of Human Rights in the Domestic Legal Order' (2005) 40 *Texas International Law Journal* 359, 359ff, and Christoph Grabenwarter, *Europäische Menschenrechtskonvention*, 4th edn (Munich, Beck, 2009) § 16, para 3.

[109] See eg, Case C-99/00 *Criminal Proceedings against Kenny Roland Lyckeskog* [2002] ECR I-4839, para 16.

[110] See Lock, 'Implications for Judicial Review' (n 10) 791.

[111] See David Edward, '*CILFIT* and *Foto-Frost* in their Historical and Procedural Context' in Miguel Poiares Maduro and Loïc Azoulai (eds), *The Past and Future of EU Law. The Classics of EU Law Revisited on the 50th Anniversary of the Rome Treaty* (Oxford, Hart Publishing, 2010) 177f.

[112] See Case 283/81 *CILFIT v Ministry of Health* [1982] ECR 3415, para 21.

[113] See Kokott and Sobotta, 'Charter of Fundamental Rights after Lisbon' (n 4) 5.

(and therewith encroach upon the Union's legal autonomy),[114] or it may declare the application inadmissible due to the applicant's potential failure to exhaust all domestic remedies. None of these findings, however, yields any desirable and worthwhile outcomes for the applicant.

It has therefore been regarded as a weakness of the preliminary ruling procedure that even though Article 267 (3) TFEU imposes an obligation on certain courts to make references, there is no real sanction for breaching this obligation.[115] Of course, failure to request a preliminary ruling from Luxembourg clearly violates the duty of loyal and sincere cooperation (Art 4 (3) TEU) and the Member States' obligation to provide remedies sufficient to ensure effective legal protection in the fields covered by European Union law (Art 19 (1), subparagraph 2 TEU).[116] Given an obvious violation of the Treaties, the European Commission may accordingly initiate infringement proceedings under Article 258 TFEU to compel a domestic court to make a reference. It has, however, so far refrained from commencing proceedings against a Member State with regard to the failure to make a reference,[117] mostly due to political inopportuneness and the difficulties involved.[118] In addition, the Commission is not bound to commence such proceedings, but has discretion in doing so which excludes the right of individuals to require that institution to adopt a specific position.[119] But most importantly, infringement proceedings against the respective Member State whose court of last resort failed to make a reference to the CJEU, would not be of any support to the applicant alleging a violation of the Convention; on the contrary, these proceedings would not necessarily cover this violation and unduly prolong the pending litigation.

ii. Preliminary Rulings and the Interpretation of Primary Union Law

Given the abovementioned findings, the following sections scrutinise whether the request for a preliminary ruling concerning the interpretation of primary law is necessary in order to satisfy the requirements under Article 35 (1) ECHR. From the outset, two essential criteria ought to be recalled at this point in order to conduct a proper line of reasoning. Firstly, the CJEU's decision is not an autonomous and stand-alone verdict, but rather an interlocutory judgment which is embedded

---

[114] See Gragl, 'Accession Revisited' (n 102) 169.

[115] See David WK Anderson, *References to the European Court* (London, Sweet & Maxwell, 1995) 178.

[116] De Schutter, *L'adhésion de l'Union européenne* (n 105) 18.

[117] See Bernhard W Wegener, 'Art 267 AEUV' in Christian Calliess and Matthias Ruffert (eds), *EUV/AEUV. Kommentar*, 4th edn (Munich, Beck, 2011) para 34, and Juliane Kokott, Thomas Henze and Christoph Sobotta, 'Die Pflicht zur Vorlage an den Europäischen Gerichtshof und die Folgen ihrer Verletzung' (2006) 61 *Juristen-Zeitung* 633, 640; see also Gert Meier, 'Zur Einwirkung des Gemeinschaftsrechts auf nationales Verfahrensrecht im Falle höchstrichterlicher Vertragsverletzungen' (1991) 2 *Europäische Zeitschrift für Wirtschaftsrecht* 11, 11ff.

[118] See Frenz, *Wirkungen und Rechtsschutz* (n 37) para 3320.

[119] See Case 247/87 *Star Fruit Company v Commission* [1989] ECR 291, para 11, and Case C-422/97 P *Sateba v Commission* [1998] ECR I-4913, para 42.

in the pending domestic litigation involving Union law. More precisely, even if a reference for a preliminary ruling is made, the principal lawsuit always starts and ends before a domestic court.[120] Secondly, individual applicants cannot compel a national court to make such a reference.

A concrete past case—namely the *Laval v Svenska Byggnadsarbetareförbundet* case—can help illustrate whether a preliminary ruling procedure is in fact indispensable to exhaust all local remedies. In its judgment, the CJEU held that the fundamental right to collective action, protected by both Article 11 ECHR and Article 28 ChFR, must be recognised as an integral part of the general principles of European Union law, but nevertheless, the exercise of such a right does not fall outside the scope of the provisions of the Treaty and must be reconciled with the requirements of the EU's fundamental freedoms. Subsequently, Luxembourg concluded that fundamental freedoms prevailed over fundamental rights in this concrete case.[121] Based on the two criteria recalled above, it is evident that, even after accession, an applicant cannot directly challenge the CJEU's *Laval* judgment before the Strasbourg Court. Before a claimant can lodge an individual application under Article 34 ECHR, they must await the judgment of the *Arbetsdomstolen*, the Swedish Labour and Employment Court, which requested the preliminary ruling and which is thence bound by Luxembourg's preliminary ruling. Only the *Arbetsdomstolen's* final judgment may then be reviewed in Strasbourg. This view is also in line with the CJEU's recent decision in *Melki*, where it again ruled that the primary purpose and objective of the preliminary ruling procedure is to guarantee the uniformity and effectiveness of European Union law. The legal protection of individuals is merely secondary to this goal.[122]

In the case where the *Arbetsdomstolen* refuses to request a preliminary ruling from the CJEU, the applicant may allege a violation of Article 6 ECHR,[123] since the arbitrary failure of a national court of last resort to make a reference might infringe on the fairness of proceedings.[124] Consequently, it may be argued that in such cases the Strasbourg Court would only rule on this violation, while refraining from reviewing the compatibility of the act complained of with the Convention. This approach would also imply that the ECtHR interprets the requirement of the 'exhaustion rule' to the effect that the applicant must have already raised the question of compatibility of the contested EU act with fundamental rights before the domestic court and have formally requested or informally suggested a

---

[120] See Thomy (n 75) 51.
[121] See Case C-341/05 *Laval v Svenska Byggnadsarbetareförbundet* [2007] ECR I-11767, paras 91 and 93.
[122] See Joined Cases C-188/10 and C-189/10 *Melki and Abdeli* [2010] ECR I-5667, paras 43f. See also Norbert Reich, 'Beitritt der EU zur EMRK—Gefahr für das Verwerfungsmonopol des EuGH?' (2010) 21 *Europäische Zeitschrift für Wirtschaftsrecht* 641, 641.
[123] See Norbert Reich, 'Wer hat Angst vor Straßburg? Bemerkungen zur europäischen Grundrechtsarchitektur—Einheit in der Vielfalt?' (2011) 22 *Europäische Zeitschrift für Wirtschaftsrecht* 379, 382.
[124] See *Lutz v Germany* App no 15073/07 (ECtHR, 13 February 2007).

preliminary reference to the Luxembourg Court. However, given the competence of the domestic courts under Article 267 TFEU to interpret European Union law and the CJEU's own case law (namely the *CILFIT* exceptions), it is also possible that the Strasbourg Court may consider that the local remedies have in fact been exhausted when a national court of last resort has adopted a final decision without having requested a preliminary ruling—even though the individual applicant requested a reference ruling from the CJEU.[125]

This scenario, however, will most certainly provoke the sceptics to doubt its compatibility with the Union's legal autonomy, since it may not entirely ensure the proper prior involvement of the Luxembourg Court. Thus, Strasbourg may adjudicate upon a case before Luxembourg has had the chance to remedy the alleged violation in the first place and the autonomy of EU law may hence be in danger.

iii. Preliminary Rulings and the Validity of Secondary Union Law

In the next step, Luxembourg's most recent case law, reinforced and intensified by the Charter's entry into force, and hence its increased readiness to annul EU legislation in conflict with fundamental rights,[126] is to be examined in light of the Union's accession to the Convention. The cases *Schecke and Eifert*[127] and *Test Achats*[128] in particular are worth investigating at this point to explore the intricate interplay of the preliminary ruling procedure and the requirements under Article 35 (1) ECHR.[129]

a. Refusal to Request a Preliminary Ruling by a Domestic Court

The national courts of last resort requested a preliminary ruling from Luxembourg in both *Schecke und Eifert* and *Test Achats* and asked whether the respective EU acts—a regulation and a directive—were compatible with the Charter. The subsequent analysis, however, explores a scenario in which those courts refused to make a reference and looks at the consequences of this refusal in relation to the 'exhaustion rule' under Article 35 (1) ECHR.

In light of *Foto-Frost*, the Luxembourg Court is the only court competent to adjudicate on the invalidity of EU legislation.[130] Domestic courts are nevertheless entitled to determine the validity of such acts and to refuse to make a reference, if the exceptions of Luxembourg's *CILFIT* case law apply.[131] But even if the

---

[125] See Council of the European Union, 'Accession of the EU to the ECHR and the Preservation of the ECJ's Monopoly on the Interpretation of EU law: Options under Discussion' 10568/10, 3f.

[126] See Benedek, 'EU Action on Human and Fundamental Rights' (n 14) 100f.

[127] See Joined Cases C-92/09 and C-93/09 *Schecke und Eifert* [2010] ECR I-11063.

[128] See C-236/09 *Test Achats* [2011] ECR I-773.

[129] See also Reich, 'Wer hat Angst vor Straßburg?' (n 123) 383.

[130] See Case 314/85 *Foto-Frost* (n 101) paras 14–15.

[131] See Case 283/81 *CILFIT* (n 112) para 21.

national courts decline to request a preliminary ruling by arguing that the Union act in question does not violate fundamental rights, there is no internal Union remedy to challenge this refusal.[132] In this situation, the applicant may lodge an individual application under Article 34 ECHR, if all other domestic remedies have been exhausted—for example, in the *Schecke und Eifert* case, in which the reference was not made by the court of last resort, but by the Administrative Court Wiesbaden, and in *Test Achats*, where the preliminary ruling was requested by the Belgian Constitutional Court.[133] Yet again, the CJEU's prior involvement and thus the internal Union redress of alleged human rights violation is not guaranteed in this scenario.

b. No Violation of the Convention by EU Law

The next scenario deviates from the real-life cases to the extent that the domestic courts did in fact request a preliminary ruling, but the CJEU found that the challenged EU acts did not violate any fundamental rights. Luxembourg's judgment on the merits of the case does of course bind the national courts which in turn decide on the case in correspondence with this judgment. In this situation, a claimant may lodge an individual application under Article 34 ECHR without the prior exhaustion of all domestic remedies, as even a court of last resort would not be entitled to depart from the judgment of the CJEU (as in the *Schecke und Eifert* case). This means that if Luxembourg finds no violation of fundamental rights, individuals must merely await the subsequent verdict by the national court. After that, applications may be lodged directly, since there are no more remedies to be exhausted in this scenario.[134]

This constellation represents the best way of guaranteeing the autonomy of Union law, in particular by involving the Luxembourg Court, and also to comply with the requirements set forth in Article 35 (1) ECHR. Nonetheless, at this point, the sceptics will recall that such a perfect scenario is simply the exception that proves the rule.

iv. *Possible Solutions and Conclusions*

The question remains how the principle of subsidiarity under Article 35 (1) ECHR and the prior involvement of the CJEU can be effectively reconciled with one another. On the one hand, one may argue that the discipline of the preliminary reference procedure and the application of the *Foto-Frost* rules ought to be strengthened, predominantly by requiring domestic courts to request a preliminary ruling in all cases in which an incompatibility of a European Union act and

---

[132] See Manfred Dauses, 'Braucht die Europäische Union eine Grundrechtsbeschwerde?' (2008) 19 *Europäische Zeitschrift für Wirtschaftsrecht* 449, 449.

[133] See Reich, 'Wer hat Angst vor Straßburg?' (n 123) 383.

[134] See ibid 383.

the Convention is invoked. After all, EU law clearly obliges the courts of last resort to cooperate with the CJEU, and it is only by way of the *CILFIT* exceptions that the CJEU loosened up on this requirement. One argument against this approach might be Luxembourg's fears that it would be flooded with such references after accession, due mainly to the fact that clever lawyers would quickly learn that the mere allegation that an act is in violation of the Convention would make the reference procedure automatic.[135] Yet, there is also a persuasive legal argument against such a *modus operandi*—the CJEU is not a superior or supreme court vis-à-vis the domestic courts. The relationship between those two judicial spheres is based rather upon cooperation, as Luxembourg itself has repeatedly held in its case law.[136] With regard to the principle of judicial independence in particular,[137] and the primary objective of the preliminary ruling procedure—namely the uniform interpretation and application of European Union law—coercion towards the Member States and the domestic courts to make a reference might not be an appropriate instrument to safeguard Luxembourg's prior involvement in such cases.

One the other hand, the applicant's situation must also be taken into account in these proceedings. If a domestic court decided that it is not obliged to make a reference, this should not be to the applicant's disadvantage. There is a substantial risk that an application alleging a violation of the Convention would not be reviewed by any of the two European courts, if Strasbourg found that the domestic remedies had not been exhausted in the absence of a reference. Beyond that, the applicant cannot enforce a request for a preliminary ruling and has thus no influence over the domestic court's decision not to make a reference.[138]

There would also be a major practical problem if a reference for a preliminary ruling was needed to satisfy the requirements of Article 35 (1) ECHR. Applicants would find themselves in a highly intricate situation if the questions brought before the CJEU or the CJEU's decision did not address the very issue of compliance with the Charter and the Convention, namely the questions which the Strasbourg Court—as a human rights court—deems relevant to adjudicate on.[139] As the *Azinas v Cyprus* case[140] demonstrates, the ECtHR might be prone to consider such negligence as insufficient to exhaust all local remedies. In this case, the applicant had claimed a violation of the right of property before the domestic courts, but had then withdrawn the grounds of the alleged fundamental rights violations. In the end, the Supreme Court of Cyprus did not rule on whether

---

[135] See Jacqué, 'Accession' (n 3) 1019f.
[136] See eg, Case 16/65 *Schwarze v Einfuhr- und Vorratsstelle für Getreide und Futtermittel* [1965] ECR 877; Case C-415/93 *Bosman* [1995] ECR I-4921, para 59; Case C-379/98 *PreussenElektra AG v Schleswag AG* [2001] ECR I-2099, para 38; Case C-35/99 *Criminal Proceedings against Manuele Arduino* [2002] ECR I-1529, para 24.
[137] See Wegener, 'Art 267 AEUV' (n 117) para 34.
[138] See Lock, 'Implications for Judicial Review' (n 10) 791f.
[139] See ibid 792.
[140] See *Azinas v Cyprus* App no 56679/00 (ECtHR, 28 April 2004).

the national legal act violated the applicant's property rights. In the opinion of the Strasbourg Court, the applicant did not provide the domestic courts with the opportunity to address the alleged violation, and thereby prevented it from putting right the particular Convention violation alleged against it. This led the ECtHR to reject the application as inadmissible for failure to exhaust all local remedies under Article 35 (1) ECHR.[141] If a preliminary reference to the CJEU under Article 267 TFEU were to become a criterion necessary to exhaust all domestic remedies, it would therefore only be consistent for the ECtHR to reject any application where the CJEU did not assess the question of the alleged violations of the Convention. When taking into account that the domestic courts enjoy discretion in determining the need for and the subject matter of a preliminary ruling and that the individual applicant thence has no influence over the actual content and the relevance of the questions the national courts refer to Luxembourg,[142] it is not acceptable for the claimant that the preliminary ruling procedure should be introduced as a new admissibility criterion before the Strasbourg Court.[143]

There is another argument against regarding the preliminary ruling procedure under Article 267 TFEU as a domestic remedy which must be exhausted lest the application be declared inadmissible by the Strasbourg Court. In some EU Member States the constitution provides for a quasi-preliminary ruling mechanism which is very similar to that on the Union level. More precisely, the ultimate decision whether to make a reference to the national Constitutional Court or not rests with the national judge, which means that in a case where the judge decides not to request such a ruling, the Constitutional Court is bypassed and does not have the opportunity to adjudicate on the matter.[144] Therefore, it may be argued that, with regard to Article 35 (1) ECHR, failure to make a reference to the CJEU is tantamount to the failure to request such proceedings before the Italian *Corte Costituzionale*.[145] However, the Italian Constitution does not entitle individuals to apply directly to this Court for a review of the constitutionality of a law or its compatibility with fundamental rights.[146] Only the court hearing the merits of a case, may it be a *Giudice di Pace* or even the *Corte Suprema di Cassazione*, has the opportunity and the right to make such a reference to the Constitutional Court, at the request of a party or of its own motion.

---

[141] See ibid paras 40–42.

[142] See Joined Cases C-332/92, C-333/92 and C-335/92 *Eurico Italia Srl, Viazzo Srl and F & P SpA v Ente Nazionale Risi* [1994] ECR I-711, para 17; Case C-189/95 *Criminal Proceedings against Harry Franzén* [1997] ECR I-5909, para 79; Case C-435/97 *World Wildlife Fund (WWF) v Provinz Bozen* [1999] ECR I-5613, paras 28–29.

[143] See Lock, 'Implications for Judicial Review' (n 10) 792 and Gragl, 'Accession Revisited' (n 102) 169.

[144] See De Schutter, *L'adhésion de l'Union européenne* (n 105) 17.

[145] See Winkler (n 10) 65.

[146] See arts 24 and 134 of the Italian Constitution. Art 24 (1) in particular prescribes that '[a]nyone may bring cases before a court of law in order to protect their rights under civil and administrative law'. No mention is made of the Constitutional Court in this provision.

Consequently, the Strasbourg Court has held that such an application cannot be regarded as a remedy whose exhaustion is required under Article 35 (1) ECHR.[147] Moreover, it observed that the Convention does not ensure any right to have a case referred by a domestic court to another national or international authority for a preliminary ruling.[148]

It would therefore constitute an undue denial of access to the ECtHR and thus a violation of Article 6 ECHR, if individual applicants were formally required to obtain a preliminary ruling from Luxembourg before bringing a case to the Strasbourg Court. It may, however, be reasonably argued that the applicant must at least suggest or even formally apply to the court to refer the case to the Luxembourg Court.[149] This approach would guarantee that the domestic court addresses the question of compatibility of EU law with the Convention in the case before it, thereby increasing the likelihood of a reference.[150]

Nevertheless, given the fact that even other national courts of last resort might end up in a situation in which they did not have the chance to decide on a case prior to the Strasbourg Court, the situation of the Luxembourg Court after accession is not particularly special when considering that the domestic courts of the Member States are the first judicial bodies to apply European Union law.[151] This book therefore concludes that a request for a preliminary reference procedure under Article 267 TFEU is not necessary in order to fulfil the requirements of Article 35 (1) ECHR, as it is not normally a legal remedy available to the claimant.[152] Applicants may of course suggest or apply that such proceedings be initiated, but in case the respective court fails to do so, the ECtHR should not declare the application inadmissible due to the applicant's failure to exhaust all domestic remedies. This conclusion disburdens the applicant from getting involved with procedural subtleties where the outcome is difficult to anticipate. Furthermore, it is now clear that specific provisions to ensure Luxembourg's prior involvement are only necessary within the legal framework of indirect actions, ie preliminary reference procedures, as they do not qualify as domestic remedies. The preceding findings do not, however, give any answers to the question of how the Luxembourg Court's prior involvement may be ensured in order to guarantee the internal review of alleged fundamental rights violations before the external review in Strasbourg and thus the autonomy of European Union law.

---

[147] See *Brozicek v Italy* App no 10964/84 (ECtHR, 19 December 1989) para 34; *Immobiliare Saffi v Italy* App no 22774/93 (ECtHR, 28 July 1999) para 42; *De Jorio v Italy* App no 73936/01 (ECtHR, 3 June 2004) para 37.

[148] See *Coëme v Belgium* App nos 32492/96, 32547/96, 32548/96, 33209/96 and 33210/96 (ECtHR, 22 June 2000) para 114.

[149] See Kokott and Sobotta, 'Charter of Fundamental Rights after Lisbon' (n 4) 5.

[150] See Lock, 'Implications for Judicial Review' (n 10) 792.

[151] See De Schutter, *L'adhésion de l'Union européenne* (n 105) 17.

[152] See Joint Communication from Presidents Costa and Skouris (n 10) 2.

III. THE SOLUTION OF THE DRAFT ACCESSION AGREEMENT

A. Preliminary Remarks on the Necessity of Internal Union Review

To ensure the CJEU's prior involvement in ECtHR proceedings and thus the internal Union review of EU acts allegedly in violation of fundamental rights, cursory guidelines on this matter have been proposed. These guidelines give a rough overview of the most basic requirements of such an internal review mechanism and what standards they ought to comply with, but without delving into any details. For instance, the CJEU's *Discussion Document* generally states that the Convention's principle of subsidiarity and the proper functioning of the Union's judicial system are closely intertwined. A special mechanism must therefore be available which is capable of guaranteeing that the question of the validity of EU legislation can effectively be brought to Luxembourg before Strasbourg then rules on the compatibility of that very act with the Convention.[153] In January 2011, Presidents Costa and Skouris tried to elaborate this view and argued that

> [...] a procedure should be put in place, in connection with the accession of the EU to the Convention, which is flexible and would ensure that the CJEU may carry out an internal review before the EC[t]HR carries out external review. The implementation of such a procedure, which does not require an amendment to the Convention, should take account of the characteristics of the judicial review which are specific to the two courts. In that regard, it is important that the types of cases which may be brought before the CJEU are clearly defined. [...].[154]

The following sections consequently investigate the mechanisms and procedures that have been devised in order to satisfy these high expectations and challenging demands. Furthermore, they illustrate the details of these procedures which aim at ensuring Luxembourg's prior involvement in ECtHR proceedings, and the advantages and disadvantages these mechanisms would bring about if they were implemented. Formal implementation of such a procedure is a necessary prerequisite given Luxembourg's view in *Opinion 1/91* on the binding nature of its decisions[155]—thus, simple and informal consultation procedures are certainly not sufficient in this respect.[156]

---

[153] See Court of Justice of the European Union, 'Discussion Document of the Court of Justice of the European Union' (n 1) para 12.

[154] See Joint Communication from Presidents Costa and Skouris (n 10) 2.

[155] See Opinion 1/91 *EEA I (Draft agreement between the Community, on the one hand, and the countries of the European Free Trade Association, on the other, relating to the creation of the European Economic Area)* [1991] ECR I-6079, para 61, where the CJEU ruled that '[i]t is unacceptable that the answers which the Court of Justice gives to the courts and tribunals in the EFTA States are to be purely advisory and without any binding effects. Such a situation would change the nature of the function of the Court of Justice as it is conceived by the EEC Treaty, namely that of a court whose judgments are binding. Even in the very specific case of Article 228 [now Art 218 TFEU], the Opinion given by the Court of Justice has the binding effect stipulated in that article.'

[156] See Jacqué, 'Accession' (n 3) 1021.

Beyond that, the following sections take a close and thorough look at the provisions of the Draft Accession Agreement and whether the presented mechanisms are in accordance with these provisions and the autonomy of European Union law. But before these issues are addressed, a preliminary question of utmost importance should be answered. In the preceding chapters, it was generally assumed that Luxembourg's prior involvement is absolutely necessary in order to preserve the Union's legal autonomy. Certainly, this would be the case if Strasbourg were given competence and jurisdiction to interpret European Union law in a binding manner and in the absence of a mechanism ensuring the prior involvement of the Luxembourg Court. But, as demonstrated above,[157] in a case where the ECtHR finds a violation of the Convention by EU law, the Union act in question will not be invalidated, as Strasbourg cannot quash or annul domestic law. Its judgments are merely declaratory in nature and even though the contracting parties are obliged under international law to redress the violations found by the ECtHR, the ultimate choice in how they go about this rests with them. It is therefore a crucial principle and the theoretical ground for the subsequent analysis that the prior involvement of the Luxembourg Court is not required in order to preserve the autonomy of the European Union's legal order.[158]

B. Article 3 (6) of the Draft Accession Agreement and the Autonomy Question

i. *The Constituent Elements of Article 3 (6) of the Draft Accession Agreement*

In the final version of the Draft Accession Agreement, the negotiators agreed that a prior involvement of the CJEU in ECtHR proceedings should be permissible under certain circumstances which are illustrated and examined below. In its entirety, Article 3 (6) of the Draft Accession Agreement reads as follows:

> In proceedings to which the European Union is *co-respondent*, if the Court of Justice of the European Union *has not yet assessed the compatibility with the Convention rights at issue of the provision of European Union law* as under paragraph 2 of this Article,[159] then *sufficient time* shall be afforded for the Court of Justice of the European Union to make such an assessment and thereafter for the parties *to make observations* to the Court. The European Union shall ensure that such assessment *is made quickly so that the proceedings before the Court are not unduly delayed*. The provisions of this paragraph *shall not affect the powers of the Court*.[160]

---

[157] See ch 8.

[158] See Lock, 'Tightrope' (n 20) 1047.

[159] See art 3 (2) of the Draft Accession Agreement which governs the conditions under which the European Union may join the proceedings against one or more Member States as a co-respondent. See also ch 9 for more details.

[160] Art 3 (6) of the Draft Accession Agreement; Council of Europe, 'Steering Committee for Human Rights—Report to the Committee of Ministers on the Elaboration of Legal Instruments

The question remains of the significance and legal ramifications of this provision for proceedings after accession, most importantly despite the fact that the prior involvement of the CJEU is not an absolute prerequisite in safeguarding the autonomy of EU law. To be exact, even though the prior involvement of Luxembourg is not necessary in order to preserve the Union's legal autonomy, such prior involvement must of course not infringe this very autonomy, for example by clandestinely introducing new types of procedures into European Union law and thereby amending the Treaties. The subsequent analysis of the constituent elements of this provision will help shed more light on this issue.

Firstly, the negotiators of the Draft Accession Agreement have been well aware of the fact that in cases in which the EU may be a co-respondent, a bypassing of the CJEU (inter alia in the form of a court of last resort failing to make a request for a preliminary ruling) is rarely expected to arise. Nevertheless, it was considered desirable that an *internal* Union procedure be put in place to guarantee that Luxembourg has ample opportunity to review the compatibility with the Convention rights at issue of the provision of Union law which triggered the participation of the Union as a co-respondent in the first place.[161] Given the problems the introduction of an external mechanism may pose for the Union's legal autonomy, this book investigates which external procedures have been proposed in the past and what internal procedures may be implemented in order to comply with the requirements of Article 3 (6) of the Draft Accession Agreement. Secondly, the question arises whether the Union institution authorised to initiate the internal proceedings before the CJEU can in fact be compelled to do so or whether such an obligation may conflict with the Union's legal autonomy. Thirdly, it is understood that the parties involved—including, of course, the applicant—will have ample opportunity to make observations in the procedure before the CJEU.[162] There is, however, a serious risk that the strict time limits in CJEU proceedings may prevent the applicants from making such observations or the Union institutions from instigating the respective actions. Fourthly, in order not to unduly delay the proceedings in Strasbourg, the Union must ensure that the Luxembourg ruling is delivered quickly, for example on the basis of an accelerated procedure.[163] It must therefore be scrutinised whether such a demand touches upon a question completely internal to Union law and thus on its autonomy. Fifthly, by virtue of Article 3 (6) of the Draft Accession Agreement, the Luxembourg Court will not assess the act or omission of which the applicant complained, but rather the legal basis of it under European Union law.[164] It is, however, doubtful whether such a

---

for the Accession of the European Union to the European Convention on Human Rights' CDDH-UE(2011)009, 8 (emphasis added).

[161] See CDDH-UE(2011)009 (n 160) 24, paras 57–58.
[162] See ibid 25, para 58.
[163] See ibid 25, para 61.
[164] See ibid 25, para 59.

marginal and limited procedure before the CJEU is possible under EU law and whether the introduction of such a mechanism would jeopardise its autonomy.

ii. *External Mechanisms: A Reference Procedure by Strasbourg to Luxembourg?*

It is obvious that the introduction of an external mechanism is itself incompatible with the autonomy of the Union's legal order as it would constitute a hidden amendment to the Treaties if it were included in the final Accession Agreement.[165] Had the drafters of the Draft Accession Agreement not included a reference to an internal mechanism, every agreement internal to the European Union would have to be measured by the same standards.[166] As *Opinion 1/91* has demonstrated, EU law does not prevent an international agreement from conferring new functions on the Union's institutions, but it is unacceptable that such a situation would change the nature of their primary function.[167] In other words, neither the Luxembourg Court nor any other EU institution must be given a role which it currently does not have under primary law. If this external mechanism resulted in a new procedure before the CJEU, which had no legal basis on the currently existing provisions or procedures, the Union's legal autonomy would thus be violated.[168]

One external mechanism to involve the CJEU in proceedings before the ECtHR would be to introduce a preliminary reference procedure between the two courts, as the French Senator Robert Badinter suggested in 2010.[169] More precisely, if the Strasbourg Court is seized by an applicant in cases where the European Union has been designated as co-respondent, the CJEU could be asked to rule on the compliance of the legal act in question with the Union's fundamental rights—ie the Charter and the Convention.[170] If Luxembourg did not find any violation, the case would be immediately referred back to Strasbourg for a definitive review on the basis of the Convention.[171] Arguably, this special reference procedure should only be initiated after the application is declared admissible in Strasbourg. This, however, may be too late, since Strasbourg's decision on admissibility might already contain an assessment of European Union law, as some past cases

---

[165] See O'Meara (n 8) 1824.
[166] See Lock, 'Tightrope' (n 20) 1048.
[167] See Opinion 1/91 *EEA I* (n 155) paras 59 and 61.
[168] See Lock, 'Tightrope' (n 20) 1048.
[169] See Sénat Français, 'Adhésion de l'Union Européenne à la Convention européenne de sauvegarde des droits de l'homme, Communication de M Robert Badinter sur le mandat de négociation' (E 5248), 25 May 2010, <www.senat.fr/europe/r25052010.html#toc1> accessed 1 November 2012, where Senator Badinter stated that '[j]e crois pour ma part qu'il faut aller plus loin et préciser que la Cour de justice devrait être saisie d'une question préjudicielle par la Cour de Strasbourg, si elle ne l'a pas été auparavant.'
[170] See Jacqué, 'Accession' (n 3) 1021.
[171] See Lock, 'Implications for Judicial Review' (n 10) 793.

expressly demonstrate.[172] It has therefore been suggested that intervention by the EU should take place when it becomes party to the dispute, either because it was addressed as the original respondent or because it has joined the proceedings as co-respondent.[173]

There are, however, several arguments against a reference procedure by Strasbourg to Luxembourg. Firstly, there is no precedent for a reference mechanism in the Convention system.[174] This means that the Convention or at least the Rules of the Strasbourg Court would have to be amended to allow for the introduction of such a specific reference mechanism between the two European courts.[175] Given the difficulties of the past, namely the delayed entry into force of Protocol No 14 to the Convention, and the expectedly lengthy ratification procession of the final Accession Agreement, such a course of action is not recommended at all. Secondly, any reference by Strasbourg to Luxembourg would lead to further delay in proceedings.[176] Beyond that, such a mechanism would grant the CJEU and the European Union undue privileges[177] which would contradict the principle that the Union should accede to the Convention on an equal footing with the other high contracting parties.[178] The Supreme and Constitutional Courts of the other parties are not entitled to request a preliminary ruling from Strasbourg and cannot thence avoid the risk of violating the Convention by obtaining such a judgment. Besides, the situation in which the CJEU has not had the opportunity of a prior internal review concerning the compatibility with fundamental rights would not be unique, since some other legal systems of the Member States do not provide for any (or only very limited) judicial review regarding the constitutionality of their domestic legislation. This means that the Strasbourg Court is in fact sometimes the first court to adjudicate on alleged human rights violations. More importantly in the context of preserving the autonomy of European Union law, the ECtHR would undoubtedly, to some extent, pre-judge the outcome of such cases and thus assess EU law.[179]

Lastly, with respect to the standards of *Opinion 1/91* and the preservation of the functional nature of the Union's institutions, the introduction of a preliminary

---

[172] See eg, *Connolly v 15 Member States of the European Union* App no 73274/01 (ECtHR, 9 December 2008); *Cooperatieve Producentenorganisatie van de Nederlandse Kokkelvisserij v The Netherlands* App no 13645/05 (ECtHR, 20 January 2009); *MSS v Belgium and Greece* App no 30696/09 (ECtHR, 21 January 2011).

[173] See Jacqué, 'Accession' (n 3) 1021.

[174] See Kokott and Sobotta, 'Charter of Fundamental Rights after Lisbon' (n 4) 5.

[175] See Council of Europe, '5th Working Meeting of the CDDH Informal Working Group on the Accession of the European Union to the European Convention on Human Rights (CDDH-UE) with the European Commission' CDDH-UE(2011)02, 4.

[176] See Lock, 'Implications for Judicial Review' (n 10) 793. But see Jacqué, 'Accession' (n 3) 1021 who argues that this factor would pose only a few problems, given the length of proceedings in Strasbourg.

[177] See Theodor Schilling, 'Der Beitritt der EU zur EMRK—Verhandlungen und Modalitäten. Fast eine Polemik' (2011) 17 *Humboldt Forum Recht* 83, 91.

[178] See CDDH-UE(2011)009 (n 160) 16, para 7.

[179] See Lock, 'Implications for Judicial Review' (n 10) 793.

ruling mechanism from Strasbourg to Luxembourg is highly problematic in light of the more recent *Opinion 1/09* on the creation of a European and Community Patents Court. In this Opinion, Luxembourg held that another international court must not take the place of national courts and tribunals and thus deprive them of the power to request preliminary rulings from the CJEU.[180] Of course, one might object that the Strasbourg Court would not take the place of the domestic courts in requesting a preliminary ruling, as those courts have failed to do so in the first place. But in contrast to a situation in which the courts of the Member States refuse to make a reference, the European Commission could not initiate infringement proceedings under Article 258 TFEU against the Strasbourg Court in case it failed to request a preliminary ruling. Thus, Strasbourg's action or rather inaction could not be subjected to infringement proceedings.[181] The introduction of an external mechanism of a preliminary reference procedure by Strasbourg to Luxembourg would therefore run afoul of the requirements of Article 3 (6) of the Draft Accession Agreement and, more importantly, would also infringe the autonomy of European Union law.

iii. Potential Internal Mechanisms

Yet, even though Article 3 (6) of the Draft Accession Agreement sets forth that the Luxembourg Court shall be afforded the opportunity to make an assessment on the compatibility of EU law with the Convention if it has not yet had chance to do so, such a procedure may be fraught with problems, especially in regards to preserving the autonomy of European Union law. The Draft Accession Agreement neither indicates any details of this procedure nor does it disclose how and by what institution or organ the review before the CJEU is to be triggered.[182] The Explanatory Report, in contrast, merely reveals that it was considered desirable that an internal Union procedure be put in place to ensure Luxembourg's prior involvement in ECtHR proceedings.[183] This general reference to internal Union rules was necessary to avoid any infringements of the EU's legal autonomy. In a case where the agreement provided for detailed and specific procedure, this would be tantamount to a hidden Treaty amendment and would thus violate the requirements for upholding the autonomy of EU law.[184] As a result, the final determination of the procedure before the Luxembourg Court has been left to the European Union. However, given the political difficulties involved in Treaty revisions, the internal procedure should be based on existing provisions and thence avoid any amendments to the Union's primary law.[185]

---

[180] See Opinion 1/09 *European and Community Patents Court* [2011] ECR I-1137, paras 79 and 89.

[181] See ibid, paras 87–88.

[182] See Lock, 'Tightrope' (n 20) 1049.

[183] See CDDH-UE(2011)009 (n 160) 25, para 58.

[184] See Case 43/75 *Defrenne II* [1976] ECR 455, para 58. See also Matthias Pechstein, 'Die Justitiabilität des Unionsrechts' (1999) 34 *Europarecht* 13, 19.

[185] See Lock, 'Tightrope' (n 20) 1049.

Therefore, the question arises as to what options are in fact available to the European Union on the basis of the existing primary law. In a working document published in January 2011, the European Commission mentions that the general features and the specific procedural rules of the prior involvement of the Luxembourg Court should be similar to those governing the preliminary ruling procedure under Article 267 TFEU.[186] Potential candidates for making such a request may be the European Commission or the respondent Member State.[187] It seems that the most appropriate place to lay down these procedural rules would be the Council decision concluding the Accession Agreement pursuant to Article 218 (6) TFEU. If more detailed and technical rules are necessary, they could be laid down in the CJEU's Rules of Procedure.[188]

Furthermore, the Commission argues that these procedural rules would not amount to conferring new competences on the Union or new powers on the CJEU within the meaning of *Opinion 1/91*. Rather, these rules would preserve the specific characteristics of the EU's legal system—as required by Article 1 of Protocol No 8 to the Treaties—and address situations in which the Luxembourg Court would exercise its power to ensure the proper observation of European Union law in the interpretation and application of the Treaties, as set forth in Article 19 (1) TEU, by annulling an EU act if it is incompatible with the Union's fundamental rights. Beyond that, as Article 51 (1) ChFR prescribes that these fundamental rights are addressed to all Union institutions, bodies, offices and agencies, the procedural rules introduced in the context of the accession to the Convention would concurrently guarantee that the obligation of the Union's institutions to 'act within the powers conferred on [them] in the Treaties' under Article 13 (2) TEU was properly respected.[189]

Nevertheless, Article 19 (1) TEU does not provide the CJEU with a legal foundation for (new) competences or procedures, but rather defines the general role and the 'constitutional' function of the Luxembourg Court.[190] As a result, any procedure suggested would still have to be compatible and reconcilable with the procedures currently in existence.[191]

a. Legal Opinions by Luxembourg

During the negotiations, the involvement of the Luxembourg Court in the course of the co-respondent mechanism by means of an opinion was suggested as an

---

[186] See European Commission, 'Working Document on the Previous Involvement of the Court of Justice in the Context of the Accession of the European Union to the European Convention for the Protection of Human Rights and Fundamental Freedoms' DS 1930/10, para 5.

[187] See ibid, para 6.

[188] See ibid, para 11.

[189] See ibid, para 12.

[190] See Franz C Mayer, 'Art 19 EUV' in Eberhard Grabitz, Meinhard Hilf and Martin Nettesheim (eds), *Das Recht der Europäischen Union. Band I* (Munich, Beck, 2010) para 4.

[191] See Lock, 'Tightrope' (n 20) 1049.

option to guarantee the CJEU's prior internal review of alleged fundamental rights violations. More precisely, this option would allow the CJEU as an organ of the European Union to submit to the Strasbourg Court a legal opinion in the form of a regular submission by a high contracting party involved in the case— possibly the original respondent. The European Commission may be a potential candidate to request that the CJEU submits such an opinion. The negotiators argued that the Convention system of fixing time limits for submissions seemed to be flexible enough to accommodate such submissions which would consist of a legal opinion by an international court and thus a very complex and time-consuming submission. The obvious advantage of this mechanism lies in the fact that it would enable Strasbourg to consider the CJEU's opinion on the matter before deciding the case and without the need for any changes or amendments to the Convention system.[192]

In this scenario, however, Luxembourg would not be in the position to formally pronounce itself on the case and thus to remedy the alleged fundamental rights violation before Strasbourg reviews the case. This approach is therefore not in accordance with the original purpose of Article 35 (1) ECHR and the basic sub-sidiarity of Strasbourg's protection system. Of course, this procedure might not necessitate specific amendments to the Convention, but adaptations to the rules of the Strasbourg and Luxembourg courts and the EU Treaties may nevertheless be required.[193] It is consequently evident that such a procedure involving the CJEU by submitting a legal opinion on a case is not capable of ensuring both the Convention's subsidiarity principle and the Union's legal autonomy.

b. Reference Procedure Requested by the Commission

Another plausible option to guarantee the CJEU's prior involvement in ECtHR proceedings is a mechanism suggested by former CJEU Judge Christiaan Timmermans in which the European Commission may request that the Luxembourg Court decides upon the compatibility of an EU act with fundamen-tal rights (or on a national measure within the ambit of EU law) after an applica-tion has been declared admissible in Strasbourg. In a case where the European Commission makes such a reference, the proceedings before the ECtHR would be suspended until the CJEU has assessed the case. If the CJEU finds a violation, the proceedings before the ECtHR would be terminated; if not, they will automati-cally be resumed.[194]

Prima facie, the introduction of such a mechanism would be a worthwhile addition to the European system of human rights protection, for the following reasons in particular. Firstly, such an action is already possible under European Union law. The European Commission, as a privileged applicant, may initiate

---

[192] See CDDH-UE(2011)02 (n 175) 3.
[193] See ibid 3.
[194] See Timmermans (n 5) 7f.

annulment proceedings under Article 263 (2) TFEU, in order to have legislation reviewed by Luxembourg as to its compatibility with the Charter.[195] Secondly, the Commission may also initiate infringement proceedings under Article 258 TFEU against the respective Member State, as the national court of last resort has failed to make a reference to the CJEU.[196] If the European Commission additionally asserted that the decision by the domestic court infringed Union law with respect to the case before the ECtHR, the CJEU could make a pronouncement on this very issue. Conversely, if the Commission regarded that the national decision complied with Union law, it could refrain from initiating infringement proceedings.[197] By and large, an extension of the Commission's power to initiate proceedings before the Luxembourg Court after accession would not violate the autonomy of European Union law. This book, however, will take a closer look and demonstrate that the EU's legal autonomy may nevertheless be in serious jeopardy.[198]

iv. Discretion or Obligation to Trigger Proceedings?

In the situation where the European Commission becomes the Union institution competent to instigate internal proceedings before the CJEU, any such action under Article 258 or 263 TFEU would then be dependent upon the discretion of the Commission, which may fail to bring a case or may be reluctant to do so, as the Commission would always have initiated or introduced the legislation in question itself[199] according to its monopoly of legislative initiative under Article 17 (2) TEU.[200] Thence, it is evident that the introduction of a provision which would in turn obligate or compel the Commission to instigate proceedings would also necessitate a Treaty revision.[201]

Since such a politically inopportune step has to be avoided, the Commission's discretion in instigating infringement proceedings[202] or actions for annulment[203] must be taken into consideration for the subsequent analysis. From the outset, it may be argued that this margin of discretion would allow the Commission to preliminarily assess whether such proceedings before the Luxembourg Court are necessary or not. Where Luxembourg has already adjudicated on the compatibility

---

[195] See Lock, 'Implications for Judicial Review' (n 10) 793.

[196] See Wegener, 'Art 267 AEUV' (n 117) para 34, and Kokott, Henze and Sobotta, 'Pflicht zur Vorlage' (n 117) 640f.

[197] See Kokott and Sobotta, 'Charter of Fundamental Rights after Lisbon' (n 4) 5.

[198] See Lock, 'Tightrope' (n 20) 1050.

[199] See Lock, 'Implications for Judicial Review' (n 10) 793.

[200] See Craig, *The Lisbon Treaty* (n 12) 33, and Bernd Martenczuk, 'Art. 17 EUV' in Eberhard Grabitz, Meinhard Hilf and Martin Nettesheim (eds), *Das Recht der Europäischen Union. Band I* (Munich, Beck, 2010) paras 50ff.

[201] See Lock, 'Tightrope' (n 20) 1050.

[202] See Case 48/65 *Lütticke GmbH v Commission* [1966] ECR 19, 27; Case C-72/90 *Asia Motor France v Commission* [1990] ECR I-2181, para 13; Case T-47/96 *SDDDA v Commission* [1996] ECR II-1559, para 42.

[203] See Case 247/87 *Star Fruit Company v Commission* (n 119) para 11.

of a specific EU act with fundamental rights, the Commission could refrain from triggering the internal procedures. It would hence be in a position to exercise a filter function,[204] which would correspond to its primary role as guardian of the Treaties.[205] In a situation where the European Commission failed to bring the case before the Luxembourg Court, Strasbourg would then decide without a prior involvement of the CJEU. This bypassing of Luxembourg would not conflict with the European Union's legal autonomy, since the prior involvement of Luxembourg is in fact desirable in order to give the Union ample opportunity to redress fundamental rights violations on the domestic level and thus to avoid a conviction by Strasbourg, but not necessary in upholding the autonomy of EU law. If the European Commission chooses not to trigger proceedings, it may be assumed that the European Union does not have any interest in remedying the alleged fundamental rights violation. The Strasbourg Court would accordingly be in a position of finding such a violation without the prior involvement of Luxembourg.[206] As a result, there is no need to oblige or compel the Commission to instigate proceedings, as its broad discretion in doing so is in accordance with both Article 35 (1) ECHR and the Union's legal autonomy.

v. *Observations by the Parties and the Time Limit under Art 263 (6) TFEU*

Even though the Explanatory Report emphasises that the parties involved—including the applicant—shall be given ample opportunity to make observations in the procedure before the CJEU,[207] there is, nonetheless, the strict time limit under Article 263 (6) TFEU which may prevent the applicants from making such observations or the Commission from instigating the proceedings in the first place. Article 263 (6) TFEU sets forth that annulment proceedings shall only be instituted within two months of the publication of the measure in question. The correct observation of and the compliance with this time limit is examined *ex officio*[208] and is, as a matter of public policy, not subject to the discretion of the parties or the Luxembourg Court, since this very time limit was established in order to ensure legal certainty.[209] After this time limit expires, Union acts become definitive

---

[204] See Lock, 'Tightrope' (n 20) 1050.

[205] See John Usher, 'The Commission and the Law' in David Spence and Geoffrey Edwards (eds), *The European Commission*, 3rd edn (London, John Harper Publishing, 2006) 116f, and Matthias Ruffert, 'Art 17 EUV' in Christian Calliess and Matthias Ruffert (eds), *EUV/AEUV. Kommentar*, 4th edn (Munich, Beck, 2011) paras 7ff.

[206] See Lock, 'Tightrope' (n 20) 1050.

[207] See CDDH-UE(2011)009 (n 160) 25, para 58.

[208] See Joined Cases T-121/96 and T-151/96 *Mutual Aid Administration Services v Commission* [1997] ECR II-1355, para 39.

[209] See Case 24/69 *Nebe v Commission* [1970] ECR 145, para 5; Case 227/83 *Moussis v Commission* [1984] ECR 3133, para 12; Case C-246/95 *Coen v Belgian State* [1997] ECR I-403, para 21; Case T-276/97 *Guérin Automobiles* [1998] ECR II-261, para 14.

and are precluded from impugnment.[210] But by the time proceedings have reached Strasbourg, the worst case scenario for the applicant might have already come to pass, as Luxembourg will declare the action for annulment inadmissible, due to the expiry of the two-month period under Article 236 (6) TFEU.[211] Therefore, the question arises as to whether this strict and admittedly short time limit may be a major obstacle to Luxembourg's prior involvement, as foreseen by Article 3 (6) of the Draft Accession Agreement. Moreover, the autonomy of European Union law would be in danger, if the nature of the CJEU's functions were affected.[212] In *Opinion 1/91*, the CJEU refused to accept that the answers it gave to the courts and tribunals of the European Free Trade Association states were intended to be purely advisory and not binding on them, since this would have changed the functional nature of the Luxembourg Court.[213] At this point, one may ask whether a dispensation or relaxation of the strict time limit in Article 263 (6) TFEU would be tantamount to such a change in the CJEU's functional nature and thus a direct violation of the Union's legal autonomy. Luxembourg's settled case law on the importance of legal certainty seems to pursue a narrow approach which would speak out against any changes to the time limit.[214]

This conclusion leads to the question as to whether there are any options other than the action for annulment the European Commission may resort to in order to guarantee Luxembourg's prior involvement in ECtHR proceedings. The preliminary reference procedure under Article 267 TFEU also provides for a review of legality and validity of European Union law by the CJEU. Of course, the Commission is not entitled to make a request for a preliminary ruling, but a closer look at the CJEU's case law on Article 267 TFEU and the respective time limit in which to make such a request may help to analogously find solutions to the aforementioned issues.

The Luxembourg Court made it clear in its decision in *TWD Textilwerke Deggendorf* that the validity of Union acts may no longer be called into question by means of a preliminary ruling procedure once the time limit laid down in Article 263 (6) TFEU has expired.[215] In other words, despite the lack of an express clause in Article 267 TFEU governing the time limit for making requests to the CJEU, the two-month time limit of Article 263 (6) TFEU is analogously applicable to procedures under Article 267.[216] As a result, in a case where a domestic court makes a request for a preliminary ruling regarding the legality of a Commission decision after the time limit for an individual application has expired, the decision

---

[210] See Oliver Dörr and Christofer Lenz, *Europäischer Verwaltungsrechtsschutz* (Baden-Baden, Nomos, 2006) paras 147 and 271, and Frenz, *Wirkungen und Rechtsschutz* (n 37) para 2817.

[211] See Bertrand Wägenbaur, 'EuGH: Verfristung der deutschen Klage gegen Tabakwerberichtlinie' (2002) 13 *Europäische Zeitschrift für Wirtschaftsrecht* 404, 406.

[212] See Lock, 'Tightrope' (n 20) 1050.

[213] See Opinion 1/91 *EEA I* (n 155) paras 58 and 61.

[214] See Lock, 'Tightrope' (n 20) 1050.

[215] See Case C-188/92 *TWD Textilwerke Deggendorf* [1994] ECR I-833, paras 15f.

[216] See Thomy (n 75) 85, and Wegener, 'Art 267 AEUV' (n 117) para 15.

becomes definitive vis-à-vis the addressee for the sake of legal certainty.[217] In this context, the CJEU ruled in the *Nachi Europe v Hauptzollamt Krefeld* case that anti-dumping regulations have a dual nature, which means that they are, at the same time, general acts of a legislative nature and acts liable to be of direct and individual concern to natural and legal persons. Thus, the regulation must be considered to be an individual decision towards the individual, which means that the plaintiff could undoubtedly have sought the annulment of the said regulation under Article 263 (4) TFEU and that the time limit of Article 263 (6) is applicable.[218]

Yet, these judgments share a common feature which may support the argument of extending or even disabling the time limit rule of Article 263 (6) TFEU. In the *Wiljo NV v Belgian State* case, the CJEU held that the validity of a Commission decision, which was directly addressed to a natural or legal person, could not be contested before a domestic court if the claimant had not applied for an annulment of that decision, even though they could undoubtedly have done so, and that they had instead brought proceedings before the domestic courts challenging the implementation of the decision by the national authorities.[219] Accordingly, the rule the CJEU found in *Textilwerke Deggendorf* only applies to acts which are addressed to the applicant or which are clearly of direct and individual concern to them.[220] It thus seems unlikely that this rule would normally extend to measures of general application for two reasons. On the one hand, Article 263 (4) TFEU must be interpreted in such a way that it complies with the principle of effective judicial protection. On the other hand, direct actions for annulment are more appropriate for determining issues of validity than (indirect) preliminary ruling procedures and thus less liable to cause legal uncertainty for individuals and the Union institutions,[221] since the requirements for submitting a direct action are strict and the opportunities for written observations and for replying to the arguments of the other parties involved are significantly greater than within the course of a preliminary ruling procedure.[222]

This approach seems the most appropriate way of tackling this issue, as the situation is entirely different when it comes to legislative acts.[223] Commission decisions are directly addressed to certain individuals, while legislative acts are in fact generally

---

[217] See Case C-188/92 *TWD Textilwerke Deggendorf* (n 215), paras 13 and 16.

[218] See Case C-239/99 *Nachi Europe v Hauptzollamt Krefeld* [2001] ECR I-1197, paras 36–38.

[219] See Case C-178/95 *Wiljo NV v Belgian State* [1997] ECR I-585, para 23.

[220] See Anthony Arnull, *The European Union and its Court of Justice*, 2nd edn (New York, McGraw-Hill Books, 2006) 129.

[221] See Case C-50/00 P *Unión de Pequeños Agricultores v Council* [2002] ECR I-6677, Opinion of AG Jacobs, para 37.

[222] See Anderson (n 115) 19f.

[223] See Morten Broberg and Niels Fenger, *Preliminary References to the European Court of Justice* (Oxford, Oxford University Press, 2010) 213f.

applicable *erga omnes*[224] and usually of an infinite duration.[225] As a result, in a case where these acts are in violation of fundamental rights, they infringe the rights of individuals every time they are implemented. In other words, one might say that if they were not impugnable for more than two months after their promulgation, situations in complete contradiction to the effective protection of human rights would be perpetuated. In conclusion, the interests involved in challenging general legislation are entirely distinct from those involved when individual decisions are contested, as legality and compatibility with fundamental rights should prevail over individual legal certainty.[226] This means that individuals may challenge the validity of a certain legislative act regardless of the time limit laid down in Article 263 (6) TFEU.[227] Luxembourg eventually confirmed these results and held that, even though the applicant had failed to bring an action for annulment within the two month time limit under Article 263 (6), there was no reason to prevent a review of legislative acts in connection with a reference for a preliminary ruling.[228] It seems that such an approach is a suitable compromise between the need for legal certainty and the principle of legality. In situations where a natural or legal person is affected by a measure with the same effect as an individual decision, the party may seek an action for annulment within the time limit of Article 263 (6) TFEU. In situations where this is not the case, the CJEU's standards found in *Textilwerke Deggendorf* do not apply. If these standards were applied in such cases, individuals would be required to file pre-emptive actions for annulment which contradict the European Union's own 'constitutional' norms and the good administration of justice.[229]

When examining the compatibility of Luxembourg's prior involvement with the autonomy of European Union law, the question remains whether the CJEU—in light of its own case law—would have the jurisdiction to review the legality of legislative acts even in cases where the time limit of Article 263 (6) TFEU has already expired. A thorough examination of the case law regarding Article 267 TFEU shows that there is ample room for such an argument. Nevertheless, it is doubtful whether giving the European Commission a comprehensive competence to request the CJEU to review legislation on a regular basis (regardless of the concrete circumstances with respect to the applicant's standing) would modify the functional nature of CJEU proceedings and thus infringe the Union's legal autonomy. Of course, there are considerable risks that the prior involvement

---

[224] See Armin von Bogdandy, Jürgen Bast and Felix Arndt, 'Handlungsformen im Unionsrecht. Empirische Analysen und dogmatische Strukturen in einem vermeintlichen Dschungel' (2002) 62 *Zeitschrift für ausländisches öffentliches Recht und Völkerrecht* 77, 82f.

[225] See Case C-137/92 P *Commission v BASF* [1994] ECR I-2555, para 48.

[226] See Lock, 'Tightrope' (n 20) 1051f.

[227] See Matthias Vogt, 'Indirect Judicial Protection in EC Law—The Case of the Plea of Illegality' (2006) 31 *European Law Review* 364, 377.

[228] See Case C-241/95 *The Queen v Accrington Beef* [1996] ECR I-6699, paras 14–16; Joined Cases C-346/03 and C-529/03 *Atzeni* [2006] ECR I-1875, para 34; Case C-119/05 *Lucchini* [2007] ECR I-6199, paras 54–55; see also Broberg and Fenger (n 223) 216f.

[229] See Balthasar (n 47) 549.

of the Luxembourg Court, as foreseen by Article 3 (6) of the Draft Accession Agreement, cannot be effectively reconciled with the autonomy of the EU's legal order without an amendment to the Treaties.[230] However, it is equally possible that this risk is being overestimated. The past case law of the Luxembourg Court on the development of unwritten fundamental rights vividly demonstrates that it is perfectly capable of balancing codified provisions of primary law with unwritten principles in order to ensure the protection of individual rights. Luxembourg is prudent enough not to interpret the requirements of the time limit under Article 263 (6) TFEU *contra legem*, but rather to mitigate or relax them, as it has done with regard to Article 267 TFEU and the preliminary ruling procedure. In other words, it can be assumed that Luxembourg would find a way to balance the time limit with the effective judicial protection of individual applicants, which is, as the CJEU has repeatedly held, not only enshrined in the constitutional traditions of the Member States and Articles 6 and 13 ECHR, but also in Article 47 ChFR which guarantees the right to an effective remedy.[231]

vi. A Quick Delivery of CJEU Rulings

Nevertheless, even though it has been emphasised that such prior proceedings before the CJEU would be sufficiently flexible to prevent unacceptable delays in proceedings,[232] it would unquestionably exceed the overall proceedings and thus complicate the applicant's situation in an unacceptable manner.[233] Therefore, Article 3 (6) of the Draft Accession Agreement sets forth that the 'European Union shall ensure that such assessment is made quickly so that the proceedings before the Court are not unduly delayed.'[234] It is apparent that this provision addresses a question internal to European Union law and might thereby constitute a hidden amendment to the Treaties, which would in turn encroach upon the EU's legal autonomy.[235]

Yet, as the Explanatory Report correctly underlines, an accelerated procedure— the so-called PPU ('*procedure préjudicielle d'urgence*')[236]—already exists which has enabled the Luxembourg Court to give rulings within six to eight months.[237]

---

[230] See Lock, 'Tightrope' (n 20) 1052.

[231] See Case C-50/00 P *Unión de Pequeños Agricultores v Council* (n 221) paras 38–39.

[232] See Timmermans (n 5) 8.

[233] See Françoise Tulkens, *Les aspects institutionnels de l'adhésion de l'Union européenne à la Convention européenne de sauvegarde des droits de l'homme et des libertés fondamentales.* L'audition du 18 mars 2010. European Parliament, Committee on Constitutional Affairs, Hearing on the Institutional Aspects of the European Union's Accession to the European Convention on Human Rights, 18 March 2010, 4.

[234] See art 3 (6) of the Draft Accession Agreement; CDDH-UE(2011)009 (n 160) 8.

[235] See Lock, 'Tightrope' (n 20) 1052.

[236] See generally on the '*procedure préjudicielle d'urgence*' (urgent preliminary procedure), Catherine Barnard, 'The PPU: Is it Worth the Candle?' (2009) 34 *European Law Review* 281, 281ff.

[237] See CDDH-UE(2011)009 (n 160) 25, para 61.

In *Jippes*,[238] for instance, the CJEU decided the case in record time, and delivered its judgment just three weeks after the hearing.[239] To be exact, such a procedure can be found in Article 23a of the CJEU Statute[240] which provides for an expedited or accelerated procedure before the Luxembourg Court. As the Statute is contained in a Protocol to the Treaties and thus forms part of primary law,[241] an accelerated procedure is not alien to the Treaties in their current form. This means that the introduction of an accelerated procedure in ECtHR cases, as envisaged by Article 3 (6) of the Draft Accession Agreement, would not represent a hidden amendment to the Treaties and would thus not jeopardise the autonomy of European Union law. The only precondition to allow for such a course of action in the context of proceedings in Strasbourg is the amendment of the CJEU's Rules of Procedure which in Articles 104a and 104b provide for such an accelerated procedure.[242] However, after accession, the CJEU itself—with the approval of the Council[243]—may modify its Rules of Procedure under Article 48 (6) TEU without the need for any amendments to primary law. Thus, a special accelerated procedure in ECtHR proceedings can easily be introduced without the burdens of a Treaty revision and the political difficulties involved.

Regarding the effective judicial protection of individuals, however, there is less cause for satisfaction.[244] The initiation of accelerated and expedited procedures, respectively, under Articles 104a and 104b Rules of Procedure, demands the existence of 'exceptional urgency' which is, under settled case law, a very high and difficult requirement to satisfy.[245] Moreover, in the context of accession, the CJEU's past case law provokes serious doubts regarding the effective judicial protection of individual applicants as there is no urgency simply because fundamental rights are at stake.[246] Nevertheless, there is the potential for a satisfactory resolution of this problem, mostly by means of inserting a new provision into the rules of procedure which would—in light of the final Accession Agreement and thus the European Union's obligations as a contracting party to the Convention—provide for an accelerated or expedited procedure of any case that is pending before the Strasbourg Court. This provision, however, must ensure that proceedings

---

[238] See Case C-189/01 *Jippes* [2001] ECR I-5689.

[239] See Eric Barbier De La Serre, 'Accelerated and Expedited Procedures before the EC Courts: A Review of the Practice' (2006) 43 *Common Market Law Review* 783, 796.

[240] Inserted by Council Decision 2008/79/EC, Euratom, of 20 December 2007 amending the Protocol on the Statute of the Court of Justice [2008] OJ L24/42.

[241] See art 281 TFEU. See also Bertrand Wägenbaur, *EuGH VerfO. Satzung und Verfahrensordnungen EuGH/EuG Kommentar* (Munich, Beck, 2008) 1, and Bernhard W Wegener, 'Art 281 AEUV' in Christian Calliess and Matthias Ruffert (eds), *EUV/AEUV. Kommentar*, 4th edn (Munich, Beck, 2011) para 5.

[242] See Lock, 'Tightrope' (n 20) 1052.

[243] See Decision 2010/214/EU, Amendments to the Rules of Procedure of the Court of Justice of the European Union [2010] OJ L92/12.

[244] See De La Serre (n 239) 802.

[245] See Joined Case T-195/01 R and T-207/01 R *Government of Gibraltar v Commission* [2001] ECR II-3915, paras 3–5.

[246] See Case C-540/03 *European Parliament v Council* [2006] ECR I-5769, paras 3 and 8.

in such PPU cases are not compromised.[247] Given the existing caseload and thus the massive backlog in the dockets before the ECtHR,[248] procedures in Luxembourg within the course of the CJEU's prior involvement should in any case be considered exceptionally urgent.[249] The Luxembourg Court is therefore highly advised to continue its judicial deference vis-à-vis Strasbourg by quickly delivering its judgments in cases where proceedings before the ECtHR have been suspended in order to allow for a prior involvement of the CJEU.

vii. Assessment of the Legal Basis of European Union Law

The final question in the context of the CJEU's prior involvement in proceedings before the Strasbourg Court is whether Luxembourg's review of the case should be restricted to violations of human rights.[250] Article 3 (6) of the Draft Accession Agreement provides that Strasbourg shall afford Luxembourg sufficient time to make an assessment of the case.[251] Beyond that, the Explanatory Report emphasises that the CJEU will not assess the act or omission complained of by the applicant, but the legal basis for it which is rooted in European Union law.[252] This seems to correspond with the European Commission's point of view. In its working document of January 2011, the Commission argued that the scope of the assessment to be carried out by the CJEU should be strictly limited to the validity of the EU act in question with regard to the respective fundamental right involved. Luxembourg's assessment would consequently not include other aspects of validity, for instance the compatibility of the EU act at issue with other fundamental rights, competency questions, legal foundation choice or respect of essential procedural requirements. Most importantly, such concentration and condensation of the procedure and the pleadings would certainty contribute to 'streamlining' the procedure in Luxembourg and thus reduce its overall length.[253] The proceedings in Luxembourg would thence mirror the test to be carried out later on in Strasbourg.[254]

Nonetheless, European Union law does not provide for a purely fundamental rights review, although the introduction of such a specific remedy has been

---

[247] See O'Meara (n 8) 1825.

[248] See eg, European Court of Human Rights, 'Annual Report 2011' 149, stating that by the end of 2011 more than 151, 000 applications were pending in Strasbourg < www.echr.coe.int/NR/rdonlyres/77FF4249-96E5-4D1F-BE71-42867A469225/0/2011_Rapport_Annuel_EN.pdf> accessed 1 November 2012.

[249] See generally on this issue Rüdiger Wolfrum and Ulrike Deutsch (eds), *The European Court of Human Rights Overwhelmed by Applications: Problems and Possible Solutions* (Berlin Heidelberg, Springer, 2009) 1ff.

[250] See Lock, 'Tightrope' (n 20) 1052.

[251] See art 3 (6) of the Draft Accession Agreement; CDDH-UE(2011)009 (n 160) 8.

[252] See CDDH-UE(2011)009 (n 160) 25, para 59.

[253] See European Commission, 'Working Document on the Previous Involvement of the Court of Justice' DS 1930/10 (n 186) para 9.

[254] See Lock, 'Tightrope' (n 20) 1053.

vigorously argued for over the last decades.[255] The only actions available, namely the action for annulment under Article 263 TFEU and the preliminary ruling procedure under Article 267 TFEU, are not intended to carry out a fundamental rights review, but rather a general review of legality and validity of the legal act at hand. Article 267 TFEU grants the domestic courts a wide range of questions they may refer to the CJEU, as long as these questions pertain to the compatibility of Union legislation with primary law. However, at the same time, Article 267 TFEU restricts the Luxembourg Court to answering only those questions referred to it by domestic courts. The CJEU is therefore neither authorised to rule on the interpretation and applicability of provisions of national law or to establish the facts relevant to the decision in the main proceedings,[256] nor to examine questions which have not been submitted to the CJEU by the national court.[257] As a result, it may be argued that the European Commission could also limit its requests. Given Luxembourg's findings of *Opinion 1/91*, however, this course of action would certainly alter the functional nature of the Commission's right to have legislation reviewed by the CJEU and would thus violate the autonomy of European Union law, as Article 263 TFEU does not allow for any such limitation by the Commission.[258]

In this context, the wording of Article 3 (6) of the Draft Accession Agreement and the Explanatory Report perfectly avoids any infringement of the Union's legal autonomy. The solution found by the negotiators does not constrain Luxembourg's right to review Union acts which are the subject of a complaint in Strasbourg; it rather sets forth that the CJEU would not assess the act or omission complained of by the applicant in Strasbourg, but the legal foundation for it in EU law.[259] The Commission could then decide on a case-by-case basis whether there is a violation of fundamental rights in a concrete case and thus whether to request that the Luxembourg Court adjudicates on the legal foundation of these alleged violations. If it chooses not to make a request, it can be assumed that the European Union does not have sufficient interest in a prior involvement of its court and the proceedings in Strasbourg may be resumed.

Moreover, the CJEU has a long-standing practice of reformulating questions submitted under Article 267 TFEU[260] and of interpreting all provisions of Union

---

[255] See also eg, Norbert Reich, 'Zur Notwendigkeit einer Europäischen Grundrechtsbeschwerde' (2000) 33 *Zeitschrift für Rechtspolitik* 375, 375f; Josef Franz Lindner, 'Fortschritte und Defizite im EU-Grundrechtsschutz—Plädoyer für eine Optimierung der Europäischen Grundrechtecharta' (2007) 40 *Zeitschrift für Rechtspolitik* 54, 54ff; Matthias Niedobitek, 'Entwicklung und allgemeine Grundsätze' in Detlef Merten and Jürgen Papier (eds), *Handbuch der Grundrechte in Deutschland und Europa. Band VI/1, Europäische Grundrechte I* (Heidelberg, CF Müller, 2010) 930; Hans-Werner Rengeling, 'Brauchen wir die Verfassungsbeschwerde auf Gemeinschaftsebene?' in Ole Due, Marcus Lutter and Jürgen Schwarze (eds), *Festschrift für Ulrich Everling. Band I* (Baden-Baden, Nomos, 1995) 1187ff.
[256] See Case C-153/02 *Neri v ESE* [2003] ECR I-13555, paras 33–36.
[257] See Case C-189/95 *Criminal Proceedings against Harry Franzén* (n 142) para 79.
[258] See Lock, 'Tightrope' (n 20) 1053.
[259] See CDDH-UE(2011)009 (n 160) 25, para 59.
[260] See, inter alia, Case 6/64 *Costa v ENEL* [1964] ECR 585; Case 54/85 *Ministère public v Xavier Mirepoix* [1986] ECR 1067, para 6; Case C-88/99 *Roquette Frères SA v Direction des services fiscaux du*

law, even if those provisions are not expressly indicated in the questions referred to the CJEU.[261] This means that it will seldom dismiss a case on the grounds of incorrectly or imperfectly posed questions,[262] but it will rather modify the questions in order to allow for a proper preliminary reference procedure.[263] However, in the context of this judicial practice, a limitation of Luxembourg's jurisdiction by restricting it to merely assessing the legal foundations for alleged fundamental rights violations might not prove very effective.[264] Presumably, the CJEU would reformulate the questions referred to it by the Commission to the effect that it would also review the act or omission complained of by the applicant. This *modus operandi* would give the CJEU the opportunity to redress the violation and thus avoid a conviction of the European Union in Strasbourg, thereby respecting both the principle of subsidiarity under Article 35 (1) ECHR and the autonomy of EU law.

IV. INTERIM CONCLUSIONS

This chapter has examined the legal issues in relation to the requirement under Article 35 (1) ECHR—namely the rule to exhaust all local remedies before calling upon the ECtHR—and the prior involvement of the CJEU in EU-related cases. There is serious concern that the Convention's exhaustion rule under Article 35 (1) would be insufficient to ensure that Strasbourg's external review would be preceded by an effective internal review by both the courts of the Member States and the courts of the EU. In other words, one might ask whether internal EU procedures must be exhausted in all Union-related cases in order to satisfy the requirements of Article 35 (1), and whether procedures in which the CJEU had no chance of delivering a judgment may infringe the Union's legal autonomy. Sceptics of the Union's accession to the Convention argue that cases in relation to EU law must not reach Strasbourg before Luxembourg itself has had the opportunity to adjudicate on them, lest the jurisdictional monopoly of the CJEU and thus the autonomy of EU law be in serious jeopardy.

It was thence assumed that the CJEU's prior involvement is only guaranteed in those proceedings under EU law which must necessarily be exhausted under the premise of Article 35 (1) ECHR in order to be declared admissible in Strasbourg. All other internal Union proceedings which do not qualify as domestic remedies and

---

Pas-de-Calais (Roquette Frères II) [2000] ECR I-10465, para 18; Case C-62/00 *Marks & Spencer* [2002] ECR I-6325, para 32.

[261] See Case C-280/91 *Finanzamt Kassel v Viessmann* [1993] ECR I-971, para 17; Case C-115/08 *Land Oberösterreich v ČEZ as* [2009] ECR I-10265, para 81.

[262] See Luigi Malferrari, *Zurückweisung von Vorabentscheidungsersuchen durch den EuGH* (Baden-Baden, Nomos, 2003) 56f.

[263] See Broberg and Fenger (n 223) 403, and Caroline Naômé, *Le renvoi préjudiciel en droit européen. Guide pratique* (Brussels, Larcier, 2010) 195f.

[264] See Lock, 'Tightrope' (n 20) 1053.

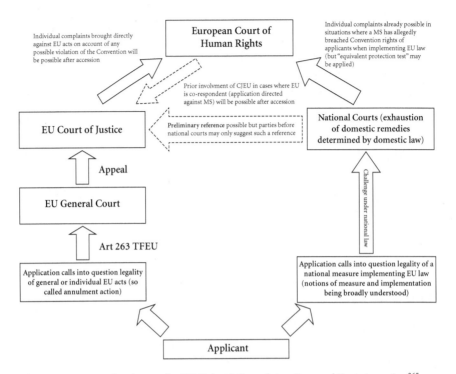

Figure 5: Access to Strasbourg for EU-Related Complaints Pre- and Post-Accession[265]

thus do not fulfil the requirement of Article 35 (1), may lead to a situation where the Luxembourg Court is simply bypassed by applicants and where Strasbourg adjudicates on a case without the CJEU's prior involvement. Accordingly, the preceding chapter analysed on the one hand, when and under what circumstances the requirements under Article 35 (1) ECHR are fulfilled in cases in which European Union law is involved, and on the other hand, how the CJEU's prior involvement in these proceedings can effectively be guaranteed.

On the European Union level, an individual seeking redress for alleged violations of the Convention by EU law may exhaust domestic remedies via a (direct) action for annulment. In situations where the Union is held responsible as the sole respondent, the action for annulment under Article 263 (4) TFEU is the only domestic remedy within the meaning of Article 35 (1) ECHR which is available to an individual at Union level. Moreover, the Convention organs have already held that the action for annulment has to be exhausted before bringing a case to Strasbourg if Union law is involved. This means that the applicant is required to file an action for annulment in order to exhaust all domestic remedies, which will also allow Strasbourg to take into account the interpretation given by Luxembourg. The European Union's legal autonomy is consequently preserved as the review exercised by the ECtHR will be preceded by the internal review exercised by the Union courts. Yet, Article 263 (4) TFEU raises considerable hurdles for individual applicants. The wording of this provision contains strict *locus standi* criteria for bringing actions for annulments and thus may preclude certain individuals from doing so. Until the precise scope of Article 263 (4) TFEU has been defined by the Luxembourg Court, individual applicants alleging a violation of the Convention by a legislative act of the Union are nevertheless highly advised to first seek a ruling by the Union's courts via an action for annulment. In a case where they do not act accordingly, they are at high risk of their application being declared inadmissible because they failed to exhaust all domestic remedies as prescribed by Article 35 (1) ECHR. A complaint to the European Ombudsman, however, does not qualify as a domestic remedy within the meaning of Article 35 (1) ECHR and is therefore not required to satisfy the criteria of this provision.

Beyond that, one may also ask whether preliminary ruling procedures under Article 267 TFEU are a necessary precondition to involve the CJEU in human rights proceedings and to satisfy the requirements of Article 35 (1) ECHR. So far, the Convention organs have not answered this question, but have simply held that a refusal by a domestic court to request a preliminary ruling might violate Article 6 (1) ECHR, particularly when it appears to be arbitrary. Even though Article 267 TFEU provides that domestic courts may request a preliminary ruling or—in cases where there is no further judicial remedy—are obliged to do so, situations may arise in which such a request is not made and thence Luxembourg is sidelined in the proceedings. For example, according to the CJEU's renowned *Foto-Frost* judgment, national courts may abstain from making a reference if they consider a Union act valid. In this case, one might ask whether a complaint to the Strasbourg Court would be admissible after accession, if the national court did not first request a preliminary ruling from Luxembourg. Such a scenario would additionally necessitate Strasbourg to adjudicate on an application involving EU law, but without the Luxembourg Court having the chance to review the compatibility of the provision in question with the Union's own set of fundamental rights beforehand. Nonetheless, this situation would not infringe the autonomy of the Union's legal order, as Strasbourg does not have the jurisdiction to declare any EU act null and void.

Yet, this does not explain whether a preliminary ruling procedure under Article 267 TFEU is necessary in order to satisfy the requirements of the 'exhaustion rule'. A domestic court might refuse to request a preliminary ruling, for example, if it erroneously assumes that there is no duty to do so in a concrete case or because it opines that one or more of the exceptions to Article 267 (3) TFEU applies, particularly those of the CJEU's *CILFIT* judgment, for example. Individual applicants, however, can neither initiate a reference to Luxembourg nor enforce the Member State's obligation to do so. If the applicant then lodges an application to Strasbourg, the ECtHR may either review the compatibility of EU law with the Convention, but without the prior involvement of Luxembourg, or it may declare the application inadmissible due to the applicant's potential failure to exhaust all domestic remedies. Of course, the European Commission may initiate infringement proceedings under Article 258 TFEU to compel a domestic court to make a reference, but these proceedings would not be of any support to the applicant alleging a violation of the Convention; on the contrary, these proceedings would not necessarily cover this violation and unduly prolong the pending litigation.

By and large, the aforementioned are considerable arguments against regarding the preliminary ruling procedure under Article 267 TFEU as a domestic remedy which must be exhausted in order to gain access to the Strasbourg Court. Apart from the fact that individuals cannot trigger the procedure or—in a case where a domestic court makes a reference to the CJEU—must face prolonged proceedings, the constitutions of some EU Member States provide for a quasi-preliminary ruling mechanism which is very similar to that on the Union level. However, the Strasbourg Court has repeatedly held that such proceedings cannot be regarded as a remedy whose exhaustion is required under Article 35 (1) ECHR. This book therefore concludes that a request for a preliminary reference procedure under Article 267 TFEU is not necessary in order to fulfil the requirements of Article 35 (1) ECHR, as it is not normally a legal remedy available to the claimant.

In a very important step within this book's line of argument, this chapter has shown that Luxembourg's prior involvement is not absolutely necessary for the preservation of the Union's legal autonomy. This would only be the case if Strasbourg were given competence and jurisdiction to interpret European Union law in a binding manner. This book has also demonstrated that Strasbourg's judgments are merely declaratory in nature and even though the contracting parties are obliged under international law to redress the violations found by the ECtHR, the ultimate choice as to how they do so rests with them. Therefore, one of the most crucial findings is that the prior involvement of the Luxembourg Court is not required in order to preserve the autonomy of the European Union's legal order.

Still, in the final version of the Draft Accession Agreement, the negotiators agreed that a prior involvement of the CJEU in ECtHR proceedings should be permissible under certain circumstances. This legal analysis explored how such prior involvement could be reconciled with the autonomy of European Union law. Firstly, it is clear that the introduction of an external mechanism is itself incompatible with the autonomy of the Union's legal order as it would constitute a hidden amendment to the Treaties. The suggested preliminary reference procedure between Strasbourg and Luxembourg would blatantly violate the EU's legal autonomy, as it would alter the functional nature of the CJEU and take the place of domestic courts in requesting preliminary rulings. Moreover, the introduction of an external mechanism would run afoul of both the requirements of Article 3 (6) of the Draft Accession Agreement and the Union's legal autonomy.

Secondly, this chapter therefore analysed the internal mechanisms—on the basis of the existing primary law—which would be available and, more importantly, compatible with the autonomy of Union law. One option would be to enable the Luxembourg Court to deliver legal opinions on pending cases. However, by doing so, the CJEU would not be in the position to formally pronounce itself on the case and thus remedy the alleged fundamental rights violation before Strasbourg reviews the case. This approach is therefore not in accordance with the original purpose of Article 35 (1) ECHR. Even though it is not mentioned in the Draft Accession Agreement, another potential candidate for ensuring the CJEU's prior involvement would be the European Commission, which may request that the Luxembourg Court decides upon the compatibility of an EU act with fundamental rights after an application has been declared admissible in Strasbourg. This would be a worthwhile addition to the European system of human rights protection, since the Commission may either initiate annulment proceedings under Article 263 (2) TFEU, in order to have legislation reviewed by Luxembourg as to its compatibility with fundamental rights, or infringement proceedings under Article 258 TFEU against the respective Member State, as the national court of last resort failed to make a reference to the CJEU. Generally, such a *modus operandi* would not violate the autonomy of European Union law. If the Commission is given this new role within the course of accession, however, serious problems would arise for the Union's legal autonomy.

Thirdly, it was consequently scrutinised whether the instigation of such proceedings would be dependent upon the discretion of the Commission, or whether the Commission was obliged to call upon the Luxembourg Court. Since the introduction of a provision which would compel the European Commission to instigate proceedings would necessitate a Treaty revision, it is obvious that the Commission enjoys a margin of discretion in whether or not to initiate proceedings. Furthermore, this discretion would allow the Commission to exercise a filter function, as it could refrain from triggering the internal procedures and thus show that the European Union does not have any interest in remedying the alleged fundamental rights violation itself. The ECtHR would then decide without the prior involvement of the CJEU. This would not conflict with the European Union's legal autonomy since the prior involvement of Luxembourg is not necessary in upholding the autonomy of EU law.

Fourthly, it was shown that the strict two-month time limit under Article 263 (6) TFEU may prevent the Commission from instigating the internal proceedings. A closer look at the CJEU's case law on the preliminary reference procedure, however, demonstrated that the Luxembourg Court would—in an analogous manner—have the jurisdiction to review the legality of legislative acts, even in cases where the time limit has already expired. Nevertheless, it is doubtful whether giving the European Commission a comprehensive competence to request that the CJEU reviews legislation on a regular basis would modify the functional nature of CJEU proceedings and thus infringe the Union's legal autonomy. But Luxembourg's past case law on the development of unwritten fundamental rights vividly demonstrates that the CJEU is perfectly capable of balancing codified provisions of primary law with unwritten principles in order to ensure the protection of individual rights. It can thus be assumed that Luxembourg would find a way to balance the time limit with the effective judicial protection of individual applicants.

Fifthly, in order to prevent the undue delay of proceedings in Strasbourg, Article 3 (6) of the Draft Accession Agreement prompts the EU to ensure that the CJEU's internal review of cases is made quickly. This provision addresses a question internal to European Union law and might thereby constitute a hidden amendment to the Treaties, which would most certainly encroach upon the EU's legal autonomy. But under the Statute of the CJEU and its Rules of Procedure, an accelerated procedure before the Luxembourg Court already exists which means that no Treaty revision is necessary. Consequently, such a procedure is not alien to the Treaties in their current form and the autonomy of Union law is perfectly preserved.

Lastly, this chapter examined whether Luxembourg's review of concrete cases should be restricted to violations of fundamental rights in order to focus on the aspects the Strasbourg Court would be most interested in. Thence it may be argued that the European Commission could also limit its requests. Given the findings of *Opinion 1/91*, however, this course of action would certainly alter the functional nature of the Commission's right to have legislation reviewed by the CJEU and would thus violate the autonomy of European Union law. Still, although EU law does not provide for a purely fundamental rights review, Article 267 TFEU restricts the Luxembourg Court to answering only those questions referred to it. Article 3 (6) of the Draft Accession Agreement and the Explanatory Report do not constrain Luxembourg's right to review Union acts which are the subject of a complaint in Strasbourg, but rather set forth that the CJEU would not assess the act or omission complained of by the applicant in Strasbourg, but its legal foundation in European Union law. Consequently, the European Commission could then decide on a case-by-case basis whether there is a violation of fundamental rights in a concrete case and thus whether to request that the Luxembourg Court adjudicates on the legal foundation of these alleged violations. If it chooses not to make a request, it can be assumed that the European Union does not have sufficient interest in a prior involvement of its court and the proceedings in Strasbourg may be resumed. Furthermore, Luxembourg may reformulate the submitted questions to the effect that it would also review the act or omission complained of by the applicant. This *modus operandi* would give the CJEU the opportunity to redress violations found in EU law and thus avoid a conviction of the European Union in Strasbourg, thereby respecting both the principle of subsidiarity under Article 35 (1) ECHR and the autonomy of EU law.

Part IV

Conclusions and Outlook

12

The Analytical Point of Departure: Revisiting and Answering the Research Question

> Institutional rivals and epistemic friends, the European courts [...] must solve the game together and [...] lose as someone tries to win over the other [...].[1]

AFTER NEGOTIATIONS BETWEEN the Council of Europe and the European Union were successfully concluded in 2011, the EU's accession to the Convention is legally tangible and imminent. Notwithstanding any political obstacles, the Union will eventually become both the 48th high contracting party to the Convention and the first non-state signatory,[2] which will unfortunately deprive many European academics and lawyers of one of their favourite research and discussion topics.[3] After more than 30 years of discussion, the adverse effects of two parallel and juxtaposed legal regimes will be overcome by the integration of the European Union into Strasbourg's human rights protection system, which means that divergences in human rights standards will expectedly cease to occur and that a greater degree of coherence in the field of human rights protection will be assured. Furthermore, the EU and its institutions will become subject to the external judicial supervision of an international treaty regime. This new situation will in turn entitle individuals to submit applications against the Union directly to the Strasbourg Court when they allege that their fundamental rights have been violated by legal acts rooted in EU law.[4]

However, Part I already made it clear that this book does not busy itself with the advantages and merits of accession, but rather focuses on the most urgent legal problems related to accession, most notably on the perils for the autonomy

---

[1] See Laurent Scheeck, 'The Relationship between the European Courts and Integration through Human Rights' (2005) 65 *Zeitschrift für ausländisches öffentliches Recht und Völkerrecht* 837, 885.

[2] See Noreen O'Meara, '"A More Secure Europe of Rights?" The European Court of Human Rights, the Court of Justice of the European Union and EU Accession to the ECHR' (2011) 12 *German Law Journal* 1813, 1813.

[3] See Jean-Paul Jacqué, 'The Accession of the European Union to the European Convention on Human Rights and Fundamental Freedoms' (2011) 48 *Common Market Law Review* 995, 995.

[4] See Council of Europe—Parliamentary Assembly, *The Accession of the European Union/European Community to the European Convention on Human Rights*, Doc 11533 (Committee on Legal Affairs and Human Rights) 2.

of European Union law. The legal analysis at hand therefore attempts to provide answers to the question on whether and how accession and the system of human rights protection under the Convention can effectively be reconciled with the autonomy of European Union law. Beyond that, it also takes into account how this objective can be attained without jeopardising the current system of individual human rights protection under the Convention. In the end, this book shows that accession certainly raises elementary problems of constitutional significance[5] which are, nevertheless, conquerable, and that there are viable solutions to overcome these legal issues.

As the introduction and the conclusion of a scientific analysis form the argumentative frame in which the legal study of this book is embedded, this chapter will now come full circle and give a succinct answer to the overall research question of this book, namely *whether and how accession and the system of human rights protection under the Convention can effectively be reconciled with the autonomy of European Union law without jeopardising the current system of individual human rights protection under the Convention.* In order to answer this question, this book has explored the definitional and theoretical basis of the term 'legal autonomy' and, in its main part, five specific legal issues relating to the European Union's accession to the European Convention on Human Rights.

By means of a comprehensive analysis, this book has made it clear that the drafters of the Accession Agreement had to take into consideration a plethora of legal pitfalls, both within European Union law and within the legal system established by the Convention. Nonetheless, this book has also clarified that the negotiators managed to overcome these difficulties. The provisions enshrined in the Draft Accession Agreement are in fact apt and adequate to reconcile the autonomy of European Union law with the Convention's system of European human rights protection. Moreover, in the light of the second part of the research question, this book could prove that the drafters of the Accession Agreement have successfully reconciled the accession of one legal system to another without impairing the Convention system and without decreasing the standards of human rights protection provided for by this legal regime. It is therefore the final conclusion of this book that the autonomy of European Union law and the EU's accession to the Convention are in fact compatible with each other without compromising the system of human rights protection established by the European Convention on Human Rights.

The subsequent and concluding chapters will, on the one hand, briefly summarise the findings of this book, including both the most urgent legal questions and the respective solutions to these questions, and on the other hand offer a preliminary outlook on the future architecture of European human rights protection after accession.

---

[5] See Tobias Lock, 'Walking on a Tightrope: The Draft Accession Agreement and the Autonomy of the EU Legal Order' (2011) 48 *Common Market Law Review* 1025, 1053.

13

The Prerequisites and Consequences of Accession: A Summary of Findings

I. THE IMPORTANCE OF THE AUTONOMY PRINCIPLE

A. Luxembourg's Sceptical View on International Law

IT WAS THE principal task of Part II of this book to lay down the theoretical framework whose boundaries and basis would allow for further analysis to operate on firm conceptual ground. To this end, it thoroughly examined the case law of the Luxembourg Court in order to define the term 'legal autonomy'. As the EU Treaties remain silent on the autonomy principle, the Court of Justice of the European Union (CJEU) developed the autonomy principle via the teleological interpretation of various cases (most notably among them *Van Gend en Loos v Netherlands Inland Revenue Administration*[1] and *Costa v ENEL*,[2] constituting the Union as a new legal order of international law and an autonomous system with supremacy over the laws of its Member States) to establish, extend and uphold its exclusive jurisdiction over Union law on the basis of Article 19 (1) of the Treaty on European Union (TEU) and Article 344 of the Treaty on the Functioning of the European Union (TFEU). The purpose of this course of action was to engird the EU's legal order from internal interference (ie the law of the Member States) and, more importantly in the context of accession, from external influences, ie international law in general and international courts and tribunals in particular. Moreover, this demonstration of active judicial activism showed that Luxembourg will protect and guard the Union's legal autonomy at any cost. Of course, the same arguments apply to the Union's accession to the Convention and the CJEU's attitude towards the European Court of Human Rights (ECtHR).

B. Luxembourg's Distaste for other International Courts

On the basis of other CJEU decisions of international relevance, further analysis showed the potential legal 'gateways' through which the Union's legal autonomy

---

[1] Case 26/62 *Van Gend en Loos v Netherlands Inland Revenue Administration* [1963] ECR 1.
[2] Case 6/64 *Costa v ENEL* [1964] ECR 585.

may be jeopardised by its accession to the Convention. For instance, *Opinion 1/91* on the EEA Draft Agreement[3] exemplifies the perpetuation of the autonomy principle and the rigid imperative that conferring jurisdiction over the division of competences between the Union and its Member States to an external court is incompatible with European Union law, since this step is likely to adversely affect the allocation of responsibilities defined in the Treaties and the autonomy of the Union's legal order. The respect for this autonomy must be exclusively guaranteed by the Luxembourg Court, by virtue of Article 19 (1) TEU. Furthermore, under Article 344 TFEU, the Member States are obliged not to submit a dispute concerning the interpretation or application of the Treaties to any method of settlement other than those provided for therein. As a consequence, it is the CJEU's sole and exclusive power to interpret and apply European Union law. The creation of and submission to mechanisms of dispute settlements between the parties in an external, international agreement may jeopardise the CJEU's own interpretation of provisions of EU law and thus restrain its judicial competences by rival interpretations of the same provisions by another court.

It is not surprising then that the Luxembourg Court referred to *Opinion 1/91* in its *Commission v Ireland (MOX Plant)* judgment[4] by restating the importance of Article 19 (1) TEU and Article 344 TFEU for its exclusive jurisdiction and the autonomy of the Union's legal order. Accordingly, submitting a dispute relating to EU law to any court or quasi-judicial body other than the CJEU involves a manifest risk that the jurisdictional order enshrined in the Treaties and, as a result, the Union's legal autonomy, may be adversely affected. Therefore, such a course of action constitutes a breach of Article 344 TFEU and thus a breach of the Court's exclusive jurisdiction as well.

In the *Kadi and Al Barakaat v Council and Commission* case,[5] Luxembourg had the opportunity to delineate European Union law from international law (in particular from the legal order of the United Nations), and held that constitutional guarantees stemming from the Treaties as an autonomous legal system cannot be prejudiced by an international agreement. As a result, such an agreement cannot affect the allocation or division of powers as set forth in the Treaties. The Union's legal autonomy, particularly towards international law, is thus carefully observed and guaranteed by the CJEU on the basis of Article 19 (1) TEU.

In a nutshell, Luxembourg's strict requirements regarding international law and international courts in the light of the European Union's legal autonomy leave the relationship between the European Union and the CJEU on the one

---

[3] Opinion 1/91 *EEA I (Draft agreement between the Community, on the one hand, and the countries of the European Free Trade Association, on the other, relating to the creation of the European Economic Area)* [1991] ECR I-6079.

[4] Case C-459/03 *Commission v Ireland (MOX Plant)* [2006] ECR I-4635.

[5] Joined Cases C-402/05 P and C-415/05 P *Kadi and Al Barakaat v Council and Commission* [2008] ECR I-6351.

hand and other international courts on the other hand with the following four imperatives:

(1)   An international court or tribunal must not be given the power to rule on the internal division of competences between the EU and the Member States.
(2)   The decisions of an international court or tribunal must not internally bind the CJEU and the other Union institutions.
(3)   An international agreement must not alter the functional nature of the EU institutions.
(4)   An international agreement must not contain hidden amendments to the Union Treaties.

If one or more of these principles is breached, the European Union's legal autonomy is inevitably violated.

Thus, pursuant to Article 19 (1) TEU, Article 344 TFEU and its respective case law, the CJEU will vigilantly protect both the legal autonomy of the Union and its own exclusive jurisdiction against any external interference. To this end, the Luxembourg Court aims at limiting the choice and utilisation of other international courts and tribunals by the EU Member States and constraining their respective jurisdiction.

C. Luxembourg and Strasbourg: A Cooperative Rivalry

From the above findings, one can deduce that an agreement between the Union and another international organisation, such as the agreement on the European Union's accession to the Convention, must not affect the EU's internal division of competences or allocation of powers. On the one hand, this means that an international court must not interfere with the *internal* division of competences between the Union and its Member States, and on the other hand, and more relevant in the context of this book, Luxembourg will not suffer that an international court, such as the Strasbourg Court, might encroach upon the CJEU's innermost right to observe the law in the proper interpretation and application of the Treaties, and thus to affect the *external* allocation of powers by transferring them to another international organisation.

However, this book has also showed that the relationship between Luxembourg and Strasbourg has been a different and, in a manner of speaking, oxymoronic interplay, as the title of this section suggests. In its quest for its own codified catalogue of fundamental rights, the CJEU had to borrow fundamental rights from the Convention by taking recourse to its explicit provisions and Strasbourg's case law. This proves that the CJEU tended to accept the Convention as a fully-fledged human rights instrument in contrast to its defensive attitude vis-à-vis other international agreements and courts. The Strasbourg Court, on the other hand, has exercised due care when dealing with human rights violations related to European Union law by granting the Union privileges in the form of the '*Bosphorus*'-formula of 'equivalent protection'. It remains to be seen whether this particular form of judicial cooperation and deference between Luxembourg and Strasbourg will be upheld in the future. In the interest of the other high contracting parties to the Convention and the principle of equality, however, the Union's privileged status should be given up after accession.

It is certain that accession will alter the landscape of human rights protection in Europe. Furthermore, Part II of this book demonstrated that the conflict between the EU's legal autonomy and effective individual human rights protection essentially leads to the question of who will be the ultimate guardian of human rights within the European Union after accession. Taking a sceptical view, one might also ask whether the Luxembourg Court will be subordinated to the Strasbourg Court and whether it will thereby lose its exclusive jurisdiction when Strasbourg implicitly or even explicitly interprets and applies European Union law. These issues also pertain to other questions which are of utmost importance with respect to the autonomy of the Union's legal order and its concurrent integration into the protection system of the Convention.

This book has therefore recast the findings of Part II into more specific research questions and asked what legal status the Convention and the final Accession Agreement will have within the European Union's legal order; whether the Strasbourg Court should exert absolute external control over the Union and whether the CJEU, according to its own case law in *Opinion 1/91*, would be bound by the ECtHR's jurisprudence; how to find the correct respondent in individual complaint procedures under Article 34 of the European Convention on Human Rights (ECHR) in EU-related cases or, in other words, whom to hold responsible in cases where Member States implement EU law. The book has also asked how Article 344 TFEU and Article 55 ECHR could be reconciled with each other and whether inter-party cases between the EU and its Member States and between Member States *inter se* should be excluded; and lastly, how Strasbourg would regard the exhaustion of the local remedies rule within the EU's legal system and how a prior involvement of the CJEU could consequently be guaranteed in EU-related human rights cases, in order to avoid a situation in which Strasbourg might rule on EU law before Luxembourg had the chance to do so.

As a result, Part II of this book showed that the agreement on the Union's accession to the Convention must take into account all of these problems in order not to affect the essential powers of the Union institutions and the autonomy of EU law, respectively.

II. LEGAL INTERFACES BETWEEN ACCESSION AND AUTONOMY

A. The Legal Hierarchy of European Union Law, the Convention and the Accession Agreement

Accession will be based on an international agreement between the Union and the other high contracting parties to the Convention. During the negotiations, it was generally agreed that an agreement would be preferable to a Protocol amending the Convention, since an agreement would preserve the principal features of the Convention system as much as possible and keep the adaptations necessary for the EU's accession to a minimum. Moreover, the negotiators emphasised that the special legal characteristics of the Union must be taken into account, but not at the price of impairing the Convention's human rights protection system. In contrast to an amending Protocol, the conclusion of an agreement allows the negotiating parties to be more flexible and to attentively consider the provisions of European Union law relevant to the conditions and procedural requirements for preserving its autonomy. This means that the final Accession Agreement will not only enable the EU to accede to the Convention, but it will also amend the Convention without any further legal complications. The agreement will thus contain dynamic references to the Convention and become an integral part of the Convention itself, since some of the provisions of the agreement will remain relevant for the future functioning of the Convention system.

However, given the constitutional significance of accession as stressed in *Opinion 2/94*,[6] it is very likely that the European Commission or one of the Union's Member States may seek an Opinion on the Accession Agreement from the Luxembourg Court under Article 218 (11) TFEU. At this very moment, there is no telling how the CJEU will decide, but its past rulings on the Union's legal autonomy demonstrate that the Accession Agreement will have to overcome considerable legal obstacles in order to receive Luxembourg's blessings and to be declared compatible with the EU's legal order.

According to the CJEU's settled case law, international treaties (including both the Convention and the Accession Agreement) concluded between the EU and third parties, become an integral part of Union law, ranking on a 'mezzanine' level below primary, but above secondary, Union law. As part of European Union law in this specific status, the Convention will not only take precedence over secondary law in violation of the Convention, but also over the legal orders of the Member States. Moreover, as part of the law which the CJEU observes in the interpretation and application of the Treaties, the Convention will consequently be interpreted and applied by the Luxembourg Court. This line of action will guarantee an effective human rights protection on the 'domestic' EU plane and ensure the principle of subsidiarity, as laid down in Article 35 (1) ECHR.

This book has also shed some light on the question of whether the Convention's newly won supremacy over domestic law may jeopardise the Union's legal autonomy. Firstly, it seemed as if the Convention's minimum protection standard, as an integral part of Union law, would take precedence over domestic laws and their higher standard of protection, leaving individuals with a lesser degree of protection than before accession. However, this dilemma can be easily avoided by taking into account a particular provision of the Charter: According to the first

---

[6] Opinion 2/94 *Accession by the Community to the European Convention for the Protection of Human Rights and Fundamental Freedoms* [1996] ECR I-1759.

sentence of Article 51 (1) of the Charter of Fundamental Rights of the European Union (ChFR), the fundamental rights of the Union, ie both the Charter and the Convention as part of EU law, are only addressed to the Member States in cases 'when they are implementing Union law'. As a result, there is no actual legal dilemma, as domestic fundamental rights and EU fundamental rights are applied in different cases and situations, and thence, there is no risk for the autonomy of EU law.

Secondly, the Convention's duplication as part of both supreme Union law and domestic law appears to seriously endanger the autonomy of Union law, as this would bind the Member States on two different legal levels. To be exact, Luxembourg's decisions would take precedence over those of Strasbourg, leading to major problems in cases where the CJEU deviated from the ECtHR's case law. The solution to this problem lies in the fact that the CJEU must comply with the Convention and Strasbourg's case law when secondary EU law is in violation of the Convention, since the Convention, as part of Union law, ranks on a higher plane than secondary law. A divergence from the Convention would thus not only lead to a violation of the Convention itself, but also to a violation of Union law. It is therefore in the best interest of the Luxembourg Court to take the provisions of the Convention and Strasbourg's case law into account in all fundamental rights cases in order to avoid serious legal complications in the future.

Thirdly, it was shown that the Member States' possibly conflicting obligations under both the Convention and EU law do not pose a risk for the autonomy of EU law. In case of conflicts between the Convention and secondary Union law, the national courts must also apply the Convention and the pertaining case law of the Strasbourg Court as higher ranking EU law. By applying the Convention in the first place, the courts of the Member States would not only avoid judicial divergences between Luxembourg and Strasbourg, but also circumvent a situation which might put the Strasbourg Court into the challenging position of deciding on the validity and conformity of secondary Union law with the Convention. Thereby, there would be no danger for the autonomy of EU law.

B. Strasbourg's External Review of European Union Law

The book at hand also explored the question of whether Strasbourg's external review of EU law might endanger the Union's legal autonomy. The answer to this question is dependent on the solution to two other questions, namely whether the ECtHR would interpret Union law in a binding manner, and whether a judgment by Strasbourg finding that legal acts of the Union violated the Convention would be in fact compatible with the concept of the EU's legal autonomy.

With regard to the first question, this book demonstrated that the ECtHR primarily regards the national authorities and courts as capable in interpreting and applying domestic law. It is therefore Strasbourg's task to interpret and apply the Convention, not national law. In some cases, however, Strasbourg must take a closer look at domestic law as well in order to scrutinise whether there has been a violation of the Convention. This means that after accession the ECtHR will also take a closer look at Union law in certain proceedings. This is especially the case when an applicant alleges that a provision was violated which refers back to domestic law, for example Articles 5, 8–11 and 13 ECHR. Nonetheless, the ECtHR does not interpret domestic law in an internally binding manner. The obligation to implement Strasbourg's decisions in accordance with their commitments under international law ultimately rests with the contracting parties themselves. Pursuant to Article 41 ECHR in conjunction with Article 46 (1), Strasbourg's decisions are not directly applicable and cannot quash domestic legal acts, since the contracting parties' obligations under international law do not automatically entail an obligation under domestic law. Beyond that, the principle of subsidiarity set forth in Article 35 ECHR ensures that Strasbourg is in no case the first place to decide on the interpretation and application of domestic law. In EU-related cases, the CJEU would interpret and apply Union law in the first place and thus redress the alleged violation. The principal responsibility for implementing and enforcing the rights enshrined by the Convention after accession therefore lies with the Union's institutions. This means that the interpretation of the provisions in question and thus the Union's legal autonomy would not be affected by Strasbourg's decisions, since the ECtHR would only interpret and apply the Convention *after* the CJEU has interpreted and applied Union law. It can subsequently be guaranteed that the external review of EU acts by the ECtHR will not endanger the legal autonomy of the Union.

Pertaining to the second question, a review by the Strasbourg Court will cover all of the Union's legal acts and measures. There have been arguments to exclude the Union's primary law from Strasbourg's scope of control, especially because the Union itself is not entitled to amend its own 'constitutional' basis and the Luxembourg Court's jurisdiction is restricted in some areas of primary law (eg the Common Foreign and Security Policy). This means that the EU itself is not able to remedy any violations of the Convention found in primary law. However, the EU's primary law should not be excluded from the ECtHR's external review since such exclusion would be tantamount to an undue privilege granted solely to the EU, but not to the other contracting parties.

Besides, as the Union's principal judicial body, the CJEU is perfectly capable of reconciling legal conflicts between primary law and fundamental rights, for example by interpreting the former in conformity with the Charter and the Convention. Lastly, and most importantly, the exclusion of primary law is not envisaged in the Draft Accession Agreement. Article 3 of the Draft Accession Agreement contains the details of the co-respondent mechanism and expressly mentions that applicants may call upon the ECtHR for violations of the Convention rooted in primary law. It is thus evident that such exclusion was never intended by the negotiators.

Still, the most convincing argument against the exclusion of primary law is that such exclusion might compel the Strasbourg Court to delineate alleged violations of the Convention found in primary law from those found in secondary law which, in turn, would necessitate the ECtHR to interpret Union law in a binding manner and to decide upon the division of competences between the Union and the Member States. This step would undoubtedly endanger the autonomy of Union law and should be avoided on any account.

C. Individual Applications: The Co-Respondent Mechanism

Given the outstanding importance of individual applications under Article 34 ECHR, this book has presented a comprehensive analysis of the questions on how the individual complaint procedure would be arranged after accession, especially in the light of the specific features of the Union's legal order, and what risks the introduction of this new procedure may pose to the EU's legal autonomy.

After accession, individual claimants will have the right to lodge applications against both the Member States and the European Union in order to hold them responsible for alleged violations of the Convention. The disadvantage of accession is, however, that individuals will not know for certain against what polity they should apply and what entity they should ultimately hold responsible for violations of the Convention stemming from Union law, as most EU acts are implemented or transposed into domestic law by the Member States. Moreover, most individual applicants commonly do not have a legal education and the involvement of legal counsel is not mandatory in ECtHR proceedings. It therefore became clear that a mechanism had to be devised to hold both the Member States and the Union responsible for EU-related cases and to avoid situations in which an application was declared inadmissible just because the applicant had directed it against the wrong respondent.

In the past, numerous models (for instance joint liability and the joint and several liability models) have been proposed to solve this issue. However, all of them have been rejected, as they would have left the ultimate designation of the correct respondent and of its respective responsibility to the Strasbourg Court, which thereby would have implicitly decided on the division of competences between the Union and its Member States. This course of action would, however, interfere with Luxembourg's exclusive jurisdiction and the Union's legal autonomy.

The negotiators therefore agreed to introduce the so-called co-respondent mechanism which will allow the European Union to join cases as a co-respondent, alongside the Member State against which the application was initially lodged (Art 3 (2) of the Draft Accession Agreement). It would also allow Member States to join cases as co-respondents, alongside the Union as original respondent (Art 3 (3)). Furthermore, individual applicants may also direct applications against both the EU and a Member State right from the onset of the proceedings (Article 3 (4)). In comparison to third party interventions under Article 36 ECHR, respondents deciding to join the proceedings as co-respondents become parties to the dispute and are therefore fully bound by Strasbourg's judgment.

Beyond that, Article 3 (5) of the Draft Accession Agreement clarifies that a high contracting party shall become a co-respondent only at its own request and by the subsequent decision of the Court. This means that a party may not be forced to become a co-respondent and thus, the decision to join the proceedings within this role rests with the respective high contracting party. The European Union's legal autonomy is consequently entirely preserved, since Strasbourg is not given any right or power to designate a party as co-respondent *proprio motu*. In its decision whether or not to apply the co-respondent mechanism, the ECtHR is additionally restricted to assessing whether the reasons stated by a high contracting party in its request are plausible in the light of certain criteria. In cases where an application is filed against one or more Member States, but not against the Union, Strasbourg may decide to join the parties as co-respondents if it appears that the alleged violation can only be ascribed to a normative conflict between the Convention and primary or secondary European Union law, notably where that violation could have only been avoided by the respective Member State by disregarding an obligation under EU law (Art 3 (2) of the Draft Accession Agreement). Conversely, in cases where an application is filed against the European Union, but not against a Member State, the ECtHR may decide to join the parties as respondent and co-respondent if it appears that the alleged violation can only be ascribed to a normative conflict between the Convention and primary European Union law, notably where that violation could have only been avoided by the Union by disregarding an obligation under primary law (Art 3 (3) of the Draft Accession Agreement). The same conditions and criteria apply in the scenario where an application is lodged against both the Union and a Member State (Art 3 (4) of the Draft Accession Agreement).

This means that the Union's legal autonomy remains untouched by Strasbourg's external review, as the ECtHR will only examine the plausibility and the mere appearance of a normative conflict between the provisions of the Convention and Union law but—especially in the context of preserving the autonomy of the EU's legal order—without delving into the details of European Union law (in particular the intricate division of competences) or without interpreting it in a binding manner. Strasbourg can thus circumvent a determination of the internal allocation of powers within the EU's legal system and can restrict itself to assessing the joint responsibility of the respondent and the co-respondent. Strasbourg must, however, show a certain degree of willingness to cooperate, particularly by dismissing any defence raised by a Member State which claims that it had only acted in strict compliance with its obligations under European Union law or that it enjoyed no discretion in implementing EU law.

In the end, this book has showed that the relevant provisions of the Draft Accession Agreement will not suffice to effectively implement the co-respondent mechanism into the Union's legal system. In conformity with the autonomy of European Union law, the agreement remains silent on the issue of how the joint responsibility of the original respondent and the co-respondent should be internally attributed between the Member States and the EU itself. The Union and the Member States, however, may have a certain interest in attributing this responsibility exactly, especially due to political and monetary reasons. The most appropriate body to decide on this matter would undoubtedly be the Luxembourg Court, but in order to enable the CJEU to do so, new provisions regarding the exact procedure would have to be introduced in the Treaties. The Member States should therefore quickly make up their mind how this issue could be tackled without any further complications.

D. The Future of Inter-Party Cases

Even though inter-state cases under Article 33 ECHR are—as opposed to the sheer amount of individual applications—practically insignificant within the Convention's protection system, a legal assessment on the compatibility of the European Union's legal autonomy with the EU's accession to an international treaty regime must take into account the potential effects of such a classic dispute settlement mechanism on EU law. Inter-party cases may actually involve several risks for the legal autonomy of the Union, especially for the exclusive jurisdiction over such disputes claimed by both the Luxembourg and the Strasbourg courts. Moreover, this book has investigated whether the European Union has the competence to lodge such complaints against third countries. These legal issues have necessitated an analysis of the legal organisation of inter-party cases after accession and their potential impact on the EU's legal system, even though it is questionable whether such a situation might actually occur in practice.

To this end, this book has explored the possible 'internal' problems between the Union and its Member States within the Convention system, the future relationship between the Luxembourg and the Strasbourg courts after accession and how their respective 'exclusive jurisdiction' clauses (namely Article 344 of the TFEU and Article 55 ECHR) for settling disputes might endanger both the effective protection of human rights within the Convention's regime and autonomy of EU law. As the *MOX Plant* case vividly showed, Article 344 TFEU ensures that Union law is uniformly interpreted and applied by the CJEU, which means that Luxembourg has exclusive jurisdiction to adjudicate on all legal disputes between the Member States which involve European Union law. Yet, as the Convention will become an integral part of the Union's legal order after accession, Luxembourg will also have jurisdiction to interpret and apply the provisions of the Convention. As a result, EU Member States will be precluded from bringing inter-party complaints against each other before the Strasbourg Court, which leaves them with the internal Union dispute settlement mechanisms provided for by the Treaties. It is nonetheless clear that not all inter-party applications concerning an alleged violation of the Convention must be exclusively submitted to the CJEU after accession. The decisive factor for Luxembourg's exclusive jurisdiction is whether genuine EU law is applicable in a given situation. The CJEU will consequently not be able to claim jurisdiction in situations relating to wholly domestic fields of law, for example criminal or family law. Proceedings between Member States before the CJEU are therefore only prescribed in cases where Member States have limited fundamental freedoms or where they have implemented Union law.

Nevertheless, jurisdictional clashes between Strasbourg and Luxembourg may arise after accession, as Article 55 ECHR grants Strasbourg exclusive jurisdiction in settling inter-party complaints. This means that both the CJEU and the ECtHR consider their respective jurisdictions to be exclusive. The solution to this problem may be found in Article 55 ECHR which allows the contracting parties, by special agreement, to waive Strasbourg's jurisdiction and settle their disputes before another court or tribunal. It was shown that the specific provisions of the Treaties, namely Article 19 (1) TEU and Article 344 TFEU, may qualify as a special agreement which would entitle the CJEU to settle inter-party disputes between the Member States and thus prevent jurisdictional conflicts. Luxembourg's exclusive jurisdiction by virtue of Article 19 (1) TEU and Article 344 TFEU, however, does not represent an explicit reference to the Convention. This means that these provisions of EU law do not satisfy the requirements of Article 55 ECHR and both the ECtHR and the CJEU will have the jurisdiction to accept and decide inter-party cases, which may again lead to conflicts between those two courts.

It has therefore been suggested to simply exclude inter-party cases between Union Member States and between Member States and the Union in order to circumvent an imminent jurisdictional conflict between Strasbourg and Luxembourg in the first place. However, as the EU should accede to the Convention on an equal footing, it must be subject to the same obligations as other contracting parties to the Convention, which means that an exclusion of inter-party cases is not a workable option.

Article 4 of the Draft Accession Agreement thus clarifies that all state parties to the Convention will be able to bring a case against the Union and vice versa. Nonetheless, the Luxembourg Court has the last say in matters regarding Union law and may determine that a Member State has failed to fulfil its obligations under Article 344 TFEU, if the said Member State first lodged an inter-party application before the Strasbourg Court. A solution to this issue is given in Article 5 of the Draft Accession Agreement which safeguards the Union's legal autonomy and contains the 'special agreement' and the explicit reference to the Convention which are necessary to satisfy the requirements of Article 55 ECHR and to uphold Luxembourg's exclusive jurisdiction over EU-related inter-party applications. Moreover, according to Article 35 (1) ECHR, the CJEU must be given a chance to remedy alleged violations of the Convention before the ECtHR can adjudicate on any application. Therefore, the Convention itself enables Luxembourg to interpret and apply Union law in order to preserve its well-guarded autonomy. The Member States and the Union are thence obliged to settle their disputes via the Union's internal mechanisms (namely infringement proceedings, the action for annulment and the action for failure to act) before they can submit their applications to Strasbourg.

Besides those potential internal conflicts within the future system of European human rights protection, this book has also examined the 'external' issues of inter-party cases after accession. To be exact, it has explored whether the European Union has the competence to direct inter-party applications against third countries, ie non-Member States, in order to promote human rights in its external relations. It is, however, of utmost importance that such a competence, included in an international agreement concluded by the Union must not change the functional nature of the Union's institutions and thus interfere with the autonomy of EU law. This book then clarified that in the case where the Union has the competence to conclude international agreements for the protection of human rights with third countries, it must *a fortiori* also have the competence to protect human rights via inter-party complaints.

After the entry into force of the Lisbon Treaty, such agreements may be based on Article 216 (1) TFEU in conjunction with Article 3 (2) TFEU. Alternatively, the Union may also take action within the legal framework of its Common Foreign and Security Policy under Article 24 (1) TEU. Most importantly, the Draft Accession Agreement neither explicitly excludes inter-party cases lodged by the EU against a third country nor does it alter or restrict the functional nature of the Union's institutions within the meaning of *Opinion 1/91*. This means that the competence to submit inter-party complaints against a third country does not involve any substantial risks to the autonomy of EU law. In addition, the Explanatory Report states that once the European Union is a party to the Convention, all contracting parties will be able to bring a case against the EU and vice versa under Article 33 ECHR, without any risk to the Union's legal autonomy.

E. Luxembourg's Prior Involvement: New Procedural Routes

In its last substantive chapter, this book scrutinised the legal problems with regard to the subsidiarity principle of Article 35 (1) ECHR—the rule that all local remedies must be exhausted before lodging an application to the Strasbourg Court—and the prior involvement of Luxembourg in EU-related cases. Sceptics have expressed their concern that the Convention's exhaustion rule would be inadequate in guaranteeing an effective internal review by both the courts of the Member States and the courts of the EU prior to the external review conducted by the ECtHR. It was also called into question whether EU-internal procedures must be exhausted in all Union-related cases in order to satisfy the requirements of Article 35 (1) ECHR, and whether procedures, in which the CJEU has no chance of delivering a judgment, may infringe the Union's legal autonomy. Thus, in order to preserve the autonomy of EU law, one may argue that cases relating to EU law must not reach Strasbourg before Luxembourg itself has had the opportunity to adjudicate on them. Accordingly, this book firstly examined when and under what circumstances the requirements under Article 35 (1) ECHR are fulfilled in cases relating to European Union law, and secondly, how the CJEU's prior involvement in these proceedings may be effectively guaranteed. Furthermore, it was ascertained that Luxembourg's prior involvement is only ensured in those proceedings under EU law which must necessarily be exhausted under the premise of Article 35 (1) ECHR in order to be declared admissible in Strasbourg. In all other internal Union proceedings which do not qualify as a domestic remedy and thus do not fulfil the requirement of Article 35 (1) ECHR, the CJEU may be bypassed by applicants, which could lead to a situation in which Strasbourg adjudicates upon a case without the CJEU's prior involvement.

Under European Union law, an applicant alleging a violation of the Convention by EU law may exhaust domestic remedies via an action for annulment under Article 263 (4) TFEU. As a result, annulment proceedings are the only domestic remedy within the meaning of Article 35 (1) ECHR which is available to an individual at Union level in situations where the Union is held responsible as the sole respondent. In the past, the Convention organs already stated that the action for annulment has to be exhausted before bringing a case to Strasbourg if Union law is involved. Therefore, the applicant is always required to file an action for annulment in order to exhaust all domestic remedies, which will also allow Strasbourg to take into account the interpretation given by Luxembourg. The European Union's legal autonomy is consequently upheld as the review exercised by the ECtHR will be preceded by the internal review exercised by the Union courts.

However, Article 263 (4) TFEU lays down significant legal impediments for individual applicants, as its wording contains *locus standi* criteria for bringing actions for annulments and thus may preclude certain individuals from doing so. Until the exact scope of Article 263 (4) TFEU has been defined by the Luxembourg Court, individual applicants alleging a violation of the Convention by a legislative act of the Union are nevertheless specifically advised to first seek a ruling by the Union's courts via an action for annulment. If they do not act accordingly, individual applicants take the risk that their application will be declared inadmissible due to their failure to exhaust all domestic remedies as prescribed by Article 35 (1) ECHR.

This book has also analysed if an applicant alleging a violation of the Convention by EU law may exhaust domestic remedies by means of the preliminary ruling procedure under Article 267 TFEU in order to guarantee the CJEU's prior involvement. However, although Article 267 TFEU prescribes that domestic courts may request a preliminary ruling, or—in cases where there is no further judicial remedy—they are obliged to do so, certain situations might arise in which such a request is not made. This would sideline the Luxembourg Court and deprive it of its prior involvement. This may occur, for example, if national courts consider a Union act valid (according to the CJEU's renowned *Foto-Frost v Hauptzollamt Lübeck-Ost* judgment[7]) and abstain from making a reference. In a situation such as this, it is doubtful whether a complaint to the Strasbourg Court

---

[7] Case 314/85 *Foto-Frost v Hauptzollamt Lübeck-Ost* [1987] ECR 4199.

would be admissible after accession, if the national court did not first request a preliminary ruling from Luxembourg. Such a scenario would furthermore impose on Strasbourg the task of adjudicating on an application involving EU law, but without the Luxembourg Court having the chance to first review the compatibility of the provision in question with the Union's own set of fundamental rights. Nevertheless, such a situation would not encroach upon the autonomy of EU law, since Strasbourg does not have the jurisdiction to declare any EU act null and void.

This finding, however, cannot explain whether a preliminary ruling procedure under Article 267 TFEU is necessary in order to satisfy the requirements of the 'exhaustion rule'. A domestic court might refuse to request a preliminary ruling, for example, if it mistakenly assumes that there is no duty to do so in a concrete case or because it holds that one or more of the exceptions to Article 267 (3) TFEU apply (for example those of Luxembourg's *CILFIT v Ministry of Health* judgment[8]). Yet, individual claimants are neither entitled to initiate a reference to Luxembourg nor enforce the Member State's obligation to do so. If the applicant then lodges an application to Strasbourg, the ECtHR may either review the compatibility of EU law with the Convention, but without the prior involvement of Luxembourg, or it may declare the application inadmissible due to the applicant's potential failure to exhaust all domestic remedies. The European Commission may certainly instigate infringement proceedings under Article 258 TFEU to compel a domestic court to make a reference, but these proceedings would not be of any support to the applicant alleging a violation of the Convention. Quite the contrary, these proceedings would not necessarily cover this violation and unduly prolong the pending litigation.

These findings represent substantial arguments against regarding the preliminary ruling procedure under Article 267 TFEU as a domestic remedy which must be exhausted under Article 35 (1) ECHR. Moreover, the constitution of some EU Member States provides for a quasi-preliminary ruling mechanism which is very similar to that on the Union level. To date, the Strasbourg Court has repeatedly held that such proceedings cannot be regarded as a remedy, whose exhaustion is required under Article 35 (1) ECHR. This book has therefore concluded that a request for a preliminary reference procedure is not a necessary prerequisite under Article 35 (1) ECHR, since it is not usually a legal remedy available to the claimant.

One of the most intriguing findings of this book is that, despite the previous concerns raised about this matter, the CJEU's prior involvement is not absolutely necessary in order to preserve the Union's legal autonomy. Such involvement would only be necessary if Strasbourg were given competence and jurisdiction to interpret European Union law in a binding manner and in the absence of a mechanism ensuring the prior involvement of the Luxembourg Court. In the preceding

---

[8] Case 283/81 *CILFIT v Ministry of Health* [1982] ECR 3415.

chapters, however, this book has also shown that the ECtHR's judgments are merely declaratory in nature and even though the contracting parties are obliged under international law to redress the violations found by the ECtHR, which way they choose to do so ultimately rests with them. Thence one of the most crucial findings is that the prior involvement of the Luxembourg Court is not required in order to preserve the autonomy of the European Union's legal order.

Notwithstanding these findings, the negotiators agreed in the final version of the Draft Accession Agreement that a prior involvement of the CJEU in ECtHR proceedings should be permissible under certain circumstances. Given this legal requirement, this book investigated how such prior involvement could be reconciled with the autonomy of European Union law. It is obvious that the introduction of an external mechanism is itself incompatible with the autonomy of the Union's legal order as it would constitute a hidden amendment to the Treaties. As a result, the suggested preliminary reference procedure between Strasbourg and Luxembourg would blatantly violate the EU's legal autonomy, since it would alter the functional nature of the CJEU and take the place of domestic courts to make requests for preliminary rulings. Moreover, the introduction of an external mechanism would run afoul of both the requirements of Article 3 (6) of the Draft Accession Agreement and the Union's legal autonomy.

This book has also examined what internal mechanisms could be devised on the basis of primary law and which of these mechanisms would be compatible with the autonomy of Union law. It was suggested that the CJEU be enabled to deliver legal opinions on pending cases, but this would not give Luxembourg the chance to formally pronounce itself on the case and thus remedy the alleged fundamental rights violation before Strasbourg reviews the case. Alternatively, the European Commission may ask the Luxembourg Court to decide upon the compatibility of an EU act with fundamental rights after an application has been declared admissible in Strasbourg. The Commission could then instigate annulment proceedings under Article 263 (2) TFEU, in order to have the legislation reviewed by Luxembourg concerning its compatibility with fundamental rights, or infringement proceedings under Article 258 TFEU against the respective Member State, if the national court of last resort failed to make a reference to the CJEU. By and large, even though this would not per se violate the autonomy of European Union law, the Union's legal autonomy would still be at serious risk if the Commission was given this new role after accession.

Further investigation into this matter demonstrated that the initiation of such proceedings would be dependent upon the discretion of the Commission. This discretion would allow the Commission to exercise a filter function, as it could refrain from triggering the internal procedures and thus show that the European Union does not have an interest in remedying the alleged fundamental rights violation. The ECtHR would then decide without the prior involvement of the CJEU which would not conflict with the European Union's legal autonomy since the prior involvement of Luxembourg is not necessary to uphold the autonomy of EU law.

Beyond that, it was shown that the strict two month time limit under Article 263 (6) TFEU may preclude the Commission from instigating these internal proceedings. However, according to the CJEU's case law on the preliminary reference procedure, the Luxembourg Court would analogously have the jurisdiction to review the legality of legislative acts, even in cases where the time limit under Article 263 (6) TFEU has already expired. Yet, it is still unclear as to whether giving the European Commission a comprehensive competence to request the CJEU to review legislation on a regular basis would modify the functional nature of CJEU proceedings and thus infringe the Union's legal autonomy. So far, however, Luxembourg has proven in its case law on the development of unwritten fundamental rights that it is perfectly capable of balancing codified provisions of primary law with unwritten principles in order to ensure the protection of individual rights. This book assumes that the CJEU would find a way to weigh the time limit with the effective judicial protection of individual applicants.

In order to prevent the undue delay of proceedings in Strasbourg, Article 3 (6) of the Draft Accession Agreement prompts the EU to ensure that the CJEU's internal review of cases is quickly made. This provision addresses a question internal to Union law and might thereby constitute a hidden amendment to the Treaties, which would most certainly encroach upon the EU's legal autonomy. But this examination clarified that under the Statute of the CJEU and its Rules of Procedure, an accelerated procedure before the Luxembourg Court already exists which means that no Treaty revision is necessary. Consequently, such a procedure is not alien to the Treaties in their current form and the autonomy of EU law is perfectly upheld.

This book eventually explored whether Luxembourg's review of a concrete case should be restricted to violations of fundamental rights in order to focus on the aspects the Strasbourg Court would be most interested in. Correspondingly, the European Commission could also limit its requests. However, according to *Opinion 1/91*, this course of action would certainly alter the functional nature of the Commission's right to have legislation reviewed by the CJEU and would thus violate the autonomy of European Union law. Still, despite the fact that Union law does not provide for a purely fundamental rights review, Article 267 TFEU limits the CJEU to answering only those questions referred to it. Article 3 (6) of the Draft Accession Agreement and the Explanatory Report do not constrain Luxembourg's right to review Union acts which are the subject of a complaint in Strasbourg, but rather set forth that the CJEU would not assess the act or omission complained of by the applicant in Strasbourg, but the legal basis for it in EU law. This means that the Commission could then decide on a case-by-case basis whether there is a violation of fundamental rights in a concrete case and thus whether to request the Luxembourg Court to adjudicate on the legal basis of these alleged violations. In case it decides not to make a request, it can be assumed that the European Union does not have sufficient interest in a prior involvement of its court and the proceedings in Strasbourg may be resumed. Moreover, the CJEU is entitled to reformulate the submitted questions to the effect that it would also review the act or omission complained of by the applicant. This course of action would give the CJEU the opportunity to redress the violation and thus avoid a conviction of the EU in Strasbourg, thereby respecting both the principle of subsidiarity under Article 35 (1) ECHR and the autonomy of EU law.

14

Outlook and Future Perspectives

W ITHOUT DOUBT, THE European Union's accession to the European Convention on Human Rights will have an unprecedented and enormous impact on the existing multi-level framework of human rights protection in Europe, oscillating between the national, supranational and international planes. Furthermore, it is evident that the new procedural routes established by the Accession Agreement between the Strasbourg and Luxembourg Courts will necessitate a tremendous degree of judicial cooperation. Whereas both courts should of course uphold their mutual comity and deference for each other, this should not be done at the expense of a comprehensible and transparent review process. For the sake of accession and its ultimate objective—which basically is the creation of a more coherent and effective system of human rights protection in Europe—the functioning of the future legal regime relies on the judges of both courts to deliver robust decisions which subordinate the principle of judicial comity to the prevalence of justice and individual protection.[1] Beyond that, it is now certain that the subsidiary nature of the Charter of Fundamental Rights will guarantee Luxembourg's role as the European Union's quasi-Constitutional or Supreme Court, while its complementary counterpart, the Convention, will ensure that Strasbourg has the final say on cases only relating to alleged human rights violations. This will also allow the individual citizen to enjoy the highest possible standard of protection in Europe, where the jurisdiction of domestic, supranational and international courts is harmonised and made more coherent.[2]

There are, however, major implications for the European Union's legal order which must be taken into account in order to allow for a smooth and uncomplicated accession. The introduction of the co-respondent mechanism is to be welcomed as an effective method of both maintaining the EU's legal autonomy and enabling individual applicants to overcome certain procedural lacunae in the European multi-level maze of human rights protection. Notwithstanding

---

[1] See Noreen O'Meara, '"A More Secure Europe of Rights?" The European Court of Human Rights, the Court of Justice of the European Union and EU Accession to the ECHR' (2011) 12 *German Law Journal* 1813, 1828.

[2] See Giacomo Di Federico, 'Fundamental Rights in the EU: Legal Pluralism and Multi-Level Protection After the Lisbon Treaty' in Giacomo Di Federico (ed), *The EU Charter of Fundamental Rights. From Declaration to Binding Document* (Dordrecht, Springer, Netherlands 2011) 52f.

this groundbreaking and innovative mechanism, there is a serious risk that the co-respondent mechanism may become so complicated that well-meant solutions might create even more issues in this regard.[3] This fact demands the adoption of detailed internal rules specifically designed to address and solve these issues. At the end of the day, the decision of the Council of the European Union to conclude the Accession Agreement under Article 218 (6) of the Treaty on the Functioning of the European Union (TFEU) is primarily dependent on the prior adoption of these new internal rules.[4]

The other aspect pertaining to the further adoption of internal rules concerns the prior involvement of the Court of Justice of the European Union (CJEU) in fundamental rights proceedings, especially in cases where the national courts refrain from requesting a preliminary ruling procedure and where they thereby sideline the Luxembourg Court. It is thence crucial for the future functioning of the judicial interplay between Luxembourg and Strasbourg that the Statute of the Court of Justice and its Rules of Procedure are accordingly and appropriately amended to ensure that Luxembourg's Union-internal review is conducted efficiently and without undue delays for individual applicants.[5] Moreover, with regard to annulment proceedings, it is recommended that the CJEU construes the *locus standi* of individuals to the extent that their right to an effective remedy is not violated.[6] Alternatively, the Member States are urged to revisit this matter within the course of the next Treaty revision.

Eventually, accession will also have extensive impact on the courts of the Member States. National judges should familiarise themselves with the legal ramifications of accession, in particular with the new procedural routes opening up for individual claimants.[7] Most importantly, however, given the procedural problems involved in such scenarios, national judges are advised to reconsider whether they should refrain from requesting a preliminary ruling from Luxembourg.

In the end, it becomes clear that the European Union's accession to the European Convention is, for the time being, the missing apex within the European edifice of human rights protection. After more than 30 years of discussion, the negotiators and drafters of the Accession Agreement provide both the European Union and the Convention regime with an instrument which is capable of resolving the legal problems regarding the EU's specific and autonomous legal system. Certainly, those negotiators could only consider those issues which had already arisen at the time of drafting. Thus, the Luxembourg and Strasbourg Courts are called upon to balance any shortcomings of the agreement by properly interpreting and

---

[3] See Tobias Lock, 'Walking on a Tightrope: The Draft Accession Agreement and the Autonomy of the EU Legal Order' (2011) 48 *Common Market Law Review* 1025, 1054.

[4] See Jean-Paul Jacqué, 'The Accession of the European Union to the European Convention on Human Rights and Fundamental Freedoms' (2011) 48 *Common Market Law Review* 995, 1022f.

[5] See O'Meara (n 1) 1826.

[6] See Julie Vondung, 'Grundrechtsschutz gegen die Europäische Union vor dem Europäischen Gerichtshof für Menschenrechte' (2011) 61 *Anwaltsblatt des Deutschen Anwaltvereins* 331, 336.

[7] See O'Meara (n 1) 1830.

applying the relevant provisions of European human rights law. Eventually, these courts must bear in mind that the purpose and objective of accession is not to distinguish themselves in judicial battles with their respective counterpart, but to cooperate in order to improve the protection of human rights for individuals in Europe.

Appendix

Draft Accession Agreement and Explanatory Report

Draft Legal Instruments on the Accession of the European Union to the European Convention on Human Rights

I. Draft Agreement on the Accession of the European Union to the Convention for the Protection of Human Rights and Fundamental Freedoms

Preamble

The High Contracting Parties to the Convention for the Protection of Human Rights and Fundamental Freedoms, signed at Rome on 4 November 1950 (ETS No. 5, hereinafter referred to as "the Convention"), being member States of the Council of Europe, and the European Union,

Having regard to Article 59, paragraph 2, of the Convention;

Considering that the European Union is founded on the respect for human rights and fundamental freedoms;

Considering that the accession of the European Union to the Convention will enhance coherence in human rights protection in Europe;

Considering, in particular, that the individual should have the right to submit the acts, measures or omissions of the European Union to the external control of the European Court of Human Rights (hereinafter referred to as "the Court");

Considering that, having regard to the specific legal order of the European Union, its accession requires certain adjustments to the Convention system to be made by common agreement,

Have agreed as follows:

Article 1—Scope of the accession and amendments to Article 59 of the Convention

1. The European Union hereby accedes to the Convention, to the Protocol to the Convention and to Protocol No. 6 to the Convention.

2. Paragraph 2 of Article 59 of the Convention shall be amended to read as follows:

> "2.*a*. The European Union may accede to this Convention and the Protocols thereto. Accession of the European Union to the Protocols shall be governed, *mutatis mutandis*, by Article 6 of the Protocol, Article 7 of Protocol No. 4, Articles 7 to 9 of Protocol No. 6, Articles 8 to 10 of Protocol No. 7, Articles 4 to 6 of Protocol No. 12 and Articles 6 to 8 of Protocol No. 13.

b. The status of the European Union as a High Contracting Party to the Convention and the Protocols thereto shall be further defined in the Agreement on the Accession of the European Union to the Convention for the Protection of Human Rights and Fundamental Freedoms.

c. Accession to the Convention and the Protocols thereto shall impose on the European Union obligations with regard only to acts, measures or omissions of its institutions, bodies, offices or agencies, or of persons acting on their behalf. Nothing in the Convention or the Protocols thereto shall require the European Union to perform an act or adopt a measure for which it has no competence under European Union law.

d. Where any of the terms 'State', 'State Party', 'States' or 'States Parties' appear in paragraph 1 of Article 10, and in Article 17 of this Convention, as well as in Articles 1 and 2 of the Protocol, Article 2 of Protocol No. 4, Articles 2 and 6 of Protocol No. 6, Articles 3, 4, 5 and 7 of Protocol No. 7, Article 3 of Protocol No. 12, and Article 5 of Protocol No. 13, they shall be understood as referring also to the European Union.

e. Where any of the terms 'national security', 'national law', 'national laws', 'national authority', 'life of the nation', 'country', 'administration of the State', 'territorial integrity', 'territory of a State' or 'domestic' appear in Articles 5, 6, 7, 8, 10, 11, 12, 13, 15 and 35 of this Convention, in Article 2 of Protocol No. 4 and in Article 1 of Protocol No. 7, they shall be understood as relating also, *mutatis mutandis*, to the European Union."

3. Paragraph 5 of Article 59 of the Convention shall be amended to read as follows:

> "5. The Secretary General of the Council of Europe shall notify all the Council of Europe member States and the European Union of the entry into force of the Convention, the names of the High Contracting Parties who have ratified it or acceded to it, and the deposit of all instruments of ratification or accession which may be effected subsequently."

Article 2—Reservations to the Convention and its Protocols

1. The European Union may, when signing or expressing its consent to be bound by the provisions of this Agreement in accordance with Article 10, make reservations to the Convention and to the Protocol in accordance with Article 57 of the Convention.

2. Paragraph 1 of Article 57 of the Convention shall be amended to read as follows:

> "1. Any State may, when signing this Convention or when depositing its instrument of ratification, make a reservation in respect of any particular provision of the Convention to the extent that any law then in force in its territory is not in conformity with the provision. The European Union may, when acceding to this Convention, make a reservation in respect of any particular provision of the Convention to the extent that any law of the European Union then in force is not in conformity with the provision. Reservations of a general character shall not be permitted under this Article."

Article 3—Co-respondent mechanism

1. Article 36 of the Convention shall be amended as follows:

a. The heading of Article 36 shall be amended to read as follows: "Third party intervention and co-respondent".

b. The following paragraph shall be added at the end of Article 36:

> "4. The European Union or a member State of the European Union may become a co-respondent to proceedings by decision of the Court in the circumstances set out in the Agreement on the Accession of the European Union to the Convention for the Protection of Human Rights and Fundamental Freedoms. A co-respondent is a party to the case. The admissibility of an application shall be assessed without regard to the participation of a co-respondent in the proceedings."

2. Where an application is directed against one or more member States of the European Union, the European Union may become a co-respondent to the proceedings in respect of an alleged violation notified by the Court if it appears that such allegation calls into question the compatibility with the Convention rights at issue of a provision of European Union law, notably where that violation could have been avoided only by disregarding an obligation under European Union law.

3. Where an application is directed against the European Union, the European Union member States may become co-respondents to the proceedings in respect of an alleged violation notified by the Court if it appears that such allegation calls into question the compatibility with the Convention rights at issue of a provision of the Treaty on European Union, the Treaty on the Functioning of the European Union or any other provision having the same legal value pursuant to those instruments, notably where that violation could have been avoided only by disregarding an obligation under those instruments.

4. Where an application is directed against and notified to both the European Union and one or more of its member States, the status of any respondent may be changed to that of a co-respondent if the conditions in paragraph 2 or paragraph 3 of this Article are met.

5. A High Contracting Party shall become a co-respondent only at its own request and by decision of the Court. The Court shall seek the views of all parties to the proceedings. When determining a request of this nature the Court shall assess whether, in the light of the reasons given by the High Contracting Party concerned, it is plausible that the conditions in paragraph 2 or paragraph 3 of this Article are met.

6. In proceedings to which the European Union is co-respondent, if the Court of Justice of the European Union has not yet assessed the compatibility with the Convention rights at issue of the provision of European Union law as under paragraph 2 of this Article, then sufficient time shall be afforded for the Court of Justice of the European Union to make such an assessment and thereafter for the parties to make observations to the Court. The European Union shall ensure that such assessment is made quickly so that the proceedings before the Court are not unduly delayed. The provisions of this paragraph shall not affect the powers of the Court.

7. The respondent and the co-respondent shall appear jointly in the proceedings before the Court.

8. This Article shall apply to applications submitted from the date of entry into force of this Agreement.

Article 4—Inter-Party cases

1. The first sentence of paragraph 2 of Article 29 of the Convention shall be amended to read as follows:

> "A Chamber shall decide on the admissibility and merits of inter-Party applications submitted under Article 33".

2. The heading of Article 33 of the Convention shall be amended to read as follows:

"Article 33—Inter-Party cases".

Article 5—Interpretation of Articles 35 and 55 of the Convention

Proceedings before the Court of Justice of the European Union shall be understood as constituting neither procedures of international investigation or settlement within the meaning of Article 35, paragraph 2.*b*, of the Convention, nor means of dispute settlement within the meaning of Article 55 of the Convention.

Article 6—Election of judges

1. A delegation of the European Parliament shall be entitled to participate, with the right to vote, in the sittings of the Parliamentary Assembly of the Council of Europe whenever the Assembly exercises its functions related to the election of judges in accordance with Article 22 of the Convention. The number of representatives of the European Parliament shall be the same as the highest number of representatives to which any State is entitled under Article 26 of the Statute of the Council of Europe.

2. The modalities of the participation of representatives of the European Parliament in the sittings of the Parliamentary Assembly of the Council of Europe and its relevant bodies shall be defined by the Parliamentary Assembly of the Council of Europe, in cooperation with the European Parliament.

Article 7—Participation of the European Union in the Committee of Ministers of the Council of Europe

1. The European Union shall be entitled to participate in the Committee of Ministers, with the right to vote, when the latter takes decisions:

> *a*. under Article 26, paragraph 2, Article 39, paragraph 4, Article 46, paragraphs 2 to 5, or Article 47 of the Convention;

> *b*. regarding the adoption of Protocols to the Convention;

> *c*. regarding the adoption or implementation of any other instrument or text addressed to the Court or to all High Contracting Parties to the Convention, or relating to the functions exercised by virtue of the Convention by the Committee of Ministers or the Parliamentary Assembly of the Council of Europe.

2. The exercise of the right to vote by the European Union and its member States shall not prejudice the effective exercise by the Committee of Ministers of its

supervisory functions under Articles 39 and 46 of the Convention. In particular, the following shall apply.

a. Where the Committee of Ministers supervises the fulfilment of obligations either by the European Union alone, or by the European Union and one or more of its member States jointly, it derives from the European Union treaties that the European Union and its member States express positions and vote in a co-ordinated manner. The Rules of the Committee of Ministers for the supervision of the execution of judgments and of the terms of friendly settlements shall be adapted to ensure that the Committee of Ministers effectively exercises its functions in those circumstances.

b. Where the Committee of Ministers otherwise supervises the fulfilment of obligations by a member State of the European Union, the European Union is precluded for reasons pertaining to its internal legal order from expressing a position or exercising its right to vote. The European Union treaties do not oblige the member States of the European Union to express positions or to vote in a co-ordinated manner.

c. Where the Committee of Ministers supervises the fulfilment of obligations by a High Contracting Party other than the European Union or a member State of the European Union, the European Union treaties do not oblige the member States of the European Union to express positions or to vote in a co-ordinated manner, even if the European Union expresses its position or exercises its right to vote.

Article 8—Participation of the European Union in the expenditure related to the Convention

1. The European Union shall pay an annual contribution dedicated to the expenditure related to the functioning of the Convention. This annual contribution shall be in addition to contributions made by the other High Contracting Parties. Its amount shall be equal to 34% of the highest amount contributed in the previous year by any State to the Ordinary Budget of the Council of Europe.

2. *a.* If the amount dedicated within the Ordinary Budget of the Council of Europe to the expenditure related to the functioning of the Convention, expressed as a proportion of the Ordinary Budget itself, deviates in each of two consecutive years by more than 2.5 percentage points from the percentage indicated in paragraph 1, the Council of Europe and the European Union shall, by agreement, amend the percentage in paragraph 1 to reflect this new proportion.

b. For the purpose of this paragraph, no account shall be taken of:

– a decrease in absolute terms of the amount dedicated within the Ordinary Budget of the Council of Europe to the expenditure related to the functioning of the Convention as compared to the year preceding that in which the European Union becomes a Party to the Convention;

– [an increase in the amount dedicated within the Ordinary Budget of the Council of Europe to the expenditure related to the functioning of the Convention, expressed as a proportion of the Ordinary Budget itself, where this results from a decrease in absolute terms of the Ordinary Budget and either no change or a decrease in absolute terms of the amount dedicated within it to the expenditure related to the functioning of the Convention.]

c. The percentage that results from an amendment under paragraph 2.a may itself later be amended in accordance with this paragraph.

3. For the purpose of this Article, the expenditure related to the functioning of the Convention comprises the total expenditure on:

a. the Court;

b. the supervision of the execution of judgments of the Court; and

c. the functioning, when performing functions under the Convention, of the Committee of Ministers, the Parliamentary Assembly and the Secretary General of the Council of Europe,

increased by 15% to reflect related administrative overhead costs.

4. Practical arrangements for the implementation of this Article may be determined by agreement between the Council of Europe and the European Union.

Article 9—Relations with other Agreements

1. The European Union shall respect the provisions of:

a. Articles 1 to 6 of the European Agreement relating to Persons Participating in Proceedings of the European Court of Human Rights of 5 March 1996 (ETS No. 161);

b. Articles 1 to 19 of the General Agreement on Privileges and Immunities of the Council of Europe of 2 September 1949 (ETS No. 2) and Articles 2 to 6 of its Protocol of 6 November 1952 (ETS No. 10), in so far as they are relevant to the operation of the Convention; and

c. Articles 1 to 6 of the Sixth Protocol to the General Agreement on Privileges and Immunities of the Council of Europe of 5 March 1996 (ETS No. 162).

2. For the purpose of the application of the Agreements and Protocols referred to in paragraph 1, the Contracting Parties to each of them shall treat the European Union as if it were a Contracting Party to that Agreement or Protocol.

3. The European Union shall be consulted before any Agreement or Protocol referred to in paragraph 1 is amended.

4. With respect to the Agreements and Protocols referred to in paragraph 1, the Secretary General of the Council of Europe shall notify the European Union of:

  a. any signature;
  b. the deposit of any instrument of ratification, acceptance, approval or accession;
  c. any date of entry into force in accordance with the relevant provisions of those Agreements and Protocols; and
  d. any other act, notification or communication relating to those Agreements and Protocols.

Article 10—Signature and entry into force

1. The High Contracting Parties to the Convention at the date of the opening for signature of this Agreement and the European Union may express their consent to be bound by:

  a. signature without reservation as to ratification, acceptance or approval; or
  b. signature with reservation as to ratification, acceptance or approval, followed by ratification, acceptance or approval.

2. Instruments of ratification, acceptance or approval shall be deposited with the Secretary General of the Council of Europe.

3. This Agreement shall enter into force on the first day of the month following the expiration of a period of three months after the date on which all High Contracting Parties to the Convention mentioned in paragraph 1 and the European Union have expressed their consent to be bound by the Agreement in accordance with the provisions of the preceding paragraphs.

4. The European Union shall become a Party to the Convention, to the Protocol to the Convention and to Protocol No. 6 to the Convention at the date of entry into force of this Agreement.

Article 11—Reservations

No reservation may be made in respect of the provisions of this Agreement.

Article 12—Notifications

The Secretary General of the Council of Europe shall notify the European Union and the member States of the Council of Europe of:

  a. any signature without reservation in respect of ratification, acceptance or approval;
  b. any signature with reservation in respect of ratification, acceptance or approval;
  c. the deposit of any instrument of ratification, acceptance or approval;
  d. the date of entry into force of this Agreement in accordance with Article 10;
  e. any other act, notification or communication relating to this Agreement.

In witness whereof the undersigned, being duly authorised thereto, have signed this Agreement.

Done at .... the ...., in English and in French, both texts being equally authentic, in a single copy which shall be deposited in the archives of the Council of Europe. The Secretary General of the Council of Europe shall transmit certified copies to each member State of the Council of Europe and to the European Union.

II. Draft Rule to be added to the Rules of the Committee of Ministers for the Supervision of the Execution of Judgments and of the Terms of Friendly Settlements

Rule 18—Judgments and friendly settlements in cases to which the European Union is a Party

Where the Committee of Ministers supervises the fulfilment of obligations either by the European Union alone, or by the European Union and one or more of its member States jointly, the High Contracting Parties shall:

a. without prejudice to the provisions under sub-paragraphs *b* and *c*, consider decisions by the Committee of Ministers as adopted if a simple majority of the representatives entitled to sit on the Committee on behalf of those High Contracting Parties that are not member States of the European Union is in favour;

b. consider decisions by the Committee of Ministers under Rules 10 and 11 as adopted if two thirds of the representatives entitled to sit on the Committee on behalf of those High Contracting Parties that are not member States of the European Union are in favour; and

c. consider decisions by the Committee of Ministers under Rule 17 as adopted if, in addition to the majority set out in Article 20.*d* of the Statute of the Council of Europe, a simple majority of the representatives casting a vote on behalf of those High Contracting Parties that are not member States of the European Union is in favour.

III. Draft Explanatory report to the Agreement on the Accession of the European Union to the Convention for the Protection of Human Rights and Fundamental Freedoms

Introduction

1. The accession of the European Union (hereinafter referred to as "the EU") to the Convention for the Protection of Human Rights and Fundamental Freedoms, signed at Rome on 4 November 1950 (hereinafter referred to as "the Convention") constitutes a major step in the development of the protection of human rights in Europe.

2. Discussed since the late 1970s, the accession became a legal obligation under the Treaty on European Union when the Treaty of Lisbon came into force on 1 December 2009. Pursuant to Article 6, paragraph 2, of the Treaty on European Union, "[t]he Union shall accede to the [Convention]. Such accession shall not affect the Union's competences as defined in the Treaties". Protocol No. 8 to the Treaty of Lisbon set out a number of further requirements for the conclusion of the Accession Agreement. Protocol No. 14 to the Convention, which was adopted in 2004 and which entered into force on 1 June 2010, amended Article 59 of the Convention to allow the EU to accede to it.

I. Need for an Accession Agreement

3. The above provisions, although necessary, were not sufficient to allow for an immediate accession of the EU. The Convention, as amended by Protocols Nos. 11 and 14, was drafted to apply only to Contracting Parties who are also member States of the Council of Europe. As the EU is neither a State nor a member of the Council of Europe, and has its own specific legal system, its accession requires certain adaptations to the Convention system. These include: amendments to provisions of the Convention to ensure that it operates effectively with the participation of the EU; supplementary interpretative provisions; adaptations of the procedure before the European Court of Human Rights (hereinafter referred to as "the Court") to take into account the characteristics of the legal order of the EU, in particular the specific relationship between an EU member State's legal order and that of the EU itself; and other technical and administrative issues not directly pertaining to the text of the Convention, but for which a legal basis is required.

4. It was therefore necessary to establish, by common agreement between the EU and the current High Contracting Parties to the Convention, the conditions of accession and the adjustments to be made to the Convention system.

5. As a result of the accession, the acts, measures and omissions of the EU, like every other High Contracting Party, will be subject to the external control exercised by the Court in the light of the rights guaranteed under the Convention. This is all the more important since the EU member States have transferred

substantial powers to the EU. At the same time, the competence of the Court to assess the conformity of EU law with the provisions of the Convention will not prejudice the principle of the autonomous interpretation of the EU law.

6. The EU is founded on the respect for fundamental rights, the observance of which is ensured by the Court of Justice of the European Union (hereinafter referred to as "the CJEU") as well as by the courts of the EU member States; accession of the EU to the Convention will further enhance the coherence of the judicial protection of human rights in Europe.

7. As general principles, the Accession Agreement aims to preserve the equal rights of all individuals under the Convention, the rights of applicants in the Convention procedures, and the equality of all High Contracting Parties. The current control mechanism of the Convention should, as far as possible, be preserved and applied to the EU in the same way as to other High Contracting Parties, by making only those adaptations that are strictly necessary. The EU should, as a matter of principle, accede to the Convention on an equal footing with the other Contracting Parties, that is, with the same rights and obligations. It was, however, acknowledged that, because the EU is not a State, some adaptations would be necessary. It is also understood that the existing rights and obligations of the States Parties to the Convention, whether or not members of the EU, should be unaffected by the accession, and that the distribution of competences between the EU and its member States and between the EU institutions shall be respected.

II. Principal stages in the preparation of the Accession Agreement

8. Before the elaboration of this Agreement, the accession of the EU to the Convention had been debated on several occasions.

9. The Steering Committee for Human Rights (CDDH) adopted at its 53rd meeting in June 2002 a study of the legal and technical issues that would have to be addressed by the Council of Europe in the event of possible accession by the EU to the Convention, which it transmitted to the Convention on the Future of Europe, convened following the Laeken Declaration of the European Council (December 2001), in order to consider the key issues arising for the EU's future development with a view to assisting future political decision making about such accession.

10. When drafting Protocol No. 14 to the Convention in 2004, the High Contracting Parties decided to add a new paragraph to Article 59 of the Convention providing for the possible accession of the EU. It was, however, noted even at that time that further modifications to the Convention were necessary to make such accession possible from a legal and technical point of view. Such modifications could be made either in an amending protocol to the Convention, or in an accession treaty between the EU and the States Parties to the Convention.

11. The entry into force of the Treaty of Lisbon in December 2009 and of Protocol No. 14 to the Convention in June 2010 created the necessary legal preconditions for the accession.

12. The Committee of Ministers adopted, at the 1085th meeting of the Ministers' Deputies (26 May 2010), ad hoc terms of reference for the CDDH to elaborate, in co-operation with representatives of the EU, a legal instrument, or instruments, setting out the modalities of accession of the EU to the European Convention on Human Rights, including its participation in the Convention system. On the EU side, the Council of the EU adopted on 4 June 2010 a Decision authorising the European Commission to negotiate an agreement for the EU to accede to the Convention.

13. The CDDH entrusted this task to an informal group of 14 members (7 coming from member States of the EU and 7 coming from non-member States of the EU), chosen on the basis of their expertise. This informal working group (CDDH-UE) held in total eight working meetings with the European Commission, reporting regularly to the CDDH on progress and on outstanding issues. In the context of these meetings, the informal group also held two exchanges of views with representatives of civil society, who regularly submitted comments on the working documents.

14. In the context of the regular meetings which take place between the two courts, delegations from the Court and the CJEU discussed on 17 January 2011 the accession of the EU to the Convention, and in particular the question of the possible prior involvement of the CJEU in cases to which the EU is a co-respondent. The Joint Declaration by the Presidents of the two European courts summarising the results of the discussion provided valuable reference and guidance for the negotiation.

15. The CDDH approved the draft Accession Agreement and sent it to the Committee of Ministers on ... . The Parliamentary Assembly adopted an opinion on the draft Accession Agreement (Opinion No. ... of ...). The Accession Agreement was adopted by the Committee of Ministers on ... and opened for signature on ...

III. Comments on relevant provisions of the Agreement

Article 1—Scope of the accession and amendments to Article 59 of the Convention

16. It was decided that, upon its entry into force, the Accession Agreement would simultaneously amend the Convention and include the EU among its Parties, without the EU needing to deposit a further instrument of accession. This would

also be the case for the EU's accession to the Protocol and to Protocol No. 6. Subsequent accession by the EU to other Protocols would require the deposit of separate accession instruments.

17. The amendments to the Convention concern paragraphs 2 and 5 of Article 59.

18. Article 59, paragraph 2, of the Convention, as amended, defines the scope of the accession of the EU to the Convention. It is divided into five sub-paragraphs.

Possible accession to other Protocols

19. Under paragraph 2.*a*, a provision is added to Article 59, of the Convention to permit the EU to accede to the Protocols to the Convention. To ensure that this provision can serve as a legal basis for the accession to those Protocols, Article 59, paragraph 2.*a*, states that the provisions of the Protocols concerning signature and ratification, entry into force and depositary functions shall apply, *mutatis mutandis*, in the event of the EU's accession to those Protocols. These are, namely: Article 6 of the Protocol, Article 7 of Protocol No. 4, Articles 7 to 9 of Protocol No. 6, Articles 8 to 10 of Protocol No. 7, Articles 4 to 6 of Protocol No. 12 and Articles 6 to 8 of Protocol No. 13.

Reference in the Convention to further provisions in the Accession Agreement

20. Article 59, paragraph 2.*b*, of the Convention provides that the status of the EU as a High Contracting Party to the Convention shall be further defined in the Accession Agreement. Such explicit reference to the Accession Agreement makes it possible to limit the amendments made to the Convention. For instance, provisions about privileges and immunities and about the participation of the EU in the Committee of Ministers of the Council of Europe are thus dealt with in the Accession Agreement. In so far as the Accession Agreement will still have legal effect after the EU has acceded, its provisions will be subject to interpretation by the Court. To implement the Accession Agreement, the EU may need to adopt internal legal rules regulating various matters, including the functioning of the co-respondent mechanism. Similarly, the Rules of Court may also need to be adapted.

Effects of the accession

21. The provision under paragraph 2.*c* reflects the requirement under Article 2 of Protocol No. 8 to the Treaty of Lisbon that the accession of the EU shall not affect its competences or the powers of its institutions. The provision also clarifies that accession to the Convention imposes on the EU obligations with regard to acts, measures or omissions of its institutions, bodies, offices or agencies, or of persons acting on their behalf. Likewise, since the Court under the

Convention has jurisdiction to settle disputes between individuals and the High Contracting Parties (as well as between High Contracting Parties) and therefore to interpret the provisions of the Convention, the decisions of the Court in cases to which the EU is party will be binding on the EU's institutions, including the CJEU.8

Technical amendments to the Convention

22. An interpretation clause is added to Article 59 of the Convention with regard to terms such as "State", "State Party" and other State-specific concepts (paragraph 2.*d* and *e*); this avoids amending the substantive provisions of the Convention and the Protocols, thereby maintaining their readability. All of the Protocols provide that their substantive provisions shall be regarded as additional articles to the Convention, and that all the provisions of the latter shall apply accordingly; this clarifies the accessory nature of the Protocols to the Convention. It follows that the general interpretation clause added to the Convention will also apply to the Protocols without their needing to be amended to that effect.

23. By virtue of paragraph 2.*d*, various terms that explicitly refer to "States" as High Contracting Parties to the Convention (that is, "State", "State Party", "States" or "States Parties") will, after the accession, be understood as referring also to the EU as a High Contracting Party.

24. Paragraph 2.*e* then addresses other terms in the Convention and the Protocols that refer more generally to the concept of a State, or to certain elements thereof ("national security", "national law", "national laws", "national authority", "life of the nation", "country", "administration of the State", "territorial integrity", "domestic", "territory of a State"); after the accession, these will be understood as relating also, *mutatis mutandis*, to the EU. As regards the application to the EU of the expression "life of the nation", it was noted that it may be interpreted as allowing the EU to take measures derogating from its obligations under the Convention in relation to measures taken by one if its member States in time of emergency in accordance with Article 15 of the Convention. The term "domestic" should be understood as "internal" to the legal order of a High Contracting Party, as confirmed by the French wording of Article 35 of the Convention.

25. An interpretation clause was not considered necessary for the expression "internal law" appearing in Articles 41 and 52 of the Convention, since this expression would be equally applicable to the EU as a High Contracting Party. There are some expressions in the Convention like those covered by Article 59, paragraph 2.*d* and *e*, that have not been included in that interpretation clause. In particular, for reasons pertaining to the specific legal order of the EU, EU citizenship is not analogous to the concept of nationality that appears in Articles 14 and 36 of the Convention, Article 3 of Protocol No. 4 and Article 1 of Protocol No. 12. Likewise, the terms

"countries" appearing in Article 4, paragraph 3.*b*, of the Convention, "civilised nations" appearing in Article 7 of the Convention, and "State", "territorial" and "territory/territories" appearing in Articles 56 and 58 of the Convention and in the corresponding provisions of the Protocols, do not require any adaptation as a result of the EU's accession. A complete table of all State-related expressions and their interpretation following the EU's accession appears in the appendix to this explanatory report.

26. Finally, a technical amendment to Article 59, paragraph 5, of the Convention takes into account EU accession for the purposes of notification by the Secretary General.

Article 2—Reservations to the Convention and its Protocols

27. The EU should accede to the Convention, as far as possible, on an equal footing with the other High Contracting Parties. Therefore, the conditions applicable to the other High Contracting Parties with regard to reservations, declarations and derogations under the Convention should also apply to the EU. For reasons of legal certainty, it was, however, agreed to include in the Accession Agreement a provision (Article 2, paragraph 1) allowing the EU to make reservations under Article 57 of the Convention under the same conditions as any other High Contracting Party. This would also include the right to make reservations when acceding to existing or future additional protocols. Any reservation should be consistent with the relevant rules of international law.

28. As Article 57 of the Convention currently only refers to "States", technical adaptations to paragraph 1 of that provision are necessary to allow the EU to make reservations under it (see Article 2, paragraph 2, of the Accession Agreement). The expression "law of the European Union" is meant to cover the Treaty on European Union, the Treaty on the Functioning of the European Union, or any other provision having the same legal value pursuant to those instruments (the EU "primary law") as well as legal provisions contained in acts of the EU institutions (the EU "secondary law").

29. In accordance with Article 1, paragraph 1, of the Accession Agreement, the EU accedes to the Convention, to the Protocol to the Convention and to Protocol No. 6 to the Convention. The EU may make reservations to the Convention and to the Protocol; no reservations are permitted to Protocol No. 6, pursuant to its Article 4. In the event of EU accession to other Protocols, the possibility to make reservations is governed by Article 57 of the Convention and the relevant provisions of such Protocols.

30. Article 2, paragraph 1, of the Accession Agreement gives the EU the possibility to make reservations to the Convention either when signing or when expressing its

consent to be bound by the provisions of the Accession Agreement. In accordance with Article 23 of the 1969 Vienna Convention on the Law of Treaties, reservations to the Convention made at the moment of the signature of the Accession Agreement shall be confirmed, in order to be valid, at the moment of expression of consent to be bound by the provisions of the Accession Agreement.

Article 3—Co-respondent mechanism

31. A new mechanism is being introduced to allow the EU to become a co-respondent to proceedings instituted against one or more of its member States and, similarly, to allow the EU member States to become co-respondents to proceedings instituted against the EU.

Reasons for the introduction of the mechanism

32. This mechanism was considered necessary to accommodate the specific situation of the EU as a non-State entity with an autonomous legal system that is becoming a Party to the Convention alongside its own member States. It is a special feature of the EU legal system that acts adopted by its institutions may be implemented by its member States and, conversely, that provisions of the EU founding treaties agreed upon by its member States may be implemented by institutions, bodies, offices or agencies of the EU. With the accession of the EU, there could arise the unique situation in the Convention system in which a legal act is enacted by one High Contracting Party and implemented by another.

33. The newly introduced Article 36, paragraph 4, of the Convention provides that a co-respondent has the status of a party to the case. If the Court finds a violation of the Convention, the co-respondent will be bound by the obligations under Article 46 of the Convention. The co-respondent mechanism is therefore not a procedural privilege for the EU or its member States, but a way to avoid gaps in participation, accountability and enforceability in the Convention system. This corresponds to the very purpose of EU accession and serves the proper administration of justice.

34. As regards the position of the applicant, the newly introduced Article 36, paragraph 4, of the Convention states that the admissibility of an application shall be assessed without regard to the participation of the co-respondent in the proceedings. This provision thus ensures that an application will not be considered inadmissible as a result of the participation of the co-respondent, notably with regard to the exhaustion of domestic remedies within the meaning of Article 35, paragraph 1, of the Convention. Moreover, applicants will be able to make submissions to the Court in each case before a decision on joining a co-respondent is taken (see below, paragraphs 46 to 50).

35. The introduction of the co-respondent mechanism is also fully in line with Article 1.*b* of Protocol No. 8 to the Treaty of Lisbon, which requires the Accession Agreement to provide for "the mechanisms necessary to ensure that … individual applications are correctly addressed to Member States and/or the Union, as appropriate". Using the language of this protocol, the co-respondent mechanism offers the opportunity to "correct" applications in the following two ways.

Situations in which the co-respondent mechanism may be applied

36. The mechanism would allow the EU to become a co-respondent to cases in which the applicant has directed an application only against one or more EU member States. Likewise, the mechanism would allow the EU member States to become co-respondents to cases in which the applicant has directed an application only against the EU.

37. Where an application is directed against both the EU and an EU member State, the mechanism would also be applied if the EU or its member State was not the party that acted or omitted to act in respect of the applicant, but was instead the party that provided the legal basis for that act or omission. In this case, the co-respondent mechanism would allow the application not to be declared inadmissible in respect of that party on the basis that it is incompatible *ratione personae*.

38. In cases in which the applicant alleges different violations by the EU and one or more of its member States separately, the co-respondent mechanism will not apply.

Third party intervention and the co-respondent mechanism

39. The co-respondent mechanism differs from third party interventions under Article 36, paragraph 2, of the Convention. The latter only gives the third party (be it a High Contracting Party to the Convention or, for example, another subject of international law or a nongovernmental organisation) the opportunity to submit written comments and participate in the hearing in a case before the Court, but it does not become a party to the case and is not bound by the judgment. A co-respondent becomes, on the contrary, a full party to the case and will therefore be bound by the judgment.

40. It is understood that a third party intervention may often be the most appropriate way to involve the EU in a case. For instance, if an application is directed against a State associated to parts of the EU legal order through separate international agreements (for example, the "Schengen" and "Dublin" agreements and the agreement on the European Economic Area) concerning obligations arising from such agreements, third party intervention would be the only way for the EU to participate in the proceedings. The introduction of the co-respondent

mechanism should thus not be seen as precluding the EU from participating in the proceedings as a third party intervener, where the conditions for becoming a co-respondent are not met.

The tests for triggering the co-respondent mechanism

41. In order to identify cases involving EU law suitable for applying the co-respondent mechanism, two tests are set out Article 3, paragraphs 2 and 3, of the Accession Agreement. These tests would apply taking account of provisions of EU law as interpreted by the competent courts. The fact that the alleged violation may arise from a positive obligation deriving from the Convention would not affect the application of these tests. They would also cover cases in which the applications were directed from the outset against both the EU and one or more of its member States (Article 3, paragraph 4, of the Accession Agreement)

42. In the case of applications notified to one or more member States of the EU, but not to the EU itself (paragraph 2), the test is fulfilled if it appears that the alleged violation notified by the Court calls into question the compatibility of a provision of (primary or secondary) EU law with the Convention rights at issue. This would be the case, for instance, if an alleged violation could only have been avoided by a member State disregarding an obligation under EU law (for example, when an EU law provision leaves no discretion to a member State as to its implementation at the national level).

43. In the case of applications notified to the EU, but not to one or more of its member States (paragraph 3), the EU member States may become co-respondents if it appears that the alleged violation as notified by the Court calls into question the compatibility of a provision of the primary law of the EU with the Convention rights at issue.

44. On the basis of the relevant case law of the Court, it can be expected that such a mechanism may be applied only in a limited number of cases.

Outline of the procedure under the co-respondent mechanism

45. The co-respondent mechanism will not alter the current practice under which the Court makes a preliminary assessment of an application, with the result that many manifestly ill-founded or otherwise inadmissible applications are not communicated. Therefore, the co-respondent mechanism should only be applied to cases which have been notified to a High Contracting Party. Article 3, paragraph 5, of the Accession Agreement outlines the procedure and the conditions for applying the co-respondent mechanism, whereby a High Contracting Party becomes a co-respondent by decision of the Court. The following paragraphs are understood as merely illustrating this provision. For those cases selected by the

Court for notification, the procedure initially follows the information indicated by the applicant in the application form.

A. *Applications directed against one or more member State(s) of the European Union, but not against the European Union itself (or vice versa)*

46. In cases in which the application is directed against one (or more) member State(s) of the EU, but not against the EU itself, the latter may, if it considers that the criteria set out in Article 3, paragraph 2, of the Accession Agreement are fulfilled, request to join the proceedings as co-respondent. Where the application is directed against the EU, but not against one (or more) of its member States, the EU member States may, if they consider that the criteria set out in Article 3, paragraph 3, of the Accession Agreement are fulfilled, request to join the proceedings as co-respondents. Any such request should be reasoned. In order to enable the potential co-respondent to make such requests, it is important that the relevant information on applications, including the date of their notification to the respondent, is rapidly made public. The Court's system of publication of communicated cases should ensure the dissemination of such information.

47. If appropriate, the Court may, when notifying an alleged violation or at a later stage of the proceedings, indicate that a High Contracting Party might participate in the proceedings as a co-respondent, but a request by that High Contracting Party would be a necessary precondition for the latter to become co-respondent. No High Contracting Party may be compelled against its will to become a co-respondent. This reflects the fact that the initial application was not addressed against the potential co-respondent, and that no High Contracting Party can be forced to become a party to a case where it was not named in the original application.

48. The Court will inform both the applicant and the respondent about the request, and set a short time limit for comments. Having considered the reasons stated by the potential co-respondent in its request as well as any submissions by the applicant and the respondent, the Court will decide whether to admit the co-respondent to the proceedings, and will inform the requester and the parties to the case of its decision. When taking such a decision, the Court will limit itself to assessing whether the reasons stated by the High Contracting Party (or Parties) making the request are plausible in the light of the criteria set out in Article 3, paragraphs 2 or 3, as appropriate, without prejudice to its assessment of the merits of the case. The decision of the Court to join a High Contracting Party to a case as a co-respondent may include specific conditions (for example, the provision of legal aid in order to protect the interest of the applicant) if considered necessary in the interests of the proper administration of justice.

B. *Applications directed against both the EU and one or more of its member State(s)*

49. In a case which has been directed against and notified to both the EU and one (or more) of its member States in respect of at least one alleged violation, either of these respondents may, if it considers that the conditions relating to the nature of the alleged violation set out in Article 3, paragraphs 2 or 3 are met, ask the Court to change its status into that of a co-respondent. As in the case described under A. above, the Court may indicate the possibility of a change of status, but a request by the concerned respondent would be a necessary precondition for such a change. The High Contracting Party (or Parties) becoming co-respondent(s) would be the Party (or Parties) which is (or are) not responsible for the act or omission which allegedly caused the violation, but only for the legal basis of such an act or omission.

50. The Court will inform both the applicant and the other respondent about the request, and set a short time limit for comments. Having considered the reasons stated in the request, as well as any submissions by the applicant and the other respondent, the Court will decide whether to make the change of status, and will inform the parties to the case of its decision. When taking such a decision, the Court will limit itself to assessing whether the reasons stated by the High Contracting Party (or Parties) making the request are plausible in the light of the criteria set out in Article 3, paragraphs 2 or 3, as appropriate, of the Accession Agreement, without prejudice to its assessment of the merits of the case.

Termination of the co-respondent mechanism

51. The Court may, at any stage of the proceedings, decide to terminate the participation of the co-respondent, particularly if it should receive a joint representation by the respondent and the co-respondent that the criteria for becoming a co-respondent are not (or no longer) met. In the absence of any such decision, the respondent and the co-respondent continue to participate jointly in the case until the proceedings end.

Friendly settlements

52. Both the respondent and the co-respondent will need to agree to a friendly settlement under Article 39 of the Convention.

Unilateral declarations

53. Both the respondent and the co-respondent will need to agree to make a unilateral declaration of a violation for which they are both responsible.

Effects of the co-respondent mechanism

54. As noted above, it is a special feature of the EU legal system that acts adopted by its institutions may be implemented by its member States and, conversely, that

provisions of the EU founding treaties agreed upon by its member States may be implemented by institutions, bodies, offices or agencies of the EU. Therefore, the respondent and the co-respondent(s) may be jointly responsible for the alleged violation in respect of which a High Contracting Party has become a co-respondent. Should the Court find this violation, it is expected that it would ordinarily do so jointly against the respondent and the co-respondent(s); there would otherwise be a risk that the Court would assess the distribution of competences between the EU and its member States. The respondent and the co-respondent(s) may, however, in any given case make joint submissions to the Court that responsibility for any given alleged violation should be attributed only to one of them. It should also be recalled that the Court in its judgments rules on whether there has been a violation of the Convention and not on the validity of an act of a High Contracting Party or of the legal provisions underlying the act or omission that was the subject of the complaint.

Referral to the Grand Chamber

55. Any Party may request the referral of a case to the Grand Chamber under Article 43 of the Convention; the respondent or co-respondent could therefore make such a request without the agreement of the other. Internal EU rules may, however, set out the conditions for such a request. Should a request be accepted, the Grand Chamber would re-examine the case as a whole, in respect of all alleged violations considered by the Chamber and with regard to all Parties.

Exclusion of retroactivity

56. Article 3, paragraph 8, of the Accession Agreement provides that the co-respondent mechanism applies only to applications made to the Court from the date on which the EU accedes to the Convention (that is, the date upon which the Accession Agreement comes into force). This includes applications concerning acts by EU member States based on EU law adopted before the EU became a Party to the Convention.

Prior involvement of the CJEU in cases in which the EU is a co-respondent

57. Cases in which the EU may be a co-respondent arise from individual applications concerning acts or omissions of EU member States. The applicant will first have to exhaust domestic remedies available in the national courts of the respondent member State. Those courts may or, in certain cases, must refer a question to the CJEU for a preliminary ruling on the interpretation and/or validity of an EU act at issue (Article 267 of the Treaty on the Functioning of the European Union). Since the parties to the proceedings before the national courts may only suggest such a reference, this procedure cannot be considered as a legal remedy that an applicant must exhaust before making an application to the Court. However,

without such a preliminary ruling, the Court would be required to adjudicate on the conformity of an EU act with human rights, without the CJEU having had the opportunity to do so.

58. Even though this situation is expected to arise rarely, it was considered desirable that an internal EU procedure be put in place to ensure that the CJEU has the opportunity to review the compatibility with the Convention rights at issue of the provision of EU law which has triggered the participation of the EU as a co-respondent. Such review should take place before the Court decides on the merits of the application. This procedure, which is inspired by the principle of subsidiarity, only applies in cases in which the EU has the status of a co-respondent. It is understood that the parties involved—including the applicant, who will be given the possibility to obtain legal aid—will have the opportunity to make observations in the procedure before the CJEU.

59. The CJEU will not assess the act or omission complained of by the applicant, but the EU legal basis for it.

60. The prior involvement of the CJEU will not affect the powers and jurisdiction of the Court. The assessment of the CJEU will not bind the Court.

61. The examination of the merits of the application by the Court should not resume before the parties and any third party interveners have had the opportunity to assess properly the consequences of the ruling of the CJEU. In order not to delay unduly the proceedings before the Court, the EU shall ensure that the ruling is delivered quickly. In this regard, it is noted that an accelerated procedure before the CJEU already exists and that the CJEU has been able to give rulings under that procedure within 6 to 8 months.

Article 4—Inter-Party cases

62. Once the EU is a Party to the Convention, all States Parties to the Convention will be able to bring a case against the EU and *vice versa* under Article 33 of the Convention.

63. The term "High Contracting Party" is used in the text of Article 33 of the Convention. Changing the heading to "Inter-Party cases" makes that heading correspond to the substance of Article 33 after the EU's accession. For the sake of consistency, the reference to "inter-State applications" in Article 29, paragraph 2, of the Convention is likewise adjusted.

64. An issue not governed by the Accession Agreement is whether EU law permits inter-Party applications to the Court involving issues of EU law between EU member States, or between the EU and one of its member States. In particular,

Article 344 of the Treaty on the Functioning of the European Union (to which Article 3 of Protocol No. 8 to the Treaty of Lisbon refers) states that EU member States "undertake not to submit a dispute concerning the interpretation or application of the Treaties to any method of settlement other than those provided for therein".

Article 5—Interpretation of Articles 35 and 55 of the Convention

65. This provision clarifies that, as a necessary consequence of the EU accession to the Convention, proceedings before the CJEU (currently consisting of the Court of Justice, the General Court and the Civil Service Tribunal) shall not be understood as constituting procedures of international investigation or settlement, submission to which would make an application inadmissible under Article 35, paragraph 2.*b*, of the Convention. In this respect, it should also be noted that in the recent judgment in the case of *Karoussiotis v. Portugal* (No. 23205/08; judgment of 1 February 2011) the Court specified that proceedings before the European Commission pursuant to Article 258 of the Treaty on the Functioning of the European Union shall not be understood as constituting procedures of international investigation or settlement pursuant to Article 35, paragraph 2.*b* of the Convention.

66. As regards Article 55 of the Convention, which excludes other means of dispute settlement concerning the interpretation or application of the Convention, it is the understanding of the Parties that, with respect to EU member States, proceedings before the CJEU do not constitute a "means of dispute settlement" within the meaning of Article 55 of the Convention. Therefore, Article 55 of the Convention does not prevent the operation of the rule set out in Article 344 of the Treaty on the Functioning of the European Union.

Article 6—Election of judges

67. It is agreed that a delegation of the European Parliament should be entitled to participate, with the right to vote, in the sittings of the Parliamentary Assembly of the Council of Europe (and its relevant bodies) whenever it exercises its functions related to the election of judges under Article 22 of the Convention. It was considered appropriate that the European Parliament should be entitled to the same number of representatives in the Parliamentary Assembly as the State(s) entitled to the highest number of representatives under Article 26 of the Statute of the Council of Europe.

68. Modalities for the participation of the European Parliament in the work of the Parliamentary Assembly and its relevant bodies will be defined by the Parliamentary Assembly in co-operation with the European Parliament. These modalities will be reflected in the Parliamentary Assembly's internal rules.

Discussions between the Parliamentary Assembly and the European Parliament to that effect already took place during the drafting of the Accession Agreement. It is also understood that internal EU rules will define the modalities for the selection of the list of candidates in respect of the EU to be submitted to the Parliamentary Assembly.

69. It is not necessary to amend the Convention in order to allow for the election of a judge in respect of the EU since Article 22 provides that a judge shall be elected with respect to each High Contracting Party. As laid down in Article 21, paragraphs 2 and 3, of the Convention, the judges of the Court are independent and act in their individual capacity. The judge elected in respect of the EU shall participate equally with the other judges in the work of the Court and have the same status and duties.

Article 7—Participation of the European Union in the Committee of Ministers of the Council of Europe

70. The Convention explicitly confers a number of functions upon the Committee of Ministers of the Council of Europe, the main one being the supervision of the execution of the Court's judgments under Article 46 of the Convention and of the terms of friendly settlements under Article 39 of the Convention. The Committee of Ministers is also entitled to request advisory opinions from the Court on certain legal questions concerning the interpretation of the Convention and the Protocols (Article 47 of the Convention) and to reduce, at the request of the plenary Court, the number of judges of the Chambers (Article 26, paragraph 2, of the Convention).

71. A number of questions directly linked with the functioning of the Convention system and its implementation are, however, not explicitly dealt with in the Convention itself. The Convention does not contain, for instance, provisions regarding its amendment and the adoption of additional protocols, nor does it specify all details regarding the exercise of some of the Convention-based functions indicated in the previous paragraph. It also does not deal with the adoption or the implementation of a number of other legal instruments and texts, such as recommendations, resolutions and declarations, which are directly related to the functions exercised by virtue of the Convention by the Committee of Ministers or the Parliamentary Assembly of the Council of Europe. Such legal instruments and texts may be addressed, for example, to the member States of the Council of Europe in their capacity of High Contracting Parties to the Convention, to the Committee of Ministers itself, to the Court or, where appropriate, to other relevant bodies.

72. After its accession, the EU will be allowed to participate in the Committee of Ministers, with the right to vote, when decisions on the issues mentioned above are taken. This principle is set out in Article 7, paragraph 1, of the Accession Agreement.

73. General rules for the majorities required for the decisions of the Committee of Ministers also apply, *mutatis mutandis,* to decisions mentioned under paragraph 1.*b* and *c* of Article 7. Under EU law, the EU and its member States (in total amounting to 28 out of 48 High Contracting Parties after accession) under certain circumstances are obliged to act in a coordinated manner when expressing positions and voting. This obligation to co-ordinate refers only to decisions to be taken under Articles 39 and 46 of the Convention. Therefore it is considered necessary to make specific provision about the participation of the EU in the Committee of Ministers' supervision process under Articles 39 and 46 of the Convention. Appropriate guarantees are therefore required to ensure that the combined votes of the EU and its member States will not prejudice the effective exercise by the Committee of Ministers of its supervisory functions under Articles 39 and 46 of the Convention. A general obligation to that effect appears in Article 7, paragraph 2, which also contains a number of specific provisions.

74. The introduction of these specific provisions should not be seen as a departure from the established practice that decisions in the Committee of Ministers are adopted by consensus, with formal votes only exceptionally being taken.

Supervision of obligations in cases where the EU is respondent or co-respondent

75. In the context of the supervision of the fulfilment of obligations either by the EU alone, or by the EU and one or more of its member States jointly (that is, arising from cases to which the EU has been respondent or co-respondent), it derives from the EU treaties that the EU and its member States are obliged to express positions and to vote in a co-ordinated manner. In order to ensure that such co-ordination will not prejudice the effective exercise of supervisory functions by the Committee of Ministers, it was considered necessary to introduce special voting rules. They will appear in a new rule to be included in the Rules of the Committee of Ministers for the supervision of the execution of judgments and of the terms of friendly settlements. The new voting rules will apply to all decisions in respect of obligations upon the EU alone or upon the EU and one or more of its member States jointly. As regards obligations upon only a member State of the EU, normal voting rules will continue to apply.

76. The general rule applicable to decisions by the Committee of Ministers in the supervision of the execution of judgments and of the terms of friendly settlements in cases in which the EU is a party appears under sub-paragraph *a* of the new rule. The new rule does not require the application of the majority rule set out in Article 20.*d* of the Statute of the Council of Europe. Provided that a decision appears (for instance, by an indicative vote) to be supported by a majority of the representatives entitled to sit on the Committee of Ministers on behalf of those High Contracting Parties that are not member States of the EU, the decision would be adopted without a formal vote. Such procedure would

be consistent with other procedures already in place in the Council of Europe, whereby delegations do not request the application of the voting rule prescribed by the Statute of the Council of Europe to block the adoption of a decision if it appears that a lower majority than the one prescribed in the Statute is attained. The EU and its member States will fully participate in discussions leading to the adoption of decisions.

77. The specific rule applicable to decisions by the Committee of Ministers under Rules 10 (Referral to the Court for interpretation of a judgment) and 11 (Infringement proceedings) of the Rules of the Committee of Ministers for the supervision of the execution of judgments and of the terms of friendly settlements in cases in which the EU is a party appears under sub-paragraph *b* of the new rule. It is based on the same approach set out in the preceding paragraph. However, in so far as the majority required for the adoption of decisions under Article 46, paragraphs 3 and 4, of the Convention, as reflected in Rules 10 and 11, is higher than the majority required by the Statute of the Council of Europe, the new rule also requires a higher majority. Therefore, a decision under Rules 10 and 11 shall be considered as adopted if it appears that two thirds of the representatives entitled to sit on the Committee of Ministers on behalf of those High Contracting Parties that are not member States of the EU are in favour of it.

78. The specific rule applicable to decisions by the Committee of Ministers under Rule 17 (Final resolutions) of the Rules of the Committee of Ministers for the supervision of the execution of judgments and of the terms of friendly settlements in cases to which the EU is a party appears under sub-paragraph *c* of the new rule. In the case of the adoption of final resolutions, it must be ensured that the decision has sufficient support also from the High Contracting Parties which are not member States of the EU. Therefore, it is required that in addition to the majority set out in Article 20.*d* of the Statute of the Council of Europe, a simple majority of the representatives casting a vote on behalf of those High Contracting Parties that are not member States of the EU is in favour of the final resolution.

79. These rules do not form part of the Accession Agreement, but will be submitted to the Committee of Ministers for adoption. They may therefore be amended if necessary at a later stage by the Committee of Ministers without requiring a revision of the Accession Agreement or the Convention.

Supervision of obligations in other cases against a member State of the EU

80. In the context of the supervision of the fulfilment of obligations under the Convention by one or more of the member States of the EU, the latter is precluded under the EU treaties, either for lack of competence in the area to

which the case relates or as a result of the prohibition on circumventing internal procedures, from expressing a position or exercising its right to vote. In such circumstances, the EU member States have no obligation under the EU treaties to act in a co-ordinated manner, and therefore they can each express their own position and vote.

Supervision of obligations in cases against States which are not members of the EU

81. In the context of the supervision of the fulfilment of obligations under the Convention by a State which is not a member of the EU, the EU and its member States have no obligation under the EU treaties to express a position or vote in a co-ordinated manner. The EU member States can therefore each express their own position and vote, even where the EU also expresses a position or exercises its right to vote.

Article 8—Participation of the European Union in the expenditure related to the Convention

82. According to Article 50 of the Convention, the expenditure on the Court shall be borne by the Council of Europe. After its accession to the Convention, the EU should contribute to the expenditure of the entire Convention system alongside and in addition to the other High Contracting Parties. [This contribution would be obligatory.] It is noted that under the current system the amount of the contribution of each High Contracting Party is not linked to the Court's workload in respect of that Party, but is based on the method of calculating the scales of member States' contributions to Council of Europe budgets established by the Committee of Ministers in 1994, in its Resolution Res(94)31. [The contribution would be regulated, as any other obligatory contribution, by Article 10 of the Financial Regulations of the Council of Europe, which sets out the conditions and the procedure for the payment of obligatory contributions, and which would apply *mutatis mutandis* to the EU contribution.] It is also recalled that the budgets of the Court and of the other entities involved in the functioning of the Convention system are part of the Ordinary Budget of the Council of Europe, and that the contribution of the EU would be clearly and exclusively dedicated to the financing of the Convention system. [For this reason, the contribution should be affected to a subsidiary budget.]

83. The participation of the EU in the expenditure related to the Convention system would not require any amendment to the Convention. However, the calculation method of the EU contribution needs to be defined in the Accession Agreement, which would provide the legal basis in this respect. The proposed method aims at being as simple and stable as possible and, as such, does not require the participation of the EU in the budgetary procedure of the Council

of Europe[, without prejudice to the application of the pertinent provisions (see above).]

84. The relevant expenditure taken into account is that directly related to the Convention, namely: the expenditure on the Court and on the process of supervision of the execution of its judgments and decisions, as well as on the Parliamentary Assembly, the Committee of Ministers and the Secretary General of the Council of Europe when they exercise functions under the Convention. In addition, administrative overhead costs related to the Convention system are considered (building, logistics, IT, etc.) as requiring an increase of the above expenditure by 15%. The total amount is then compared to the [total amount of the] Ordinary Budget of the Council of Europe (including the employer's contributions to pensions), in order to identify the relative weight, in percentage, of such expenditure. On the basis of the relevant figures for the last years and of those foreseen for 2012 and 2013, this percentage is fixed in paragraph 1 of Article 8 of the Accession Agreement at 34 %. [The EU contribution, which is affected to a subsidiary budget, is not taken into account for the purpose of this calculation.]

85. As to the rate of contribution of the EU to the relevant expenditure, it is agreed that it shall be identical to that of the State(s) providing the highest contribution to the Ordinary Budget of the Council of Europe for the year, pursuant to the method of calculating the scales of member States' contributions to Council of Europe budgets established by the Committee of Ministers in 1994. Accordingly, for each year (A), the amount of the contribution of the EU shall be equal to 34% of the highest amount contributed in the previous year (A-1) by any State to the Ordinary Budget of the Council of Europe (including employer's contribution to pensions).

86. In order to ensure the stability of the calculation method proposed, a safeguard clause is added in paragraph 2 of Article 8 of the Accession Agreement of the Accession Agreement to the effect that, if the actual relative weight of the expenditure related to the Convention system within the Ordinary Budget varies substantially, the percentage indicated in paragraph 1 of Article 8 (to date, 34%) shall be adapted by agreement between the EU and the Council of Europe. Such adaptation is triggered by the fact that, in each of two consecutive years, the difference between the percentage calculated on the real figures and the percentage in paragraph 1 of Article 8 is more than 2.5 percentage points (that is, if the real figure is below 31.5%, or above 36.5%). This mechanism shall obviously apply also to any new percentage resulting from subsequent agreements between the EU and the Council of Europe.

87. In addition, [, two clauses are added in order] to avoid any possible unintended effects of the safeguard clause[, and in particular. First, in order]to avoid that the EU's accession could lead to a situation in which there would be fewer

resources available to the Convention system than before the accession, it is foreseen that no account shall be taken of a change in the percentage indicated in paragraph 1 of Article 8 (34%) that results from a decrease in absolute terms of the amount dedicated within the Ordinary Budget to the functioning of the Convention as compared to the year preceding that in which the EU becomes a Party to the Convention. [In case of major changes in the equilibrium set out in the Agreement, the revision mechanism set out in the previous subparagraph would apply in order to preserve the relative level of the contribution. Second, in order to avoid an unjustified increase in the EU's contribution in the event of a decrease in absolute terms of the Ordinary Budget, combined with no change or a decrease in absolute terms of the amount dedicated within the Ordinary Budget to the functioning of the Convention, it is foreseen that no account shall be taken of a possible increase in the percentage indicated above, resulting from it.]

88. The technical and practical arrangements for the implementation of the provisions set out in the Accession Agreement will be determined in detail by the Council of Europe and the EU.

Article 9—Relations with other Agreements

89. A number of other Council of Europe conventions and agreements are strictly linked to the Convention system, even though they are self-standing treaties. It is for this reason necessary to ensure that the EU, as a Party to the Convention, respects the relevant provisions of such instruments and is, for the purpose of their application, treated as if it were a Party to them. This is the case, in particular, for the European Agreement relating to Persons Participating in Proceedings of the European Court of Human Rights (ETS No. 161), and for the Sixth Protocol to the General Agreement on Privileges and Immunities of the Council of Europe (ETS No. 162), which sets up the privileges and immunities granted to the judges of the Court during the discharge of their duties. In addition, in its accession to the Convention, the EU should also undertake to respect the privileges and immunities of other persons involved in the functioning of the Convention system, such as the staff of the Registry of the Court, members of the Parliamentary Assembly and representatives in the Committee of Ministers; these are covered by the General Agreement on Privileges and Immunities of the Council of Europe (ETS No. 2) and its first Protocol (ETS No. 10).

90. The accession of the EU to such instruments and their amendment would require a cumbersome procedure. Moreover, the system of the General Agreement on Privileges and Immunities of the Council of Europe is only open to member States of the Council of Europe. Therefore, the Accession Agreement imposes an obligation on the EU, as a Contracting Party to the Convention, to respect the relevant provisions of these instruments, and a further obligation on other Contracting Parties to treat the EU as if it were a Party to these instruments.

These provisions are accompanied by other operative provisions about the duty to consult the EU when these instruments are amended, and about the duty of the Secretary General, as depositary of these instruments, to notify the EU of relevant events occurring in the life of these instruments (such as any signature, ratification, acceptance, approval or accession, the entry into force with respect to a Party and any other act, notification or communication relating to them).

Article 10—Signature and entry into force

91. This article is one of the usual final clauses included in treaties prepared within the Council of Europe. It has been amended to provide that the Agreement should be open only to the High Contracting Parties to the Convention at the date of its opening for signature and to the EU.

92. Should any State become a member of the Council of Europe, and consequently a High Contracting Party to the Convention, between the opening for signature of this Accession Agreement and the date of its entry into force, that State will be required as part of its commitments for the accession to the Council of Europe to give an unequivocal binding statement of its acceptance of the provisions of this Agreement. The Committee of Ministers' resolution inviting that State to become a member of the Council of Europe shall contain a condition to that effect.

93. Should any State become a member of the Council of Europe and a High Contracting Party to the Convention after the entry into force of this Agreement, it will be bound by those provisions of the Agreement which have legal effects beyond the mere amendment of the Convention; this is ensured by the new Article 59, paragraph 2.*b*, of the Convention, which creates an explicit link between the Convention and the Accession Agreement.

Article 11—Reservations

94. It is agreed that no reservations to the Agreement itself shall be allowed. This is without prejudice to the possibility for the EU to make reservations to the Convention, as provided for by Article 2.

Article 12—Notifications

95. This article contains one of the usual final clauses included in treaties prepared within the Council of Europe.

Bibliography and References

I. BOOKS AND JOURNAL ARTICLES

Akehurst, M, 'Custom as a Source of International Law' (1974/1975) 47 *British Yearbook of International Law* 1.

Alber, S and Widmaier, U, 'Die EU-Charta der Grundrechte und ihre Auswirkungen auf die Rechtsprechung' (2000) 27 *Europäische Grundrechte-Zeitschrift* 497.

Alston, P, Bustelo, M and Heenan, J (eds), *The EU and Human Rights* (Oxford, Oxford University Press, 1999).

—— and Tomaševski, K (eds), *The Right to Food* (The Hague, Kluwer Law, 1984).

—— and Weiler, JHH, 'The European Union and Human Rights: Final Project Report on an Agenda for the Year 2000' in A Cassese (ed), *Leading by Example: A Human Rights Agenda for the European Union for the Year 2000* (Florence, European University Institute, 1998).

—— and Weiler, JHH, 'An 'Ever Closer Union' in Need of a Human Rights Policy: The European Union and Human Rights' in P Alston, M Bustelo and J Heenan (eds), *The EU and Human Rights* (Oxford, Oxford University Press, 1999).

Ambos, K, 'Der europäische Gerichtshof für Menschenrechte und die Verfahrensrechte: Waffengleichheit, partizipatorisches Vorverfahren und Art. 6 EMRK' (2003) 115 *Zeitschrift für die Gesamte Strafrechtswissenschaft* 583.

Amerasinghe, CF, *Jurisdiction of International Tribunals* (Leiden, Brill, 2003).

Anderson, DWK, *References to the European Court* (London, Sweet & Maxwell, 1995).

Arai-Takahashi, Y, *The Margin of Appreciation Doctrine and the Principle of Proportionality in the Jurisprudence of the ECHR* (Antwerp, Intersentia, 2002).

von Arnauld, A, 'Normenhierarchien innerhalb des primären Gemeinschaftsrechts. Gedanken im Prozess der Konstitutionalisierung Europas' (2003) 38 *Europarecht* 191.

Arnull, A, *The European Union and its Court of Justice*, 2nd edn (New York, McGraw-Hill Books, 2006).

Balthasar, S, 'Locus Standi Rules for Challenges to Regulatory Acts by Private Applicants: The New Article 263 (4) TFEU' (2010) 355 *European Law Review* 542.

Barents R, *The Autonomy of Community Law* (The Hague, Kluwer Law, 2004).

Barnard C, 'The PPU: Is it Worth the Candle?' (2009) 34 *European Law Review* 281.

Bast, J (ed), *Die Europäische Verfassung—Verfassungen in Europa* (Baden-Baden, Nomos, 2005).

—— 'Handlungsformen und Rechtsschutz' in A von Bogdandy and J Bast (eds), *Europäisches Verfassungsrecht. Theoretische und dogmatische Grundzüge* (Berlin Heidelberg, Springer, 2009).

Baudenbacher, C, Tresselt, P and Örlygsson, T (eds), *The EFTA Court. Ten Years On* (Oxford, Hart Publishing, 2005).

Bauer, L, *Der Europäische Gerichtshof als Verfassungsgericht?* (Vienna, Facultas, 2008).

Baumann, J, 'Auf dem Weg zu einem doppelten EMRK-Schutzstandard? Die Fortschreibung der Bosphorus-Rechtsprechung des EGMR im Fall Nederlandse Kokkelvisserij' (2011) 38 *Europäische Grundrechte-Zeitschrift* 1.

Baumgartner, G, 'EMRK und Gemeinschaftsrecht' [1996] *Zeitschrift für Verwaltung* 319.

Benedek, W, 'EU Action on Human and Fundamental Rights in 2010' in W Benedek, F Benoît-Rohmer, W Karl and M Nowak (eds), *European Yearbook on Human Rights 2011* (Vienna, NWV, 2011).

——, Benoît-Rohmer, F, Karl, W and Nowak, M (eds), *European Yearbook on Human Rights 2010* (Vienna, NWV, 2010).

—— *European Yearbook on Human Rights 2011* (Vienna, NWV, 2011).

Benoît-Rohmer, F, 'Completing the Transformation: Values and Fundamental Rights in the Treaty of Lisbon' in W Benedek, F Benoît-Rohmer, W Karl and M Nowak (eds), *European Yearbook on Human Rights 2010* (Vienna, NWV, 2010).

Berger, M, 'Der Beitritt der Europäischen Union zur EMRK' in *Österreichische Juristenkommission* (ed), *Grundrechte im Europa der Zukunft* (Vienna, Linde, 2010).

Berka, W, 'EU-Recht und EMRK' in W Schroeder (ed), *Europarecht als Mehrebenensystem* (Baden-Baden, Nomos, 2008).

Bernhardt, R, 'Probleme eines Beitritts der Europäischen Gemeinschaft zur Europäischen Menschenrechts-Konvention' in O Due, M Lutter and J Schwarze (eds), *Festschrift für Ulrich Everling. Band I* (Baden-Baden, Nomos, 1995).

Beyerlin, U (ed), *Recht zwischen Umbruch und Bewahrung. Völkerrecht, Europarecht, Staatsrecht, Festschrift für Rudolf Bernhardt* (Berlin Heidelberg, Springer, 1995).

Biehler, G, *Procedures in International Law* (Berlin Heidelberg, Springer, 2008).

Björklund, M, 'Responsibility in the EC for Mixed Agreements—Should Non-Member Parties Care?' (2001) 70 *Nordic Journal of International Law* 373.

von Bogdandy, A and Bast, J (eds), *Europäisches Verfassungsrecht. Theoretische und dogmatische Grundzüge* (Berlin Heidelberg, Springer, 2009).

——, Bast, J and Arndt, F, 'Handlungsformen im Unionsrecht. Empirische Analysen und dogmatische Strukturen in einem vermeintlichen Dschungel' (2002) 62 *Zeitschrift für ausländisches öffentliches Recht und Völkerrecht* 77.

Borraccetti, M, 'Fair Trial, Due Process and Rights of Defence in the EU Legal Order' in G Di Federico (ed), *The EU Charter of Fundamental Rights. From Declaration to Binding Document* (Dordrecht, Springer Netherlands, 2011).

Blackburn, R and Polakiewicz, J (eds), *Fundamental Rights in Europe. The ECHR and its Member States, 1950–2000* (Oxford, Oxford University Press, 2001).

Brandtner, B, 'The "Drama" of the EEA. Comments on Opinions 1/91 and 1/92' (1992) 3 *European Journal of International Law* 300.

Broberg, M and Fenger, N, *Preliminary References to the European Court of Justice* (Oxford, Oxford University Press, 2010).

Bröhmer, J, 'Die Bosphorus-Entscheidung des Europäischen Gerichtshofs für Menschenrechte' (2006) 17 *Europäische Zeitschrift für Wirtschaftsrecht* 71.

Bronckers, M, 'The Relationship of the EC Courts with other International Tribunals: Non-Committal, Respectful or Submissive?' (2007) 44 *Common Market Law Review* 601.

Brown, C, 'The Proliferation of International Courts and Tribunals: Finding Your Way Through the Maze' (2002) 3 *Melbourne Journal of International Law* 453.

Brownlie, I, *Principles of Public International Law*, 6th edn (Oxford, Oxford University Press, 2003).

Buffard, I, Crawford, J, Pellet, A and Wittich, S (eds), *International Law between Universalism and Fragmentation. Festschrift in Honour of Gerhard Hafner* (Leiden, Brill, 2008).

Busse, C, 'Die Geltung der EMRK für Rechtsakte der EU' (2000) 53 *Neue Juristische Wochenschrift* 1074.

Calliess, C and Ruffert, M (eds), *EUV/AEUV. Kommentar*, 4th edn (Munich, Beck, 2011).

Cannizzaro, E (ed), *The Law of Treaties Beyond the Vienna Convention* (Oxford, Oxford University Press, 2011).

Canor, I, 'Primus inter pares. Who is the Ultimate Guardian of Fundamental Rights in Europe?' (2000) 25 *European Law Review* 1.

Cassese, A (ed), *Leading by Example: A Human Rights Agenda for the European Union for the Year 2000* (Florence, European University Institute, 1998).

Churchill, R and Scott, J, 'The *MOX Plant* Litigation: The First Half-Life' (2004) 53 *International and Comparative Law Quarterly* 643.

Clapham, A, 'Where is the EU's Human Rights Common Foreign Policy, and How is it Manifested in Multilateral Fora?' in P Alston, M Bustelo and J Heenan (eds), *The EU and Human Rights* (Oxford, Oxford University Press, 1999).

Coppel, J and O'Neill, A, 'The European Court of Justice: Taking Rights Seriously?' (1992) 29 *Common Market Law Review* 669.

Council of Europe, *Collected edition* of the 'Travaux préparatoires' *of the European Convention on Human Rights*, Vol 3. Committee of Experts (2 February–10 March 1950) (Leiden, Brill, 1976).

—— *Collected edition* of the 'Travaux préparatoires' *of the European Convention on Human Rights*, Vol 5. Legal Committee, Ad hoc Joint Committee, Committee of Ministers, Consultative Assembly (23 June–28 August 1950) (Leiden, Brill, 1979).

Craig, P, *The Lisbon Treaty. Law, Politics, and Treaty Reform* (Oxford, Oxford University Press, 2010).

——'The Classics of EU Law Revisited: CILFIT and Foto-Frost' in MP Maduro and L Azoulai (eds), *The Past and Future of EU Law. The Classics of EU Law Revisited on the 50th Anniversary of the Rome Treaty* (Oxford, Hart Publishing, 2010).

—— and De Búrca, G, *EU Law. Text, Cases and Materials*, 5th edn (Oxford, Oxford University Press, 2011).

Cremer, H, 'Entscheidung und Entscheidungswirkung' in R Grote and T Marauhn (eds), *EMRK/GG: Konkordanzkommentar zum europäischen und deutschen Grundrechtsschutz* (Tübingen, Mohr Siebeck, 2006).

Cremer, W, 'Der Rechtsschutz des Einzelnen gegen Sekundärrechtsakte der Union gem. Art. III-270 IV Konventsentwurf des Vertrags über eine Verfassung für Europa' (2004) 31 *Europäische Grundrechte-Zeitschrift* 577.

—— 'Gemeinschaftsrecht und Deutsches Verwaltungsprozessrecht—Zum dezentralen Rechtsschutz gegenüber EG-Sekundärrecht' (2004) 37 *Die Verwaltung* 165.

Cremona, M, 'The Draft Constitutional Treaty: External Relations and External Action' (2003) 40 *Common Market Law Review* 1347.

Czerner, F, 'Inter partes- versus erga omnes-Wirkung der EGMR-Judikate in den Konventionsstaaten gemäß Art. 46 EMRK' (2008) 46 *Archiv des Völkerrechts* 345.

Da Cruz Vilaça, JL and Piçarra, N, 'Y a-t-il des limites matérielles à la révision des Traités instituant les Communautés européennes?' (1993) 29 *Cahiers de Droit Européen* 3.

von Danwitz, T, *Europäisches Verwaltungsrecht* (Berlin Heidelberg, Springer, 2008).

D'Aspremont, J and Dopagne, F, '*Kadi*: The CJEU's Reminder of the Elementary Divide between Legal Orders' (2008) 5 *International Organizations Law Review* 317.

Dauses, M, 'Braucht die Europäische Union eine Grundrechtsbeschwerde?' (2008) 19 *Europäische Zeitschrift für Wirtschaftsrecht* 449.

De Búrca, G, 'The Road Not Taken: The European Union as a Global Human Rights Actor' (2011) 105 *American Journal of International Law* 649.

De La Serre, EB, 'Accelerated and Expedited Procedures before the EC Courts: A Review of the Practice' (2006) 43 *Common Market Law Review* 783.

Delmas-Marty, M, *Towards a Truly Common Law. Europe as a Laboratory for Legal Pluralism* (Cambridge, Cambridge University Press, 2002).

De Schutter, O, 'Art 52—Portée des droits garantis' in EU Network of Independent Experts on Fundamental Rights, *Commentary of the Charter of Fundamental Rights of the European Union* (2006).

—— 'Art 53—Niveau de protection' in EU Network of Independent Experts on Fundamental Rights, *Commentary of the Charter of Fundamental Rights of the European Union* (2006).

De Witte, B, 'European Union Law: How Autonomous is its Legal Order?' (2010) 65 *Zeitschrift für Öffentliches Recht* 141.

Dickens, C, *A Tale of Two Cities* (first published 1859; London, Penguin 2012).

Di Federico, G (ed), *The EU Charter of Fundamental Rights. From Declaration to Binding Document* (Dordrecht, Springer Netherlands, 2011).

—— 'Fundamental Rights in the EU: Legal Pluralism and Multi-Level Protection after the Lisbon Treaty' in G Di Federico (ed), *The EU Charter of Fundamental Rights. From Declaration to Binding Document* (Dordrecht, Springer Netherlands, 2011).

van Dijk, P, van Hoof, F, van Rijn, A and Zwaak, L (eds), *Theory and Practice of the European Convention on Human* Rights, 4th edn (Antwerp Oxford, Intersentia, 2006).

Dörr, O and Lenz, C, *Europäischer Verwaltungsrechtsschutz* (Baden-Baden, Nomos, 2006).

—— and Schmalenbach, K (eds), *Vienna Convention on the Law of Treaties. A Commentary* (Berlin Heidelberg, Springer, 2012).

Douglas-Scott, S, 'A Tale of Two Courts: Luxembourg, Strasbourg and the Growing European Human Rights *Acquis*' (2006) 43 *Common Market Law Review* 629.

Due, O, Lutter, M and Schwarze, J (eds), *Festschrift für Ulrich Everling. Band I* (Baden-Baden, Nomos, 1995).

Economidès, C and Kolliopoulos, A, 'La clause de déconnexion en faveur du droit communautaire: Une pratique critiquable' (2006) 110 *Revue Générale de Droit International Public* 273.

Edward, D, '*CILFIT* and *Foto-Frost* in their Historical and Procedural Context' in MP Maduro and L Azoulai L (eds), *The Past and Future of EU Law. The Classics of EU Law Revisited on the 50th Anniversary of the Rome Treaty* (Oxford, Hart Publishing, 2010).

Eeckhout, P, *External Relations of the European Union. Legal and Constitutional Foundations* (Oxford, Oxford University Press, 2005).

—— *EU External Relations Law* (Oxford, Oxford University Press, 2011).

Ehlers, D (ed), *Europäische Grundrechte und Grundfreiheiten* (Berlin, De Gruyter, 2009).

—— 'Allgemeine Lehren der EMRK' in D Ehlers (ed), *Europäische Grundrechte und Grundfreiheiten* (Berlin, De Gruyter, 2009).

EU Network of Independent Experts on Fundamental Rights, *Commentary of the Charter of Fundamental Rights of the European Union* (2006).

Everling, U, 'Durch die Grundrechtecharta zurück zu Solange I?' (2003) 14 *Europäische Zeitschrift für Wirtschaftsrecht* 225.

—— 'Lissabon-Vertrag regelt Dauerstreit über Nichtigkeitsklage Privater' (2010) 21 *Europäische Zeitschrift für Wirtschaftsrecht* 572.

Fassbender, B, 'The United Nations Charter as Constitution of the International Community' (1998) 36 *Columbia Journal of Transnational Law* 531.

—— 'Die Völkerrechtssubjektivität der Europäischen Union nach dem Entwurf des Verfassungsvertrages' (2004) 42 *Archiv des Völkerrechts* 26.

Fennelly, N, 'The European Court of Justice and the Doctrine of Supremacy: Van Gend en Loos; Costa v ENEL; Simmenthal' in MP Maduro and L Azoulai (eds), *The Past and Future of EU Law. The Classics of EU Law Revisited on the 50th Anniversary of the Rome Treaty* (Oxford, Hart Publishing, 2010).

Frenz, W, *Handbuch Europarecht. Band 4: Europäische Grundrechte* (Berlin Heidelberg, Springer, 2009).

—— *Handbuch Europarecht. Band 5: Wirkungen und Rechtsschutz* (Berlin Heidelberg, Springer, 2010).

Frowein, J and Peukert, W (eds), *EMRK-Kommentar* (Kehl am Rhein, NP Engel, 2009).

Frühwirth, R and Stern, J, 'Vorabentscheidungsverfahren und einstweiliger Rechtsschutz. Zur Pflicht, Abschiebungen nach Griechenland im Rahmen der Dublin II-VO auszusetzen' (2010) 22 *juridikum* 274.

Funk, B (ed), *Der Rechtsstaat vor neuen Herausforderungen: Festschrift für Ludwig Adamovich zum 70. Geburtstag* (Vienna, Verlag Österreich, 2002).

Galetta, D, *Procedural Autonomy of EU Member States: Paradise Lost?* (Berlin Heidelberg, Springer, 2010).

García, RA, 'The General Provisions of the Charter of Fundamental Rights of the European Union' (2002) 8 *European Law Journal* 492.

Geiger, R, Kahn, D and Kotzur M (eds), *EUV/AEUV. Kommentar*, 5th edn (Munich, Beck, 2010).

van Gerven, W, 'Remedies for Infringements of Fundamental Rights' (2004) 10 *European Public Law* 261.

Grabenwarter, C, *Europäische Menschenrechtskonvention*, 4th edn (Munich, Beck, 2009).

—— 'Die Grundrechte im Verfassungsvertrag der Europäischen Union' in S Hammer, A Somek, M Stelzer and B Weichselbaum (eds), *Demokratie und sozialer Rechtsstaat in Europa, Festschrift für Theo Öhlinger* (Viennam, WUV, 2004).

—— and Thienel, R (eds), *Kontinuität und Wandel der EMRK. Studien zur Europäischen Menschenrechtskonvention* (Kehl am Rhein, NP Engel, 1998).

Grabitz, E, Hilf, M and Nettesheim, M (eds), *Das Recht der Europäischen Union. Band I* (Munich, Beck 2010).

Gragl, P, 'Accession Revisited: Will Fundamental Rights Protection Trump the European Union's Legal Autonomy' in W Benedek, F Benoît-Rohmer, W Karl and M Nowak (eds), *European Yearbook on Human Rights 2011* (Vienna, NWV, 2011).

—— 'Anwendungsbereich und Tragweite der Europäischen Grundrechte' (2011/2012) 22 *Juristische Ausbildung und Praxisvorbereitung* 47.

—— 'Der rechtliche Status der EMRK innerhalb des Unionsrechts—Zu den Auswirkungen auf die Rechtsautonomie der Europäischen Union nach ihrem Beitritt zur EMRK' (2011) 14 *Zeitschrift für Europarechtliche Studien* 409.

Grote, R and Marauhn, T (eds), *EMRK/GG: Konkordanzkommentar zum europäischen und deutschen Grundrechtsschutz* (Tübingen, Mohr Siebeck, 2006).

Groussot, X, Lock, T and Pech, L, 'EU Accession to the European Convention on Human Rights: A Legal Assessment of the Draft Accession Agreement of 14th October 2011' [2011] *Fondation Robert Schuman—European Issues* No 218, 1.

Guckelberger, A, 'Das Petitionsrecht zum Europäischen Parlament sowie das Recht zur Anrufung des Europäischen Bürgerbeauftragten im Europa der Bürger' (2003) 56 *Die öffentliche Verwaltung* 829.

Härtel, I, *Handbuch Europäische Rechtsetzung* (Berlin Heidelberg, Springer 2006).

Hakenberg, W and Stix-Hackl, C, *Handbuch zum Verfahren vor dem Europäischen Gerichtshof* (Vienna, Verlag Österreich, 2005).

Hammer, S, Somek, A, Stelzer, M and Weichselbaum, B (eds), *Demokratie und sozialer Rechtsstaat in Europa, Festschrift für Theo Öhlinger* (Vienna, WUV, 2004).

Haratsch, A, 'Die *Solange*-Rechtsprechung des Europäischen Gerichtshofs für Menschenrechte. Das Kooperationsverhältnis zwischen EGMR und EuGH' (2006) 66 *Zeitschrift für ausländisches öffentliches Recht und Völkerrecht* 927.

—— 'Der kooperative Grundrechtsschutz in der Europäischen Union' in A Haratsch and P Schiffauer (eds), *Grundrechtsschutz in der Europäischen Union* (Berlin, BWV, 2007).

—— and Schiffauer, P (eds), *Grundrechtsschutz in der Europäischen Union* (Berlin, BWV, 2007).

Harpaz, G, 'The European Court of Justice and its Relations with the European Court of Human Rights: The Quest for Enhanced Reliance, Coherence and Legitimacy' (2009) 46 *Common Market Law Review* 105.

Harris, D, O'Boyle, M, Bates, E and Buckley, C (eds), *Law of the European Convention on Human Rights*, 2nd edn (Oxford, Oxford University Press, 2009).

Hartley, TC, 'The European Court and the EEA' (1992) 41 *International and Comparative Law Quarterly* 841.

—— 'International law and the Law of the European Union—A Reassessment' (2001) 72 *British Yearbook of International Law* 1.

Heer-Reißmann, C, *Die Letztentscheidungskompetenz des Europäischen Gerichtshofs für Menschenrechte in Europa* (Frankfurt am Main, Peter Lang, 2007).

Heißl, G, 'Happy End einer unendlichen Geschichte? Der Beitritt der EU zur EMRK und seine Auswirkungen auf Österreich' in M Holoubek, A Martin and S Schwarzer (eds), *Die Zukunft der Verfassung—Die Verfassung der Zukunft? Festschrift für Karl Korinek zum 70. Geburtstag* (Vienna New York, Springer, 2010).

Helfer, L and Slaughter, A, 'Toward a Theory of Effective Supranational Adjudication' (1997) 107 *Yale Law Journal* 273.

Heliskoski, J, *Mixed Agreements as a Technique for Organising the International Relations of the European Community and its Member States* (The Hague, Kluwer Law, 2001).

Hendler, R, Ibler, M and Martínez Soria, J (eds), *Für Sicherheit, für Europa. Festschrift für Volkmar Götz* (Göttingen, Vandenhoeck & Ruprecht, 2005).

Hillion, C, '*ERTA, ECHR* and *Open Skies*: Laying the Grounds of the EU System of External Relations' in MP Maduro and L Azoulai (eds), *The Past and Future of EU Law. The Classics of EU Law Revisited on the 50th Anniversary of the Rome Treaty* (Oxford, Hart Publishing, 2010).

Holoubek, M, Martin, A and Schwarzer, S (eds), *Die Zukunft der Verfassung—Die Verfassung der Zukunft? Festschrift für Karl Korinek zum 70. Geburtstag* (Vienna New York, Springer, 2010).

Holzinger, K, *EMRK und internationale Organisationen* (Baden-Baden, Nomos, 2010).

van Hoof, GJH, 'The Legal Nature of Economic, Social and Cultural Rights: A Rebuttal of Some Traditional Views' in P Alston and K Tomaševski K (eds), *The Right to Food* (The Hague, Kluwer Law, 1984).

Ibing, S, *Die Einschränkung der Europäischen Grundrechte durch Gemeinschaftsrecht* (Baden-Baden, Nomos, 2006).

Jacobs, FG, 'Judicial Dialogue and the Cross-Fertilization of Legal Systems: The European Court of Justice' (2003) 38 *Texas International Law Journal* 547.

Jacqué, J, 'The Accession of the European Union to the European Convention on Human Rights and Fundamental Freedoms' (2011) 48 *Common Market Law Review* 995.

—— 'L'adhésion de l'Union européenne à la Convention européenne des droits de l'homme et des libertés fondamentales' in W Benedek, F Benoît-Rohmer, W Karl and M Nowak (eds), *European Yearbook on Human Rights 2011* (Vienna, NWV, 2011).

Janik, C, 'Die EMRK und Internationale Organisationen. Ausdehung und Restriktion der *equivalent protection*-Formel in der neuen Rechtsprechung des EGMR' (2010) 70 *Zeitschrift für ausländisches öffentliches Recht und Völkerrecht* 127.

Jarass, HD, *Charta der Grundrechte der Europäischen Union. Kommentar* (Munich, Beck, 2010).

Kant, I, *Grundlegung zur Metaphysik der Sitten* (first published 1785; Berlin, Walter de Gruyter Akademie-Ausgabe, 1900).

Keller, H, Fischer, A and Kühne, D, 'Debating the Future of the European Court of Human Rights after the Interlaken Conference: Two Innovative Proposals' (2010) 21 *European Journal of International Law* 1025.

Klabbers, J, *Treaty Conflict and the European Union* (Cambridge, Cambridge University Press, 2009).

—— Peters, A and Ulfstein, G (eds), *The Constitutionalization of International Law* (Oxford, University Press, 2011).

Klein, E, 'Das Verhältnis des Europäischen Gerichtshofs zum Europäischen Gerichtshof für Menschenrechte' in D Merten and J Papier (eds), *Handbuch der Grundrechte in Deutschland und Europa. Band VI/1, Europäische Grundrechte I* (Heidelberg, CF Müller, 2010).

Klein, N, *Dispute Settlement in the UN Convention on the Law of the Sea* (Cambridge, Cambridge University Press, 2005).

Klein, O, 'Straßburger Wolken am Karlsruher Himmel. Zum geänderten Verhältnis zwischen Bundesverfassungsgericht und Europäischem Gerichtshof für Menschenrechte seit 1998' (2010) 29 *Neue Zeitschrift für Verwaltungsrecht* 221.

Köngeter, M, 'Völkerrechtliche und innerstaatliche Probleme eines Beitritts der Europäischen Union zur EMRK' in J Bast (ed), *Die Europäische Verfassung—Verfassungen in Europa* (Baden-Baden, Nomos, 2005).

Kokott, J, Dervisopoulos, I and Henze, T, 'Aktuelle Fragen des effektiven Rechtsschutzes durch die Gemeinschaftsgerichte' (2008) 35 *Europäische Grundrechte-Zeitschrift* 10.

—— Henze, T and Sobotta, C, 'Die Pflicht zur Vorlage an den Europäischen Gerichtshof und die Folgen ihrer Verletzung' (2006) 61 *Juristen-Zeitung* 633.

—— and Sobotta, C, 'The Charter of Fundamental Rights of the EU after Lisbon' [2010] *EUI Working Papers, Academy of European Law* 1.

Koskenniemi, M, 'International Law: Constitutionalism, Managerialism and the Ethos of Legal Education' (2007) 1 *European Journal of Legal Studies* 1.

Krüger, HC, 'Reflections Concerning Accession of the European Communities to the European Convention on Human Rights' (2002) 21 *Penn State International Law Review* 89.

—— and Polakiewicz, J, 'Vorschläge für ein kohärentes System des Menschenrechtsschutzes in Europa' (2001) 28 *Europäische Grundrechte-Zeitschrift* 92

Kühling, J, 'Grundrechte' in A von Bogdandy and J Bast (eds), *Europäisches Verfassungsrecht. Theoretische und dogmatische Grundzüge* (Berlin Heidelberg, Springer, 2009).

Kuijper, PJ, 'The European Courts and the Law of Treaties: The Continuing Story' in E Cannizzaro (ed), *The Law of Treaties Beyond the Vienna Convention* (Oxford, Oxford University Press, 2011).

Kumin, AJ, 'Die Verhandlungsvorbereitungen für den Beitritt der Europäischen Union zur Europäischen Menschenrechtskonvention—Ein Erfahrungsbericht' in S Stadlmeier (ed),

Von Lissabon zum Raumfahrzeug: Aktuelle Herausforderungen im Völkerrecht. Beiträge zum 35. Österreichischen Völkerrechtstag (Vienna, NWV, 2011).

Lavranos, N, 'Das Rechtsprechungsmonopol des EuGH im Lichte der Proliferation internationaler Gerichte' (2007) 42 *Europarecht* 440.

—— 'Judicial Review of UN Sanctions by the European Court of Justice' (2009) 78 *Nordic Journal of International Law* 343.

—— *Jurisdictional Competition. Selected Cases in International and European Law* (Groningen, Europa Law Publishing, 2009).

—— 'The MOX Plant and IJzeren Rijn Disputes: Which Court Is the Supreme Arbiter?' (2006) 19 *Leiden Journal of International Law* 223.

—— 'The Scope of Exclusive Jurisdiction of the Court of Justice' (2007) 32 *European Law Review* 83.

Lawson, R, 'Confusion and Conflict? Diverging Interpretations of the European Convention on Human Rights in Strasbourg and Luxembourg' in R Lawson and M De Bois (eds), *The Dynamics of the Protection of Human Rights in Europe: Essays in Honour of Henry G. Schermers, Vol. 3* (Leiden, Martinus Nijhoff, 1994).

—— and De Bois, M (eds), *The Dynamics of the Protection of Human Rights in Europe: Essays in Honour of Henry G. Schermers, Vol. 3* (Leiden, Martinus Nijhoff, 1994).

Lebeck, C, 'The European Court of Human Rights on the Relation between ECHR and EC-Law: The Limits of Constitutionalisation of Public International Law' (2007) 62 *Zeitschrift für Öffentliches Recht* 195.

Lenaerts, K, Arts, D, Maselis, I and Bray, R, *Procedural Law of the European Union*, 2nd edn (London, Sweet & Maxwell, 2006).

—— and De Smijter, E, 'A "Bill of Rights" for the European Union' (2001) 38 *Common Market Law Review* 273.

—— and De Smijter, E, 'The Charter and the Role of the European Courts' (2001) 8 *Maastricht Journal of European and Comparative Law* 90.

Liisberg, JB, 'Does the EU Charter of Fundamental Rights Threaten the Supremacy of Community Law? Article 53 of the Charter: A Fountain of Law or Just an Inkblot?' (2001) 38 *Common Market Law Review* 1171.

Lindner, JF, 'Fortschritte und Defizite im EU-Grundrechtsschutz—Plädoyer für eine Optimierung der Europäischen Grundrechtecharta' (2007) 40 *Zeitschrift für Rechtspolitik* 54.

Lock, T, 'Beyond *Bosphorus*: The European Court of Human Rights' Case Law on the Responsibility of Member States of International Organisations under the European Convention on Human Rights' (2010) 10 *Human Rights Law Review* 529.

—— *Das Verhältnis zwischen dem EuGH und internationalen Gerichten* (Tübingen, Mohr Siebeck, 2010).

—— 'EU Accession to the ECHR: Implications for Judicial Review in Strasbourg' (2010) 35 *European Law Review* 777.

—— 'The ECJ and the ECtHR: The Future Relationship between the Two European Courts' (2009) 8 *The Law and Practice of International Courts and Tribunals* 375.

—— 'Walking on a Tightrope: The Draft Accession Agreement and the Autonomy of the EU Legal Order' (2011) 48 *Common Market Law Review* 1025.

Ludwigs, M, 'Die Kompetenzordnung der Europäischen Union im Vertragsentwurf über eine Verfassung für Europa' (2004) 7 *Zeitschrift für Europarechtliche Studien* 211.

Maduro, MP and Azoulai, L (eds), *The Past and Future of EU Law. The Classics of EU Law Revisited on the 50th Anniversary of the Rome Treaty* (Oxford, Hart Publishing, 2010).

Malferrari, L, *Zurückweisung von Vorabentscheidungsersuchen durch den EuGH* (Baden-Baden, Nomos, 2003).

Manin, P, 'L'Adhésion de l'Union Européenne à la Convention de sauvegarde des droits de l'homme et des libertés fondamentales' in LS Rossi (ed), *Vers une nouvelle architecture de l'Union européenne: Le Projet de Traité-Constitution* (Brussels, Emile Bruylant, 2004).

Manzini, P, 'The Priority of Pre-Existing Treaties of EC Member States within the Framework of International Law' (2001) 12 *European Journal of International Law* 781.

Markard, N, 'Die "Rule 39" des Europäischen Gerichtshofs für Menschenrechte. Vorläufige Maßnahmen des EGMR bei drohenden Abschiebungen' [2012] *Asylmagazin* 3.

Marsch, N, Sanders, A, 'Gibt es ein Recht der Parteien auf Stellungnahme zu den Schlussanträgen des Generalanwalts? Zur Vereinbarkeit des Verfahrens vor dem EuGH mit Art. 6 I EMRK' (2008) 43 *Europarecht* 345.

Marschik, A, *Subsysteme im Völkerrecht. Ist die Europäische Union ein 'Self-Contained Regime'?* (Berlin, Duncker & Humblot, 1997).

Matscher, F, 'Kollektive Garantie der Grundrechte und die Staatenbeschwerde nach der EMRK' in B Funk (ed), *Der Rechtsstaat vor neuen Herausforderungen: Festschrift für Ludwig Adamovich zum 70. Geburtstag* (Vienna, Verlag Österreich, 2002).

Mayer, FC, 'Verfassungsgerichtsbarkeit' in A von Bogdandy and J Bast (eds), *Europäisches Verfassungsrecht. Theoretische und dogmatische Grundzüge* (Berlin Heidelberg, Springer, 2009).

Mayer, H (ed), *EUV/AEUV Kommentar* (Vienna, Manz, 2010).

Meier, G, 'Zur Einwirkung des Gemeinschaftsrechts auf nationales Verfahrensrecht im Falle höchstrichterlicher Vertragsverletzungen' (1991) 2 *Europäische Zeitschrift für Wirtschaftsrecht* 11.

Merten, D and Papier, J (eds), *Handbuch der Grundrechte in Deutschland und Europa. Band VI/1, Europäische Grundrechte I* (Heidelberg, CF Müller, 2010).

Meyer, J (ed), *Charta der Grundrechte der Europäischen Union* (Baden-Baden, Nomos, 2010).

Meyer-Ladewig, J, *Europäische Menschenrechtskonvention*. Handkommentar, 3rd edn (Baden-Baden, Nomos, 2011).

Moore, JB (ed), *History and Digest of the International Arbitrations to which the United States has been a Party—Vol. 1* (Washington, 1898).

Naômé, C, *Le renvoi préjudiciel en droit européen. Guide pratique* (Brussels, Larcier, 2010).

Nettesheim, M, 'Die Kompetenzordnung im Vertrag über eine Verfassung für Europa' (2004) 39 *Europarecht* 511.

Niedobitek, M, 'Entwicklung und allgemeine Grundsätze' in D Merten and J Papier (eds), *Handbuch der Grundrechte in Deutschland und Europa. Band VI/1, Europäische Grundrechte I* (Heidelberg, CF Müller, 2010).

Österreichische Juristenkommission (ed), *Grundrechte im Europa der Zukunft* (Vienna, Linde, 2010).

Okresek, W, 'Die Umsetzung der EGMR-Urteile und ihre Überwachung' (2003) 30 *Europäische Grundrechte-Zeitschrift* 168.

O'Leary, S, 'Current Topic: Accession by the European Community to the European Convention on Human Rights—The Opinion of the CJEU' [1996] *European Human Rights Law Review* 362.

O'Meara, N, '"A More Secure Europe of Rights?" The European Court of Human Rights, the Court of Justice of the European Union and EU Accession to the ECHR' (2011) 12 *German Law Journal* 1813.

Pechstein, M, 'Die Justitiabilität des Unionsrechts' (1999) 34 *Europarecht* 13.

Pernice, I, 'Kompetenzabgrenzung im Europäischen Verfassungsverbund' (2000) 55 *Juristen-Zeitung* 866.

Peters, A, *Elemente einer Theorie der Verfassung Europas* (Berlin, Duncker & Humblot, 2001).

Petzold, HA, *Individualrechtsschutz an der Schnittstelle zwischen deutschem und Gemeinschaftsrecht. Zugleich ein Beitrag zur Interpretation von Art. III-365 Abs. 4 VerfV* (Baden-Baden, Nomos, 2008).

Philippi, N, 'Divergenzen im Grundrechtsschutz zwischen EuGH und EGMR' (2000) 3 *Zeitschrift für Europarechtliche Studien* 97.

Piedimonte Bodini, S, 'Fighting Maritime Piracy under the European Convention on Human Rights' (2011) 22 *European Journal of International Law* 829.

Polakiewicz, P, 'The Status of the Convention in National Law' in R Blackburn and J Polakiewicz (eds), *Fundamental Rights in Europe. The ECHR and its Member States, 1950–2000* (Oxford, Oxford University Press, 2001).

Posch, A, 'The *Kadi* Case: Rethinking the Relationship Between EU Law and International Law?' (2009) 15 *Columbia Journal of European Law Online* 1.

Prechal, P and van Roermund, B (eds), *The Coherence of EU Law. The Search for Unity in Divergent Concepts* (Oxford, Oxford University Press, 2008).

Quinn, G, 'The European Union and the Council of Europe on the Issue of Human Rights: Twins Separated at Birth' (2001) 46 *McGill Law Journal* 849.

Rabe, H, 'Zur Metamorphose des Europäischen Verfassungsvertrages' (2007) 60 *Neue Juristische Wochenschrift* 3153.

Reich, N, 'Beitritt der EU zur EMRK—Gefahr für das Verwerfungsmonopol des EuGH?' (2010) 21 *Europäische Zeitschrift für Wirtschaftsrecht* 641

—— 'Wer hat Angst vor Straßburg? Bemerkungen zur europäischen Grundrechtsarchitektur— Einheit in der Vielfalt?' (2011) 22 *Europäische Zeitschrift für Wirtschaftsrecht* 379.

—— 'Zur Notwendigkeit einer Europäischen Grundrechtsbeschwerde' (2000) 33 *Zeitschrift für Rechtspolitik* 375.

Rengeling, H, 'Brauchen wir die Verfassungsbeschwerde auf Gemeinschaftsebene?' in O Due, M Lutter and J Schwarze (eds), *Festschrift für Ulrich Everling. Band I* (Baden-Baden, Nomos, 1995).

Ress, G, 'The Effect of Decisions and Judgments of the European Court of Human Rights in the Domestic Legal Order' (2005) 40 *Texas International Law Journal* 359.

Röben, V, 'The Order of the UNCLOS Annex VII Arbitral Tribunal to Suspend Proceedings in the Case of the MOX Plant at Sellafield: How Much Jurisdictional Subsidiarity?' (2004) 73 *Nordic Journal of International Law* 223.

Rodríguez Iglesias, GC, 'Zur Stellung der Europäischen Menschenrechtskonvention im europäischen Gemeinschaftsrecht' in U Beyerlin (ed), *Recht zwischen Umbruch und Bewahrung. Völkerrecht, Europarecht, Staatsrecht, Festschrift für Rudolf Bernhardt* (Berlin Heidelberg, Springer, 1995).

Rossi, LS (ed), *Vers une nouvelle architecture de l'Union européenne: Le Projet de Traité-Constitution* (Brussels, Emile Bruylant, 2004).

Ruffert, M, 'Anmerkung zu Gutachten 2/94' [1996] *Juristen-Zeitung* 624.

—— 'Schlüsselfragen der Europäischen Verfassung der Zukunft: Grundrechte— Institutionen—Kompetenzen—Ratifizierung' (2004) 39 *Europarecht* 165.

Sauer, H, *Jurisdiktionskonflikte in Mehrebenensystemen* (Berlin Heidelberg, Springer, 2008).

Schäfer, P, *Verletzungen der Europäischen Menschenrechtskonvention durch Europäisches Gemeinschaftsrecht und dessen Vollzug. Verantwortlichkeit und Haftung der Mitgliedstaaten* (Baden-Baden, Nomos, 2006).

Schaller, W, 'Das Verhältnis von EMRK und deutscher Rechtsordnung vor und nach dem Beitritt der EU zur EMRK' (2006) 41 *Europarecht* 656.

Scheeck, L, 'The Relationship between the European Courts and Integration through Human Rights' (2005) 65 *Zeitschrift für ausländisches öffentliches Recht und Völkerrecht* 837.

Schilling, T, 'The Autonomy of the Community Legal Order: An Analysis of Possible Foundations' (1996) 37 *Harvard International Law Journal* 389.

—— 'Der Beitritt der EU zur EMRK—Verhandlungen und Modalitäten. Fast eine Polemik' (2011) 17 *Humboldt Forum Recht* 83.

Schlette, V, 'Das neue Rechtsschutzsystem der Europäischen Menschenrechtskonvention. Zur Reform des Kontrollmechanismus durch das 11. Protokoll' (1996) 56 *Zeitschrift für ausländisches öffentliches Recht und Völkerrecht* 905.

Schmalenbach, K, 'Struggle for Exclusiveness: The CJEU and Competing International Tribunals' in I Buffard, J Crawford, A Pellet and S Wittich (eds), *International Law between Universalism and Fragmentation. Festschrift in Honour of Gerhard Hafner* (Leiden, Brill, 2008).

Schorkopf, F, 'The European Court of Human Rights' Judgment in the Case of *Bosphorus Hava Yollari Turizm v. Ireland*' (2005) 6 *German Law Journal* 1255.

Schott, M, 'Die Auswirkungen eines Beitritts der EU zur EMRK auf die Durchsetzung des Grundrechtsschutzes in Europa' (2010) *Jusletter* 1.

Schroeder W (ed), *Europarecht als Mehrebenensystem* (Baden-Baden, Nomos, 2008).

Sevón L, 'The EEA Judicial System and the Supreme Courts of the EFTA States' (1992) 3 *European Journal of International Law* 329.

Shakespeare, W, *Hamlet* (Oxford, Oxford University Press, 2008).

Shany, Y, *The Competing Jurisdictions of International Courts and Tribunals* (Oxford, Oxford University Press, 2003).

—— 'The First *MOX Plant* Award: The Need to Harmonise Competing Environmental Regimes and Dispute Settlement Procedures' (2004) 17 *Leiden Journal of International Law* 815.

Shaw, MN, *International Law*, 6th edn (Cambridge, Cambridge University Press, 2008).

Shelton, D, *Remedies in International Human Rights Law* (Oxford, Oxford University Press, 2005).

Siems, K, *Das Kohärenzgebot in der Europäischen Union und seine Justitiabilität* (Baden-Baden, Nomos, 1999).

Siess-Scherz, I, 'Das neue Rechtsschutzsystem nach dem Protokoll Nr. 11 zur EMRK über die Umgestaltung des durch die Konvention eingeführten Kontrollmechanismus' in C Grabenwarter and R Thienel (eds), *Kontinuität und Wandel der EMRK. Studien zur Europäischen Menschenrechtskonvention* (Kehl am Rhein, NP Engel, 1998).

Simon, D, 'Des influences réciproques entre CJCE et CEDH: "Je t'aime, moi non plus?"' (2001) 96 *Pouvoirs, Les cours européennes* 31.

Skouris, V, 'The ECJ and the EFTA Court under the EEA Agreement: A Paradigm for International Cooperation between Judicial Institutions' in C Baudenbacher, P Tresselt and T Örlygsson (eds), *The EFTA Court. Ten Years On* (Oxford, Hart Publishing, 2005).

Slaughter, A, Stone Sweet, A and Weiler, JHH (eds), *The European Courts and National Courts: Doctrine and Jurisprudence* (Oxford, Hart Publishing, 1998).

Spence, D and Edwards, G (eds), *The European Commission*, 3rd edn (London, John Harper Publishing, 2006).

Spielmann, D, 'Human Rights Case Law in the Strasbourg and Luxembourg Courts: Conflicts, Inconsistencies, and Complementarities' in P Alston, M Bustelo and J Heenan (eds), *The EU and Human Rights* (Oxford, Oxford University Press, 1999).

Stadlmeier, S (ed), *Von Lissabon zum Raumfahrzeug: Aktuelle Herausforderungen im Völkerrecht. Beiträge zum 35. Österreichischen Völkerrechtstag* (Vienna, NWV, 2011).

Starck, C, 'Der Vertrag über eine Verfassung für Europa' in R Hendler, M Ibler and J Martínez Soria (eds), *Für Sicherheit, für Europa. Festschrift für Volkmar Götz* (Göttingen, Vandenhoeck & Ruprecht, 2005).

Stock, S, *Der Beitritt der Europäischen Union zur Europäischen Menschenrechtskonvention als Gemischtes Abkommen?* (Hamburg, Verlag Dr. Kovac, 2010).

Storr, S, 'Rechtsstaat und Grundrechte in Europa' in Österreichische Juristenkommission (ed), *Grundrechte im Europa der Zukunft* (Vienna, Linde, 2010).

Strasser, K, *Grundrechtsschutz in Europa und der Beitritt der Europäischen Gemeinschaften zur Europäischen Menschenrechtskonvention* (Frankfurt am Main, Peter Lang, 2001).

Strebel, H, 'Erzwungener, verkappter Monismus des Ständigen Internationalen Gerichtshofs?' (1971) 31 *Zeitschrift für ausländisches öffentliches Recht und Völkerrecht* 855.

Streinz, R (ed), *EUV/EGV. Vertrag über die Europäische Union und Vertrag zur Gründung der Europäischen Gemeinschaft* (Munich, Beck, 2003).

Sumner, S, 'We'll Sometimes Have Strasbourg: Privileged Status of Community Law Before the European Court of Human Rights' (2008) 16 *Irish Student Law Review* 127.

Szczekalla, P, 'Vertrauensvorschuss aus Straßburg: Der Europäische Gerichtshof für Menschenrechte klärt sein Verhältnis zum Europäischen Gerichtshof—Anmerkungen zu EuGHMR (Große Kammer), Urteil vom 30. Juni 2005, 45036/98' (2005) 2 *Zeitschrift für Gemeinschaftsprivatrecht* 176.

—— 'Grenzenlose Grundrechte' (2006) 25 *Neue Zeitschrift für Verwaltungsrecht* 1019.

Tettinger, PJ and Stern, K (eds), *Kölner Gemeinschaftskommentar zur Europäischen Grundrechte-Charta* (Munich, Beck, 2006).

Thomy, P, *Individualrechtsschutz durch das Vorabentscheidungsverfahren* (Baden-Baden, Nomos, 2009).

Thym, D, 'Auswärtige Gewalt' in A von Bogdandy and J Bast (eds), *Europäisches Verfassungsrecht. Theoretische und dogmatische Grundzüge* (Berlin Heidelberg, Springer, 2009).

Tomuschat, C, 'Lisbon—Terminal of the European Integration Process? The Judgment of the German Constitutional Court of 30 June 2009' (2010) 70 *Zeitschrift für ausländisches öffentliches Recht und Völkerrecht* 251.

Torres Pérez, A, *Conflicts of Rights in the European Union: A Theory of Supranational Adjudication* (Oxford, Oxford University Press, 2009).

Toth, AG, 'The European Union and Human Rights: The Way Forward' (1997) 34 *Common Market Law Review* 491.

Uerpmann-Wittzack, R, 'Völkerrechtliche Verfassungselemente' in A von Bogdandy and J Bast (eds), *Europäisches Verfassungsrecht. Theoretische und dogmatische Grundzüge* (Berlin Heidelberg, Springer, 2009).

Ulfstein, G, 'The International Judiciary' in J Klabbers, A Peters and G Ulfstein (eds), *The Constitutionalization of International Law* (Oxford, University Press, 2011).

Usher, J, 'The Commission and the Law' in D Spence and G Edwards (eds), *The European Commission*, 3rd edn (London, John Harper Publishing, 2006).

Vedder, C and Heintschel von Heinegg, W (eds), *Europäischer Verfassungsvertrag. Handkommentar* (Baden-Baden, Nomos, 2007).

Verwey, D, *The European Community, the European Union and the International Law of Treaties* (The Hague, Asser Press, 2004).

Villiger, ME, *Commentary on the 1969 Vienna Convention on the Law of Treaties* (Leiden, Brill Academic Publishers, 2009).

Vogt, M, 'Indirect Judicial Protection in EC Law—The Case of the Plea of Illegality' (2006) 31 *European Law Review* 364.

Volbeda, MB, 'The MOX Plant Case: The Question of "Supplemental Jurisdiction" for International Environmental Claims Under UNCLOS' (2006) 42 *Texas International Law Journal* 211.

Vondung, J, *Die Architektur des europäischen Grundrechtsschutzes nach dem Beitritt der EU zur EMRK* (Tübingen, Mohr Siebeck, 2012).

——'Grundrechtsschutz gegen die Europäische Union vor dem Europäischen Gerichtshof für Menschenrechte' (2011) 61 *Anwaltsblatt des Deutschen Anwaltvereins* 331.

Wägenbaur, B, 'EuGH: Verfristung der deutschen Klage gegen Tabakwerberichtlinie' (2002) 13 *Europäische Zeitschrift für Wirtschaftsrecht* 404.

——*EuGH VerfO. Satzung und Verfahrensordnungen EuGH/EuG Kommentar* (Munich, Beck, 2008).

Walter, C, 'Constitutionalising (Inter)national Governance—Possibilities for an Limits to the Development of an International Constitutional Law' (2001) 44 *German Yearbook of International Law* 170.

——'Die Europäische Menschenrechtskonvention als Konstitutionalisierungsprozess' (1999) 59 *Zeitschrift für ausländisches öffentliches Recht und Völkerrecht* 961.

Warbrick, C, 'The Structure of Article 8' [1998] *European Human Rights Law Review* 32.

Webb, P, 'Scenarios of Jurisdictional Overlap among International Courts' (2006) 19 *Revue québecoise de Droit International* 277.

Weiler, JHH, 'Eurocracy and Distrust: Some Questions Concerning the Role of the European Court of Justice in the Protection of Fundamental Human Rights within the Legal Order of the European Communities' (1986) 61 *Washington Law Review* 1103.

——'The Transformation of Europe' (1991) 100 *Yale Law Journal* 2403.

——and Fries, SC, 'A Human Rights Policy for the European Community and Union: The Question of Competences' in A Alston, M Bustelo and J Heenan (eds), *The EU and Human Rights* (Oxford, Oxford University Press, 1999).

——and Haltern, UR, 'The Autonomy of the Community Legal Order—Through the Looking Glass' (1996) 37 *Harvard International Law Journal* 411.

——and Haltern UR, 'Constitutional or International? The Foundations of the Community Legal Order and the Question of Judicial Kompetenz-Kompetenz' in A Slaughter, A Stone Sweet and JHH Weiler (eds), *The European Courts and National Courts: Doctrine and Jurisprudence* (Oxford, Hart Publishing, 1998).

Wetzel, JR, 'Improving Fundamental Rights Protection in the European Union: Resolving the Conflict and Confusion between the Luxembourg and Strasbourg Courts' (2003) 71 *Fordham Law Review* 2823.

Wiethoff, JH, *Das konzeptuelle Verhältnis von EuGH und EGMR* (Baden-Baden, Nomos, 2008).

Wildhaber, L, 'About the Co-Existence of Three Different Legal Systems and Three Jurisdictions' (2005) 60 *Zeitschrift für Öffentliches Recht* 313.

——'Bemerkungen zum Vortrag von BVerfG-Präsident Prof. Dr. H.-J. Papier auf dem Europäischen Juristentag 2005 in Genf' (2005) 32 *Europäische Grundrechte-Zeitschrift* 743.

——'The European Convention on Human Rights and International Law' (2007) 56 *International and Comparative Law Quarterly* 217.

Williams, A, *EU Human Rights Policies. A Study in Irony* (Oxford, Oxford University Press, 2005).

Winkler, S, *Der Beitritt der Europäischen Gemeinschaften zur Europäischen Menschenrechtskonvention* (Baden-Baden, Nomos, 2000).

Wolfrum, R and Deutsch, U (eds), *The European Court of Human Rights Overwhelmed by Applications: Problems and Possible Solutions* (Berlin Heidelberg, Springer, 2009).

Wouters, J, 'National Constitutions and the European Union' (2000) 27 *Legal Issues of Economic Integration* 25.

Young, E, 'Protecting Member State Autonomy in the European Union: Some Cautionary Tales from American Federalism' (2002) 77 *New York University Law Review* 1612.

Zaru, D, 'EU Reactions to Violations of Human Rights Norms by Third States' in W Benedek, F Benoît-Rohmer, W Karl and N Nowak M (eds), *European Yearbook on Human Rights 2011* (Vienna, NWV, 2011).

Ziegler, KS, 'Strengthening the Rule of Law, but Fragmenting International Law: The *Kadi* Decision from the Perspective of Human Rights' (2009) 9 *Human Rights Law Review* 288.

Zwaak, L, 'General Survey of the European Convention' in P van Dijk, F van Hoof, A van Rijn and L Zwaak (eds), *Theory and Practice of the European Convention on Human Rights*, 4th edn (Antwerp Oxford, Intersentia, 2006).

II. DOCUMENTS, REPORTS AND WORKING PAPERS

Benoît-Rohmer, F, in Council of Europe—Parliamentary Assembly, *The Accession of the European Union/European Community to the European Convention on Human Rights*, Doc 11533 (Committee on Legal Affairs and Human Rights).

Christoffersen, J, *Institutional Aspects of the EU's Accession to the ECHR*. European Parliament, Committee on Constitutional Affairs, Hearing on the Institutional Aspects of the European Union's Accession to the European Convention on Human Rights, 18 March 2010.

Commission of the European Communities, 'Commission Staff Working Paper. Council of Europe Draft Convention on Cybercrime—Accession of the EC and Disconnection Clause' SEC(2001) 315.

—— 'Memorandum on the Accession of the European Communities to the Convention for the Protection of Human Rights and Fundamental Freedoms' Bulletin Supplement 2/79, COM (79) 210 final.

—— 'Memorandum from the Commission to the Working Group' SEC(93)1678.

Council of Europe, '1st Meeting of the CDDH Informal Working Group on the Accession of the European Union to the European Convention on Human Rights (CDDH-UE) with the European Commission' CDDH-UE(2010)01.

——'3rd Working Meeting of the CDDH Informal Working Group on the Accession of the European Union to the European Convention on Human Rights (CDDH-UE) with the European Commission' Meeting Report, CDDH-UE(2010)14.

——'4th Working Meeting of the CDDH Informal Working Group on the Accession of the European Union to the European Convention on Human Rights (CDDH-UE) with the European Commission' CDDH-UE(2010)17.

——'5th Working Meeting of the CDDH Informal Working Group on the Accession of the European Union to the European Convention on Human Rights (CDDH-UE) with the European Commission' CDDH-UE(2011)01.

——'5th Working Meeting of the CDDH Informal Working Group on the Accession of the European Union to the European Convention on Human Rights (CDDH-UE) with the European Commission' CDDH-UE(2011)02.

——'6th Working Meeting of the CDDH Informal Working Group on the Accession of the European Union to the European Convention on Human Rights (CDDH-UE) with the European Commission' CDDH-UE(2011)04.

——'6th Working Meeting of the CDDH Informal Working Group on the Accession of the European Union to the European Convention on Human Rights (CDDH-UE) with the European Commission' CDDH-UE(2011)05.

——'6th Working Meeting of the CDDH Informal Working Group on the Accession of the European Union to the European Convention on Human Rights (CDDH-UE) with the European Commission' CDDH-UE(2011)06.

——'7th Working Meeting of the CDDH Informal Working Group on the Accession of the European Union to the European Convention on Human Rights (CDDH-UE) with the European Commission' CDDH-UE(2011)08.

——'7th Working Meeting of the CDDH Informal Working Group on the Accession of the European Union to the European Convention on Human Rights (CDDH-UE) with the European Commission' CDDH-UE(2011)10.

——'8th Meeting of the CDDH Informal Working Group on the Accession of the European Union to the European Convention on Human Rights (CDDH-UE) with the European Commission' CDDH-UE(2011)16.

——'Press Release 545 (2010)'.

——Parliamentary Assembly, *The Accession of the European Union/European Community to the European Convention on Human Rights*, Doc. 11533 (Committee on Legal Affairs and Human Rights).

——'Steering Committee for Human Rights—Report to the Committee of Ministers on the Elaboration of Legal Instruments for the Accession of the European Union to the European Convention on Human Rights' CDDH(2011)009.

Council of the European Union, 'Draft Council Decision Authorising the Commission to negotiate the Accession Agreement of the European Union to the European Convention for the Protection of Human Rights and Fundamental Freedoms (ECHR)' Doc 9689/10 (partly classified).

——'Accession of the EU to the ECHR and the Preservation of the ECJ's Monopoly on the Interpretation of EU law: Options under Discussion' 10568/10.

——'Accession of the EU to the ECHR—Working Document from the Presidency' DS 1675/11.

——'Accession of the European Union to the European Convention for the Protection of Human Rights and Fundamental Freedoms—State of Play' 18117/11, FREMP 112.

Court of Justice of the European Union, 'Discussion Document of the Court of Justice of the European Union on certain aspects of the accession of the European Union to the European Convention for the Protection of Human Rights and Fundamental Freedoms', 5 May 2010.

De Búrca, G, 'The European Court of Justice and the International Legal Order after *Kadi*' Jean Monnet Working Paper No 1/09, 2009, 2ff <http://centers.law.nyu.edu/jeanmonnet/papers/09/090101.html> accessed 1 November 2012.

Drzemczewski, A, 'The European Human Rights Convention: Protocol No. 11—Entry into Force and First Year of Application' 226 <www.gddc.pt/actividade-editorial/pdfs-publicacoes/7980-a.pdf> accessed 1 November 2012.

De Schutter, O, *L'adhésion de l'Union européenne à la Convention européenne des droits de l'homme: feuille de route de la négociation.* European Parliament, Committee on Constitutional Affairs, Hearing on the Institutional Aspects of the European Union's Accession to the European Convention on Human Rights, 18 March 2010.

——*L'adhésion de l'Union européenne à la Convention européenne des droits de l'homme: feuille de route de la négociation.* European Parliament, Committee on Constitutional Affairs, Hearing on the Institutional Aspects of the European Union's Accession to the European Convention on Human Rights, 10 April 2010.

——in Council of Europe—Parliamentary Assembly, *The Accession of the European Union/European Community to the European Convention on Human Rights*, Doc 11533 (Committee on Legal Affairs and Human Rights), 18 March 2008.

European Commission, 'Working Document on the Previous Involvement of the Court of Justice in the Context of the Accession of the European Union to the European Convention for the Protection of Human Rights and Fundamental Freedoms' DS 1930/10.

——'2011 Report on the Application of the EU Charter of Fundamental Rights' COM(2012) 169 final.

——'28th Annual Report on Monitoring the Application of EU Law (2010)' COM(2011) 588 final.

European Convention, 'Modalities and consequences of incorporation into the Treaties of the Charter of Fundamental Rights and accession of the Community/Union to the ECHR' CONV 116/02, WG II 1.

——'Final Report of Working Group II' CONV 354/02, WG II 16.

——'Draft of Articles 1 to 16 of the Constitutional Treaty' CONV 528/03.

——'Final Report of the Discussion Circle on the Court of Justice' CONV 636/03, 25 March 2003.

——'Articles on the Court of Justice and the High Court' CONV 734/03.

European Council in Copenhagen, 21–22 June 1993, Conclusions of the Presidency, SN 180/1/93 REV 1.

European Council, 'The Stockholm Programme—An Open and Secure Europe Serving and Protecting Citizens' 4 May 2010 OJ C115/1.

——'Conclusions 16-17 December 2010' EUCO 30/1/10 REV 1.

European Court of Human Rights, 'Annual Report 2011'.

——'Inter-State Applications' < www.echr.coe.int/NR/rdonlyres/5D5BA416-1FE0-4414-95A1-AD6C1D77CB90/0/Requ%C3%AAtes_inter%C3%A9tatiques_EN.pdf> accessed 1 November 2012.

Explanatory Report to Protocol No. 14 to the Convention for the Protection of Human Rights and Fundamental Freedom, amending the control system of the Convention, CETS No 194, Agreement of Madrid.

Holdgaard, L and Holdgaard, R, 'The External Powers of the European Community' [2001] Retsvidenskabeligt Tidsskrift Publications 108, 114 <http://law.au.dk/fileadmin/site_files/filer_jura/dokumenter/forskning/rettid/artikler/20010108.pdf> accessed 1 November 2012.

Holovaty, S, *Institutional Aspects of the EU's Accession to the ECHR.* European Parliament, Committee on Constitutional Affairs, Hearing on the Institutional Aspects of the European Union's Accession to the European Convention on Human Rights, 18 March 2010.

International Law Association, 'Third Interim Report: Declining and Referring Jurisdiction in International Litigation' London Conference (2000).

Jacqué, J, *L'adhésion à la Convention européenne des droits de l'homme. Note à l'attention de la Commission institutionnelle en vue de l'audition du 18 mars 2010.* European Parliament, Committee on Constitutional Affairs, Hearing on the Institutional Aspects of the European Union's Accession to the European Convention on Human Rights, 18 March 2010.

Joint Communication from Presidents Costa and Skouris, 17 January 2011.

Kraemer, H, 'The Logistics and Technicalities of the Accession' Lecture at the UCL Institute for Human Rights Conference: 'Who Will be the Ultimate Guardian of Human Rights in Europe?' at the University College London, 20 May 2011.

Lavranos, N, 'Concurrence of Jurisdiction between the CJEU and other International Courts and Tribunals, EUSA Ninth Biennial International Conference', 31 March–2 April 2005, Austin, Texas, Conference Paper 1.

van der Linden, R, *Accession of the EC/EU to the European Convention on Human Rights.* European Parliament, Committee on Constitutional Affairs, Hearing on the Institutional Aspects of the European Union's Accession to the European Convention on Human Rights, 18 March 2010.

Lock, T, 'Accession of the EU to the ECHR: Who Would be Responsible in Strasbourg?' Working Paper Series, 3 October 2010, 18 <http://papers.ssrn.com/sol3/papers.cfm?abstract_id=1685785> accessed 1 November 2012.

Øby Johansen, S, 'The EU's Accession to the ECHR: Negotiations to resume after 7 Month Hiatus' <http://blogg.uio.no/jus/smr/multirights/content/the-eus-accession-to-the-echr-negotiations-to-resume-after-7-month-hiatus#sdfootnote10sym> accessed 1 November 2012.

Office of the United Nations High Commissioner for Human Rights, 'The European Union and International Human Rights Law' 2011, 27 <www.europe.ohchr.org/Documents/Publications/EU_and_International_Law.pdf> accessed 1 November 2012.

Response of the European Group of National Human Rights Institutions, 'EU Accession to the ECHR' CDDH-UE, 15–18 March 2011.

Sénat Français, 'Adhésion de l'Union Européenne à la Convention européenne de sauvegarde des droits de l'homme, Communication de M. Robert Badinter sur le mandat de négociation' (E 5248), 25 May 2010, <www.senat.fr/europe/r25052010.html#toc1> accessed 1 November 2012.

Steering Committee for Human Rights (CDDH), 'Study of Technical and Legal Issues of a Possible EC/EU Accession to the European Convention on Human Rights' DG-II(2002)006 of 28 June 2002.

——'Technical and Legal Issues of a Possible EC/EU Accession to the European Convention on Human Rights' CDDH(2002)010 Addendum 2.

Submission by the AIRE Centre and Amnesty International, *Informal Working Group on the Accession of the European Union to the European Convention on Human Rights* (CDDH-UE), AI Index: IOR 61/003/2011, 14 March 2011.

Timmermans, C, *L'adhésion de l'Union Européenne à la Convention européenne des Droits de l'homme,* Audition organisée par la Commission des affaires constitutionnelles du 18 mars 2010. European Parliament, Committee on Constitutional Affairs, Hearing on the Institutional Aspects of the European Union's Accession to the European Convention on Human Rights, 18 March 2010.

Tulkens, F, *Les aspects institutionnels de l'adhésion de l'Union européenne à la Convention européenne de sauvegarde des droits de l'homme et des libertés fondamentales.* L'audition du 18 mars 2010. European Parliament, Committee on Constitutional Affairs, Hearing on the Institutional Aspects of the European Union's Accession to the European Convention on Human Rights, 18 March 2010.

Index